D0845795

Tibet

Plate 1 *frontispiece* Fra Mauro's map of Tibet, 1459

Tibet,

A Chronicle of Exploration

John MacGregor

PRAEGER PUBLISHERS
New York · Washington

BOOKS THAT MATTER

Published in the United States of America
in 1970 by Praeger Publishers, Inc.,
111 Fourth Avenue, New York, N.Y. 10003

Library of Congress Catalog Card Number: 70–109482

Printed in Great Britain

For Stephanie and Maria

Contents

List of Maps

List of Illustrations

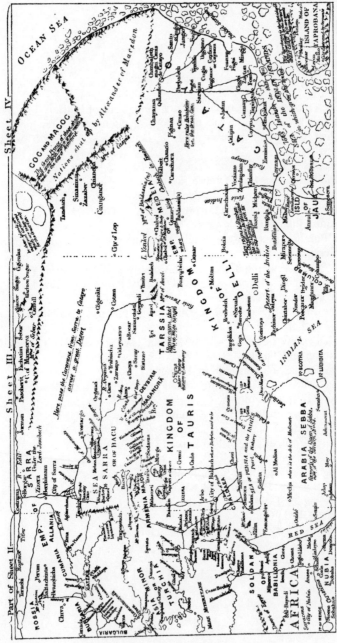

ASIA, from Sheets II, III & IV, of the CATALAN MAP of 1375, reduced and condensed from the fac-similes in Notices et Extraits, &c. Tom.XIV.

Prologue

Sometimes shadowy, sometimes confused, persistent legends of Christian kingdoms in Cathay fascinated Europe in the Middle Ages. In 1145 Bishop Otto of Freisingen described a great king of the Christians called 'Prester John'. Otto's startling report – perhaps the first on this subject to be considered authoritative – was based on information brought to Europe by the Syrian Bishop of Gabala who appeared before Pope Eugene III in 1145 as Ambassador from the King of Armenia. The Syrian bishop referred to 'Presbyter Joannes', or Prester John, as a great Nestorian priest-king, a descendent of Magian kings who ruled over a rich and powerful realm in Asia. The medieval scholar, Albericus, in 1145 also reflected this report in his influential historical work, *Chronicon*.[1] John was credited with a major victory over the Medes and Persians. This story, possibly a distortion of the defeat of the Seljuk Sultan, Sanjar, near Samarkand by the Turkish Kara-Khitan chieftain, Ye-lü Ta-shih, in 1141, added to the Nestorian's fabled reputation.

One of history's most ingenious and still unsolved forgeries also played a role in spreading the Prester John myth. In 1165 there appeared in Europe a letter addressed to Manuel I, Emperor of Byzantium, purporting to be from Prester John, 'ruler of the three Indias'. The text invited Manuel to visit him and promised 'the highest and most dignified position in the household', adding enticingly, 'Shouldst thou desire to return, thou shalt go laden with treasures.' On a note of sheer braggadocio the letter stated, 'If indeed thou desirest to know wherein

---

1 William Woodville Rockhill, *The Journey of William of Rubruck to The Eastern Parts of the World, 1253–55* (London, Bedford Press, 1900) (Hakluyt Society, Second Series, No. IV), p. xxii.

I

consists our great power, then believe without hesitation that I, Prester John, who reign supreme, surpass in virtue, riches and power all creatures under heaven.'

In this strange communication the ghost author, in the name of Prester John and for unclear motives, promised 'to visit the sepulchre of our Lord with a very large army, in accordance with the glory of our Majesty to humble and chastise the enemies of the cross of Christ and to exalt His blessed name.'[1]

Manuel forwarded this remarkable letter to Emperor Frederick Barbarossa and copies were widely circulated among other kings and princes of Europe. The crude forgery found ready acceptance, perhaps because it seemed to confirm stories of Christian influence in far Asia which were beginning to filter into Europe through pilgrims and travellers, and because this influence provided hope of assistance against the Saracens in the Holy Land.

Mongol expansion toward the Moslem Kingdom of Khorasmia, or Khiva, seemed to provide substance to such hope in so far as this campaign in the beginning had been interpreted wishfully by Christendom as a Nestorian holy war against Islam. Reports of Prester John's power, wealth and righteousness continued to spread throughout Europe and were exaggerated so much it became accepted as fact that this Christian conqueror was pushing relentlessly westward against the unbelieving Saracens.

When it finally became painfully clear that the early Mongol invaders would not spare the eastern European border lands of Christendom any more than they had the kingdoms of Islam, an alternative legend gained currency that the feared Mongol leader, Genghiz Khan, had been a rebellious vassal of Prester John. In this version, Genghiz Khan was alleged to have slain the good Nestorian king and taken his daughter in marriage.[2] Still another variation of the story, attributed to Rabban-ata, an Uighur Nestorian priest at the Mongol headquarters in Armenia,

---

[1] Arthur Newton (ed.), *Travel and Travellers of The Middle Ages*, Chapter IX, 'Prester John and the Empire of Ethiopia', by Sir E. Denison Ross (London, Routledge & Kegan Paul Ltd, 1926), pp. 175–8.

[2] R. A. Skelton, Thomas Marston and George O. Painter, *The Vinland Map and the Tartar Relation* (New Haven & London, Yale University Press, 1965), p. 48.

tells how Genghiz Khan in 1202 killed David, son of Prester John, and married his daughter.[1]

After crushing the Khorasmian Empire in 1222, a Mongol army under Genghiz Khan's grandson, Batu, struck ruthlessly southward through the Caucasus bringing ruin in its wake. In their terror and confusion the beleaguered Moslems concluded that the Mongols must be the 'nation of Satan', the lost tribes of Gog and Magog, which had forsaken Mosaic law and had for their sins been imprisoned behind the mountains of the Caucasus by Alexander the Great. The Ismaeli Moslem sect, south of the Caucasus, hurriedly sent embassies in 1238 to King Louis IX of France and King Henry II of England pleading for help. The frantic envoys described the Mongol invaders as 'devils from the Tartarus' come to challenge the followers of the Book.

The entreaties of the Ismaelis fell on deaf ears. Christendom could neither comprehend the full scope of the Mongol threat nor make common cause with an old antagonist which had shed so much Crusader blood. The Bishop of Winchester summed up Western sentiment when he growled, 'Let these dogs destroy one another . . . then we shall see the universal Catholic Church founded on their ruins.'[2] But at least reports of Batu's appalling destruction put to rest any lingering hopes that the Mongol army was from the saviour, Prester John, marching to the rescue of the Holy Land.

Soon afterward, in 1240, Mongol armies attacked southern Russia, Poland and Hungary. Kiev was taken on 6 December 1240. The northern unit, which seized Krakow, smashed a Polish-Silesian defence force near Liegnitz in Silesia on 9 April 1241. The main army under Batu and Sabutay then pressed onward into Hungary and Moravia, destroying the Magyar army near Buda on 11 April. The southern Mongol force marched virtually unopposed across Hungary to the Adriatic. Faced with an undeniable threat to Europe and suspicious that Emperor Frederic may have reached a secret understanding with the invaders, Pope Gregory IX pressed hard for a unified defence against the Mongols.

---

[1] *Ibid.*, p. 23.
[2] Matthew Paris, *Chronica Majora*, ed. H. R. Luard, 7. vols (London, 1872–83), pp. iv, 112, 119.

In the midst of Mongol terror new evidence bearing on the lost Christians of Asia and their influence on the Mongols reached Europe. A Russian bishop called Peter, who had fled before the Mongol invaders sweeping across southern Russia, reported in 1243 to Gregory's new successor, Pope Innocent IV, that some of the Mongols worshipped but one god. The prelate told of a Christian leader called John who lived far to the east. It was this kind of testimony that caused the Genoese pontiff, who had a reputation for diplomatic acumen, to hope that he could find among the Mongols partisans of the Faith to whom he could appeal. If Prester John existed, surely there must be followers of Christ who could leaven the onslaughts of the anti-Christ. Or at least the Christian element would provide allies and a point of approach for missionaries who could convince the heathen Mongols of the error of their ways. The Pope at the very least needed intelligence on the Mongols so that he might know the full extent of this threat.

Innocent IV chose two Franciscans, Friar John of Plano Carpini and Friar Ascelin, to lead separate embassies to the Mongols. Both were given letters of credence when they received the Pope's blessings at Lyons on 9 March 1245. Friar John was given a message to the Mongol Great Khan, exhorting the latter 'to repent for the wrath of God'. The letter complained that he had 'exterminated other nations'. The Pope asked bluntly: 'What are your future intentions?'[1]

John, accompanied on his epic journey by Franciscan brothers Benedict of Poland and Ceslaus of Bohemia, reached Batu's winter camp near present-day Astrakhan on the Volga delta without difficulty. There, by coincident and good fortune, Russia's medieval hero, Alexander Nevsky, was visiting the great Mongol commander and could serve as Carpini's interpreter.

Batu sped the friar's party on its way eastward to the Mongol capital at Karakorum so that it could arrive in time to see Genghiz Khan's grandson (Ogadai's son), Kuyuk, elected Great Khan by an assembly of Mongol chieftains. The Congress of Khans, or *Kurtilai* as it was known by the Mongols, was attended

---

[1] R. A. Skelton, Thomas Marston and George O. Painter, *op. cit.*, p. 35.

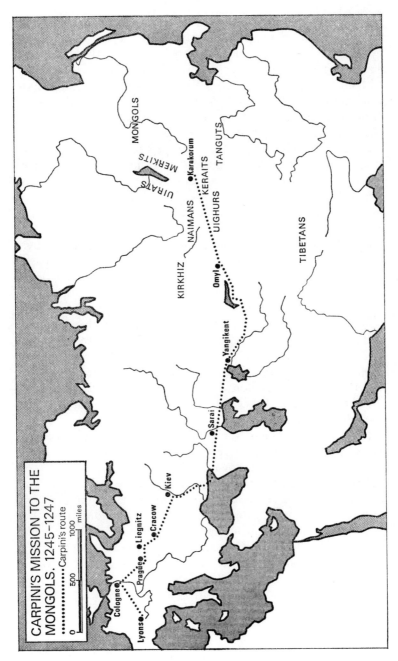

CARPINI'S MISSION TO THE
MONGOLS. 1245–1247

······· Carpini's route

0   500   1000 miles

MONGOLS

MERKITS

UIRATS

Karakorum

NAIMANS

KIRKHIZ

KERAITS

UIGHURS

TANGUTS

TIBETANS

Omyl

Yangikent

Sarai

Kiev

Cracow

Liegnitz

Prague

Cologne

Lyons

by some 3,000 envoys. Such notables as Yaroslav, Duke of Susdal in Russia (and father of Alexander Nevsky), waited to be received by the new Emperor. Marred only by an abortive plot by a dissident pretender to the throne, the ceremony took place with all the splendour which the court could muster. Its climax was marked by wild revels and orgies of drinking. The pious Franciscans discreetly retired early from such heathen excesses – much to the disgust of the lusty Kuyuk.

Centuries would pass before Europe's scholars succeeded in removing the shrouds of mystery surrounding the legend of Prester John. Carpini, however, found in Kuyuk's encampment, south of Lake Baikal, remnants of Nestorian power and clues to substantiate the long-rumoured existence of a great Christian capital in far-off Tartary.

Kuyuk, himself, owed his new throne to the shrewd manœuvring of his Christian mother – the widow of Ogadai. Turakina, as this Naiman princess was known, ignored her husband's dying request that his grandson, Siremun, succeed him. Instead she used her four and a half years as regent to manipulate Mongol politics so that her son, Kuyuk, could inherit the standard. Turakina proved to be a good friend in court for the Franciscan envoys and did what she could to make up for the new Khan's coolness toward them. Another influential Nestorian Christian was the Court Chancellor, Chingay, an official of Kerait origins who befriended the friars and was finally able to introduce them to the Great Khan.

Friar John's version of Mongol history, learned at Karakorum, includes an interesting but distorted contribution to the Prester John myth, which places the great Christian leader in India as an antagonist of the Mongols. Genghiz Khan's son, Tolui, according to Carpini's information, led a strong force against India. Reaching first 'lesser India', the region west of the Indus River, the marauding horde encountered dark-skinned people. The Mongol force then moved on into 'Greater India', the Indian subcontinent east of the Ganges River, and attacked the king called Prester John.[1]

Suggesting that his account of the battle was founded on biased

---

[1] *Ibid.*, p. 68.

Nestorian sources, Friar John concluded by describing the humiliating defeat of the Mongols. In this version of the legend, the 'Indian' cavalry of Prester John deployed a new and secret weapon which the Mongols blamed for their rout. This was a bronze statue containing live coals, mounted on each saddle. Before the Tartar's arrows could reach the Indian horsemen, 'they began to shoot forth fire against them by blowing it with bellows which they carried on either side of the saddle under both thighs.[1]

Carpini's story may have been a distorted version of the Battle of Perwan, which is believed to have occurred north of Kabul, Afghanistan, in 1221. But in that actual battle the Mongol general, Shigikituku, was defeated by the Moslem Khorasmian leader, Jelal-ed-Din – not by anyone resembling Prester John. The incendiary device may have been any one of several weapons used by both sides in the Khorasmian wars, but it strongly resembles a technique used by Alexander the Great in his battle against Porus, King of India. The great Macedonian commander is alleged to have put to flight Porus's elephants with a squadron of wagons carrying bronze statues kept hot by burning embers inside them. On scorching their trunks, the elephants bolted, trumpeting in pain as they fled the battlefield.

Carpini noted that Nestorian influence was particularly concentrated in the Great Khan's secretariat. Certain members of the secretariat hinted to Friar John that the new Emperor was about to embrace Christianity, the religion of his mother. But Kuyuk's arrogant attitude toward Innocent IV's entreaties makes this unlikely, and there is no evidence that Friar John took them seriously.

The Franciscan emissaries returned to Europe in 1247 without having reached accord or even improving relations with the new Khan. But they did bring considerable intelligence of value to Innocent IV and the still-worried Christian kings of Europe. For one thing, Friar John could report to the Pope at Lyons that Ogatai's son Batu withdrew suddenly from Europe upon 'learning secretly of his father's death'. Actually it was news of a stroke suffered by Ogatai in 1241, not his death, which caused Batu to

---

[1] *Ibid.*, p. 68.

redeploy his forces and march homeward. His father's illness brought closer to reality the succession problem, and Batu could anticipate much manœuvring for power and position at the Karakorum court. Carpini in another passage reported more accurately that Batu, while fighting in Hungary in 1242, learned of the death of Ogatai Khan after the latter had been poisoned by his sisters. He predicted that Batu's return to the court of the newly-crowned Kuyuk would create dissention. His analysis that this discord could provide the Christian world respite 'from the Tartar for many years' proved to be accurate, although Europe could not yet be certain that the high watermark of the Mongol invasions had passed.

However useful Carpini's mission was as a vital reconnaissance, Innocent's diplomacy failed. The Great Khan expressed understandable bewilderment at the Pope's request that he be baptized. As for peace, he thundered that if the West wanted peace, then the Pope, emperors, kings and all leaders of men must come to him without delay to learn *his* will. Kuyuk left the friars with a scarcely-veiled threat that if this were not the case, 'We know not what will come of it – but God knows!'[1]

In 1245,[2] at approximately the same time Carpini left on his mission to Karakorum, Pope Innocent IV sent the Dominican friar, Ascelin, to the camp of Baiju, Mongol commander and pro-consul of Armenia. The record of Ascelin's journey was kept by his travelling companion, Friar Simon of St Quentin, and preserved in Vincent of Beauvais' medieval encyclopedia, *Speculum Majorum*.[3]

As in the case of Carpini, Friar Ascelin's party met only arrogance on the part of the Mongols. The Dominican envoys were poorly housed and fed and generally neglected – even humiliated. Like Carpini, Ascelin returned with a rude and essentially hostile reply from the Mongol general, which he tendered to Innocent IV in 1250. In all fairness to Baiju, however, it should be noted that Ascelin appeared to have little of the tact expected of envoys.

Ascelin reported that he had encountered Nestorian Christians

---

[1] *Ibid.*, p. 38.
[2] Sometimes this date is mistakenly given as 1247.
[3] William Woodville Rockhill, *op. cit.*, pp. xxiv, xxv.

at Baiju's camp and had learned from them new details of Mongol history. However distorted and biased Nestorian records may have been, they did provide invaluable new insight with which to fill the void in Christendom's knowledge of its greatest threat.

A Syrian priest, known variously as Simeon and Rabban-ata, who befriended the forlorn party of Dominicans, was particularly helpful in describing the rise of the Mongols and the role played by the Nestorians in the fortunes of the great Genghiz Khan. Rabban-ata was an important source of one legend attributing to Genghiz Khan the murder in 1202 of his one-time Christian overlord, David King of India and the son of Prester John. In this version of the Prester John saga, Genghiz soon thereafter married King David's daughter. This is a highly garbled account of Genghiz Khan's victory over the Kerait tribes in 1203. Actually, at this time he killed the Kerait leader, Wang Khan Toghril, believed to be the real Prester John of Asian history, and married the latter's niece, Ibaka-beki.

According to Rabban-ata, to whom Ascelin owed his account of the Mongol invasion of Armenia in 1236, Ogadai personally decreed that Christian communities would be protected. Earlier fragmentary reports of such tolerance of Christians contrasted with reports of Mongol savagery against Moslems south of the Caucasus perhaps contributed to Europe's false hope that an alliance with the Mongols against Islam was possible.

King Louis IX of France, later canonized as Saint Louis, was among those who believed that there was still room for diplomatic manœuvre with the Mongols despite Pope Innocent's signal lack of success. Louis, who set out on an ill-fated crusade in 1248, seems to have entertained dreams of an alliance with the Mongols, permitting an envelopment of the Saracens. The Mongols would strike the Holy Land from inland while the Christian crusaders mounted a seaborne attack from their base in Cyprus.

Louis was encouraged in this hope by the unexpected arrival of a Mongol envoy at his Cyprus camp in late 1248. The visitor, known as Sabeddin Morrifat David, had been met casually by Ascelin in Armenia so was not a total stranger; but neither was he known to be reliable. He announced to Louis that he had been sent by General Ilchikadai, Mongol pro-consul in Persia, with an offer of Mongol assistance against the forces of Islam. The French king was addressed in the letter from Ilchikadai as one 'whose reknown had . . . spread throughout western Asia.'[1] The Mongol envoy also praised the Pope whom he claimed was famous among the Tartars. Presumably to build credibility, David alleged that the mother of the Great Khan was Christian and that the Great Khan himself had been converted to Christianity by a Saracen bishop called Mallachias.

David's knowledge of Christian influence among the Mongols seemed to corroborate information contained in a letter from the Constable of Armenia, which reached Louis in Cyprus at almost the same time. Thus encouraged, the great French crusader decided to send a return mission to Ilchikadai and, if possible, on to Emperor Kuyuk Khan himself.

A Christian embassy, led by the Dominican friar, Andrew of Longumeau, and guided by David, was sent off in mid-February 1249. Following a stay at the encampment of Ilchikadai, the group continued on to the great Mongol court with high hopes, despite news of the recent death of Kuyuk Khan. Andrew found in command the Regent-Empress Ogul Gaimish, a she-devil every bit as formidable as any male Mongol emperor. Not only was the defenceless friar unable to reach accord, but he was mercilessly exploited by the crafty Regent-Queen who exhibited her visitors before several visiting kings and princes and told them, 'My Lords, the King of France has come under my subjection and here is the tribute he sends us.' The scheming Queen added, 'And if you come not to our mercy, we will send for him to confound you.'[2]

Only later did King Louis learn that the plausible David spoke only for Ilchikadai – if even for him – and had no mandate from the Mongol court to negotiate. Upon assuming the throne, Kuyuk's successor, Mangu Khan, was disturbed enough to write Louis that David had been an outright imposter.[3] But had he not at least been the legitimate agent of Ilchikadai, why was he willing to lead Friar Andrew to the Mongol commander's camp? One can only speculate that Ilchikadai felt himself strong

---

[1] William Woodville Rockhill, *op. cit.*, p. xxvii.
[2] *Ibid.*, pp. xxix, xxx.   [3] *Ibid.*, p. xxvii, note 2.

enough to take independent diplomatic initiatives without clearing them with Karakorum.

By the time Andrew returned empty handed from the Great Khan's court in 1251, Louis' forces had been crushed by the Egyptians at the Battle of Mansurah. He found his monarch and the tattered remnant of the Crusaders holed up in the fortress of Caesarea on the Palestine coast. The disillusioned friar, who still smarted from his treatment by Ogul Gaimish, described her to Louis as a 'most abominable sorceress – viler than a dog.'[1]

Louis IX could, however, find satisfaction in the Franciscan friar's intelligence – however inaccurate – on the Mongols and the Christians in their midst. Andrew traced Mongol origins to a vast desert which began at the eastern end of an 'impenetrable wall'. This wall was popularly supposed to keep imprisoned the evil tribes of Gog and Magog which, according to prophecy, would one day burst forth with the anti-Christ to herald the end of the world. This clearly can be sourced to Nestorian influences, but it is interesting to speculate whether the Mongol substitution for the Caucasian ranges, which more traditionally confined the followers of Gog and Magog, was meant to be the Great Wall of China or some particularly awesome mountain range.

Friar Andrew told of a great Mongol king – presumably Genghiz Khan – who had been miraculously converted to Christianity by a vision in which God rewarded him with victory over Prester John. This vision revealed to him a vast encampment in which there were 800 chapels, each mounted on huge ox-drawn carts. Genghiz is also supposed to have gazed in his dream upon vast battlefields strewn with mounds of human bones through which Mongol legions marched westward to new victories.

Despite Ogul Gaimish's waspish performance, Louis IX could not yet abandon hope that there were influential Christian forces in Mongol-dominated Asia with which he could negotiate. Had not Louis' emissary brought news that Batu's son, Sartach, who ruled south-eastern Russia for the Great Khan, was a convert to Christianity? And had not Philip of Toucy, son of the one-time Regent of Byzantium, described his own mission to the Coman

---

[1] *Ibid.*, p. xxx.

people of southern Russia and to the Mongol court at Karakorum on behalf of Emperor Baldwin II of Byzantium as one in which he made contact with local Nestorians?

King Louis chose as his next emissary to the Mongols the Flemish friar, William of Rubruck, who had accompanied him throughout his disastrous crusade. Friar William had the benefit of both Philip of Toucy's and Friar Andrew's experiences. Given a small purse by his king and an illuminated psalter by his queen, Friar William set out in 1253 from Constantinople on what was to be the most useful of all Christian missions to the Mongols.

Still angry about Ogul Gaimish's trickery, Louis carefully avoided giving William plenipotentiary credentials. But he did provide the Flemish friar with a personal letter of introduction to Sartach, whom he hoped would help him on his way to the Great Khan himself. In a 5,000 mile epic journey William reached the encampments of Sartach and Batu, then pushed eastward to meet Mangu Khan at Karakorum. He returned in 1255 and gave King Louis – by now back in France – a complete account of his extraordinary adventures. History is indebted to Roger Bacon for including many of the details of Friar William's remarkable achievement in his *Opus Majus*, but otherwise this unique record of the thirteenth-century Mongol empire has been largely over-looked. Not until 1600 were additional details published by Richard Hakluyt, Britains foremost chronicler of adventure and discovery. The fame which came to Marco Polo might just as well have been Friar William's for his lively record of travel and discovery many years earlier.

Rubruck was the first to bring accurate and detailed intelligence on the Christians living within the Mongol realm. His reconstruction of the Prester John saga and the role played by this Christian king in the rise of Genghiz Khan is in broad outline correct although understandably inaccurate in detail. He told of a 'mighty shepherd', leader of a partially Mongolized Turkish people known as the Naiman, who called himself King John. John's brother, Unc Chan or Unc Khan Toghril, 'Lord of Caracorum (Karacorum) and ruler over the Crit (Kerait[1]) and

---

[1] The Keraits were another semi-Mongolized tribe living to the south-east of the Naimans and south of Lake Baikal.

Merkit[1] Nestorian people', seized command of the Naiman on their king's death and became the semi-mythical leader known to Christendom as Prester John.

Friar William in his *Journey to the Eastern Parts of the World*[2] appears to believe that Unc Khan Toghril later abandoned Christianity for idolatry. But this would be the natural reaction of a Franciscan monk to the Nestorian doctrine which had been moulded in many curious ways by its close exposure to Turkish-Mongol Shamanism.

In Rubruck's historical sketch of the Mongols, a Mongol blacksmith and cattle thief named Genghiz provoked Unc Khan to launch a punitive campaign against certain of the Mongol-Tartar tribes which harboured this young outlaw. In retaliation, a tribal coalition under Genghiz's leadership defeated Unc Khan and sent him fleeing eastward to his death.[3]

Modern historical research indicates that Genghiz, or Temujin as he was originally known, submitted himself as a vassal to Toghril – or Prester John – in 1185. This was a natural act by the young blacksmith since Toghril had been his father's former overlord. Angered by repeated raids from the forest-dwelling Merkits to the north, Temujin and Toghril joined forces to campaign against the marauders. They soon overwhelmed their adversary. Unc Khan Toghril thereafter assumed the title Wang Khan, or 'Prince of Princes', while Temujin earned the honorific, 'Commander of Hundreds'. In 1197 Temujin again helped Toghril, this time to defeat his Merkit adversaries and restore him to the Kerait throne from which he had been earlier driven by a hostile brother. In 1203 the alliance broke up with Temujin driving Toghril into exile among the Naimans. After a series of successful campaigns to consolidate power, Temujin declared himself 'Supreme Khan' in 1205 and adopted the new title, Genghiz Khan – 'Conqueror of the World' – by which he is best known today.[4]

Friar William took notice of the Nestorian Christian com-

---

[1] The Merkits were a Mongol tribe inhabiting the forests bordering Lake Baikal on the east.
[2] William Woodville Rockhill, *op. cit.*   [3] *Ibid.*, p. 115.
[4] Sir Henry Yule, *Cathay and the Way Thither*, Vol. I (London, Hakluyt Society, edited by Henri Cordier, 1916), pp. 178–81.

munities which existed among the Mongols. But predictably parochial in his outlook, he commented critically that the Nestorians 'know nothing', and while 'they say their offices and have sacred books in Syrian', they 'chant like those monks among us who do not know grammar and they are absolutely depraved.' Friar William accused them of being 'usurers and drunkards', and some he alleged 'even had several wives like their Tartar neighbours' and, equally reprehensibly, 'wash their lower parts like Saracens'.[1] William noted also the presence of Armenian Christians whom he unfairly judged by a rogue of a monk called Sergius.

Tibetan Buddhism, or Lamaism as it is commonly called, first began to appear among the Mongols about the time of Friar William's visit to Karakorum. Because of marked similarities between certain Christian and Lamaist rituals, the latter were frequently misinterpreted by early European travellers as aberrant Christian rites. Some scholars believe – interestingly but not wholly convincingly – that Lamaist ritual was in fact influenced by the Nestorians with whom Tibetan lamas had begun to come in contact at about this time.[2]

It is known from other sources that a renowned Tibetan lama named Saskya Pandita visited the court of Kuyuk Khan in 1247, and Mangu Khan appointed a Tibetan lama called Namo as religious overseer a few years later. But not until the reign of Kublai Khan, who formally embraced Lamaism as the state religion, did this religion become generally accepted among the Mongols. In 1260 Kublai named Drogon P'agapa as 'Imperial Advisor' and head of the Buddhist Church with the title, 'Great Precious Prince of the Faith'. It was this act which provided the Mongols with a claim of suzerainty over Tibet even though Mongol troups never occupied that high plateau.

Friar William is the first European traveller to observe, or at least make reference to 'incarnate lamas', the ranking clerics in Tibetan Buddhism. He specifically mentioned a young 'living Buddha', as the incarnate lamas are sometimes known, who had reached his 'third incarnation', William also commented on 'a

[1] William Woodville Rockhill, *op. cit.*, pp. 157, 158.
[2] W. Y. Evans-Wentz, *The Tibetan Book of The Dead* (New York, Oxford University Press, 1960), pp. 232–8.

priest from Cathay' who, on one occasion, had been seated near him, 'dressed in red stuff of the finest hue'.[1] Judging by the costume, this curiosity was in all probability also a Lamaist priest.

The Franciscan traveller's knowledge of the Tibetan people was minimal, and it is likely that they were then still somewhat of a mystery to the Mongols themselves. He heard only that the Tibetan people 'were held an abomination among all nations' because of a habit they once had of eating their parents upon death. The Friar colourfully credited this custom to more primitive religious ritual which dictated that 'for piety's sake they [the Tibetans] should not give their parents any other sepulchre than their bowels'. William observed that the Tibetans 'make handsome cups of the skulls of their parents, so when they drink out of them while merrymaking, they may have their parents well in mind.'[2]

Rubruck commented briefly on the Uighur tribes settled south-west of Karakorum between the Mongol capital and Lake Balkash. Their towns were a *mélange* of Nestorian Christians and Saracens. In a town called Cailac, Friar William was dismayed at the state of idolatrous degeneration in which he found their church: but in fact, he had mistaken a Buddhist temple for a Christian place of worship. Unaware of his error, he asked the priest, 'Have you not here the cross and figure of Jesus Christ?' The startled prelate replied simply – and one can assume with a certain amount of puzzlement – 'It is not our custom.' Still the good Friar persisted in believing that the idolatrous worshippers were the degenerate remnants of early Christianity, and he set about searching for clues to substantiate this theory.

On the basis of rituals and sacred images which resembled those in his own Catholic Church, Friar William concluded that this strange sect had simply atrophied with time or isolation and had become unrecognizable. He described the clergy as having cleanly shaven heads, wearing saffron-coloured robes and living communally in large monasteries. His descriptions of course fit the symbols and dress of Lamaism. A winged St Michael, which he described, could have been one of the many saints in the Lamaist pantheon; figurines of 'praying bishops' similarly could

---

[1] William Woodville Rockhill, *op. cit.*, p. 199.
[2] *Ibid.*, pp. 151, 152.

have been Bodhisattwas – or preaching Buddhas. And the bald, saffron-robed priests perfectly described Lamaist monks.

An exploratory trip to the Great Khan's court by the Venetian merchants, Nicola and Maffeo Polo, was different from that of their missionary predecessors in so far as it was motivated by commerce. When a younger brother, Marco, returned with them to Kublai's court in 1275 and entered into the Great Khan's service, a seventeen-year epic exploration of Cathay began. The Western world would ultimately be the beneficiary of his acute observations, made from the vantage point of an emperor's agent.

While Marco Polo did not dwell on the Nestorian Church, he did note that the great Mongol leader had a certain sympathy for Christians who were then dispersed throughout the Mongol Empire.[1] But once, when asked by the Polos why he did not embrace this faith, Kublai Khan complained: 'The Christians of these countries are ignorant, inefficient persons who do not possess the faculty of performing miracles, whereas, you see, the idolaters can do whatever they will.'[2] Earlier he had asked Marco Polo's brothers, during their first trip, to petition Pope Gregory X for 'a hundred persons well skilled in law, who being confronted with the idolaters shall have power to coerce them'. The Mongol Emperor explained how Christians must be endowed with the same occult powers as idolaters; but, unlike the latter, these powers would be used for good, not evil. He added, 'When I am witness of this, I shall allow myself to be baptized.'[3]

According to one story, probably exaggerated, Kublai Khan had brought before him both Christian missionaries and Buddhist lamas. He demanded of each a miracle by which method the relative strength of their faiths could be tested. The Christians were unable to produce a miracle on demand (or unwilling to participate in such sacrilege), while one of the lamas obligingly caused his cup of wine to rise of its own accord to his lips.[4]

While it is fascinating to speculate how the history of the world might have been changed had the Christians at Kublai's court

---

[1] Sir Henry Yule, *op. cit.*, Vol. I, pp. xcvii, xcix.
[2] *The Travels of Marco Polo, The Venetian*, translated and edited by William Marsden, re-edited by Thomas Wright (Garden City, Garden City Books, 1948), p. 114.
[3] *Ibid.*, pp. 114, 115.
[4] L. A. Waddell, *Lhasa and its Mysteries* (London, 1950), p. 26.

been willing and able to produce a conjurer at the right moment, it is likely that the Great Khan had less capricious reasons for embracing Buddhism. In 1270 he placed on Tibet's throne a Lamaist monk of the so-called 'Red Hat' sect. This began a dynasty of Sakya priest-kings in Tibet who drew support and protection from the Mongols. The Tibetan kings, who, by virtue of their isolation, could escape the usual bonds of vassalage, nevertheless, had a 'patron-priest' relationship which provided the Mongols with a measure of influence which was essential to protect the southern boundaries of their empire.

Nearly a decade after Marco Polo left China a Franciscan ascetic named Odorico of Pordenone arrived at the court of the Great Khan. His observations, while surely embellished and in some cases perhaps invented, are classics of their kind.[1] In Hangchow Odoric recalls his revulsion at watching a Christian convert summon and feed a weird collection of assorted animals from the surrounding woods, which, he explained, had 'the souls of gentlemen'. In what sounds like a distorted version of the Buddhist doctrine of reincarnation, the 'Christian' added that 'if a man be noble, his soul (after death) entereth the form of someone of these noble animals; but the souls of boors enter the forms of baser animals and dwell therein!'[2] The shocked friar was unable to dissuade him from this idolatrous belief.

Travelling down the Yangtze-Kiang River, the Franciscan came to the city of Yamzai – probably Yangui of Marco Polo's time and the Yangchufu of later years – where there was a Franciscan mission and 'three churches of the Nestorians'. Odoric praises Yamzai as 'a noble and great city, containing 400,000 tributary fire places and offering an abundance of all kinds of things on which Christian people live.' Ten miles from Yamzai at the mouth of the Yangtze, perhaps Chinkiangfu, Friar Odoric gazed upon 'shipping finer and more numerous . . . than in any other port in the world'. The ships were white as snow and had sumptuous accommodations 'which no man would believe unless he had seen them with his own eyes'.[3]

---

[1] Some of Odoric's stories became better known through the pen of John Mandeville, an English plagiarist, who claimed certain of Odoric's experiences as his own.
[2] Sir Henry Yule, *op. cit.*, Vol. I, pp. 119, 120.
[3] Sir Henry Yule, *op. cit.*, Vol. I, pp. 119–27.

Odoric's memory – or imagination – was most vivid when describing Canbaluc, the Peking of today, where the seat of Mongol power had been located. His stay there from 1322 to 1324 obviously made a deep impression on him. His awe shines through the pages of his journal as he describes the court of the Great Khan.[1] The Mongols had come a long way from the dusty encampment at Karakorum. The decadence which accompanies power was now clearly visible. The crude but vital court of Kuyuk seen by Carpini could never have boasted a spectacle such as this one described by Odoric in writing of a great state banquet:

The barons are ranged . . . in their appointed places . . . arrayed in divers colours; for some, who are the first in order, wear green silk; the second are clothed in crimson; the third in yellow. And all these have coronets on their heads, and each holds in his hand a white ivory tablet and wears a golden girdle of half a span in breadth; and so they remain standing and silent. And round about them stand the players with their banners and ensigns. And in one corner . . . abide the philosophers. . . . [When] the hour and conjunction awaited by the philosophers arrives, one of them calls out with a loud voice saying, 'Prostrate yourselves before the Emperor, our mighty Lord!' And immediately all the barons touch the ground three times with their heads. Then he will shout again: 'Rise all of you!' and immediately they get up again. And then they wait for another auspicious moment, and when it comes he will shout out again, 'Put your fingers in your ears!' And so they do. And then, 'Take them out' and they obey. And then he will say, 'Bolt your meal!' And so they go on with a number of such other words of command, which they allege have deep import.[2]

Odoric was not adverse to embroidering his narrative to titillate his readers. For example, in the grand finale of the banquet he describes lions, 'doing obeisance unto the Great Khan', and jugglers causing golden goblets of wine to fly up and down in the air and 'offer themselves to the lips of all who lust to drink of it'. The good friar tantalizes his readers by concluding: 'Such things and many more are done in that [Mongol] lord's presence; and any account that one can give of his magnificence,

---

[1] Probably Dua-Timur was Great Khan when Odoric first arrived in Canbaluc.
[2] Sir Henry Yule, *op. cit.*, Vol. I, pp. 141, 142.

and of the things that are done in his court must seem incredible to those who have not witnessed it.'[1]

The small Franciscan mission had a place of respect at the court and was regularly called upon to bestow their blessing on the Great Khan. The mission was then headed by Friar John of Monte Corvino, who had been sent to the court of Kublai Khan at the end of the thirteenth century (probably 1292 or 1293) by Pope Clement V.[2] This famous missionary, who died an old man in 1328, was the first archbishop of Canbaluc. During his long and successful mission he had an important impact on the Mongol capital. According to one report, he converted and baptized the Mongol Emperor (probably Ayur Balibatra, grandson of Kublai Khan) who was buried in 1311 with full Christian service in the mission's church.[3] In a memoir of his mission, Friar John describes the kindnesses bestowed on Christians by the Great Khan, but accuses the Nestorians of jealously opposing him. With understandable satisfaction, however, Monte Corvino notes that he converted to the Roman faith a certain Nestorian, King George, 'of the illustrious family of Prester John'.[4]

After three years in Canbaluc, Odoric set out to reach Europe overland through uncharted Central Asia. Fifty marches brought him to Tozan, which he referred to as the capital of the 'Empire of Prester John'.[5] The imaginative Franciscan was perhaps the last European chronicler to have placed the lands of Prester John in Asia.[6]

Odoric pressed on to Kansan – the Quengianfu of Marco Polo – which was one of the farthest provinces of the Mongol realm. Beyond this lay Tibet. It is doubtful that he ever reached Lhasa or, for that matter, actually crossed Tibet proper, as he implies in the chronicle of his journey. But his descriptions, which pre-

---

[1] *Ibid.*, pp. 143, 144.

[2] It is not clear whether or not Kublai Khan was still living when Monte Corvino arrived.

[3] Sir Henry Yule, *op. cit.*, Vol. III, p. 10.

[4] *Ibid.*, Vol. I, p. 173; Vol. III, pp. 46, 47.

[5] This appears to be the Tenduc of Marco Polo, which the latter described as the chief seat of Prester John when he ruled the Tartars. Yule, *op. cit.*, Vol. I, pp. 146, 147.

[6] A treatise written by the Italian, Giovanni da Carignano makes an imaginative case for Prester John being an Abyssinian, and thereafter the search for this Christian king's traces seems to centre on that ancient Christian nation of Africa.

sumably were based on the observations of persons whom he met and talked with, provide the first real information on this remote plateau to reach Europe. With his own imagination or credulity showing through, he wrote:

I came to a certain great kingdom called Tibet, which is on the confines of India proper, and is subject to the Great Khan. . . . The chief and royal city, Lhasa, is built with walls of black and white, and all its streets are well paved. In this city no one shall dare to shed the blood of any, whether man or beast, for the reverence they bear a certain idol which is there worshipped. In that city dwelleth the *Abassi*, i.e. in their tongue, the Pope (Dalai Lama) who is the head of all idolaters.

And the fashions of this kingdom are thus: the women have their hair plaited in more than one hundred tresses, and they have a couple of tusks as long as those of wild boars. And another fashion they have in this country is this: Suppose one's father is to die, then the son will say, 'I desire to pay respect to my father's memory' and so he calls together all the priests and monks and players in the country round, and likewise all the neighbours and kinsfolk. And they carry the body into the country with great rejoicings. And they have a great table in readiness, upon which the priests cut off the head, and then this is presented to the son. And the son and all the company raise a chant and make many prayers for the dead. Then the priests cut the whole of the body to pieces, and when they have some, so they return to the city . . . praying for him as they go. After this, the eagles and vultures come down from the mountains and [each] one takes his morsel and carries it away. Then all the company shout aloud, saying, 'Behold! the man is a saint! for the angels of God come and carry him to Paradise.' And in this way the son deems himself to be honoured in no small degree, seeing that his father is borne off in this creditable manner by the angels. And so he takes his father's head, and straightway cooks it and eats it; and of the skull he maketh a goblet, from which he and all of the family always drink devoutly to the memory of the deceased father. And they say that by acting in this way they show their great respect for their father. And many other preposterous and abominable customs they have.[1]

Odoric's journey allegedly took him westward to the realm of the 'Old Man of the Mountain', leader of the Ismaeli sect of Shia Islam. Located just south of the Caspian Sea in Alamut, Persia, this citadel was once centre of a kingdom which stretched

---

[1] Sir Henry Yule, *op. cit.*, Vol. I, pp. 148–52.

westward into Syria and southward as far as Isfahan. European Crusaders came to hear of certain members of this sect in Syria who systematically used murder as an instrument of politics. Because they killed while under the influence of *hashish*, these zealots came to be known as 'Hashishins', or 'assassins' – a term since used generically to describe all political murderers.

Odoric described this remarkable citadel as containing delightful fountains of water beside which lounged 'the most charming virgins on the face of the earth'. Wine and milk flowed through conduits 'and the place had the name of Paradise'.[1]

After 'Paradise' Odoric journeyed on, eventually reaching a dreadful valley inhabited by demons, which seemed a hell. Here fantasy appears to have taken over altogether. In this evil place, which it is now believed may have been in eastern Turkey, Odoric was appalled by the litter of dead corpses and terrified by strange, unearthly music which reached his ears. Unbelievers who dared venture into this perilous valley could not survive, but Odoric, with the help of constant prayer and Divine intercession, made his way safely through. Resisting a final temptation in the form of a mound of silver coins at the end of the valley, the good friar emerged unscathed. He reported that 'all the Saracens, when they heard of this, showed me great worship, saying that I was a baptized and holy man; but those who had perished in that valley . . . belonged to the devil.'[2]

Mandeville's Travels, written by an unknown author in about 1357 under the pseudonym Sir John Mandeville, drew heavily on Odoric's experiences. Falsely attributing much of Odoric's journey and many of his adventures to himself, this unknown plagiarizer took particular delight in embroidering Odoric's account of his descent into the perilous valley, and it is likely that this, in turn, inspired John Bunyan's 'Valley of the Shadow of Death'.[3]

After other adventures, Friar Odoric finally reached home in 1330. When he later died, the legends surrounding his life and

---

[1] Sir Henry Yule, *ibid*., pp. 153, 154.
[2] *Ibid*., pp. 157–9.
[3] M. C. Seymour (ed.), *The Bodley Version of Mandeville's Travels* (London, Oxford University Press, 1963), pp. 104, 105, 107.

adventures gave rise to rumours of miracles, which electrified the crowd of townsfolk attending his funeral and spread his fame throughout Italy. Ultimately, he became a *Beatus* or semi-saint and a shrine was erected to his memory in Udine. Seventy miracles were officially credited to him by Rome after his death.

Odoric bequeathed to history a record of his journey. His unique description of Tibet, however embellished if not invented, would be the last for 300 years, and Cathay was to vanish from Europe's consciousness for almost as long. Yet the Church would not forget completely that the steppes, deserts and high plateaus of Central Asia were once peopled by Christians as well as idolaters. Though the tendrils of Mongol power had contracted, denying to the Western world even the few glimpses of Asia's heartland which had been possible in the Middle Ages, the memory of Prester John would linger to haunt Christendom. The records of early travellers would in time reappear like a bad conscience to spur latter-day missionaries to re-explore those remote stretches of Asia denied them for so long. But this time they would approach from a different direction.

Part One

The Missionaries

1

The Jesuits

Whatever else the unwelcome Mongols may be remembered for, they provided Europe with a land link to Cathay by which came new knowledge of mythical lands long shrouded in darkest legend, and new commerce to make the more adventurous rich. The thirteenth-century 'Mongol peace' brought the silk trade to Europe as caravans from Cathay in ever-increasing numbers crawled across the empty steppes and deserts of Central Asia to supply the looms of Italy. The caravans brought disease as well. The bubonic plague, or 'black death', as it was all too appropriately called, struck Europe in 1347. It is said that the dread disease reached a Genoese trading port in the Crimea when the outpost was overrun by marauding Tartars. It spread quickly from there to Constantinople and then to the Continent itself. Before it had run its course more than a third of Europe lay dead of its lethal touch.

The mid-fourteenth century also brought the beginning of the Hundred Years War between England and France. This marathon conflict, which bled Europe dry and plunged it into profound chaos, left neither will nor resources for intercourse with Asia. But even if Europe had not been agonized by war and pestilence, the disintegration of the Mongol monolith would soon make commerce unpredictable and unprofitable.

By 1368 the Mongols had been expelled from China by the Ming warriors, cutting off the silk and causing the caravan traffic to dwindle still further. No less a block to trade was the rise of Moslem power astride the western approaches to Asia. With the Turkish capture of Constantinople in 1453, Venetian and Genoese traders were cut off from their customary Black Sea staging depots for onward, overland travel to Cathay. The southern route by way of Alexandria was similarly cut off by the greed of the Sultan who sought to take advantage of the situation by extorting ruinous taxes for the privilege of transit.

With eastern egress from the Mediterranean blocked by Islam it was inevitable that maritime power would shift to the Atlantic. Only by the long route around Africa could the spices of India or the silks of Cathay now be brought to Europe. Whichever power controlled the sea lanes would have the rewards of trade with the Orient. The Portuguese, whom geography had destined to become a great maritime people, had systematically explored the west coast of Africa and thus taken the lead in pioneering the new route to Asia. Under Prince Henry the Navigator's leadership Portuguese mariners probed Africa's west coast, pushing ever southward. Portuguese ships finally rounded the Cape of Good Hope in 1434, and for the first time it could be said that the Moslem flank had been turned.

The ghost of Prester John still provoked the devout Portuguese to seek lost Christian colonies in the new lands they found on the far side of Africa. Abyssinia, with its early Christian culture, had by then largely replaced Central Asia as the imagined redoubt for John's descendents. India, however, was still linked with the legendary Christian king: Portuguese mariners were, therefore, not too astonished to find indigenous Assyrian Christians along India's south-west coast when Vasco da Gama reached there in 1497 in his search for spices. But the Christians in Travancore, whose origins probably date from the fourth century, said nothing about Prester John; they claimed instead (as they still claim today) that their ancestor's original conversion had been made by the Apostle, Thomas, in the first century.

Portuguese efforts to monopolize the Indian spice trade brought them into conflict with Hindu merchants who had traditionally sold their products to Arab traders plying their dhows between Calicut and South Arabia. This led to the establishment in 1510 of a Portuguese base at Goa, halfway up India's west coast, from where the Arabian Sea could be controlled. Portuguese methods were cruel and earned for them the lasting antagonism of the Indians, but at least a permanent foothold on the sub-continent was secured and Portuguese maritime supremacy in the Indian Ocean was ensured for some time to come.

Coincident with the landing of the Portuguese in India was the invasion of the Mongols who were destined to rule most of the sub-continent. In 1517 Babur, a chieftain of predominantly Turkish blood – fifth in descent from the great Tamerlaine – marched into India to begin what is now known as the Moghul dynasty. After nearly two decades of defending his hereditary lands in Badakhshan from Uzbek harassment and trying in vain to recapture the ancestral capital of Samarkand, Babur took Kabul and Kandahar to create for himself a new kingdom to the south made up of the lands which are now called Afghanistan. India next was ripe for the picking. Recognizing that the Afghan Lodi rule was weakened by dissension, Babur struck on 21 April 1526, defeating Delhi's defenders at the Battle of Panipat. One year later at the Battle of Kawaha near Agra, Babur's cavalry, deployed in the classic Mongol 'wheeling' manœuvre, defeated a Rajput effort to contest his drive for control of north India. By the time of his death in 1530, Babur ruled Afghanistan, the Punjab and the north Indian plains to the borders of Bengal.

After a precarious rule of twenty-six years Babur's successor, Homayun, died leaving a much weakened and very insecure realm to Akbar, his son. Akbar ruled for forty years. He defeated Rajputs, Gugeratis and Bengalis. In 1586 he took Kashmir, then he conquered Orissa in 1592 and the Sind in 1595. By 1605, when he died, Akbar's empire stretched from Badakhshan to the Bay of Bengal and southward through the Sind to the Arabian Sea.

The Portuguese first came in contact with Akbar at the time of the Great Moghul's conquest of Gujerat. Negotiations between them took place in 1573. Four years later two Portuguese emissaries were sent from Goa to Akbar's court at Fatehpur Sikhri near Agra to discuss further the relationships between the Portuguese and the Moghuls in India. Julian Pereira, one of the envoys, discussed Christianity with Akbar as well and described in what must have been irresistible terms the mission work of the Jesuits at Goa. Perhaps searching for the eclectic religion he was ultimately to formulate, or simply for reasons of state, Akbar sent two emissaries to Goa in 1579 to request the Jesuits to open a mission at his court. Thus it was that Rudolph Aquaviva, accompanied by Fathers Antonio Monserrate and Francisco Henriques, opened the first Jesuit mission to the Moghul court.

The first Jesuit missionaries at the Moghul court of India found the mysteries of Himalaya and Trans-Himalaya irresistible. As the sixteenth century drew to a close the world which lay beyond the highest and most awesome mountain barrier remained shrouded in obscurity. Was it the edge of Cathay, then but a vague geographic concept only dimly understood in the West, or was it a separate region with its own identity? Long buried records left by the few medieval travellers who reached the court of the Great Khans referred loosely to the heartland of the Mongol empire as Cathay[1] but its limits were never defined. Not until the sixteenth century did Portuguese mariners and missionaries who reached China by sea provide Europe with intelligence on the littoral of the Orient. But even then confusion persisted as to whether or not the land seen from the coastal approaches was identical to the Cathay of Kublai Khan, described so vividly by Marco Polo three centuries before.

The early Jesuits in India generally shared the view of European geographers who believed that Cathay was one realm, China another. The opposite conclusion had been reached by Mathew Ricci, the great Jesuit pioneer in China. But if China and Cathay were the same, what had become of the once influential Nestorian Christian communities? While they were known to have been strongly rooted in Cathay by the end of the thirteenth century, there existed no trace of them when the first Portuguese ships touched the China coast in the sixteenth century. Did this substantiate the theory that China and Cathay were not the same? If so, what were the limits of Cathay and what remote corner of that empire still harboured the missing Christians?

Father Nicolas Pimenta, Jesuit Provincial in Goa, was probably the first to propose seriously that exploratory probes be made beyond the Himalayas in search of Christian enclaves.[2] Adding urgency to his recommendations were tantalizing stories, repeated by Indian pilgrims and wandering Hindu ascetics from the Himalayas, describing Tibetan religious rites that sounded disturbingly similar to those of the Catholic Church. Moreover,

---

[1] Cathay is a term which came into Europe's geography in the thirteenth century at the time of Mongol conquests. The word is a corruption of 'Khitan', a Manchu tribe which, until the tenth century, lived in north-east China. The Khitan conquered the entire territory from the Sea of Korea to the Altai mountains and southward as far as the Hoang-ho River. The 'Iron dynasty' of the Khitans lasted two centuries and gave the region the name of Khitai, or Cathay as it is known in English.

[2] Sir Edward Maclagan, *The Jesuits and the Great Mogul* (London, Burns, Oates & Washbourne Ltd, 1932), p. 336.

Tibetans were said to revere sacred images and relics in their temples. They also held religious processions and conducted liturgical chanting reminiscent of Gregorian ritual.[1]

The Jesuit mission at the court of Emperor Akbar became seriously interested in trans-Himalayan exploration in 1581 on the basis of new reports alleging Christian practices in Tibet. Father Monserrate of the Moghul, or 'Mogor' mission – as it was then known – was intrigued by one particular story related by a native traveller who alleged that in a western Tibetan town which he had visited a weekly symbolic offering of wine was made by the local priest. Monserrate thought this must surely be a Eucharistic rite traceable to Christian influence.[2]

Father Rudolph Aquaviva, also of the first Mogor mission, reflected the Jesuits' increasing fascination with Tibet in a letter to Rome. With breathless enthusiasm, he wrote in 1582: 'We have discovered a new nation of heathen called Bottan (Tibet) which is beyond Lahore toward the River Indus – a nation very well inclined and given to pious works. They are white men, and Mohammedans do not live among them, wherefore we hope that if two earnest Fathers are sent thither, a great harvest of other heathen may be reaped.'[3]

With the withdrawal of the Mogor mission in 1583, the Jesuits were forced to suspend plans for a trans-Himalayan expedition. A revival of concern for the fate of Asia's lost Christians had to wait until the closing years of the century when Father Jerome Xavier – grand nephew of Saint Francis Xavier – stirred new interest in it among the priests of the third Mogor mission. Looking well beyond the Himalayas, Xavier advocated an exploratory journey northward to the Cathay of the Mongols.

Medieval church histories preserved the most reliable descriptions of Asia's Nestorian communities, written by the thirteenth-century Catholic emissaries to the court of the Great Khans. Such records provided at least some knowledge of Central

---

[1] *Ibid.*, p. 337.

[2] *Ibid.*, p. 337. According to the Tibet scholar W. Y. Evans-Wentz (*op. cit.*, p. 237), 'Some of the rituals of Northern Buddhism may seem to suggest a Christian-like theory of the forgiveness . . . of sins, which, more than any other subsidiary doctrine peculiar to northern Buddhism may possibly yet be shown to have been shaped . . . by Christianity.'

[3] *Ibid.*, p. 38.

Asian Christianity. Recollections of medieval Christendom's contact with its Asian co-religionists and the spectre of lost congregations – however idolotrous they may have become – provided the basis of Xavier's concern. His interest was further stimulated by a stay in Kashmir. Driven from the Lahore palace on Easter day by a raging fire, Akbar's court, including Father Xavier, was obliged to move to this cool retreat earlier than usual in the spring of 1597. From here Xavier wrote often of his plan for a northern probe. Again the next year from Lahore and the year after that from Agra he tried to excite interest in the subject of Christians in Cathay. In one letter he quoted an old Moslem merchant, returning from thirty years residence in Canbaluc (or Peking), who alleged that most of the people in Cathay's capital were Christian; that there were temples adorned with figurines of the crucified Jesus. The merchant described a priesthood whose black robes were identical to those worn by Xavier.

In 1601 King Philip III of Spain and the Pope both endorsed Xavier's proposal to explore Cathay and reclaim for the Church the peoples 'lying between India and Cathay'. The Jesuit plotted alternative routes. One led from the Vale of Kashmir through Ladakh, along the western edge of Tibet where he had heard in 1597 that there were colonies of Christians. He preferred, however, a route via Lahore and Kabul since this one lay for a longer stretch within the protected boundaries of Akbar's realm.

Bento de Goes, a member of the Mogor mission and Xavier's earlier companion in Kashmir, was selected to lead the mission. Born in 1562 at Villa Franca do Campo on the Azore island of San Miguel, de Goes had shipped to India as a professional soldier while a very young man. A biographer of de Goes named Jose de Torres[1] attempted to prove that the explorer's name had been Luiz Conçalves, and attributed his sudden departure for India to an unhappy love affair. Perhaps more revealing was his restlessness of character which caused him to abandon suddenly the freebooting ways of a mercenary and seek admittance to the Society of Jesus in 1584; and then leave the order just as suddenly before completing his novitiate and run off to Ormuz in the Persian Gulf.

---

[1] Jose de Torres, *Bento de Goes* (Ponta Delgada, Azores, 1854).

De Goes rejoined the Jesuits as lay brother in 1588 and, despite his erratic career, was selected to accompany Father Xavier and Emmanuel Pinheiro to reopen in Lahore the (third) Mogor mission. The three Jesuits reached Akbar's court on 5 May 1595 and within a remarkably short time had earned the Great Moghul's confidence. So great did de Goes's own personal influence become that he was able to dissuade the Emperor from attacking the Deccan where many Portuguese settlements were precariously located. One next hears of de Goes as Akbar's ambassador to the Portuguese viceroy at Goa with instructions to improve the strained relations between the two countries.[1]

While at Goa, de Goes met Father Nicholas Pimenta, Jesuit Superior, and so impressed him that when the question of Central Asian exploration arose there was no question in Pimenta's mind as to who should be chosen to head the expedition.

Disguised as an Indian and travelling under the pseudonym, Banda Abdullah, de Goes and three companions – two Greeks and one Armenian – followed the route recommended by Xavier. They struck northward from Lahore to Peshawar where they heard distorted tales about the Pathans. This gave rise to a faint hope that these remote hill tribesmen who 'drank wine' and 'dressed in black', might even be Christians.[2]

On reaching Kabul the two Greeks dropped out of the expedition. But the Jesuit explorer pushed on, now with only his Armenian friend, Isaac, to accompany him. From Kabul they crossed the lands of the King of Badakhshan whose welcome was assumed since he had once served in Akbar's court. The next major stop was Yarkand in the western part of what is now Sinkiang. Here the Jesuit once again could hope that he had found at least a faint trace of Asia's Christian heritage when a relative of the King of Kashgar claimed ancestors who 'were professors of [the Christian] faith'.[3]

At Turfan, near today's Sinkiang capital of Urumchi, de Goes met merchants from Cathay who knew Father Ricci in Canbaluc and were able to provide geographic details of their journey from

---

[1] C. Wessels, S.J., *Early Jesuit Travellers in Central Asia, 1603–1721* (The Hague, Martinus Nijhoff, 1924), pp. 10, 11.
[2] Sir Edward Maclagan, *op. cit.*, p. 340.
[3] *Ibid.*

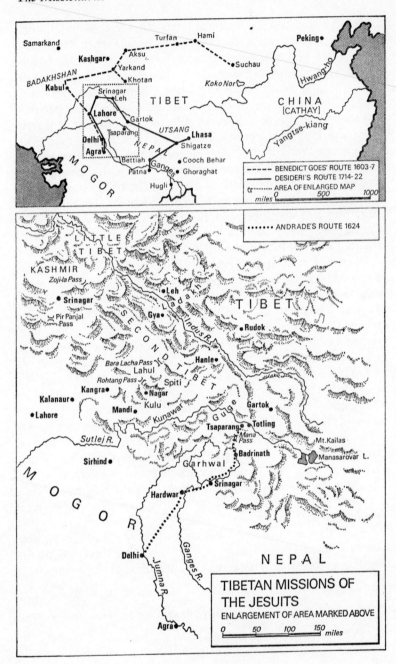

Samarkand

Turfan Hami

Peking●

Kashgar● Aksu

BADAKHSHAN Yarkand

Khotan Suchau

Kabul● Srinagar● Koko Nor Hwang-ho

Leh● T I B E T C H I N A

Lahore● Gartok [CATHAY]

Tsaparang *UTSANG* **Lhasa** Yangtse-kiang

Delhi● *NEPAL* Shigatze

Agra● Bettiah ● Cooch Behar

M O G O R Patna Ganges ● Ghoraghat

Hugli

——— BENEDICT GOES' ROUTE 1603-7
- - - - DESIDERI'S ROUTE 1714-22
········ AREA OF ENLARGED MAP

miles 0   500   1000

●●●●●●● ANDRADE'S ROUTE 1624

L I T T L E
T I B E T

KASHMIR

Zoji-la Pass ●**Leh**

● Srinagar **Gya**● T I B E T

Pir Panjal
Pass ● **Rudok**

Bara Lacha Pass **Hanle**●

Lahul

Rohtang Pass Spiti

Kangra● **Nagar**● Guge **Gartok**●

Kalanaur● **Mandi**● Kulu Tsaparang● **Totling**

● **Lahore** Kunawar *Mana* Mt.Kailas
  Pass

Sutlej R. Manasarovar L.

● **Sirhind** **Badrinath**●

Garhwal

Hardwar● **Srinagar**●

M O G O R

● **Delhi** Jumna R. Ganges R.

N E P A L

**TIBETAN MISSIONS OF
THE JESUITS**

ENLARGEMENT OF AREA MARKED ABOVE

● **Agra** 0   50   100   150 *miles*

the Chinese capital to Turfan. They were also able to produce papers written in Portuguese by Father Ricci. With this evidence, the last remaining link could be joined; de Goes could prove convincingly that China and Cathay were identical. Thus one of his major objectives had been achieved. But the unfortunate Jesuit explorer would never reach home to announce his historic discovery. Hardships endured on his long journey caused him suddenly to become ill and die at Su-cheu, north of Lop Nor. As a Jesuit brother later phrased it; 'Seeking Cathay, he found heaven.'

De Goes's detailed diary was unfortunately stolen by Moslem travellers whom he had befriended along the route. The culprits were probably anxious to remove all records of their indebtedness to this generous missionary who had loaned them money. But de Goes's faithful companion, Isaac, after enduring still more hardships at the hands of the hostile and suspicious Moslems, reached Ricci to reconstruct the details of the Jesuit's remarkable journey.

In identifying Cathay with China, de Goes resolved a geographic mystery. He also established the perimeters of Tibet and provided it with an identity of its own. But his journey, which half encircled the high Tibetan plateau, revealed no Christian enclaves. De Goes had had but faint clues to encourage the hopes that Christians would be found. In Kashgar he had talked with the King of 'Second Tibet', or Ladakh, who described a form of worship which could have been Christian. But this was vague and inconclusive. Perhaps it seemed to confirm earlier rumours of Christianity in Tibet. But it was not much to go on.

Yet despite de Goes's experience, this sort of story in the early 1620s fired the zeal and imagination of still another Jesuit. Father Antonio de Andrade, Portuguese Superior of the Jesuit Mogor mission, like Xavier, was obsessed with the possibility that there still existed forgotten Christian pockets – remnants of the once prospering Nestorian communities of the Middle Ages. He vowed to breach the Himalayas and find the lost flocks which he was convinced were hidden there.

Accompanied by Manuel Marques, a remarkable lay brother who was to figure prominently in the exploration of western Tibet, Andrade set out from the Mogor court at Agra in March 1624, on a reconnaissance of Tibet. They travelled in the retinue of Emperor Jehangir as far as Delhi, keeping secret their real objective. In Delhi the two travellers donned elaborate disguises permitting them to join unnoticed a Hindu pilgrim caravan departing for the holy shrine of Badrinath in south-western Tibet.

Following the rushing Ganges, the pilgrim column reached Hardwar, 'the Gate of Vishnu', then on to Srinagar, the capital of Garhwal province. Chanting 'Ye Badrinat, ye, ye,' the pilgrims wound their way up the Himalayan slopes. Sometimes the path as it clung to the sheer face of towering canyon walls narrowed to inches. The travellers were compelled to edge carefully by these dangerous stretches, gripping the rock where they could to avoid losing their balance and plunging to their death in the rushing Ganges far below. Andrade's descriptions of the forest slopes whose primeval pines towered 'two or three times the height of the church tower of Goa', betray understandable awe.[1] No European had ever before penetrated this part of the Himalayas to feast his eyes on the Cinnamon trees, Cypresses, Lemon and Chestnut trees and endless profusion of wild flowers.

In Garhwal the two Jesuits were uncovered. Somehow unconvincing in their disguises, they were reported to the Rajah of Garhwal who had them seized as spies and subjected to rigorous interrogation. Unruffled, Andrade fell back on an unlikely but apparently plausible story to explain his presence on the Tibetan border: he pretended to be a Portuguese merchant, accompanying the pilgrim caravan into Tibet to visit a sick brother. Black priestly robes found in his luggage were ingeniously explained away on the grounds they would be needed for mourning in the event his brother succumbed.

Finally released after nearly a week of abuse, Andrade and Marques climbed toward the Hindu shrine at Badrinath. As the pilgrim caravan crept forward, passage became even more tortuous. Andrade wrote: 'Not as hitherto by difficult rope-bridges, but over bridges formed by frozen snow, which fill up the whole width of the river, and underneath which the river water breaks itself a foaming passage, we had to cross and recross

---

[1] C. Wessels, S.J., *op. cit.*, p. 48. From *Novo Descobrimento do Gram Cathayo ou Reinos de Tibet* (Lisbon, 1626), based on a letter written by Andrade from Agra on 8 November 1624.

the Ganges, to reach after a journey of a month and a half the pagoda of Badrid (Badrinath).'[1] No other non-believer had ever visited Holy Badrinath and nearly two centuries would pass before another European would brave the upper Himalayas to see this famous shrine.

Of the shrine itself, the Portuguese priest noted that 'it is situated at the foot of a rock from which several springs issue, one of which is so hot that it is impossible for the hand to bear the heat of the water even for a moment.' He added: 'This spring divides into three rivulets which run into their several basins; in these basins the pilgrims bathe to cleanse their souls, the hot water being tempered with cold.' Hindu folklore traces the origin of the sacred springs to the remorse of a fire deity which '. . . was very sorry for all the harm he had done on earth by burning houses, woods and fields, and came to this temple to find a cure for his affliction of spirit.' He found that he could be pardoned only if he remained at the shrine. Thus, 'Fire stayed at the feet of the god and heated the water of the spring.' Unfortunately, a small part of Fire refused to atone and henceforward continued to 'walk the earth' causing untold damage.[2]

Climbing above Badrinath – now without the protection of a caravan – the two Jesuits made their way to Mana, the last town before the great divide which separates India from Tibet. The suspicious Rajah evidently had second thoughts about releasing the two strangers since he sent orders to Mana that they were to be detained again for questioning. Andrade slipped out of town, evading apprehension, and made for Mana Pass with their two servants, while Marques remained behind to deal with the Rajah's agents.

The courageous Jesuit struggled to reach the crest of the pass where he would be beyond the jurisdiction of the Rajah. He had reason to recall with some horror the hardships he had to endure:

Immediately beyond this place there rise lofty mountains, behind which lie an awful desert, which is passable only during two months of the year. The journey requires twenty days. As there is an entire absence of trees and plants here, there are no human habitations, and

---

[1] C. Wessels, S.J., *op. cit.*, p. 50.
[2] *Ibid.*, p. 51.

the snowfall is almost uninterrupted; there being no fuel, travellers live on roasted barley meal, which they mix with water and drink, taking with them nothing that requires fuel to cook. According to the natives, many people die on account of the noxious vapours that arise, for it is a fact that people in good health are suddenly taken ill and die within a quarter of an hour; but I think it is rather owing to the intense cold and the want of meat, which reduce the heat of the body.[1]

As the weary party approached the pass, three provincial agents caught up with them and gave stern warning that retribution would be taken if they didn't immediately obey the Rajah's order to return. On the threat of death, the local guide understandably abandoned the party. But Andrade, ignoring warnings that Marques would be held accountable for his obduracy, pushed on with his two Christian servants.

Snow was to be their most formidable enemy. They floundered in deep drifts – sometimes almost drowning in them. As the pitiful party neared the crest, a blizzard struck with such velocity that they could not see each other, although huddled together. Andrade was so numbed by the piercing cold that a spurt of blood was the only indication he had that part of his finger had been lost in an accident. He complained, 'Having no sense of pain, I should not have believed it had not a copious flow of blood shown it to be a fact. Our feet were frozen and swollen, so much so that we did not feel it when later on they touched a piece of red-hot iron.'[2]

Thirst added to their misery. The valiant Portuguese recalled that 'it was so violent that it could not be quenched by eating snow.' They were also forced to endure the crippling effect of snow blindness. 'It was all one dazzling whiteness to our eyes . . . we could make out no sign of the road we were to follow.'[3] Finally staggering to the top, the Jesuit saw a large glacial pool which he credited correctly as the ultimate source of the Holy Ganges.[4] But whatever exhilaration he felt at this discovery was

---

[1] *Ibid.*, p. 54. From *Novo Descobrimento do Gram Cathayo ou Reinos de Tibet* (Lisbon, 1626), based on a letter written by Andrade from Agra on 8 November 1624.

[2] C. Wessels, S.J., *op. cit.*, p. 56.

[3] *Ibid.*, p. 62.

[4] Sven Hedin, *Trans-Himalaya, Discoveries and Adventures in Tibet*, Vol. III (London, Macmillan & Co Ltd, 1913), pp. 301, 302.

dampened by terrible fatigue. The strain and crippling effect of his climb were beginning to tell; the exhausted priest was forced to retreat from the pass and await a break in the impenetrable curtain of snow which kept him from his goal.

Andrade was joined by Marques who had satisfied the suspicious Rajah, and they once again began an assault on Mana Pass – this time with the assistance of a party of Tibetans. Four months from their departure from Agra they crossed the Himalayan crest and entered Tibet, the first Europeans to do so if one does not accept Odoric's claim three centuries earlier. Unlike the suspicious reception given the two friars in Garhwal, the Tibetans greeted them with surprising friendliness. The King and Queen of Guge, in whose domain along the Upper Sutlej River they found themselves, were particularly cordial and welcomed them to the capital, Tsaparang.

Andrade and Marques could remain less than a month since they had to return to India before the pass was closed by autumn snows. But it had been a good beginning: the King consented to daily religious lessons and gratefully received from the Jesuits an image of the Virgin and Child. So impressed was the petty monarch with Andrade that he insisted that the missionary return the following year. He promised that the mission would have his full support. In a letter to this effect, the King also promised to protect them, hinting that opposition by the Ladakhi Moslems could be expected.

We, the King of the Kingdom of Potente [Tibet], rejoicing in the arrival in our lands of Padre Antonio Frangim [Andrade] to teach us the holy law, take him for our Chief Lama and give him full authority to teach the holy law to our people. . . . We shall not allow that anyone molest him in this, . . . we shall not give credence to any intrigues of the Moors [Moslems] against the Padres, because we know that as they have no law, they oppose those who follow the truth.[1]

Guge was also troubled in its relations with the Hindu regions in India to the south. Andrade and Marques were delayed at Mana on their return journey by a spirited war between Tsaparang and Hindu Garhwal forces. Three petty chieftains,

---

[1] Sir Edward Maclagan, *op. cit.*, p. 345.

vassals of the Tibetan king, had rebelled. This had encouraged the Rajah of Garhwal to attack his northern neighbour. Andrade could do nothing but wait in Mana for hostilities to die down. Snow, this time, came to his rescue by blocking the passes which had been stoutly defended by the Tibetans so that the invaders could advance no further.

Andrade arrived back in Goa in November 1624 where he wrote up his report for the benefit of the Provincial. He could claim no discoveries of lost Christian civilizations, but he felt Guge provided a particularly good environment for propagating the Faith. So well did Andrade make his case that three additional priests were named to join him in establishing a permanent mission at Tsaparang.

By August 1625, Andrade, Marques and a Father Gonzales de Sousa were in Tsaparang as an advance contingent to open the mission. Construction of a permanent church was begun on Easter Day, slightly more than a year later. The King, himself, had donated the necessary funds and had officiated at the corner stone ceremony. Dedicated to 'Our Lady of Good Hope', the church was decorated by New Testament scenes painted by the fathers themselves.

Before the new church was completed the remaining priests arrived in the persons of Fathers João de Oliveira, Alano dos Anjus and Francisco Godīnho. Andrade dismissed with contempt his religious opponents, the lamas of Tsaparang, describing them as 'souls bred in laziness'. He heaped scorn on their beliefs in public disputations. Andrade was confident. He wrote back to Goa of his ambitious plans for expansion.

Andrade always looked upon Tsaparang as a 'gate to many other kingdoms'. Some members of the Tsaparang mission – though possibly not Andrade, himself – travelled northward to Rudok and a branch mission may even have existed there for a while. Probes were also made westward into Ladakh. In Jesuit correspondence there were references to Kashgar in western Chinese Turkestan, which suggested mission activity even that far north.[1] But the most significant initiative taken by Andrade was that which led in 1626 to the establishment of a

---

[1] *Bibliotheca Marsdeniana*, 1827, p. 306.

Jesuit outpost at Shigatse in the southern Tibetan province of Utsang.[1]

Andrade's first knowledge of Utsang was gleaned from itinerant merchants. He learned that the southern province was six weeks' hard journey from Tsaparang over well travelled but difficult trails. Later he realized there were relationships between Utsang and Guge that seemed to provide the entrée he needed for evangelical expansion. The betrothal of a daughter of the King of Utsang with the Crown Prince of Guge offered further possibilities. Andrade wrote: 'I see in this, work of Providence, who thus opens to us a gate into that country.'[2]

A year later Andrade could report to the General of the Society of Jesus that a *firman*, or royal decree, and letter of invitation from Utsang's monarch had been received. In August 1626 the missionary wrote the Jesuit Malabar Provincial, in whose parish lay the Bengal approaches to Utsang, saying that he was considering sending some of his staff to investigate opportunities in southern Tibet. But by then the Provincial, presumably acting on Andrade's earlier advice, had already despatched a mission to Utsang consisting of Father Estevão Cacella, previously an associate of Andrade's in Tsaparang, and Father João Cabral.[3]

Pausing at Hugli on the Ganges delta where there was a Jesuit mission, the small party sought information on the route ahead. Cacella wrote hopefully, 'the road to Cathay is much frequented and offers no serious hindrances.' (The assumption that Tibet was part of Cathay died hard.) Still hopeful that co-religionists would be found in Tibet, Cacella added, 'the people are said to behave as if they were Christians.'[4]

On 2 August 1626 Cacella and Cabral left Hugli and passed through the Kingdom of Cooch Behar. Their journey was held up for nearly four months while they waited in the Himalayan

---

[1] This province, in fact, contained the two distinct areas of U in the vicinity of Lhasa, and Tsang to the south which was dominated by Shigatse.

[2] Filippo de Filippi (ed.), *An Account of Tibet, the Travels of Ippolito Desideri of Pistoia, S.J.*, 1712–1727 (London, George Routledge & Sons Ltd, 1931, revised edition 1937), p. 7.

[3] The mission also included an Italian lay brother named Bartolomeo Fonteboa, who died before the group reached Shigatse.

[4] Filippo de Filippi (ed.), *op. cit.*, p. 20.

border town of Runate for the snows in the passes to melt. Not until February 1627 could they go on.

From Runate the two Jesuits travelled northward and crossed into Bhutan – the first Europeans ever to enter this remote Himalayan kingdom. They found departure, however, more difficult than arrival: the ruler, or Dharma Rajah as he was called, was so delighted with his unique visitors that he offered them every hospitality rather than see them go. The Rajah felt that their departure would somehow reflect adversely on him. Possibly he feared that their mission in Shigatse would somehow upset the power equilibrium he sought to maintain in his relationship with Utsang. To keep the Jesuits at his own court the worried ruler expansively promised them full permission to evangelize and even offered to have built for them a church in the border town of Paro.

Becoming more restless with every day they were restrained, Cacella seized the first opportunity to escape. With the furtive help of a friendly lama he set out for Shigatse one day when the King had left town on a hunting trip. Cabral agreed to remain behind to appease the King who would surely be infuriated when he discovered that Cacella had left. He would await rescue which Cacella would hopefully arrange with Utsang's ruler. Royal intervention was in fact secured soon after Cacella arrived in Shigatse and the Dharma Raja reluctantly relinquished his guest. In the dead of winter, 1627, a greatly relieved Cabral was finally able to leave his enforced residence.

Friction between the Dharma Rajah of Bhutan and the King of Utsang was sharpened with the establishment of a Jesuit mission in Shigatse. The Rajah saw in the Christian mission a threat to Lamaism as well as a political threat to Bhutan. The Dharma Rajah struck back by investigating intrigues against Cacella and Cabral, which to some extent at least had the desired effect. They soon discovered that two lamas from Bhutan had secret instructions from the Bhutanese Rajah to agitate among the monks of the powerful Tashilhunpo monastery near Shigatse and drive a wedge between the Jesuit missionaries and the King.

Religious wars had created serious strains on Tibetan unity. In central Tibet, known as Wu province, the 'Yellow Hat' reformists, known more formally as the *Gelugpa* sect of Lamaism, had the upper hand. But in Utsang province the older 'Red Hat', or

Urgyenist sect, which enjoyed the patronage of the powerful Sakya monastery near Lhasa, was predominant.

Cacella and Cabral had arrived in Shigatse as tension was rising between the Red Hats and the Yellow Hats. Not fully aware of the intricacies of Tibetan politics, the Jesuits nevertheless felt the tension of the times. They may have attributed too much of their difficulties to the machinations of the Bhutanese Rajah and too little to more far-reaching religious dissension. But whatever the case, developments in Shigatse persuaded the missionaries that they should report back to India. Nearly two years had passed since they had left Cochin and it was time for taking stock.

The Dharma Rajah's attitude convinced Cacella and Cabral that they should not return the way they had come. The latter volunteered to find a new route which would by-pass Bhutan. He left Shigatse in January 1628, armed with letters of introduction from the King, and followed a trail well to the west of the one which had brought them to Tibet. This took him through Nepal – the first European to take this particularly difficult route over some of the highest passes of the Himalayas. The journey from Tibet to Nepal is difficult in the best of seasons, but in mid-winter crossing the high passes can be terrifying.

The King of Nepal, who received Cabral at his court in Kathmandu, responded hospitably to the introductions sent by his Utsang neighbour. The Jesuit traveller recalled that he 'very kindly directed me to Patans (Patna)', a town near the India-Nepal border clear of the mountains from where he could easily follow the flat Ganges plains to Hugli.

At the Hugli mission, Cabral joined Father Manuel Diaz who had been recently directed to the Shigatse mission. Together they made for Utsang by way of the Chumbi Valley, skirting Bhutan rather than encounter the hostile Dharma Rajah. The route was hazardous and Cabral had written Cacella, asking that he send an escort to meet them. When none arrived and, even more puzzling, no answer acknowledging his letter was received from Cacella, the two priests halted at an obscure border village called Cocho rather than risk the trip alone.

What Cabral could not know was that Cacella had left Shigatse in an attempt to test the route to Tsaparang. Having had no word from Cabral, Father Cacella feared the worst. He felt it prudent to make his own way westward along the southern trail toward Andrade's mission in Guge and from there travel southward to Garhwal rather than attempt a Himalayan crossing as the missing Cabral had set out to do. The Tsaparang mission was still looked upon as a feasible base of support for Shigatse, and Cacella had already sent several of his reports to his Cochin headquarters in Malabar by way of Tsaparang. Communications would logically seem easier along this lateral route rather than over the forbidding Himalayan passes to Bengal.

Actually, heavy snowfall forced Cacella to turn back well before he reached Tsaparang. Thus after all, he was forced to work his way southward to Hugli. The journey was exhausting but at Hugli his spirits were buoyed by news that Cabral was safe and waiting at Cocho. Cacella finally caught up with his partner and they could for the first time in many months exchange experiences.

It was decided that Cacella and Diaz would risk the trip to Shigatse without escort. Cabral would stay behind to guard the heavy stores which would only attract brigands if an attempt were made to transport them without guard. This was to prove a fatal decision. Diaz died along the way as a result of the extreme rigors of the trip, while Cacella, already weakened by months of exertion in the Himalayas, died within a week of reaching Shigatse.

In the wake of this tragedy the King sent an escort to bring Cabral safely to Shigatse. After some delay the Jesuit reached his destination in 1631. But clearly the problem of communications with India had not been solved and there seemed to be no ready solution.

Cabral made one last effort to have the Shigatse mission placed under Tsaparang in the hope that communications could be maintained despite Cacella's unfortunate experience. But by then a new Jesuit Provincial at Cochin was clearly unenthusiastic about trying to maintain a mission in southern Tibet against such odds. In 1632 Cabral was finally recalled to Malabar and the brave mission's fate was decided three years later when Father Coresma delivered the opinion that 'the risks were too great, and the promise of success too uncertain; the King's only object being to obtain presents from the missionaries.'[1] Shigatse was abandoned; a more auspicious time awaited.

In the meantime Tsaparang seemed to be prospering. Indicative of the progress made by this mission, the Jesuit fathers could report in 1627: 'we hope that the King will receive baptism, and he says he will though he wishes first to know thoroughly the errors of their ['the lamas'] book in order to refute them in meetings which he intends having with the most learned of his ecclesiastics.'[2] As it turned out, the Jesuits were unwilling to baptize him because he would never agree to giving up fornication. But this in no way strained the relationship and the King remained their obliging patron.

Andrade became fascinated by a comparative analysis of the two faiths. Despite his uncompromising opposition to Lamaism, he was intrigued by its apparent similarities with Christianity. These similarities were taken as evidence that Lamaism is but a degenerate form of Christianity, corrupted by its years of isolation. The missionaries saw in Tibetan worship a recognition of the Trinity of God. The Tibetans, according to Andrade, 'know that there are three hierarchies of the Angelic Spirits, divided into nine choirs according to the differences in their excellencies and dignities; that there is a Hell which awaits the wicked and a Paradise for the reward of the good.'[3] The tunics and mitres worn by Tibetan lamas could, with some imagination, be compared with the robes of Christian priests, and elements of baptism, confession and communion seemed to have been present in Lamaism. Andrade wrote that no less an authority than the Head Lama told how the 'Grand Lama in Utsang Province of Tibet offers small quantities of bread and wine, that he drinks of them himself and distributes the remainder to the other lamas and that he blows . . . over the wine which he presents to God.'[4]

Yet Andrade saw also the Shamanistic side of Tibet's religion; the influence of the primitive pre-Buddhist cult of 'Bon' which had been absorbed into Buddhism to form Lamaism. With a

[1] Filippo de Filippi (ed.), *op. cit.*, p. 26.
[2] Sir Edward Maclagan, *op. cit.*, p. 347.
[3] Sir Edward Maclagan, *op. cit.*, pp. 347, 348.
[4] Sven Hedin, *Trans-Himalaya, Discoveries and Adventures in Tibet*, Vol. III (London, Macmillan & Co Ltd, 1913), p. 308.

shudder he described one custom: 'when they prepare for worship, they blow trumpets . . . made of leg and arm bones of dead men, and they also make use of rosaries with beads made from dead men's skulls.'[1] With obvious contempt for his arch-rival, the Head Lama of Tsaparang, Andrade paraphrased remarks made by him on this same subject: 'they used such trumpets in order that the people might remember the dead when they heard the blare, and they often drank out of skulls that they might retain a lively remembrance of death.'[2]

The King's brother, as Head Lama, became fiercely jealous of Andrade's growing influence. While the Jesuits found gratification in the King's help (including financial subsidization), and were moved by visible testimony of royal sympathy, they failed to sense in time the growing public resentment whipped up by the disgruntled lamas. It was inevitable that the blatant royal favour shown the alien mission would inflame the lamas and lead ultimately to a clash with the Jesuits. The priests' frontal attack on Lamaism, made possible by their growing power at court, was in part responsible for the fall from favour of the King's brother. He had long antagonized the King by taking the best of Tsaparang's young men for the monasteries, thereby depriving the army of their services; but Jesuit influence was the critical factor in the schism which developed between the two brothers. This in turn led to further unrest throughout the country.

Much of the strength and momentum of the Tsaparang mission was lost in 1630 when Father Andrade left to take up new duties as Provincial at Goa. He had been the mission's driving force and continuing inspiration. Without him, Jesuit influence could not be sustained. So when the King fell ill in 1633 the dissident lamas, led by the King's brother, saw their chance. With the help and secret encouragement from the King of neighbouring Ladakh, the seething clergy and warrior monks rose against the throne.

The fortifications protecting the King were nearly impregnable. His castle, located on top of a high plateau overlooking Tsaparang, was accessible only by a narrow stairway carved out

---

[1] *Ibid.*, p. 305.   [2] *Ibid.*, p. 308

of the mountain. Amply supplied with food and having access to hidden springs of fresh water, the castle was well prepared to sustain a long siege. But the Chief Lama, always treacherous in dealing with his hated brother, counselled submission with the promise that the King of Ladakh would raise the siege and satisfy himself with a loose suzerain power over Guge. After a month of stout resistance, the King took his brother's advice, only to find that he and his family would henceforward be prisoners of Ladakh. They were carried off to Leh and never heard of again. Tibetan records make sparse reference to this event, noting only that a King of Guge had offended the lamas. Not even his full identity, much less his fate was recorded.[1]

The Christian converts of Guge suffered at the hands of the revengeful lamas. Many were carried off by force to Ladakh as slaves. The church was sacked and five Jesuits in residence at the time of the assault became virtual prisoners of the Ladakhis.

Andrade's response to the catastrophe was to send Father Francis de Azevado, a former colleague at Tsaparang to investigate. Accompanied by the indefatigable Marques, Azevado reached Srinagar in Garhwal where they were held up by mourning ceremonies following the Rajah's sudden death. The missionaries were shocked witnesses of the *sutee* ritual in which sixty women from the harem leaped to horrible deaths on the Rajah's funeral pyre. The friars arrived in Tsaparang on 25 August 1631 to find the situation as bad as they had anticipated. What was left of the mission was unable to serve the small community of converts. The pathetic collection of Christians was anyway too frightened to practise the rituals of its new faith.

Azevado decided that a bold and direct approach would be best. Recognizing that only in the capital could he hope to get satisfaction, he went on to Leh. This proved not only to be a wise political decision but it provided the West with its first glimpse of Ladkh's capital. Toward nightfall Azevado arrived at the gates of Leh. In his first view of the town he saw that it was 'built on the slope of a small mountain, and numbering some 800 families'.[2] Observing the customary formalities, the group

---

[1] Leh chronicles refer to the King only as 'Loslong' which means 'the blind'.
[2] C. Wessels, S.J., *op. cit.*, p. 108.

dismounted and waited patiently for permission to enter. On orders of the King they were finally admitted and provided with food and lodging.

Shortly after arrival they were sent for by the King – 'less to see us personally than to receive our presents', commented Azevado. The Jesuit described King Senge-Namgyal as 'a man of tall stature, of a brown colour, with something of the Javanese in his features, and of stern appearance. He wore a rather dirty upper garment of some red material, a mantle of the same, and a threadbare cap; his hair hung down to his shoulders, either ear was adorned with turquoise and a large coral, whilst he wore a string of skull bones round his neck to remind himself of death.'[1]

The first meeting was also attended by the Queen whom Azevado recalls was short and fat with sore eyes. Chinese tea was served, then the Jesuits were given a piece of raw meat and a ball of husked barley. Azevado's overall impression was that the palace was generally dirty and full of cobwebs.

Not for four days could Azevado get down to business. Listening sympathetically, the King heard the Jesuits' *démarche* and soon afterwards sent royal approval to continue evangelistic work, not only in Guge, but in Rudok and even in his own capital. Azevado and Marques could return to India with this good news, and as tangible proof of the King's good-will they brought with them a gift horse, a broken-down bag, 'very like that of Don Quixote'.[2]

Father Andrade was so encouraged by the success of Azevado's mission that he sought permission to resign as Provincial and to go back, himself, to Tsaparang. This was where he had been happiest. But death in 1634 denied him his wish. It also gave rise to dark rumours that he had been poisoned. There were those in Goa who whispered that this courageous veteran of the first Tibet mission met an agonizing end by the act of an assassin who disapproved of his uncompromising conduct of the Inquisition in Goa.

The death of Andrade seemed to signal another round of misfortunes for the Tsaparang mission. Two priests died *en route* to their new post, while a third became seriously ill and

---

[1] *Ibid.*, p. 109. [2] Sir Edward Maclagan, *op. cit.*, p. 351.

never reached his destination. The two survivors, Fathers Coresma and Correa, reached the mission only to find it still harassed by the Tibetans despite promises made to Azevado by the Ladakhi King.

Coresma found little to be optimistic about. He wrote: 'The people in general are incapable of understanding and realizing anything of the mysteries of our faith. They are very poor and uncivilized and rude to a degree I have never yet seen or read of. ... There is not a shadow of any religious sense; they only frequent their temples to eat and drink.'[1] He was equally disparaging about the mission's conversion record. In ten years no more than a hundred baptisms had been made and many of these were retainers of the mission whose motives were questionable. He felt that the sacrifices which the Christians would have to make in this hostile environment were out of proportion to any success which the mission could reasonably expect to have. He therefore recommended closing the mission. In 1635 everyone was evacuated.

A last effort to re-open Tsaparang failed in 1640 when three new priests with Marques as their guide were unable to reach Tsaparang. The party was attacked as it entered Tibet and all were forced to retreat hastily toward India. Marques unluckily was captured before he could reach safety and held by the Tibetans. In a pathetic letter, which the unfortunate Jesuit veteran wrote in late 1641, he admitted that he was being very badly treated – 'even injured' – and 'had no hope of getting out'.[2] A last attempt to free Marques was made through the Queen of Lahore who appealed to the King of Guge for the Jesuit's release. But nothing came of this and Andrade's old comrade met an unknown, but probably violent end at the hands of the Tibetans.

But for the vagaries of local politics, Guge might have become a Christian state. As it turned out, no remaining trace of Christianity could be found in western Tibet when the next Western travellers passed through many years later. Andrade's brave efforts seemed to have dissolved in thin air.

---

[1] Filippo de Filippi (ed.), *op. cit.*, p. 13.   [2] *Ibid.*, p. 17.

2

Grueber and D'Orville

Not until 1661 was Tibet again penetrated by European travellers. The German Jesuit, John Grueber, and his Belgian companion, Albert d'Orville,[1] crossed the high wastelands of Tibet from north to south to become the first Occidentals to give a reliable report on Lhasa. The record of their journey is tantalizingly brief; so much more could have been told. Yet Grueber's account, incomplete as it was, provided welcome knowledge of this strange and remote world.

While still a theological student, Grueber volunteered for duty with the China Mission. This had brought the young Jesuit into contact with the learned Jesuit scholar, Athanasius Kircher, who was even then planning his monumental book of Asia to be called *China Illustrata*.[2] Before Grueber left in 1656, Kircher secured his agreement to keep a record of the journey. It was thus Kircher's classic work, published in 1667, that introduced Grueber's remarkable story to the world and provided the first meaningful description of Lhasa itself.

Beginning his journey in Venice, the young traveller in 1656 sailed to Smyrna in Turkey. He travelled with Father Bernard Diestel who had originally invited him to join the China Mission. The two missionaries interrupted their sea journey at Smyrna

---

[1] D'Orville may be described more fully as Albert Le Comte, son of the Seigneur of Orville. Kircher, however, uses the form 'Dorville'. In two letters written by the Father, himself, he uses the form, 'de Dorville'. In Baron Isidore de Stein Altenstein's genealogy of the family the form 'd'Orville' is used and this spelling is preferred by Wessels, who is considered one of the best authorities on Grueber and d'Orville. (C. Wessels, S.J., *op. cit.*)

[2] Full title: *China Monumentis Qua Sacris Qua Profanis Nec Non Variis Naturae et Artis Spectaculis, Aliarumque Rerum Memorabilium Argumentis Illustrata* (Amsterdam, 1667).

and travelled overland through the Middle East to the Persian Gulf rather than follow the traditional ocean route. No record remains to explain this departure from the usual. One can speculate that Grueber, even this early in his mission career, was more concerned with exploration than evangelism, and sought to chart a shorter and safer land alternative to the long sea voyage around the Cape from Portugal. Or possibly politics entered into it: it could have been an effort to break the Portuguese monopoly on transport to the Far East. Certainly the Jesuits chaffed under Portuguese insistence that all missionaries, regardless of nationality, travel on Portuguese ships. King Alfonso VI of Portugal had found cause to complain to the Jesuit Order in 1664 of non-compliance with this edict, which is another indication of Rome's attitude towards Lisbon.

Grueber's and Diestel's onward journey took them through Asia Minor, Armenia and Persia – no small accomplishment. From the Persian Gulf island of Hormuz, they again took ship, this time for Surat on the Gulf of Cambay, north of Bombay. After a frustrating ten-month delay in India, the travellers finally found passage on an English ship to the Portuguese colony of Macao on the China coast where they arrived in late July 1658.

The Jesuit mission in Peking, paced by the talented but controversial priest, Adam Schall, had a distinctively scientific bent. At the court of Shun-chi, first Manchu Emperor, Schall served as Director of the Bureau of Astronomical Observation, which is indicative of the prestige he enjoyed among the Manchus. Grueber, a mathematician by training, was a useful addition to Schall's group at the Imperial observatory.

The death of the Emperor and a growing criticism against the unorthodox Schall in the Jesuit hierarchy brought the Peking mission to a point of crisis in early 1661. Consultation in Rome was clearly required. Grueber, who had at the beginning been one of Schall's detractors but later a supporter of the much maligned Jesuit, was chosen for this task, and was specifically commissioned to carry to Rome a bill of charges against Schall for adjudication.[1]

---

[1] George H. Dunne, S.J., *Generation of Giants* (Notre Dame, Indiana, University of Notre Dame Press, 1962), pp. 330, 337.

Unfortunately, however, a return voyage by sea was no longer possible. While the Portuguese still held the port of Macao from which the missionaries customarily sailed, control of the sea approaches had passed to the Dutch. Captains Bort and Speelman, Dutch raiders operating under the orders of Jan Maet Suiker, Governor General of Batavia, attacked Portuguese shipping and blockaded Chinese ports. Macao felt the full force of this harassment. Thus an overland route home had to be found. De Goes's tragic death in Central Asia was still fresh testimony that this method of travel was strenuous and dangerous. His experience also suggested that the route he chose was not a good one. Passage through Tibet to India would perhaps provide a safer, if not shorter, way to Europe. Moreover, it would provide an opportunity to explore the Tibetan highlands which were still totally unknown.

Father Bosmans, a Jesuit scholar and biographer of d'Orville,[1] found evidence to convince him that Grueber's mission from the outset had been to survey a new overland route from China to Europe. Whatever ostensible function he had been given in China, there had never been any intention to leave him there longer than required to prepare himself for the return journey of exploration and survey. Bosmans quotes from a letter written by Father de Rougemeont on 27 July 1661, saying that Grueber, 'sent to China by our Very Reverend Father General to try and find some overland route from Persia to China, wants to have Father Albert [d'Orville] as the companion of his arduous undertaking.'[2] This might also explain why Grueber took the overland route across Asia Minor on his way to China. But it is curious that in none of his correspondence nor in his talks with Kircher did Grueber say anything which would lend credence to Bosman's contention.

Whether he had or had not intended to return so soon to Europe, Grueber was a logical choice to undertake the long overland journey to Rome: he had the endurance of youth and

[1] H. Bosmans, *Documents sur Albert Dorville de Bruxelles, Missionaire de la Companie de Jesus au XVII e Siècle et Notament sur les Épisodes de son Voyage vers Lisbonne et la Chine* (Louvain, 1911).

[2] C. F. Waldack, *Le Père Philippe Couplet, Malinois, S.J. Missionaire en Chine, 1633–94* (Louvain-Bruxelles, 1872).

had received geographical training. Since much of his voyage to China had been by land he had had an opportunity to prove himself a resourceful land traveller – one able to meet the challenges of an untested route.

Grueber's travelling companion, Father Albert d'Orville, had arrived in China before him and had spent more than a year in Shansi Province learning the language. Highborn as Albert Le Compte, son of the Seigneur of Orville, d'Orville left his home-land in Belgium to join the court of the Duke of Neuberg. In 1646 he decided on a religious career and began his Jesuit novi-tiate in Lorraine. It was while studying theology at Louvain University in Belgium that he fell under the spell of Father Martini, one of the more eminent Jesuit missionaries in China. Martini's lectures on China at Louvain so inspired d'Orville that he was one of the first to volunteer to return with Martini to China.

In 1660 d'Orville joined Grueber at the Peking observatory where he took geographical and surveying training in preparation for the trip home. Equipped with Imperial passports and laden with surveying equipment, the two Jesuits set out from Peking on 13 April 1661. They followed an ancient caravan route which approached Tibet by way of Sining-fu. Reaching this Chinese frontier town after a two-month journey, Grueber described it as 'a great and populous city built at the vast wall of China'. Here merchants from India were forced to pass beneath 'three rows of guns'[1] which pointed accusingly from a fort, guarding this gate of empire. They had to petition for imperial licences before they were allowed to enter the 'celestial' realm.

Today the Great Wall of China does not reach to Sining-fu, presumably because it has been obliterated by successive Mongol invasions. But Grueber's vivid description attests to its one time existence. He pictured it as being 'so broad that six horsemen may run abreast on it'.[2] The Jesuit added that the citizens of Sining-fu stroll along the wall and travel on it 'to the next [gate] at Sochow – an eighteen-day journey'. He recounted strange and improbable stories he had heard of wild bulls, tigers, lions,

[1] Athanasius Kircher, *China Illustrata* (Amsterdam, 1667), p. 318. C. Wessels, *op. cit.*, p. 181.
[2] C. Wessels, S.J., *op. cit.*, p. 179.

elephants, rhinoceroses and monoceroses [a legendary kind of horned ass], which were alleged to inhabit this route.

Leaving the Wall behind them, the travellers struck out across the sands of the 'Tartar desert'. Grueber had heard that the great desert began 'in the middle part of India'. He had been astonished by allegations that nobody had yet discovered its bounds, 'which may stretch to the frozen ocean'.

Three days of difficult travel brought the two Jesuits to Koko Nor, the great 'Blue Sea'. After skirting this large, brackish lake and crossing the south Koko Nor range they plunged again into wasteland. The arid Baian Gol plains, part of the Tsaidam Basin, were anything but hospitable. The only evidence of human habitation was the occasional bleak cluster of black felt tents pitched by nomads.

The lonely party crossed the Burkhan Buddha Range and then the Shuga mountains before reaching a 12,000-foot plateau, which was more forbidding than anything they had experienced before. Impossibly barren plains, strewn with the bones of less lucky travellers, faced them for days on end. Grueber complained of the need to be constantly alert for brigands, known to harass unprotected caravans.

Crossing the Baian-kars mountains and the Mur Ussa, or Blue River, on its south flank, the travellers attacked the towering Tangla range. The pass which caravans customarily used is more than 15,000 feet high, though fortunately both ascent and descent are gradual.

Grueber and d'Orville, wearied by their ordeal, could rest briefly at Reting monastery, some forty-five miles north of Lhasa. Here they noted that the lamas wore white coats and red girdles with red caps to match. Sketches of them made by the talented Grueber somehow betray the Germanic hand which drew them. However exotic the costumes, the faces would seem more natural on the streets of Grueber's birthplace, Linz. While clearly a good draftsman, the Jesuit seemed unable to capture the Mongoloid features of the Tibetans.

Grueber and d'Orville reached Lhasa, the Kingdom of Barantola as it was then known by the Tartars, on 8 October 1661 – three months after leaving Sining-fu. On entering the city they were immediately struck, as all subsequent visitors to Lhasa have been, by the sight of the Potala hill rising abruptly at the edge of the town. A sketch by Grueber of the 'European fashioned' palace on top of it remains today the only visual record of the famous landmark as it looked before the present-day Potala was built. In the foreground of the picture is a carriage, which one can excuse only on the grounds of artistic licence since wheeled carriages of this type were then unknown in Tibet.

Grueber told of two kings: one, the 'Deva' of Tartar origin who handled the affairs of state; and the other, the Great Lama, or Dalai Lama, who was worshipped as a deity and exercised supreme religious authority. The Tibetans ascribed to the Great Lama various occult powers and believed implicitly in his omniscience. In approaching him the faithful 'fall prostrate with their heads to the ground and kiss him with incredible veneration.' Thus, believed Grueber, 'hath the Devil, through his innate malignity, transferred to the worship of this people that veneration which is due only to the Pope of Rome, Christ's Vicar.'[1]

The Head Lama, referred to as the 'Lama Kongji' by Grueber, was Ngawang Lobzang Gyatso – the Great Fifth Dalai Lama. This pontiff's powerful religious hold on the Tibetans seemed to Grueber a most formidable obstacle to Christian conversions. That 'devilish God the Father puts to death those that refuse to adore him', observed the Jesuit with obvious exasperation. Yet he was struck with the impression that this 'Pope of the Chinese and Tartars' was guardian of a faith which in all essential points seemed similar to Roman Catholicism. Grueber marvelled that, despite the absence of Christians in Tibet, 'their religion agrees with the Romish'. As eyewitness he reported that they 'celebrate the sacrifice of the Mass with bread and wine, give extreme unction, bless married folks, say prayers over the sick, make processions, honour the relics of idols, have monasteries and nunneries, sing in the service of the choirs, observe fasts during the year, undergo most severe penances, and among the rest, whippings, consecrate Bishops and send out missionaries who live in extreme poverty, and travel barefoot through the deserts as far as China.'[2]

---

[1] Thomas Astley, *New General Collection of Voyages and Travels*, Vol. IV (London, 1747), p. 462.
[2] *Ibid.*, p. 459.

The Fifth Dalai Lama, then in his nineteenth year of power, owed his position to an Öelot Mongol chieftain from the Koko Nor region of 'Lower Tartary', on Tibet's northern border. Gushi (or Gusri) Khan, as the chieftain was known, had driven the Khalka Mongols from that area in 1636. Two years later he had seized the province of Kham. Then in 1641 the victorious Khan had invaded Tibet proper at the invitation of the Fifth Dalai Lama whose Yellow Hat sect of Lamaism had long been subjugated by the rival Red Hat sect headed by Prime Minister Tsangpa. After seizing control of Tibet the Mongol commander for political reasons deeded supreme religious authority to the Yellow-mitred Dalai Lama with whom he had collaborated. This enabled the Yellow, or *Gelugpa*, church to gain ascendency over the Red Hat sect. It also established a 'patron-priest' power formula between suzerain and Dalai Lama which was to repeat itself frequently throughout Tibetan history.

Gushi reigned as patron and ruled in secular matters until his death in 1655. This fulfilled a prophecy supposed to have been made in the ninth century by the Indian Tantric Buddhist scholar, Padma Sambhava – or Urgyen, as he is known in Tibet. This great teacher whose lives and transmigrations of soul in Tibetan history closely resemble the life of Buddha, prophesied 800 years earlier that the 'Tartars of Lower Tartary would become masters of Tibet'.[1]

Upon Gushi Khan's death, his son and successor, Dayan, retained control of the Mongol armies, but relinquished all secular power to the Dalai Lama. The office of Prime Minister, or Grand Vizier, was revived, but the incumbent, Sangye Gyatso, was subservient to the Great Fifth. Thus by the time Grueber and d'Orville arrived in Lhasa, the Dalai Lama held full power in his hands.

Grueber sketched the Dalai Lama and thus brought back to Europe a likeness of one of Tibet's greatest rulers. The Fifth Dalai united Tibet under the Yellow Church and extended the influence of his office throughout the Mongol world. It was also the Great Fifth who ordained his beloved tutor, Ch'ösgyi

[1] Tibet's Book of Lungh-ten, the *Prophecies of Urgyen*, from Filippo de Filippi (ed.), *An Account of Tibet: The Travels of Ippolito Desideri of Pistoia, S.J. 1712–1727* (London, George Routledge & Sons Ltd, 1931, revised edition 1937), p. 280.

Gyaltsän, as 'Panchen Rimpoche', High Priest of Tashilhunpo monastery near Shigatse.[1] The Panchen Lama, as he is known today, is second only to the Dalai Lama in the incarnate Lama hierarchy of Tibet.

The 'Deva' whom Grueber also referred to as King, should more accurately be called Prime Minister. And while Grueber was under the impression that he was a brother of the Dalai Lama, it is now believed that he was the Great Fifth's illegitimate son. The Mongol, Dayan Khan, son and successor of Gushi Khan, still held the title 'King of Tibet', although he was completely subservient to the Dalai Lama.

Grueber's description of life in Lhasa was more accurate than his political observations, though still not as full as one would have liked. Grueber noted that the courtiers had luxurious taste, which in dress ran to gold brocade. The common people, in contrast, were slovenly. He observed, 'neither men nor women wear shirts or lie in beds, but sleep on the ground'. They 'eat their meat raw and never wash their hands or face.'[2]

Grueber was shocked by much he saw. For example, he divulged a 'most detestable' feast day custom in which a committee of high priests empowered a youth of their selection 'to kill without distinction whomever he meeteth with'. The young assassin, dressed in a 'very gay habit, decked with little banners, and armed with a sword, quiver and arrows,' wandered at will through the streets, killing people at his pleasure – none making any resistance.'[3] This fatal ritual was based on the belief that 'whomever he slays obtains eternal happiness'.

Grueber's stay in Lhasa, however brief, provided other less lugubrious details of Tibetan life. He was the first to mention the prayer wheel – that cylindrical container of prayer scrolls – which plays such an important role in the religious life of Tibet. By spinning the small cylinder, the prayers within are believed to be transmitted without need for further thought or articulation. He was also the first of several horrified foreign observers to

---

[1] He was declared to be an incarnation of Amitabha, whose spiritual son is the Tibetan God, Avolokita, incarnate in the Dalai Lama. In the nineteenth century the British in India became accustomed to calling the Panchen Lama the Teshu Lama, or Teshi Lama, after the Tashilhunpo monastery where he resided.

[2] Thomas Astley, *op. cit.*, p. 457.

[3] *Ibid.*, p. 461 (from p. 22 Grueber's letters in Thevenot's Collection).

discover that a rare and much sought after 'curative' pill was, in fact, made from the Dalai Lama's excrement.[1]

From Lhasa, Grueber and d'Orville travelled southward across the high passes of the Himalayas. Crossing Thung La at nearly 17,000 feet, the travellers arrived at ice-bound Nilam. The path beyond became progressively more tortuous. They were repeatedly forced to cross deep chasms of the Bhotia river by flimsy, swinging Tibetan suspension bridges. At some points the trail hung from the face of sheer rock cliffs, supported only by iron pegs. These buttressed toe-holds, sometimes no more than nine inches in width, were poised over canyons as deep as 1,500 feet. After a harrowing eleven-day march they reached Nepal's capital, Kathmandu.

At the time of their visit, Nepal's King Pratap Malla was at war with a troublesome chieftain named Varkam. Leading the Nepalese forces in the field was the King's brother, Mahendra Malla. Grueber, on being received by the warrior prince, presented him with a European telescope from his stock of presents, carried for such occasions. Prince Mahendra, unfamiliar with the optical illusion of a telescope, leaped into action when he saw the greatly magnified image of the enemy forces. Believing them to be nearer than they actually were, he waved his astonished troops forward to the attack.[2]

Grueber's impressions of Nepal were not flattering. He particularly criticized the lack of personal cleanliness which he found among the mountain people. He wrote: 'The women, out of a religious whim, never wash but daub themselves with a nasty kind of oil, which not only causes them to stink intolerably, but renders them extremely ugly and deformed.' The Jesuit priest was also disturbed by certain Nepalese burial customs: 'When they judge their sick people to be past hopes of recovery, they carry them into the fields, and casting them into deep ditches

---

[1] Athanasius Kircher, *op. cit.*, p. 74: 'beatum ille se reputet, cul Lamarum benignitate aliquid ex naturalis secessus sordibus ant urina magni Lamai obligerit; es huius – modi enim collo portatis, urina quique cibis commixta . . . contra omnium infirmitatum insultus tutissimos ac probe munitos se fore stolidissime sibi imaginatur.'

Also: C. Wessels, S.J., *op. cit.*, pp. 191, 192, note 6.

[2] C. Wessels, S.J., *op. cit.*, p. 194. From Thevenot, *Viaggio del P. Giovanni Grueber Tornando per Terra da China in Europa*, Part IV, 1672, p. 2.

full of dead corpses, there leave them to perish, and their bodies when dead, to be devoured by birds and beasts of prey, esteeming it an honour to have living creatures for their tombs.'[1]

The King was loathe to allow the travellers to proceed since the surveying instruments which they carried fascinated him. Only with the promise that they would return, did he allow them to go on their way.

The two missionaries reached India a month after leaving Lhasa – eleven months after departing Peking. Their route from Nepal took them to Patna, Benares and finally Agra. Here, at the Mogor Mission, d'Orville died at age thirty-nine. One can only assume that the hardships of the trip, particularly the gruelling crossing of the Himalayas at a most savage time of the year, caused his sadly premature death. The brave Belgian was put to rest in the 'Martyr's Chapel' of the Catholic cemetery.

Grueber, who went on to Rome by way of Persia and Turkey, submitted his report and made plans to return again to China. For a variety of reasons, this was not to be the case. But what he had accomplished must be considered not only an exceptional feat of human endurance but an extremely useful contribution to geography. His calculations along the route have proven remarkably accurate in the light of later, more elaborately arrived at findings. Moreover, he was the first European to bring back a firsthand account of Tibet and its people. What is perhaps difficult to understand is why he did not provide more details than he did. He said nothing, for example, about the landscape, nor did he have much insight into the everyday life of the Tibetans.

Grueber later commented to the Grand Duke of Tuscany that 'to add anything to what had already been said by so great a man [as Father Kircher] and to write a separate book would be a waste of trouble.'[2] This reference to Kircher's *China Illustrata*, published in 1667, may have contained a note of sarcasm. While Grueber was perhaps being genuinely deferential, there were other indications that he had been disappointed with Kircher's account of his experiences. He wrote from Tyrnau in September 1669, after returning from army chaplain duty in Transylvania:

---

[1] C. Wessels, S.J., *op. cit.*, p. 194.
[2] Sven Hedin, *Trans-Himalaya*, p. 124.

I wish you had at least sent me the headings of the chapters before going to press; I should certainly have supplied you with several data of no small importance. These I intend to send you at some future time— perhaps shortly, together with the whole of my journal, which as yet I have not been able to finish on account of my continuous work among the soldiers.

There are certainly points in *China Illustrata* that need correction, especially the drawings, but it is better to leave things as they are, though I shall send you the recommendations for insertion in case the work should be reprinted.[1]

The tone of subsequent correspondence with Kircher suggested that Grueber intended to write his own book. But, as he wrote in a letter; 'Being engaged in laborious and incessant work among the soldiers, I have, as yet, been unable to finish the work I have begun; but now that I have more leisure, I hope with God's help to have the whole completed before the end of Autumn.'[2]

If Grueber completed his manuscript, no trace of it has ever been found. Should it come to light, one could hope to read a more complete description of the seventeenth-century Tibet than that contained in *China Illustrata*. One could also hope to make a closer acquaintance with the remarkable German priest whose journey must be ranked amongst the more important achievements of exploration.

Despite plans to return to China, Grueber's health forced him to remain in Europe. He spent two years as army chaplain with the Imperial Austrian troops in Transylvania. From his correspondence it is known that from September 1669 on he remained at Tyrnau. But little else is recorded about the last few years of his life. Quietly he died on 30 September 1680 at Saros Patak in Hungary at the age of fifty-seven, carrying to the grave a unique knowledge of a still unknown land.

---

[1] C. Wessels, S.J., *op. cit.*, pp. 167, 168.
[2] *Ibid.*, p. 169. From a letter dated 2 May 1671 from Trencsin.

3

Ippolito Desideri

An optimistic belief that after seventy years there may still remain some of Andrade's original converts in Tsaparang prompted the Jesuits to approve the re-opening of a western Tibet mission. But not until 1712, when Ippolito Desideri – then a twenty-seven year old, fledgling Italian priest – volunteered, was a qualified and willing candidate found for the assignment. As introduction to his remarkable odyssey, Desideri modestly wrote, 'Who brings new and rare fruits from a foreign land need not make excuses if their flavour is not perfect . . . their quality and their rarity must be their excuse.' Unfortunately, the rare fruits of knowledge about Tibet were not shared for nearly two centuries. His manuscripts did not come to light until 1875 when they were discovered among the papers of Cavaliere Rossi-Cassigoli, an Italian gentleman of Pistoia. But then, for one reason or another, they were not published until 1904.

Desideri reached Lhasa on 18 March 1716, having pushed on from his original goal in western Tibet. Three and a half years had passed since he received in Rome the Apostolic benediction for his mission from Pope Clement XI. He was the first Westerner to see holy Mount Kailas, to travel the length of trans-Himalaya and one of the first half-dozen to see Lhasa. The wonderment which he felt during his five years in Tibet is reflected in his warning that those who hear his story 'must not be imbued with the baneful prejudice that a thing out of the common must necessarily be false.'[1]

Desideri's object, of course, was to make converts to Roman Catholicism. He began in Lhasa by working on Tibet's Mongol

---

[1] Filippo de Filippi (ed.), *op. cit.*, p. 50.

king. If the latter could be won over the rest would be easy. This had been Andrade's technique in western Tibet. Desideri lived most of the time in Tibetan monasteries among the lamas he hoped to convert so that he might observe as closely as possible the religion which he was determined to expose as false. Such audacity was extraordinary, particularly when one realizes that Tibet was probably the most completely theocratic state the world has known.

Desideri learned much about Lamaism, although it is curious that he apparently never quite realized that Tibet's religion is a form of Buddhism. He also learned about the Tibetan people whom he came to admire. Perhaps the greatest praise a missionary can give to non-believers was expressed when Desideri wrote: 'I was ashamed to have a heart so hard that I did not honour [my] Master as this people did their deceiver.' Desideri's journal also provides a unique window on the history of a little known part of the world. During his stay in Tibet he was witness to a power struggle between the Tibetan clergy and the royal family. He saw the Mongols sack Lhasa. He also saw a massive Chinese army invade Lhasa to drive the Mongols out and thereby establish a claim of suzerainty over Tibet which remained to plague the Tibetan people down to the present day.

Desideri set out on his epic journey from Genoa on 22 November 1712. Travelling in the Mediterranean was then not without hazards; the fledgling Jesuit noted – perhaps too casually – that his ship, *La Madonna Delle Vigne*, was menaced near Cadiz by Turkish pirates, and later forced to seek shelter from storms three times before passing the Straits of Gibraltar. Not until the following April could the young priest embark at Lisbon for the second leg of his journey, a long and tedious voyage around the Cape of Africa.

The monotony of the voyage was relieved briefly off the west coast of Africa when the passengers were subjected to the traditional equator crossing rites. Desideri may even have been included in the mock ceremony which required everyone to be baptized by pails of sea water and to swear solemnly on nautical charts to pay the tribute demanded of Neptune's novitiate. But he was more interested in searching for a rational explanation of a widely held belief that people can be mysteriously stricken and even die while crossing the equator. Aware that ships were often becalmed for days in the intense heat of the West African coast, he reasoned that this alone was enough to cause all but the sturdy to 'suffer from sickness, insomnia and languor'. And, observed Desideri logically, if a person were already in poor health he 'may be affected by the want of air and die'.

Three and a half months out of Lisbon Desideri went ashore at the Portuguese East African port of Mozambique. His ship was held up awaiting cargoes of 'elephant tusks, gold, silver, black amber and slaves from Sienna'. The impressionable young Jesuit reacted with undisguised horror to the common scene of 'kaffir', or negro, slaves, bound for the Goan market place, being loaded aboard ship in conditions of filth and overcrowding. He was also offended by the practice of insisting on the baptism of the slaves before they were shipped from Mozambique so that the local priests could receive one *crusado* coin per head in payment.

Desideri also remembered Mozambique for the wide-spread cultivation of herbs – particularly *calumba* and *lopo* roots. *Calumba* roots were ground to powder against stone, then the powder dissolved in water. He described the potion as being 'excellent for obstruction of the bowels'. Being a versatile brew, it could also be used to produce a 'contrary effect' by simply immersing in it a red-hot poker.

Desideri's ship reached the port of Aguada in Goa on the west coast of India on 20 September. It had been at sea more than a month crossing the Indian Ocean. From Goa Desideri sailed up the Indian coast to Bassein from where he travelled overland to the tiny Portuguese colony of Daman. The next stop was Surat.

Surat had a special significance for the Europeans in India. This was the sea gate to the Moghul Empire and thereafter the site of fierce competition between the Portuguese, who got there first, and the British East Indian Company which was determined to gain a foothold in the rich Indian sub-continent despite Portuguese hostility.

Desideri was forced to stay in Surat until late March owing to widespread disturbances in the countryside which followed in the wake of Farrokh Shah's seizure of the Moghul crown from Emperor Jehundar Shah. The young priest's arrival in India, or Mogor as it was called, occurred only seven years after the death of Aurangzeb, the last great Moghul. He witnessed, therefore, the rapid disintegration and spreading chaos in the Moghul Empire. Jehundar Shah and his vizier, Zulfiquar Shah, had been murdered less than a year before, and Farrokh Shah had embarked on a reign of cruelty which would hasten his own downfall only four years later. Even while Desideri waited in Surat, intelligence was received that Farrokh had ordered the eyes of the princes of the royal house to be 'burned out with red hot irons' so as to eliminate competition for the throne.

Desideri finally resumed his journey on 25 March. He passed through Ahmadabad in the princely state of Gujerat where he noted the flourishing commercial house of the British East India Company. The caravan next crossed the Rajput Kingdom, pausing briefly at its capital, Udaipur. Desideri considered the Rajputs to be 'pagans, bold by nature, tall and most warlike'. Always alert for heathen heresies, he was fascinated to find that the Rajputs held peacocks to be sacred. He also discovered for the first time that Hindu taboo against killing and eating animals.

Finally, on 10 May, the caravan reached Delhi, seat of the decaying Moghul Empire. This was to be the staging spot for Desideri's evangelistic assault on Tibet. Here he met his patroness, a Portuguese lady named Donna Juliana Diaz da Costa, whom history has inexplicably passed by with virtually no notice. Donna Juliana is admiringly described by the young and obviously adoring priest in his journal as an 'ornament of our Holy Faith in the Empire'. It is understandable that he felt gratitude for her since she financed his mission to Tibet. But it is equally understandable that he admired her because she was a most admirable person.

Donna Juliana's Portuguese parents had fled Cochin on the south-west coast of India when the Dutch seized it from the Portuguese in 1663. The dispossessed family made its way northward, eventually reaching Delhi. By good fortune they were taken into the court of Shah 'Alam, Moghul prince and son of the Emperor, Aurangzeb. Even after Shah 'Alam had fallen from royal favour and had been imprisoned by his father, Donna Juliana continued to serve his wife and mother. When Shah 'Alam was released in 1693 after seven years' confinement and banished to the far reaches of Afghanistan, she stayed with him, bearing the same deprivations. Upon Aurangzeb's death, Shah 'Alam returned to Delhi from exile and ascended the Peacock

Throne as Bahadur Shah. It was during this reign that Donna Juliana, reaping the rewards of her loyalty, gained her greatest influence within the Moghul court.

Desideri credited Donna Juliana with 'rare intelligence, eloquence, amiability and sagacity'. She tutored the princes and princesses of the court. 'Difficult and intricate business, precious treasures and important family secrets were entrusted to her. She settled disputes, comforted those in pain (she was a skilled physician according to the standards of the day) or in sorrow and shielded many from grave disasters.' He alleged that so strong was her influence over Bahadur Shah that 'the real government was in her skilful and prudent hands'. Bahadur Shah loved her as a mother and 'confided to her the most important secrets and submitted every despatch to her judgment'. To use Desideri's description, she was 'the choicest jewel in Bahadur's crown'.[1]

Even more remarkable was the Christian influence Donna Juliana exerted on a Moslem court. It is astonishing that a king – son of the great Aurangzeb and defender of Islam – could 'forsake the rituals of this false sect and kneel before a large and sacred image of our Lord Jesus Christ.' It is perhaps more astonishing that in this Moslem court the prayers of Donna Juliana were generally credited with invoking the divine intercession of St John the Baptist and thereby enabling Bahadur Shah's daughter-in-law 'miraculously' to conceive a son.[2] In gratitude the son at birth was named Yahya, a Moghul equivalent of John; although he was eventually crowned Mohammed Shah, an obviously more suitable name for a Moslem monarch.

Desideri was stirred by still another apparent miracle attributed to his patroness. He related how Bahadur Shah and many in his court had been once trapped in a palace fire and were in serious danger of perishing in the flames. Donna Juliana, an island of calm in a sea of panic, fetched a consecrated palm branch from her room and flung it into the flames. The fire was miraculously extinguished and a tragedy averted. This phenomenon so affected the Emperor that he thereafter kept a palm branch in his own chambers, renewing it yearly on Palm Sunday.

After Bahadur's death in 1712, Donna Juliana enjoyed royal

---

[1] Filippo de Filippi (ed.), *op. cit.*, pp. 64, 65.   [2] *Ibid.*, p. 66.

favour under his two successors, Jehundar Shah, who lasted but one year, and Farrokh Shah whose reign began just before Desideri arrived in India. Her influence on Farrokh Shah seems to have been more political than spiritual; certainly his brief but cruel rule was not tempered by any trace of Christian compassion.

Donna Juliana's help seems to have been recognized by several benefactors. Desideri credited her with Farrokh Shah's acceptance of John Surman's British embassy. The King of Portugal in 1712 officially thanked her for her services to Christianity and Portugal. The Dutch East Indian Company similarly acknowledged its obligations to her. The Jesuit order named her a member of its confraternity in recognition of her contribution, and the Vatican, itself, also saw fit to honour her.

Father Emanuel Freyre, a Portuguese Jesuit, joined Desideri in Delhi to make the journey with him to Tibet. Desideri wrote little about Freyre and it is likely that they were not very congenial companions. Freyre had been a missionary for twenty years in the Indian plains and was obviously less than enthusiastic about changing so abruptly his routine of life. Being much older and senior to Desideri, Freyre was leader of the expedition. Desideri, however, was clearly the driving force which kept it going.

Unlike Andrade, Desideri and Freyre decided to approach western Tibet through Kashmir. This route was longer but avoided a frontal attack on the Himalayas. The Kashmir route was difficult enough, however, and Desideri compared the Kashmir approaches to 'staircases piled one on the top of another' made of ice 'resembling marble in hardness'. But it was the 'continual wading through cold streams' which the Jesuit travellers found most trying, and Desideri blamed this for a severe case of dysentery which sapped his strength for months thereafter.

The two Jesuits entered the valley of Kashmir on 13 November 1714. The Moghuls called the vale *Behesht*, or paradise; and paradise it seemed to Desideri when he stumbled wearily into Srinagar nearly a month after leaving Delhi. He thought Srinagar's delightful gardens formed 'a most ornamental garland round the city'. According to Sanscrit mythology the valley was originally a great lake. The *Rajatarangini*, or *Chronicle of Kings*, discovered by

Akbar the Great when he invaded Kashmir in 1588, describes how it was transformed. Kasyapa, son of Marichi who was son of the Hindu God, Brahma, trenched the pass at Baramulla. This enabled the water to flow out. Kasyapa then invited his Brahman brothers to occupy the earthly paradise which was created in the lake's place.

Freyre's description of early eighteenth-century Srinagar is more vivid than Desideri's but reflects a very sour personality. It is little wonder Desideri did not find him congenial. To Freyre, Srinagar was surrounded by 'stagnant waters' rather than by an 'ornamental garland' of gardens. In the lovely river which winds through Srinagar Freyre saw only a drain for the city's 'refuse'. He disdained the inhabitants as 'Muslims and heathens'. They were 'timid and not very much to be relied on'. Parochial to the core, Freyre observed, 'instead of ruling their actions by the will of God [the Kashmiris] consult their Taqivimum or, in other words, the prognostic of the stars; and instead of resting on the mercy of Providence they trust in the auguries of the Brahmans.'[1]

While in Srinagar Desideri and Freyre learned all they could about Tibet. They studied the routes, the people and the climate. They were told that the sparse population consists mainly of nomadic shepherds who lead their flocks to pasturage as the snows melt. They were informed that there were neither shrubs nor trees in Tibet. The timid Freyre wrote: 'I will not repeat what they told us about the depths of the snow . . . and such fearful things about the rivers being frozen with the cold, for if I should venture to repeat everything those people told us you might easily think I was trading on human credulity.'

Following the track of the Kashmiri wool gatherers, Desideri and Freyre began their journey eastward to Ladakh on 17 May 1715. By this date the snows had melted enough to make the way passable. It was during the summer that caravans brought fine wool and goat hair to Srinagar from Leh, capital of Ladakh. From this wool was made the shawls for which Kashmir is still famous. Desideri described the best quality shawl as being 'so fine, delicate and soft that, though very wide and long, they can be folded into so small a space as almost to be hidden in a closed hand.'

---

[1] *Ibid.*, pp. 351, 352.

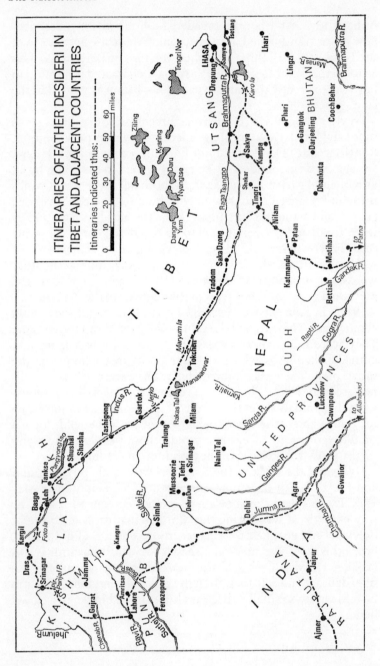

With a sly attempt at humour Desideri noted that they began their ascent of Kantel mountain on 'Ascension Day'. This peak divides Ladakh from 'Lesser Tibet', or 'First Tibet' as it was then known. Freyre's sufferings became more severe as they began the climb. He complained of heavy snows which made the climb so hazardous that their native porters begged them to turn back and take an easier, but longer route to the south. He later recalled that in several places it was necessary for porters to precede them with hatchets, 'cutting away the snow and hewing steps for their feet'. Once Desideri avoided being crushed by an avalanche only because some fortunate instinct caused him to step off the trail and examine a large rock which curiously resembled an elephant.

Desideri and his companion endured snow-blindness in the high passes where they were forced to climb for hours in the unbroken whiteness of fresh snowfall. Only by threatening, cajoling and finally bribing did Freyre succeed in dissuading the porters, equally afflicted, from turning back to avoid the piteous glare of intense sunlight reflected into their eyes by the mirrored crusts of snow. Desideri himself was so stricken that at one point he could not see the porters who stood before him in a delegation to beg him to return. At length the miserable party found that they could improvise masks out of cloth impregnated with charcoal from the charred wood of spent camp fires, and in this way lessen the painful glare.

On 20 June the weary party dragged themselves into Leh, capital of Ladakh – or 'Second Tibet' as Desideri referred to it. This was to have been Desideri's destination. It was here or near here that he had planned to open his mission and carry on the work which his Jesuit predecessors at Tsaparang had been forced to abandon seventy years before. But the forty-day ordeal of travelling from Srinagar to Leh had been too much for the faint-hearted Freyre who insisted on returning to the Indian plains, even if he had to do so alone. Determined not to relive the hardships which he had already suffered, Freyre looked for another route home. His investigations showed that only by travelling far to the east – as far as Lhasa – could he find lower or at least easier passes piercing the Himalayas permitting him passage to his beloved Indian flat lands.

Desideri claims to have been reluctant to abandon his original plan to work in western Tibet. The friendliness and cooperation which he found in Leh were good omens for the future of a mission there. He later wrote, 'I can hardly tell you how great the temptations to do missionary work in a place which seemed to offer so good a field for our labour.' But, in the end, Desideri gave in to Freyre and accompanied him to Lhasa rather than let him run the risks of travelling alone. Desideri explained his decision on the grounds that 'Third', or 'Principal Tibet', as the Lhasa area was known, harboured 'the head and centre of that false sect', and because 'Father Antonio de Andrade and other missionaries of our Society after him had once been there'. Actually Andrade had never actually reached Lhasa and anyway this was quite beside the point. Certain Tibet scholars, including Sir Thomas Holdich, considered Desideri a Jesuit agent, specifically intent on discrediting the Capuchin mission in Lhasa so that the Jesuits could replace it.[1] This accusation, based on unreliable data, is not borne out by Desideri's own testimony and is probably grossly unfair.

Freyre, for his part, justified their leaving Leh in a somewhat forced and unconvincing way. He wrote in his own record of the trip:

After twenty one days in Ladakh we felt that our quest was in vain. Not only was there not a trace of the Capuchin Fathers, but not a person in that place had even heard of them. But, at least, we met with a native returned from Rudok who told us of a Third Tibet, larger than the others and said that in that Third Tibet he had seen with his own eyes some poor-looking men clad in robes who were distributing medicine to the people and he was sure that these men were Europeans.[2]

This was odd. A search for the Capuchin missionaries was hardly their mission. In fact, the presence of a Capuchin mission in Lhasa would have been reason enough for the Jesuits to stay away. Founded in 1708 by four friars of that order, the Capuchin mission in Lhasa had been temporarily abandoned. Rome, however, did not want two competing orders in Lhasa and Desideri's

---

[1] Sir Thomas Holdich, *Tibet, The Mysterious* (London, Alston Rivers Ltd, 1906), p. 78.
[2] Filippo de Filippi (ed.), *op. cit.*, p. 354.

ultimate arrival in Lhasa precipitated a jurisdictional dispute which was ultimately to force him to withdraw in favour of a returning Capuchin mission. Freyre's statement was thus clearly an excuse, and a clumsily contrived one at that, to justify his refusal to remain in Tsaparang. But he was in charge of the expedition and had his way. Therefore, on 17 August 1715 the two Jesuit fathers, pulling uneasily in harness, set out from Leh.

After a week of tedious travel the two priests arrived at Tashigong – which translated means 'abode of mirth'. However appropriate the Tibetans may have thought the name to be, Tashigong is in fact on the edge of a cheerless waste called Chang Thang. In this immense desert no unescorted traveller could hope to survive. Desideri wrote of 'pools of stagnant and putrid water and sulphur' which 'produced noxious gases causing painful inflammation of the gums and lips'. Tashigong was then a frontier town, heavily fortified against frequent raids from the predatory Dzungar Mongol tribes to the north. Desideri and Freyre could not proceed without escort and guides. But letters of introduction provided them by the King of Ladakh assured their finding help and cooperation at Tashigong. Their introduction to the Lama of Tashigong was particularly helpful as he undertook to arrange onward travel.

During his wait in Tashigong Freyre took disapproving notice of the Lamaist priesthood. He wrote in his journal that 'lamo' in Bhotia (Tibetan) language means 'way', thus a lama is one 'who shows the way', i.e. a priest. Lamas, as seen by Freyre were 'dressed in gaiters of leather or wool and in breeches; their chests protected by a vest and their long tunic tied at the waist by a belt or a cord'. He observed that their heads were 'adorned by a hat which is sometimes shaped like a mitre and sometimes worn transversally over the ears; the whole is in red.' But, according to the suspicious Freyre, their habits were scarlet in more than one way: he noted that lamas, who customarily are 'admitted to the dignity' while still adolescent and who are supposed to remain celibate, actually have 'no shame about sexual intercourse, nor even hid it'.[1] Freyre was obviously describing the 'Red Hat' sect in which marriage is commonly permitted.

---

[1] *Ibid.*, p. 356.

Freyre was also confused about the Tibetan belief in re-incarnation and the transmigration of the soul. His analysis of these phenomena was, if nothing else, original. He wrote:

When it happens that a Superior (Head Lama) dies – when he goes, not into another body as they vainly believe, but down into the pit of Hell – instead of choosing a new Superior by election, they choose him by the work of the Demon. What happens is this: the Demon takes possession of some person – generally a kinsman of the deceased – and tells him of various hiding places: 'In such and such a place there is this or that amount of gold; hurry and take it.' Or: 'In dying I left my gaiters on the bench; take care that they do not rot.' . . . Or: 'Hurry to the stable and secure a heap of musk skins I hid under the she-ass's manger; I hid them there against thieves.' And so on. Thus does the Devil triumph over souls, making them believe that the person has been born again. And that person possessed of the Demon becomes the Head Lama of the whole monastery.[1]

The Head Lama of Tashigong, whether or not demon-inhabited, was the soul of help and hospitality. Most particularly, he was successful in arranging onward escort for the Jesuit fathers. By good fortune the nearby Gartok garrison troops were returning to Lhasa on rotation and could provide safe convoy. Moreover, the two priests would have the company of the garrison commander who – wonder of wonders – was a charming Tartar princess. This inspired Desideri to comment, 'God, who never abandons those who put their trust in Him, provided us with the best escort which can be imagined.' Princess Casals, as she was known, was the widow of the original garrison commander and had taken over his command when he died two years before. Freyre was obviously touched by his first encounter with the princess. He recounted, 'The Lady whose pretty face was radiant at our gifts, raised her eyes to ours and asked us with womanly curiosity: 'To what do we owe your presence in this kingdom and where is Fate leading you now?'[2] Freyre relates how they told her through an interpreter that they were bound for Lhasa but 'were ignorant of the climate and roads, so were very desirous of joining her party.' They offered to

---

[1] *Ibid.*, p. 357.   [2] *Ibid.*

pay their passage if necessary. She replied graciously: 'If I help you on the journey and give of my provisions, it will not be because of money but because of God. In the meantime listen to my counsel. Horses are not dependable for they die of hunger; in the desert there is no fodder but grass withered by the cold or covered with snow; so besides horses, be sure to take some oxen which, moreover, are better for your loads.' She added, 'I am travelling with orders from the King; wheresoever I meet with Botian (Tibetan) shepherds they are bound to carry my loads on their oxen till we meet with other shepherds; the new shepherds shall carry my loads till I meet with others, and so on ... for advantages so great as these you must not be afraid to spend a little money.'[1]

There were exceptionally heavy snows while Desideri and Freyre waited for the princess's caravan to leave. Freyre's shudderings can be felt in the following lines he wrote: 'The air was strangely heavy which filled us with great forebodings, so we took the precaution of tightening the ropes of our tent.' According to Freyre, 'the snow fell all during the night and in such quantities that Desideri feared that the Last Day was at hand.' Desideri suddenly rushed from the tent, took refuge in the kitchen, then sent servants to bring the others with their baggage. No sooner had this been done when the tent collapsed and was buried beneath mountains of heavy snow. This was the second incident in which Desideri was saved by premonition – a fact which no doubt added to Freyre's general uneasiness.

Toward the end of October the caravan was assembled and finally left from the town of Gartok, just south of Tashigong. In the lead were guards of Tartar cavalry, followed on horseback by the Princess, her ladies in waiting, her ministers and principal officers. Next came the two Jesuits, bundled in sheepskin great coats. They were flanked by squadrons of cavalry. Bringing up the rear was more cavalry – Tartar and Tibetan. Then, straggling along behind, came the baggage and assorted unmounted servants and followers.

The trip was not easy. Freyre recalled: 'the terrible cold and wind would chafe my face so severely as to make me exclaim (I

---

[1] *Ibid.*, pp. 357, 358.

confess it) "A curse on this cold!" But at such trying moments Princess Casals would comfort us with hot *cha* (tea) and through the mouth of her interpreter she would tell us to have courage, for no dangers from the mountains nor avalanches had power to harm us if we kept to her side.'[1]

On 9 November the caravan came within sight of a dramatic peak which Desideri called *Ngnari Giongar*. Desideri and Freyre were thus the first Europeans to see Mount Kailas, as it is known in India and the Western world. Not only is 22,000-foot Kailas one of the more impressive peaks of the Himalayas but it has been considered sacred in India and Tibet since earliest times. The Aryan tribes which invaded the plains of the Indus and Ganges came originally from the Central Asian steppes. They entered India through the mountain passes of the north-west. The everlasting snows and jagged heights of the mountain ranges which had to be crossed must have staggered the imagination of a steppe-dwelling people. The impressions made in dim antiquity have been woven into the fabric of religion and folklore. Just as the ancient Greeks placed their gods on Olympus, this people chose Kailas, which seemed to reach the heavens, as citadel of their gods.

Tibetan Lamaism, which has borrowed heavily from Hindu scriptures, also accepts Kailas as centre of the universe, pantheon of the gods and source of the 'divine rivers'. Its four sides are likened to the facets of some great jewel; the eastern face is believed to be of crystal, the southern sapphire, the western ruby and the northern, gold.

In early Sanscrit literature Kailas was worshipped as the abode of the great Hindu God, Shiva and his divine wife, Parvati. In the Tibetan version, the presiding deity of Mount Kailas is known as Demchhok rather than Shiva. Very near Kailas is a smaller peak which went unnoticed by Desideri. In Tibetan mythology this pyramidal peak, called Tijung, is the abode of Demchhok's consort known as Dorje Phangmo – the Parvati of the Hindu version. In Tibetan art, just as in Indian art, she is sometimes shown standing on ler left leg with her right thrust around Demchhok's waist. In another variation on this theme she is

---

[1] *Ibid.*, p. 358.

shown with both legs embracing her lover. These poses are meant to symbolize the consummation of their union in the fire of Supreme Wisdom.

Desideri and Freyre were, of course, oblivious to the details and derivations of the complex lore inspired by Kailas. In fact, the many variations of Hindu and Buddhist scriptures, blended as they are in Tibet with pre-Buddhist folklore, are very confusing. Desideri did, however, note the ritual at Kailas which is still practiced today; pilgrims from all over India and Tibet, upon arrival at this mountain shrine, circle many times its base, thereby earning great indulgences. The total distance for each circumambulation is thirty-two miles. The more pious believe the indulgences to be even greater if the circuits are made on one's belly – much in the manner of an inch worm.

Desideri heard that the watershed formed by Kailas's peak provides the 'fountainhead, not only of the river Ganges, but also of the Indus'. He was told that the eastern slopes of Kailas drains into nearby Lake Manasarovar and then into the Indus. Technically, the priest's information was wrong. The precise source of the Indus was not actually located until 1907 when the great Swedish explorer, Sven Hedin, found it on the far watershed of a divide well north of Kailas. Influenced by earlier writers who told fabulous accounts of gold sand in the Ganges, Desideri concluded reasonably, but erroneously, that Manasarovar, whose shores also yield gold, must be the source of the Ganges. A river which does originate at Lake Manasarovar, however, and collects the waters from both of Kailas's watersheds, is the Sutlej. This great river flows westward from the adjacent lakes Manasarovar and Rakal, through the Punjab plains until it finally joins the Indus in what is now Pakistan. To this extent Desideri was right about Kailas being the 'fountainhead of the Indus'.

Desideri and Freyre both felt the agonies of the Tibetan plateau. The former was struck by the emptiness of the desert. He wrote that, 'for three whole months the traveller finds no village nor any living creature; he must therefore take with him all provisions.' He described his bed at night as 'the earth off which you often have to scrape the snow and your room is the sky from which falls snow and sleet. 'Desideri found it particularly hard to maintain minimum standards of cleanliness. He later wrote: 'you are exposed to the bitter cold and run the risk of losing nose, fingers, toes and even your life.' But, added Desideri, 'if you look to utility instead of cleanliness, you must bear the great weight of sheepskins and put up with the dirt and insects which accumulate after long wear.' The nights were, as Desideri put it, 'a cessation of fatigue more than real repose, for the intense cold and intolerable annoyance of the insects harboured in our clothes prevented any real sleep.' The fragile Freyre suffered even more than Desideri. He very nearly died; in his own words he described the near-tragedy which befell him:

One day it happened that my horse began to bleed from the nostrils and stagger from hunger, and at last toward night sank dead in the snow. Having fallen behind the rest, I had no one near me but a Mussulman servant, and when daylight vanished I lost the traces of the others. All I could do was to lie against the horse's belly for the sake of warmth and wait for the morning.

Desideri, who first thought his companion was ahead of him, finally realized that Freyre had been left behind on the trail. Bursting in on the princess, he announced the disappearance of Freyre. She met the crisis by sending riders back along the trail. The unfortunate priest was found, but not before he had suffered from exposure and almost mortally from indignation. He was bundled up and brought back to camp where a warm fire, food and the genuine concern of the princess brought him back to normal. Desideri thanked 'Divine assistance which provided . . . such an escort.' Later when reflecting on his remarkable journey, Desideri expressed deep regret that he had not, at that stage of his Tibetan adventure, mastered the Tibetan language enough to express his thanks to Princess Casals. He was sorry that he would not, as he 'so heartily wished, see her again and have the opportunity to initiate her into our Holy Faith.'

On 18 March 1716 the caravan, which brought Desideri and Freyre safely across the length of Tibet's high wastelands, arrived in Lhasa. They were among the first few Westerners to see Tibet's holy city. The journey from Delhi, which had taken a year and a half, was a remarkable one, but Desideri's real discoveries still lay ahead. He had arrived in time to see a great upheaval in Tibet and to see the Chinese Empire push southward to the Himalayas.

4

Dzungar Invasion

As Desideri wearily drew near to the western gate of Lhasa he must surely have been exhilarated by the sight of the Potala rising before him. As palace of the Dalai Lama, the Potala was the Holy See of Lamaism – the citadel which Desideri had pledged himself to storm, armed only with the weapon of 'superior doctrine'.

The origins of the Potala are obscure. According to legend the hill on which the Potala stands was, in the beginning, the home of the progenitors of the Tibetan people. Tibet's Eve was an ogress named Dras-rin-mo while her Adam was Hilumanju, 'King of the monkeys'.[1] Anticipating Darwin, Tibetan legend relates how generations passed before the descendants of Dras-rin-mo and Hilumanju evolved into true human form. Tibetans believe that the beginnings of human civilization came when their God, Chenrezi – an equivalent of the Hindu God, Avalokitesvara – provided the ogress and her mate with seeds of wheat, rice and barley, then bade them cultivate the soil.

The name 'Potala' is probably a corruption of 'Potaraka', the hilltop abode of Avalokitesvara which, according to Hindu legend, was located at Cape Comorin – India's southernmost point. Not until the seventh century was the first palace built atop Lhasa's Potala hill. In 1645 the Fifth Dalai Lama began the structure which Desideri knew and which exists, basically un-changed to this day. Desideri described it as 'a sumptuous palace, five stories high'. Mirroring the towering structure is a small lake in the middle of which perches a smaller palace where, as

---

[1] Hilumanju is the equivalent of the Hindu monkey god, Hanuman.

gossips later confided to Desideri, 'The Grand Lama . . . used to go and divert himself with the ladies.'

Freyre apparently saw nothing extraordinary in the Potala; at least he didn't mention it in his account of the journey. His only observation on Lhasa was to comment that it was 'little suited to Europeans on account of the extreme cold and poverty of food.'[1] Having reached this gloomy conclusion, Freyre left Lhasa within a few days of his arrival, returning to India by way of Nepal. With some bitterness, Desideri felt that Freyre had abandoned him. But he was probably glad to be rid of his companion and the endless grumbling which went on.

They found no Capuchin friars in Lhasa, the mission having been withdrawn four years before. Thus with Freyre's departure, Desideri found himself the sole European in Tibet's capital. The Tibet which he found was ruled by an alien king. Ginghiz Khan, or Latsang Khan[2] as he was more simply known, was a great grandson of the powerful Mongol Chieftain, Gushi Khan, chief of the Qösot Mongols from the Koko-nor region near China's border, who had conquered Lhasa in 1642. The power of the Tibetan kings had declined after Gushi Khan's death, but the death of the Great Fifth Dalai Lama enabled the monarchy to re-establish its authority over the ecclesiastic influence of the Grand Lamas. Actually, there is some question as to the exact date of the Great Fifth's death because his Grand Vizier (and suspected bastard son) Sangye Gyatso, went to great lengths to conceal the death of his master for many years. By this remarkable feat Gyatso was able to prolong his own power. By the time it became known that the Fifth Dalai Lama was dead, Sangye Gyatso had firmly established himself in Lhasa as regent. But only through a succession of petty wars was he able to push his authority into the provinces surrounding Lhasa.

The hero of these wars was Latsang – then only a Qösot prince who commanded Sangye Gyatso's forces. Jealous of Latsang's personal popularity and afraid of the increasing power which he derived from the army, Sangye Gyatso twice tried to poison him. Enraged at the Regent's treachery, Latsang and his principal

---

[1] Filippo de Filippi (ed.), *op. cit.*, p. 360.
[2] Also transliterated Lha-bzan, Lhabsang and Latsan by various authorities.

officer, Targum Tresij,[1] staged a military *coup d'état* and seized
Lhasa in 1705. The Qösot Prince settled the score completely
soon afterward when he lured Sangye Gyatso from a redoubt
near Lhasa and summarily executed him.

Latsang was able to consolidate his power only with the strong
support of K'ang Hsi, Manchu Emperor of China. The Emperor
believed that a Qösot Mongol ally in Tibet would provide a
buffer against the hostile Dzungar Mongols who were menacing
the western reaches of his empire. Manchu supremacy in China
was relatively safe so long as Tibet remained a friendly neighbour or, at least, a neutral buffer. But, if Lhasa were to fall under
Dzungar domination and if Tibet were absorbed into a greater
Mongolia, united by common religion, Manchu rule would be
in grave jeopardy. Latsang, for his part, needed Manchu support
– not only to ward off the predatory Dzungars, but to maintain
his secular rule in the face of opposition from the 'Yellow Hat'
sect of Lamaist clergy which resented his suppression of ecclesia-
tical power.

Still resentful that the King had deprived the clergy of much of
its traditional authority and had established his own supremacy
over the Dalai Lama, the Yellow Hats intrigued with the Dzungars and the Dzungars' allies, the Oelot Mongols to the north-
west. The key to the conspiracy was the Dalai Lama. As Desideri
disapprovingly described him, the Sixth Dalai Lama drank,
gambled and behaved so badly that 'no girl or married woman or
good looking person of either sex was safe from his unbridled
licentiousness.'[2] More charitable historians describe the Dalai as a
young man of great talent. In one quatrain he described himself
quite accurately:

> I dwell apart in Potala,
> A god on earth am I;
> But in the town, the chief of rogues
> And boisterous revelry.[3]

---

[1] Referred to as K'an-cen-nas by certain authorities.
[2] Filippo de Filippi (ed.), *op. cit.*, p. 150.
[3] Sir Charles Bell, *Tibet, Past and Present* (Oxford, Oxford University Press, 1924),
p. 39.

He was nevertheless loved by the Tibetan people who believed that his transgressions were divinely inspired to test their faith. He was a potential rallying point for any uprising. For this reason Latsang had to get rid of him. Desideri, whose bias was clearly in favour of the throne, commented naively that Latsang had been forced to 'stamp out an evil which was contaminating the whole kingdom'. In reality, Latsang was moved by more than moral indignation; his kingdom was at stake.

In 1707 Latsang sent the Dalai Lama on a journey to China – allegedly for ceremonial purposes. But the Dalai's Tartar escorts stopped in Li-tang, short of the Chinese border, to carry out secret orders to murder their charge. Before he was put to death the Dalai Lama is alleged to have asked friends in his entourage to solace the Tibetan people; he promised to be re-born near the spot of his execution and here they should search for his new incarnation. The Dalai's death near Li-tang was an enactment of an earlier prophecy which he had written in verse:

> It is now far that I shall roam,
> Lend me your wings, white crane;
> I go no further than Li-tang,
> And thence return again.[1]

The second part – his return – would later appear to come true. But first, with no regard for the traditional method of finding a new incarnation, Latsang arbitrarily selected a twenty-five year old monk to be his puppet Dalai. This further enraged the orthodox Tibetans, particularly the Yellow Hat clergy who refused to recognize Latsang's choice. Even Latsang's ally and protector, Emperor K'ang Hsi, thought he had gone too far and delayed China's recognition of the new Dalai. Alarmed at the King's political blundering and recognizing that he needed counsel if he were to avoid aggravating an already ugly situation, K'ang Hsi sent to Lhasa an advisor – a high-ranking official named Ho-shou. This Manchu pro-consul in 1709 shrewdly extracted tribute from Latsang in return for Chinese protection. Thus, for the record, China established its first claim to suzerain power over Tibet. Although Tibetans, with some justice on their side,

---

[1] *Ibid.*

would later claim that the acts of a foreign king cannot be considered binding on the Tibetan people, the Chinese henceforward refused to concede that Tibet was wholly independent of China.

The dissident monks who refused to recognize Latsang's puppet Seventh Dalai Lama found a child whom they believed to be the true reincarnation. Consistent with the Sixth Dalai's prophecy, his new incarnation was discovered near Li-tang on the eastern border of Kham Province, near the spot where his earlier body had been killed. Emissaries of the King investigated and, of course, disputed the claim. But to deprive the monks of a new rallying symbol and to forestall a situation in which the puppet Seventh Dalai's authority would be undermined, Latsang conspired with the Chinese to have the alleged new Dalai kidnapped and spirited off to China.

The atmosphere in Lhasa was understandably tense when Desideri arrived. He was first interviewed by General Tondrup Sering, Commander-in-Chief of Latsang's army who wanted to know who Desideri was and what brought him to Lhasa. Desideri described himself bluntly as a priest, 'bound by his religion to rescue [the Tibetans] from error and to teach them the Holy Faith by which alone they could attain Heaven and eternal salvation.' Desideri assured the General that he had no other motive than 'to disperse the dark cloud of ignorance in which Tibetans are enveloped'.[1] One might assume that Desideri's words would unsettle the General who had quite enough to worry about in the Tibetan clergy without encouraging zealous competitors who could only aggravate the tense situation.

Desideri was quickly steered to Targum Tresij, Latsang's comrade in arms and now Prime Minister, who also questioned him closely before arranging an audience with the King. The royal audience would be the critical test and would determine the future of the young Jesuit's mission.

The royal palace bordered the north side of the main square. With his usual eye for detail, Desideri described the palace as, 'fine, strong, and with symmetrically distributed windows and balconies'. It was three stories high and solidly built of brick.

---

[1] Filippo de Filippi (ed.), *op. cit.*, pp. 91, 92.

Viewing it from the square, it had a spotted, granulated appearance but was basically red in colour. The palace had been built by the Great Fifth Dalai Lama who, according to Desideri, used to amuse himself there by 'seeing the ladies of Lhasa dance'.

Adjacent to the palace on the western side of the square stood an old temple called Lha-brang, or Palace of the Gods. Covered with a richly gilded, pagoda-like roof and intricately decorated with gilded bas-reliefs, Lha-brang contained several chapels, cluttered with idols of religious significance. Desideri wrote that, 'All day long troops of Tibetans walk round and round the temple to gain great indulgences; some of the more devout even lie down flat and, marking where their head touches the ground, get up and lie down, putting their feet where their head has been and thus go round and round the temple.' So sacred is this spot that even the King is not permitted to ride by; he must dismount and lead his horse.

On the day appointed for the royal audience Desideri approached the palace bearing rare gifts with which to please the King. He brought two 'Gaspar Antonio stones', a healing agent unknown to modern pharmacology, and a pot of 'balsam' to be used against apoplexy.[1] Surrounded by his court and a large gallery of suspicious lamas, the King formally received Desideri and demanded his reasons for coming to Lhasa from such a great distance. Undaunted by the charged atmosphere of the great hall, the Jesuit father announced righteously that his object was to bring the 'light of Gospel' to the people of Tibet; to 'free them from the fetters by which they were bound or the precipices into which they would fall headlong and go to eternal perdition.' He begged the King's permission 'to speak freely and without hindrance and to explain the truth of the Holy Faith in public and in private to him, to his court, and all his subjects.'[2] This approach could not have endeared him to the surly Yellow Hats, but the King was cheerfully indulgent.

The dramatic audience ended with the King politely praising

---

[1] The balsam compound, then popular in Tibet, consisted of beeswax, butter of nutmeg, Peruvian balsam, amber oil, clove and lavender essence.

[2] Filippo de Filippi (ed.), *op. cit.*, pp. 93, 94.

him as an 'emphatic, persuasive speaker' and granting him permission to establish a mission. Moreover, the King promised graciously to care for Desideri as a 'father cares for his son'. Desideri had won his first objective – his relationship with the King had somehow begun on the right note.

Having dimly heard of the role already played by the Jesuit missionaries in China, Latsang may have concluded that Desideri was an ally of the Manchus, thus a friend of his. Desideri theorized that, 'The King, being a relation of the Emperor of China and well informed about that court, knows well that for many years European missionaries have been employed in that Empire in the same duties which I had come here to fulfill.' Perhaps jealous of the Capuchins, Desideri did not suggest as a reason for his quick acceptance the fact that his predecessor mission had paved the way. But whatever Latsang's reasons, Desideri was accepted with good grace and welcomed with genuine hospitality.

After such an auspicious reception Desideri had nothing but praise for Latsang. He found him, 'by nature gay, joyous and affable'. Latsang was described as 'courteous to all, easy to approach; he listened to and comforted those to whom he gave audience and was very liberal with money'. His intellect was 'keen and prompt'. His administration of justice 'was most equitable'. The young priest admired his prudence but observed that it 'would have been more useful to him had it been accompanied by suspicion, a quality very necessary to rulers'. Predicting darkly a tragedy yet to be described, Desideri commented that the lack of a suspicious mind would cost him his kingdom, his family and his life.

Desideri further ingratiated himself with the King by producing from his stores an antidote for the residual poison which lingered in Latsang's system as a result of the earlier attempts on his life by Sangye Gyatso. The medicine prescribed by the versatile Jesuit was 'theriac', an opium based drug which is believed to have been invented in imperial Rome by Andromachus, Nero's personal physician. So effusive was Latsang's gratitude that Desideri dared to hope that the King's conversion to Christianity was near. Latsang had gone so far as to promise that he would submit to Desideri's teachings and, if persuaded, 'he, his whole family, his court and all his people would become followers of Jesus Christ.'[1] In gratitude for the progress which he had been able to make, Desideri took a vow to fast until his mission in Tibet succeeded – to let nothing pass his lips during daylight hours except tea. He was to stick to this stern regimen for the more than five years he remained in Tibet.

It is ironic that opposition to Desideri's mission came from his own church, not from the Lamaist clergy of Tibet. On 1 October 1716 Desideri's hopeful start suffered its first setback when three Capuchin monks appeared unexpectedly. Orazio della Penna, accompanied by Domenico da Fano – another veteran of the earlier Capuchin group – and Francesco Fossombrone asserted their rights to the Lhasa parish. Orazio della Penna described how his order had petitioned the Pope who would certainly issue a formal order to the Jesuits to leave Lhasa.

Desideri replied, somewhat caustically, that 'they had done well to write to Rome and ask for orders from the *College de Propaganda Fide* and His Holiness, the Pope' because only when such orders arrived would he be ready 'humbly to obey'. Knowing that communications from Europe would take months to arrive, and perhaps hoping that, in the meantime, the Jesuits might succeed in reversing the decision, Desideri made no plans to leave. Instead he began a steady stream of correspondence with his headquarters in Goa, urging that the Jesuits be permitted to work in Tibet's capital. He clearly had the confidence of the King and, if he could bring off the feat of converting him, the case for a Jesuit mission would be immeasurably strengthened. The competing missions settled down to a long wait for Rome's formal decision and, as far as can be told from the record, they got along tolerably well. But it is perhaps not surprising that Desideri wasted few words on the Capuchin mission in the record of his Lhasa mission.

The receptivity of the King had inspired Desideri to learn Tibetan and compose in that language a treatise on Christianity which he hoped would finally convert the King. By January 1717, the work was completed and Desideri with high hopes presented it to the King. Latsang read it patiently and with interest but noted that there were various dogma set forth in it diametrically

---

[1] *Ibid.*, p. 98.

opposed to his own religion. He was particularly disturbed by the Christian belief in a 'Supreme Being' and the Christian refusal to accept transmigration of the soul.

Latsang cannily proposed that Desideri pit his dogma against that of the Lamas in a public disputation so that the court could better decide which had the most merit. But, so that Desideri would not be handicapped by ignorance of his 'adversaries' arms', Latsang urged Desideri to enter a monastery and master the dialectics and dogma of Lamaism. This had the signs of a diplomatic solution. But, at least, it provided Desideri with an unprecedented opportunity to penetrate the secrets of the Tibetan religion and study its monastic system. It was with enthusiasm that he accepted admittance to the monastery of *Ramo-che*, or 'The Big Goat'.

Although a keen student, Desideri did allow his strong religious bias to influence his judgments. The Tibetans' belief in 'miracles', for example, provoked troublesome theological problems for the Jesuit. He could neither debunk them as delusions of a superstitious people nor accept them. Instead he explained them as the work of the Devil – Desideri's devil, that is, since it was certainly not any of the legion of heathen devils who inhabit Lamaism.

Transmigration of the soul provided Desideri with a particularly knotty doctrinal problem to ponder. Tibetans believe that before a Dalai Lama dies he somehow indicates the time and place of his rebirth as a new incarnation of the God, Chenrezi. With these clues high ranking monks search for the new child Dalai. Authentication of likely candidates is made by a special council of lamas and other learned men who conduct searching interrogations. A child candidate is tested on his familiarity with the life of his earlier incarnation. He is asked to identify belongings of his preceding self. If satisfied, the council members declare the boy to be the new Grand Lama and prostrate themselves before him. In seeking an explanation for this phenomenon, Desideri found some doubters – probably among the less pious Mongols of the court. Scoffers were convinced that the whole thing was a fraud arranged between the child's relations and some lamas to deceive the credulous Tibetans. Desideri, however, concluded that it was a true phenomenon – not a fraud. But he was convinced that it was a phenomenon perpetrated by the Devil. He thought it impossible that anyone except the Devil could 'deceive, not only the people of Tibet, but those of Upper and Lower Tartary, of Second Tibet, of Nepal and of the vast empire of China as well.' In a detailed dissertation on the subject, the pious Jesuit solemnly concluded that the Tibetans are universally deceived by the machinations of the Devil because their Grand Lama is, himself, a manifestation of the Devil.

Desideri's conviction that the Devil had the upper hand in Tibet is belied by a system of ethics in Lamaism very similar to Christian ethics; and a multitude of hells to discourage transgressions. Lamaist ethics, like the Mosaic commandments, recognizes ten sins – three sins of the body, four of the tongue and three of the heart. The corporeal sins are murder, lust and theft. The sins of the tongue are lying, grumbling and reviling. Those of the heart are coveting the goods of another, desiring to do evil to others and secret dissent from the maxims of their faith. Capital vices considered to be the source of sin, are the 'five poisons of the soul: pride, immoderate love of things, anger, envy and ignorance. The virtues found in Lamaist doctrine include the Christian virtues of faith, hope, charity, prayer, alms giving, compassion, diligence and contemplation. Even Desideri admitted that the only missing virtue in their 'false religion' was humility.

The distressed prelate found even more evidence of the Devil's work in Tibetan customs than in Tibetan beliefs. Particularly deplorable to Desideri were Tibetan marriage practices. According to custom the bridegroom, but not the bride, knows when their pre-arranged marriage will occur. On the day appointed, accomplices of the bridegroom surround the bride-to-be and carry her kicking and screaming to her future home where the bridegroom awaits her. After a magician casts spells to ensure the success of the marriage and exorcises evil spirits by raucous shouting, the bride, bridegroom and entire wedding party enter the house. The bridegroom then smears large gobs of butter into the hair of his bride. With this ritual, the couple is inseparably joined in wedlock – at least according to the interpretation of the ceremony heard by Desideri. But, not only does the butter-soaked bride find herself united with her husband, but with all his brothers as well, in this land where polyandry is still commonly practised.

The treatment of the dead in Tibet was equally strange and particularly abhorrent to Desideri. It was commonplace for a fresh corpse to be chopped into small pieces and thrown to dogs which, in anticipation, had congregated outside the house of the deceased. In the case of wealthy families the corpse was expertly dismembered on some venerated mountain top by professional undertakers and left to be devoured by eagles. The very poor who couldn't afford undertakers to cut up the remains of their loved ones simply threw the corpse into a river where it was presumed to have been eaten by the fish. Tibetans regard the funeral rituals as an act of compassion, or as Desideri put it, 'a step toward arriving after many transmigrations, at the supreme heroism of giving their flesh and therefore their life to other living creatures.'

The Jesuit singled out for special condemnation the 'Lhoba', or Bhutanese who, he had heard, consoled their dying relatives with promises that their friends would join them in death. When a Lhoba died certain of his relatives – true to their word – killed a number of his friends so that he may not be lonely in death. As a symbol that the promise had been fulfilled, the dutiful relatives made for themselves necklaces of teeth – one tooth for every person thus killed.

On 17 August 1717, Desideri moved to Sera monastery on the outskirts of Lhasa. In his studies, which he took very seriously, he grappled earnestly with strange dogma. He learned of the five stages of attainment, the last and final being *Nirvana*, or supreme exaltation and perfect grace. These stages can be reached by a succession of reincarnations provided the conduct of each life earns the reward of a higher incarnation. But the bliss of Lamaist heaven is matched by the agonies of many hells designed to accommodate those whose life cycles spiral downward because of misdeeds.

The animal state, for example, is a severely retrogressive stage in a being's striving for *Nirvana*. A still more retrograde incarnation is called *Itaa*. In this state of damnation one's mouth 'is only the size of the eye of a needle, the neck is many miles long, the eyes emit pestiferous gases and the belly is distended.' Desideri described the suffering of one who finds himself in a state of *Itaa*. He undergoes incredible hunger and thirst. To quench his thirst he runs toward a flowing stream only to have it turn to blood.

To assuage his perpetual hunger he must search for food. But when he discovers it, either he cannot fit it into his pinhole mouth or it is suddenly changed into loathsome filth. The ultimate state of damnation is Hell, which is divided and subdivided so that there may be exquisite refinements of torture to suit every gradation of sin. The torture of the many hells include burning, boiling, crushing, mangling and mutilation. In the eighth hell, to describe but one, the Devil's custodians drive the inmates over red-hot filings and up and down spikes of iron. The tongues of the damned are then stretched and pierced with nails.[1]

Bothering Desideri most about Lamaism was not, however, the proliferation of heathen hells, but the fact that the Tibetans acknowledge no Supreme Judge. Good men are rewarded according to their merits while evil-doers are punished according to their sins; merit and demerit have within themselves an innate power over reward and punishment. Desideri felt that the 'source of all [the Tibetan] false dogmas . . . is the absolute denial of the existence of any God.'[2] This negation of a prime mover of the universe was an all-important obstacle to Desideri's finding common ground with Lamaism. It was around this presumed vulnerability that he planned to build his case for Christianity and thereby win Latsang to his side. To use the Jesuit's own words, Desideri had 'discovered the site of the enemy's camp, the quality of their arms' and had, toward the end of November 1720, 'resolved to challenge them and begin war'. But before the King could referee Desideri's war on Lamaism, as he had earlier promised to do, he was caught up in another war – one which would prove his undoing.

Finding themselves unable to resist Latsang's authority by themselves, the disgruntled Yellow Hat monks plotted secretly with the Dzungar Mongols, traditional enemies of the Qösot tribes. The Dzungarian homeland was located in the northern part of what is now known as Sinkiang. It was in an arid basin framed by the Altai mountains on the north-east, the *T'ien Shan*, or 'Heavenly mountains' on the south, and the Ala Tau and Tarbagatai ranges on the north-west. Triangular in shape, its

---

[1] Filippo de Filippi (ed.), *ibid.*, pp. 232–8.   [2] *Ibid.*, p. 245.

base stretched along the T'ien Shan, which separated it from the huge Tarim Basin to the south. But however far away, many of the monks from the large monasteries near Lhasa, including Sera where Desideri was studying, slipped away to join the Dzungar and Oelot armies which were preparing secretly to invade Tibet. Clandestine contact was established between those monks remaining as a fifth column in Lhasa and the Oelot Mongol King, Tse-wang Rabden.

The Mongol strategy was well conceived. First to gain Latsang's confidence, Tse-wang Rabden had in 1714 arranged for the marriage of his daughter to Latsang's son. Later he appealed to Latsang for troop reinforcements, claiming that he was being menaced by Russia in the province of Yarkand. Innocent of any suspicion, Latsang sent off many of his finest fighters to the Oelot leader, thereby weakening the Lhasa garrison. Tse-wang Rabden raised two armies. One, which he commanded personally, would invade China to regain the child Dalai Lama and block the Emperor from sending reinforcements to Latsang. Tse-wang Rabden's ultimate goal, of course, was to conquer China and seize the throne from the Manchus. But first Tibet must be wrested from Latsang. This would be the task of the second army, a 6,000-man expeditionary force of combined Mongols and Tibetans under the command of a Tsering Dundup. The latter, a warrior monk and learned graduate of a Tibetan monastery, was described by Desideri as 'proud, intrepid and warlike'. The Jesuit noted that Tsering's 'favourite seat was the saddle, his bed a horse rug and his softest pillow, a shield, a sword, a quiver and arrows.' Desideri likened Tsering Dundup to Alexander the Great – both being examples of his theory that 'the great victors in war are those who have been educated in the school of liberal arts, and who have submitted to the discipline of an Aristotle.'

Rabden used a cruel ruse to catch Latsang off guard. In June 1717, he sent Latsang a message in the name of Latsang's son asking that they meet for a reunion at Dam, the King's summer place north of Lhasa. Eager to see his eldest son again, Latsang with his customary escort of troops marched toward Dam, un-aware that Tsering Dundup's army would be lying in ambush. But, as Latsang approached the trap his younger son, who had by chance gotten wind of the treachery, rode fast to warn his father. Latsang acted quickly. He arrested those members of his entourage whom he suspected of being implicated in the plot and deployed his small forces to attack. With the advantage of surprise now on his side, Latsang won his first battle against Tsering Dundup. The time won by this victory was used to fortify Dam. This enabled Latsang to hold back the superior Mongol force throughout the summer. As winter approached, however, the vicious winds which whipped Dam became less and less endurable. By October Latsang was forced to withdraw his forces to Lhasa which had been prepared for a long siege with the help of Chinese military advisors.

In the meantime, Tse-wang Rabden's invasion of China had failed completely. He was neither able to 'liberate' the child Dalai from the Chinese nor prevent the Emperor's army from mauling his forces. The defeat, however, was kept a secret. And according to the original strategy, Tsering Dundup let the word reach the Yellow Hat monks in Lhasa that his approaching army was accompanied by the true reincarnation of the Sixth Dalai Lama.

Tsering Dundup attacked Lhasa from four directions on 1 December 1717 and triggered a mass uprising of the Yellow Hat monks within Tibet's capital. Ladders were dropped from the city's walls so that the besiegers could scale the ramparts. The northern and eastern gates of the city were thrown open by secret sympathizers at a precisely agreed upon time. By first dawn, Tsering Dundup was master of Lhasa. His troops sacked the town, engaging in orgies of looting which threatened to empty Lhasa of its treasures and relics. Desideri described the scene dramatically:

They rushed with arms in their hands into the houses . . . robbing the treasures which had been deposited and hidden in the temples. Not satisfied, they returned again and again to the houses, sparing neither age nor sex; wounding and savagely beating some, tying the arms of others behind their backs and suspending them to beams and scourging them to make them reveal where their riches were concealed.[1]

The ravages of the Mongols were matched by the excesses of their confederates, the Yellow Hat monks, who savagely set upon

---

[1] Filippo de Filippi (ed.), *op. cit.*, p. 157.

their Red Hat rivals, massacring all they could find. Desideri heard grim details of this blood-letting from the Red Hat Head Lama of Lungar monastery who escaped through a secret rear exit of the monastery just moments ahead of a Yellow Hat lynch mob which had battered down the monastery entrance. The terrified Head Lama had immediately sought out his friend, Desideri, for help and protection. At considerable risk to himself, Desideri gave money to the unfortunate abbot and made possible his escape from the city.

The Potala was held until the end by Latsang and a handful of loyal lieutenants. But by the third day, it too was stormed. Ladders had been erected on the walls of the south entrance and a passage finally forced open. Bursting into the Potala, the insurgents found only the Queen with her youngest son. Latsang with Targum Tresij, General Tondrup Sering and his second son had escaped through a passage leading to the north side of the Potala just ahead of their pursuers. King Latsang might have made good his escape if his horse had not become frightened and thrown him. Left alone and unaided, the doomed monarch fought a furious hand to hand battle with his pursuers, killing several of them with his sword. With one final desperate lunge Latsang lopped off the arm of one of his attackers before he fell dead of his own wounds. News of Latsang's death quickly reached Tsering Dundup who had hoped to receive Lhasa's valiant defender in honourable defeat. Tsering rushed to the place where Latsang fell and, overcome with grief, 'threw himself on the body and bathed the wounds with his tears.'[1]

Unaware until too late that the King had been cornered, the other three fugitives rode on. They managed to escape into the night and reach the northeastern province of Taze on horseback. They sought refuge with the Governor, or *Deba Taze*, as he was known. But, as bad luck would have it, the Governor had been a rival of Latsang's. He was, in fact, a close relative of the former King of Tibet whose death at the hands of Latsang had deprived him of a claim to the throne. Recognizing this accident of fate as an opportunity to eliminate rivals and at the same time to curry favour at Lhasa's new court, the Governor took the

---

[1] *Ibid.*, p. 159.

three fugitives into custody and sent them back to Lhasa. General Tondrup Sering was spared – the new Mongol conqueror admired his fighting qualities and hoped to win him over to his service. Latsang's second son and the luckless Prime Minister were, however, imprisoned and treated most cruelly. Targum Tresij was particularly badly handled since he was suspected of having hidden many of the treasures of the Potala which had been found missing by the invaders. He was starved and forced to endure Lhasa's winter in an unheated, unlighted cell. So miserable was his plight that Desideri, at considerable risk to himself, arranged to have a bed delivered to his cell so that he would not have to continue sleeping on the freezing cobblestones. Desideri also smuggled to him money with which he could bribe his jailer to provide him with extra rations of food and tea. But these gestures could do little to alleviate the distress and mental anguish of the Prime Minister who, after the King's death, became the main symbol of the defeated regime.

Mindful that the old regime still had followers, Tsering Dundup decided that the presence of the Queen, her two sons and Targum Tresij were dangerous. As the princes grew up they would be tempted to plot against the regime and avenge their father. They were all sent under escort in great secrecy away from Lhasa. Latsang's loyal commander, Tondrup Sering, who had steadfastly refused to accept a position in the new regime, but who enjoyed the freedom of the city, heard of this plan. Fearing that the trip covered a plan to murder all of them, he pursued and overtook the caravan in which they travelled. Desideri described the confrontation: 'Attacking the escort . . . and fighting valiantly, one against many, [the general] succeeded in delivering the half-dead viceroy [Tresij] and inducing him to seek safety in flight.'[1]

News of Tondrup Sering's attack and Tresij's escape quickly reached Lhasa. Tsering Dundup was infuriated and as reprisal had Tondrup Sering's wife tortured and 'cut into small pieces'. This provoked the General, who was still shadowing the slow-moving caravan, to attack again, this time in a terrifying rage. Desideri's description of this episode is particularly moving:

---

[1] *Ibid.*, p. 163.

The tears [the General] shed only served to inflame his valor. He threw himself into the very midst of the enemy, where he saw the unhappy Queen and the two princes, miserable survivors of the royal family. Like lightning he fell on their escort, his flashing eyes inspired terror as he trod over the corpses of so many adversaries, when unmindful of the severe wounds he received . . . he suddenly lost consciousness and fell within an arms length of the wretched prisoners. With loud shouts of inhuman joy the Tartars seized him, cut off his hands, feet, ears and nose and set him on a horse.[1]

Thus the brave General died. According to Desideri, the Queen and her two sons met a 'lamentable end' which he found too awful to describe. Actually they spent the remainders of their lives in Ili, capital of Dzungaria, captives of their conquerors.[2] But the Dzungars and Oelots would not enjoy for long the spoils of their victory.

---

[1] *Ibid.*, p. 163.
[2] L. Petech, *China and Tibet In The Early Eighteenth Century, History of the Establishment of a Chinese Protectorate in Tibet* (Leiden, E. J. Brill, 1950, 'Monographies du T'oung Pao, Vol. I'), p. 41.

5

The Capuchins

While Lhasa was under Dzungar attack, Desideri wisely remained secluded at Sera monastery. But after the occupation of
Lhasa by the victorious Mongols his position became more
precarious. The Jesuit's friendship with the murdered king and
his well-known anti-Yellow Hat bias made him extremely
vulnerable. He therefore moved to the Takpo-Khier district, a
several-day journey from the capital. Here, toward the end of
December 1717, he found safe refuge in a monastery at a place
called Trong Gnee.

Desideri settled in to complete his ambitious three-volume
work 'exposing Lamaism'. Famous for two Lamaist shrines,
Takpo-Khier served the priest's scholarly research well. One
shrine perched on a 'summit of a very high and terrible mountain' was watched over by a high-ranking, incarnate lama, and
was held in great reverence. Wealthy Tibetans would specify in
their wills that their remains be brought here to be dismembered
and then devoured by vultures, as is customary in Tibet. At
another shrine near Desideri's new sanctuary troops of pilgrims
walked endlessly 'in procession round the foot of the mountain',
collecting religious indulgences with each circuit.

As Desideri studied in the tranquillity of the provinces, Lhasa
remained tense. The Tibetans still expected Chinese retaliation;
K'ang Hsi could ill afford to leave Lhasa in Dzungar hands. The
invasion of Tibet's capital fulfilled the Chinese Emperor's worst
fears; this could be a serious step toward unification of the
Mongols. Moreover, the Emperor realized that the Mongols'
ultimate goal was the conquest of China. So long as Tibet remained under the hostile rule of the Dzungars, K'ang Hsi was
dangerously vulnerable to Mongol attack.

In March 1718, before his defeat and death, Latsang had

urgently appealed to K'ang Hsi for help. The Chinese Emperor responded quickly by sending two armies. Both were despatched well before the Dzungars subjugated Lhasa. One staged in Sining, preparing to take the southern route through Tachienlu in Kham Province. This route had the advantage of crossing a more cultivated area, permitting troops to live off the land, but it was the longer of the two. The other army, selected to attack first, cut across the northern desert from Sining through Koko Nor and Tsaidam. It passed through relatively empty lands where, because few people could exist, the columns were spared harassment by lawless or hostile inhabitants.

The Manchu commander, Erentei, led a force along this latter route made up of local Moslem levies from Chinese Turkestan, encadred by a relatively few regular Chinese. The levies were generally inferior to the Emperor's regulars but they were thought adequate for what K'ang Hsi originally believed would be a minor campaign to rescue Latsang. Moreover their use made it unnecessary to redeploy crack regiments needed at home to guard the 'Celestial Realm' itself.

It was at Koko-Nor that news of the Dzungar seizure of Lhasa and Latsang Khan's death reached Erentei. This changed the situation; his was no longer simply a rescue mission, essentially defensive in nature. Now Tibet must be liberated from the Dzungars, and this would demand a stronger force and an offensive capability. At least a year's delay would be required before a major campaign could be properly prepared. Thus, instead of leading with the main force, Erentei sent ahead a smaller reconnaissance unit under a commander named Sereng to probe the route to Lhasa.

Unfortunately for the Chinese, Sereng over-extended his supply line. Finally realizing that he had penetrated too deeply into Dzungar-infested territory, he stopped at the banks of the Nag-chu river, north of Lhasa – the first place where new provisions could be had. Sereng was aware of his predicament and called for reinforcements. His soldiers dug in behind a hastily built stone fortification and waited for a relief force under Erentei. Despite Dzungar harassment along the way, the Manchu commander managed to reach Nag-chu to bolster Sereng's forces. But, tired by the gruelling march, the Chinese were careless. Adding to the problem was appallingly bad coordination between the two commanders. In the confusion the Dzungars were able to take them by surprise. The Chinese were quickly surrounded and imprisoned behind their own flimsy fortifications. Reduced to eating their pack animals and in some cases the corpses of their fallen comrades, the beleaguered army of Erentei finally surrendered after a month's siege. As 7,000 emaciated Chinese prisoners huddled in corrals they were systematically slaughtered by the Mongols.[1] Not a single survivor escaped to describe the débâcle to his Emperor.

However elated the Dzungars might have been, they knew that K'ang Hsi would mount another and larger offensive to avenge this humiliating defeat. Moreover, they soon realized that their Lhasa garrison could not be reinforced with fresh troops from Dzungaria. The western route to Lhasa, on which the Mongols depended for communications with their homeland, was not safe from the harassment of remnants of Latsang's broken army.

Latsang's Prime Minister, Targum Tresij, who had fled to Gartok[2] in western Tibet after the fall of Lhasa, collected and regrouped the soldiers in this area still loyal to the old regime. The bitter and vengeful vazir reasoned that if he could control the route between Gartok and 'High Tartary', the homeland of the Dzungars to the north, he could prevent reinforcements from reaching Lhasa. In this way he could help the Chinese oppose his enemy.

Targum's forces, trained in guerrilla tactics, intercepted Dzungar messengers and were able to repulse small units of Dzungar replacements headed for Lhasa. These tactics were so successful that communications between Lhasa and Dzungaria were completely disrupted. At first Tsering Dundup was not aware of the cause and feared that lack of response from home meant that he had fallen from favour. In an effort to please his monarch so that his urgent requests for replacements would be acted upon, the Dzungar commander sent an exceptionally large convoy laden with treasure stolen from Lhasa's monasteries.

The convoy arrived in Gartok after four months on the road.

---

[1] L. Petech, *op. cit.*, p. 56.
[2] Gartok was called 'Cartoa' by Desideri whose account of this episode is quite complete. See; Filippo de Filippi (ed.), *op. cit.*, p. 167.

News of its coming preceded it and gave Targum time to devise a scheme to overcome the obviously superior force. The tired Dzungar soldiers were received with feigned hospitality by Targum's troops disguised as townfolk. The latter had erected large and festive tents in which to welcome the Mongol column. A great feast was prepared and countless jars of *chang*, or Tibetan beer, were urged upon the thirsty guests. After the Dzungars had drowned their caution in *chang*, Targum cajoled them into observing the Tibetan custom of laying aside arms in a gesture of friendship. The drunken Dzungars cheerfully complied and continued their drinking until, one by one, they fell unconscious to the floor. This was the signal for the ex-vizier and his men to set upon the sodden soldiers, cutting them down without mercy. The stolen treasure was confiscated – guarded in Gartok until it could be restored to the monasteries from which it had been looted. No further effort to force the western route was made by the Dzungars. They had no choice but to reconcile themselves to meeting K'ang Hsi's imminent attack with the limited forces at hand.

Many of the Chinese Emperor's ministers had strongly opposed a second campaign against Lhasa. It would be enormously expensive and difficult to sustain. Also the Emperor's already tarnished prestige could not stand a second defeat. But K'ang Hsi was confident and more than ever determined to crush the Mongols.

First, however, he tried diplomacy. In the spring of 1719 he sent envoys to the Dzungar general, Tsering Dundup, inviting him to 'give up the throne he had so unjustly seized, or to prepare for being ignominiously ousted.'[1] The Mongol leader, now pro-consul of Tibet, arrogantly reminded the emissaries that he had seized Tibet by force and meant to retain it by force if need be. He bragged that more kingdoms would fall under his sword. The Emperor's envoys retired in confusion with threats against their Emperor ringing in their ears.

There was now no alternative to war. K'ang Hsi began in earnest preparations to invade Lhasa. This time the Chinese paid well to attract the best mercenaries of the realm. Desideri wrote,

---

[1] *Ibid.*, p. 166.

'the Emperor ordered an innumerable number of men to be summoned, among them many Tartars from the outlying provinces of the Empire.' Only Mongol mercenaries would be a match for the seasoned Dzungar garrison defending Lhasa. The Jesuit missionary added, 'Only he who knows the immense riches of the Emperor of China can at all realize the quantities of arms, ammunition, instruments of war, and animals provided for this huge army.'

Desideri witnessed the inflationary effect caused by the highly paid mercenaries, commenting: 'Shortly after the Chinese entered Tibet ... the whole vast kingdom was flooded with silver, which so diminished in value that ... severe punishments were necessary to force the people to accept it as payment.'[1] Most of this unminted silver was ultimately traded for Nepalese coinage, more convenient to use. The ultimate result was a windfall for the King of Nepal who grew rich on the trade.

The main expeditionary force, which invaded Tibet in 1720, was commanded by Prince Yün-t'i, the Emperor's fourteenth son. This time the Chinese planned the invasion by way of Tachienlu, through more densely populated areas where the troops could forage for supplies.

With the Chinese army rode the Seventh Dalai Lama. Recognized by the Yellow Church as the true reincarnation of the Sixth Dalai Lama, the young lama had been earlier spirited off to China to prevent the Tibetans from exploiting him as a symbol of resistance to Latsang's rule. The invading Dzungars for psychological effect had pretended he was in their custody and had promised the Tibetans he would be reinstated in the Potala. The Emperor reckoned that Tibetan disillusionment with the unfulfilled Dzungar promise would help undermine their regime and soften the populace for the Chinese invasion. It was shrewd of K'ang Hsi to attach the Dalai to the imperial army and dramatize the campaign as a 'Holy War'. The Chinese could urge the Tibetans along the way to rise and join their Dalai Lama in the great crusade to drive the alien Dzungars from the land.

As the Chinese army was making its final preparations to move, an Imperial announcement was read before the Dalai

---

[1] Filippo de Filippi (ed.), *op. cit.*, p. 167.

Lama at the Kumbun monastery and disseminated widely among the faithful. It promised: 'Within the fourth month of the next year, four great officials together with the commanders of the great army of fulgent splendour, will lead the most excellent Lama towards . . . Tibet; they will place the lotus of his feet upon the great golden throne, built by the five fearless demons of the matchless grand palace of Lokesvara, the second Potala.'[1]

The role of the Dalai Lama was an important one. A prince of the Chinese Imperial Court had met with the young Dalai Lama's father at Kumbun monastery in February, on the eve of the invasion, to explain the Emperor's design. Accompanied by 3,000 men, the royal prince was received by the Dalai with appropriate pomp. The young lama and the Koko Nor chiefs also in attendance, solemnly approved of the Emperor's plan and pledged an army of local men to augment his invasion forces.

The Dalai Lama's cooperation, having been received, K'ang Hsi officially recognized him by bestowing on him the Great Seal which had belonged to his predecessor. This splendid symbol of office was encrusted with gold and jewels and bore the inscription, 'Seal of the Sixth Dalai Lama, leader of the creatures, diffuser of the Teaching.'[2] On 28 May, the Dalai Lama officially joined the great army for the long march.

Slowly the Chinese advanced. Desideri recalled, 'from all parts people assembled to acclaim the Grand Lama and hear the orders given by the representatives of the Emperor of China.' These orders called on all Tibetan men from the age of twelve to join the invading force. Even Desideri, who thought himself secure in the Governor's palace at Trong Gnee, was not overlooked in the draft. He recalls with distaste: 'After sundown on the evening of the 28th of September 1720, I received an order from the general in command of the troops in that province to go next day, armed with a horse, a baggage mule, and two armed serving-men on foot to the camp, under pain of death if I disobeyed. My character as a lama was of no avail as several lamas . . . had been forced to obey.'[3] The Vice-Governor consoled Desideri with the promise that he would intervene with the

---

[1] L. Petech, *op. cit.*, p. 59.   [2] *Ibid.*
[3] Filippo de Filippi (ed.), *op. cit.*, p. 169.

general, and in fact the worried priest was spared the discomfort and danger of military service. Had he not been exempted he would doubtless have been deployed with other untrained Tibetans astride routes leading northward from Lhasa to prevent both the Dzungars from reinforcing Lhasa and the Lhasa garrison from retreating to Dzungaria.

Desideri reconstructed a fairly accurate description of the Dzungar defeat. The 4,000-man Dzungar garrison, unable to retreat and unwilling to surrender, seized the offensive. Moving up, north of Lhasa, they engaged the Chinese in a savage early dawn attack. Again the following night the desperate Mongols attacked and again they slaughtered thousands of Chinese. They struck hardest at that sector of the enemy's line where the Dalai Lama was believed to be camped, 'making violent attempts to break through the ranks of the terrified Chinese, killing them without mercy.' Had they been able to seize the Dalai Lama and use him as a hostage, their negotiating position could perhaps have saved them.

Noting that over-aged Chinese reserves bore the brunt of the Dzungar's first two attacks, Desideri concluded that 'China is so densely populated that she cares little for the loss of thousands of men while the enemy exhausts himself thoroughly by slaughtering.' This seemed indeed to have been the case as the hard core of the Chinese attacking force was held back, waiting for the Dzungars to tire.

History is indebted to Desideri for his vivid account of the final defeat of the doomed Mongols. He wrote:

On the fourth night the Chinese did not wait for the Dzungars to attack. As evening closed in, the lights and fires illuminated their tents and pavilions to show they were being guarded, while in truth they were almost denuded of troops. Meanwhile the Tartars of China and Lower Tartary under cover of night had been formed into three detachments. The first remained to guard the Grand Lama: the second took up a position, after the Chinese had all been withdrawn, facing the enemy; the third marched out in silence and by a circuitous route got to their rear. At a given signal these two divisions attacked the Dzungars, who soon became aware of the difference between these troops and their former antagonists. After heavy fighting the Dzungars were defeated.[1]

---

[1] *Ibid.*, p. 170.

After the defeat of the Mongols Desideri commented, 'after nigh twenty years of tumult and disaster . . . Tibet was thus subjugated by the Emperor of China in October 1720.' Lhasa was actually first occupied by the Chinese Szechwan army which entered the capital unopposed on 24 September 1720 after the Dzungar garrison had moved north to Dam to meet the main Chinese force from Koko Nor.[1] Desideri, who described this latter battle, seemed unaware of the two-pronged pincer strategy used by the Chinese and the several-day earlier occupation of Lhasa by the Chinese.

While Chinese influence in Tibet would fluctuate throughout history according to its 'mandate from heaven', K'ang Hsi had by this campaign secured China's flank. And by controlling the See of Lamaism and binding the Dalai Lama to him in a suzerain-vassal relationship, he had gained an important measure of influence over the Mongols as well. He had also fulfilled a prediction by Urgyen, the founder of Tibet's Lamaism many centuries before, that 'China would attack and defeat the tyrannical usurpers (from Upper Tartary or Dzungaria) and conquer the kingdom.'[2]

Desideri's description of the aftermath of victory paints a lurid scene. Aside from its historical interest, it reveals another side of the Jesuit priest's personality. While Desideri was understandably antagonistic to the Yellow Hat Clergy whose excesses he had observed at the time of the Dzungar invasion, one somehow is brought up short by the vindictive note he struck when he wrote:

By the written order of the Emperor of China . . . infamous traitors were condemned to a public and ignominious death. Many were the supplications for mercy. But all were sternly refused, and even the Grand Lama was warned not to interfere. . . . Barefoot and bareheaded, with hands bound, surrounded by Chinese and Tartar guards fully armed, these miserable traitors were led round the magnificent temples of the idols, called Lha-brang, or the Palace of the Gods, and then through the principal streets to the place of execution. The deposed

[1] L. Petech, *op. cit.*, pp. 56, 57.
[2] Filippo de Filippi (ed.), *op. cit.*, p. 280.

Lama was beheaded; the *Deba Taze* and others were tied to a certain instrument of torture, tortured and then shot at with arrows until they were dead. Thus perished those iniquitous traitors.[1]

The Emperor had played his hand shrewdly. He had eliminated the Mongol threat to his Empire. He could appear to have 'liberated' Tibet and to have restored to that war-torn country the 'rightful' Dalai Lama. The Chinese victory also saved Desideri from the dangerous position in which he found himself under Dzungar rule. As a close friend of Latsang, Desideri's fate would have been sadly sealed had he come to Tsering Dundup's attention. Now, however, he could emerge from hiding and openly resume his objectives. Latsang's death deprived him of a permissive patron and set back the timing of his plan. But still he had his major work to finish. The logic of his arguments would speak eloquently enough to overcome the loss of his privileged position in court.

While Desideri continued to work at Takpo Khier the fate of his mission had long since been decided in Rome. As early as December 1718, the judgment was rendered, awarding the Tibet parish to the Capuchins. Father Michelangelo Tamburini, General of the Society of Jesus, was ordered to withdraw Desideri immediately. Tamburini wrote Desideri to this effect on 16 January 1719, but communications being what they were, the letter did not reach Takpo Khier until January 1721 – two years later. The mid-winter weather of the Tibetan plateau, which discourages travel, gave Desideri a valid excuse not to leave immediately. But in April the unhappy Jesuit returned to Lhasa.

Father Domenico da Fano, then Prefect of the Capuchin Mission, had the thankless task of showing the disappointed priest the official decree confirming the Jesuit General's letter and making official Capuchin jurisdiction in Tibet. Another Capuchin, Giuseppe Felice, pleaded with Desideri to leave behind his three-volume work. But this Desideri would not do. His masterpiece, which had absorbed so much of his time in Tibet, was his monument and he meant to take it with him.

On 25 April 1721 Desideri left Lhasa, a sadly disappointed man.

---

[1] *Ibid.*, pp. 171, 172.

While the balance of his career would bring him high office in the Jesuit missions of India, his inability to finish the job which he had set for himself in Lhasa must always have rankled. That the Capuchins – not he – would have the challenge of converting Tibetans in the Holy See of Lamaism, itself, must have deeply hurt the dedicated Jesuit.

The defeat of the Dzungars by the Chinese army in 1720 ushered in a period of Manchu influence in Tibet. A Chinese army garrisoned in Lhasa kept the peace while a new experiment in government was tried. Tibet was administered by a council of four ministers. Khangchennas, Governor of western Tibet, bearing the title *Dai-ching Batur*, served as chairman of the council. Another senior minister named Ngabo and two junior ministers, Jaranas and Lumpa, all well known for their anti-Mongol stand during the Dzungar occupation, were joined in 1733 by a fifth minister. This latter was a man of destiny named Pholhanas; Tibet would be indebted to this remarkable leader for years of relative peace and good government.

The ruling council soon split into two mutually antagonistic factions, each reflecting the sectional bias of its members. Chairman Khangchennas and Pholhanas, whose first interests were in western and southern (Tsang) Tibet, respectively, and who favoured close alliance with the new Manchu Emperor, Yung-chen, were resented by the other three ministers whose interests were mainly in Lhasa and Ü provinces and who advocated a diminution of Chinese influence. The tension between these rivals and their partisans throughout the government grew steadily worse. Pholhanas, after a falling out with Khangchennas over a matter of religious doctrine, retired to his provincial estates in 1727, leaving the council chairman alone and in the midst of his enemies.

Reminiscent of Caesar's murder, Khangchennas was set upon and killed one day when he found himself surrounded by the drawn knives of council men Ngabo, Lumpa and Jaranas in a chamber of the Jokhang temple. The despised Khangchennas paid with his life for his own ruthlessness as his three enemies repeatedly plunged their daggers into his lacerated body.

On hearing this news, Pholhanas fled to the Nepalese border, recognizing that he too was marked for assassination. He raised a force of loyal Tsang troops and in alliance with forces from western Tibet marched on Shigatse. Pholhanas's seizure of Shigatse, which earned him the accolade 'Miwang Phola', or Mighty Phola, provoked the Lhasa council men to send an army to suppress what was now a full-scale rebellion by the western and southern provinces. The contest ended in a truce negotiated by the Panchen (Teshu) Lama, the Sakya Lama and a representative of the Dalai Lama on 11 April 1728. But taking advantage of an incident in Lhasa which involved alleged outrages against Tsang people, Pholhanas ignored the truce and marched on Lhasa. By 3 July he was master of Tibet.

Within two months a new Manchu army arrived in Lhasa to prevent further civil war. This replaced the earlier occupation force which had been withdrawn when Yung-chen succeeded his father as Emperor of China and implemented a policy of retrenchment. Now backed by a powerful Chinese garrison, Pholhanas took his revenge against his enemies. Ngabo, Lumpa and Jaranas and fourteen of their more influential supporters were executed in the shadow of the Potala. Before a crowd of Tibetan townsfolk the three ministers were killed slowly and hideously by an excruciating process, perfected by the Chinese, of being sliced into small pieces. Two lamas who had been sentenced to death with the ministers were strangled in front of the crowd while the rest, more humanely, were decapitated. Not content with this, Pholhanas ordered that the families of all the victims also be killed. The Dalai Lama and his father, who had strongly supported the three council ministers, were exiled to Litang in eastern Tibet where they remained for seven years.

It was at this time that the Manchus originated the political resident, or *Amban* system in Tibet. Two Manchu pro-consuls, backed by a Chinese military garrison, were to reside in Lhasa to protect the Emperor's suzerain interests.

Against this backdrop of developments, the struggling Capuchins with the field to themselves carried on after Desideri's departure. Francisco Orazio della Penna di Billi, who succeeded Fra Domenico as mission head in 1725, left records claiming the conversion to Christianity of certain Tibetan leaders. This is probably an exaggeration but what does seem to be true is that they enjoyed sufficient favour – probably because of their medical contribution – so that they were permitted in 1724 to build a church.

Della Penna described in some detail an interchange of letters with the Dalai Lama in 1723 devoted to a spirited religious controversy. Although again della Penna may be guilty of exaggeration, the Capuchin fathers believed that the Dalai Lama had at last been convinced 'of the palpable truth and sweet attractiveness' of Christianity. 'He experienced a deep sense of pleasure ... because his reasons could now be fully satisfied ...'[1] To show 'his good-will in a practical form' the Dalai Lama had drawn up a document empowering the Capuchins to build a monastery and a public church 'to be used for the free and unhindered exercise of the Christian religion.' This was in recognition of the fact the Capuchins lived in Tibet 'for no other purpose than to help other people and to do good to all.'[2]

Della Penna wrote fleetingly of the only layman who saw Lhasa and explored Tibet in the eighteenth century. He was Samuel Van de Putte, a Dutch adventurer and scholar who, according to the Capuchin chronicler, passed through Lhasa in 1728. Unhappily, all that Van de Putte left behind to testify to his accomplishments is a sketch map of Tibet. On his death bed in Batavia, the remarkable Dutchman ordered that his extensive notes, written in his own cipher, be burned. It may be that he feared an improper popularization of it after his death. But whatever his motives, the loss of this record of travel in Tibet is a tragic one. The only opportunity for a collateral account of the Capuchin mission and a lay view of early eighteenth-century Lhasa were lost.

What can be pieced together is that Van de Putte, on a voyage of high adventure, travelled by caravan across the Middle East from Aleppo to Isfahan. From Persia's fabled city of Shahs he proceeded to India where he donned the disguise of a Hindu. He then crossed the Himalayas – probably by way of Ladakh – and made his way to Lhasa, much as Desideri had done. His reception in Tibet's capital was cordial. He was treated well, both by the Capuchins and by the Tibetans themselves.

In 1729, Van de Putte, now dressed as a Mandarin, joined a

---

[1] Samuel Louis Graham Sandberg, *The Exploration of Tibet, Its History and Particulars, 1623–1904* (Calcutta; Thacker Spink & Co, 1904), p. 41.
[2] *Ibid.*

merchant caravan travelling northward to China. He is believed
to have been well received in Peking where he arrived after
what must have been a difficult but fascinating journey. Returning as he had come, Van de Putte passed through Lhasa a second
time in 1730, where he was again greeted by the Capuchins.
After leaving Tibet he reached Delhi in time to witness its
assault by the Persian conqueror, Nadir Shah. This story, which
he could also have bequeathed to Western history, was destroyed
with his other notes in Batavia while the strangely secretive Van
de Putte lay dying.[1]

An antagonistic local clergy and a calamity of nature conspired
to make the position of the Capuchins precarious. The Kyi Chu
River, swollen by unusually heavy rains in August 1725, overflowed its banks to flood a large part of Lhasa. The highly superstitious Tantric lamas blamed this catastrophe on the foreign
intruders who, they believed, had enraged the Tibetan gods of
the earth. Incited by the lamas, a Tibetan mob of townsfolk, who
had lost their property in the flood, besieged the Christian
mission. The beleaguered priests narrowly escaped death during
this incident but were thereafter forced to suffer frequent
indignities. Finally it took an official proclamation blaming the
flood on the sins of the Tibetans themselves to save the Capuchins
from further torment, or perhaps even violent death.

The Lhasa mission was chronically troubled by financial
worries which the Capuchins were inclined to blame on Jesuit
intrigues in Rome. By 1729 the available funds could only support
two fathers in Lhasa – Orazio della Penna and Gioachino da San
Anatolia. Adding to difficulties which these two survivors
experienced in that year was an edict forbidding Tibetans to have
religious dealings with the mission. While this was soon lifted,
there remained a serious breach between the lamas and the
Capuchin fathers which could never be healed. The ill health of
della Penna forced this courageous missionary to leave at last his
Lhasa home in April 1933. Gioachino da San Anatolia, continually
plagued by local hostility, also left only a few months later. For
their long labours in Lhasa the Capuchins could show only a
scanty harvest of Christian souls: seven new converts. In all there

[1] Sir Thomas Holdich, *op. cit.*, pp. 87–9.

were but thirteen Tibetans, five Newars and seventeen Chinese who belonged to the Christian church in Lhasa.

The indefatigable Orazio della Penna successfully lobbied in the Vatican for support. He was successful enough to be able in 1738 to start out with nine colleagues for Lhasa to reopen the Capuchin mission. An account of their experiences was kept by a highly literate member of the mission named Cassiano Beligatti de Macerata. His chronicle, discovered years later in the Biblioteco Communale at Macerata in Italy – the friar's place of birth – was generously illustrated with water-colour sketches. This represented the first serious effort since Grueber to present graphically the flavour of Lhasa.

The new mission was welcomed by Pholhanas who received them with full courtesies on 11 January 1741. Beligatti's journal notes that Tibet's ruler greeted the new mission with 'the greatest affability', and appeared to be pleased with their arrival.[1]

At this first audience Chinese officials were also in attendance. These representatives of the *Ambans*, noted Beligatti, were treated with great distinction. This simple observation of Beligatti's reflected in a phrase Chinese paramountcy in Tibet. In the seven and a half years the Capuchins had been gone, much had happened, but the basic pattern of a strong Tibetan administration under Pholhanas with Chinese power in the background still remained. Pholhanas had been given a free reign. He was an efficient administrator who brought order to the chaotic government administration; he looked out for the interests of the monasteries, and brought fiscal order to the debt-ridden treasury in Lhasa.

In 1731 and 1732 there had been a resurgence of the Dzungar threat. This had been another reason why it had been thought prudent to have the Dalai Lama removed from Lhasa where his father might have been tempted to plot secretly with the Dzungars. But by 1734 the Dzungar forces were defeated in battle by the Chinese and forced to sue for peace. The Dalai Lama's father who had been called to Peking for 'discussions', gave solemn promises not to interfere in Tibetan politics. In return he and the Lama were granted the Emperor's permission

---

[1] Samuel Louis Graham Sandberg, *op. cit.*, p. 84.

to return to Lhasa. Thus in September 1735, with a Chinese honour guard, the Dalai Lama returned to the Potala.

In recognition of his able rule and presumably because of his loyal acceptance of Manchu suzerainty, Pholhanas in 1740 was given the title, Chüm-wang, or 'Prince of the Second Class'. This was awarded by Chien-lung, the new Chinese Emperor who had succeeded to his father's throne in 1736. For practical purposes Pholhanas was now King of Tibet. The *Ambans*, having initially played a prominent role in government, were now only the eyes and ears of the Emperor. So long as Pholhanas did nothing to upset the suzerain-vassal relationship, the Chinese were content to remain in the background. Characteristic of the *Ambans'* new role, was the reduced size of the Chinese military guard attached to them. Since 1733 the Chinese force had been no more than 500 men – a quarter of what it previously had been. For that matter the Emperor for several years had been content to keep but one *Amban* in Lhasa.

The day after the Capuchins paid their initial call on the Dalai Lama, they visited the *Amban*. Beligatti noted that he was a 'fine young man of about thirty years'. The Chinese representative's first question was a practical one of inquiry. He wanted to know to which country the Capuchins belonged. When he discovered they were Europeans, 'he made many demonstrations of friendliness', saying that 'he greatly esteemed Europeans with whom he had been acquainted in China'. After a lunch, washed down with 'cold spirits', the missionaries were each presented with a long stole – a signal mark of honour. On leaving, they wore the prestigious scarfs for the 'whole length of the piazza . . . [so] that it might be seen that the Chinese at headquarters regarded us not as vagabonds.'[1] In this way they hoped to ensure respectful treatment by the Tibetans.

It is likely that the universally good reception given the Capuchins by the court can be traced to their medical contribution. Commenting on his own practice, Beligatti admits he was but a novice. He was learning as rapidly as he could from Father Gioachino but he did not presume to be a full fledged doctor. Yet he talks of treating the sick 'in considerable numbers'. He

---

[1] Samuel Louis Graham Sandberg, *op. cit.*, pp. 86–8.

recalls trying unsuccessfully to save a Nepalese youth whose frost-bitten hands and feet were infected with gangrene. The patient died and his corpse was cast into the river by the Nepalese. But 'certain Tibetans hastened to rescue it. Having got it, they detached the head from the body in order to make from the skull a bowl to eat and drink out of, a custom followed by the Retroba religious community – who are practicers of magic.'[1]

A few passages from Beligatti's journal reflect the genuine cordiality shown the mission by members of Pholhanas's family. On 11 February, Beligatti and Father Gioachino called on the King's second son and the King's sister. 'Both received us ... more as intimate friends than as strangers; they entertained us upwards of two hours in familiar conversation; they gave us tea; and the sister, by way of paying a particular compliment, put with her own hands the *tsampa* in our cups.'[2]

On the following day the two missionaries visited the eldest son of the King, 'who showed ... similar cordiality, but with more gravity, perhaps to sustain the character of a lama-elect whose garments he wore.' Beligatti and Gioachino stayed for dinner which consisted of a 'large wooden dish on which was half a sheep, braised and stewed, another dish with a quarter of dried sheep, also another containing a large slice of raw yak flesh ...' Beligatti remembers all too vividly:

The constraints under which we had endured so long a journey had imparted to us the stomach of a Tibetan, that is to say, a fine hog. Accordingly it was by no means difficult for us to overcome our repugnance to eat the cooked flesh so rudely severed apart; also the *satu* made into a paste with water and rolled into a ball. However, the dried and raw flesh we refused.[3]

Beligatti provides a brief glimpse into the politics of Lhasa in describing the career of the Dalai Lama's father whom he also visited soon after arrival. 'He was an old man, upwards of seventy years of age and of singular stature, being seven and a half feet in height, of robust build and well-proportioned. In his youth he had been a novice in the [Depung] monastery from whence, because of his poverty, he was expelled. Incensed at this treatment and

---

[1] *Ibid.*, pp. 89, 90.   [2] *Ibid.*, p. 90.   [3] *Ibid.*, pp. 90, 91.

being a man of great deceit, he left the monastery the husband of three young Tartar women, all sisters.' One of these sisters gave birth to the reigning Dalai Lama but all three 'were abandoned ... in order to [permit his marrying] a Tibetan, which woman also had to yield up her bed to two other Tartar females.' Next in succession were 'two daughters of the Prime Minister'.[1]

Beligatti alludes to the events of 1727 and their aftermath: 'On account of the murder of the King (actually Council Head, Khangchennas), all the conspirators were exemplarily punished by the Chinese; (the Dalai Lama's father) himself being summoned before the Emperor of China, whither he was conducted, chained together to his new wives.' He was, however, again permitted to return to Lhasa on the condition he would not become a permanent resident of the capital.

Of all Tibetan ceremonies, none are more colourful than the great *Monlam* celebration. While originally a twenty-three-day period of prayer, this observance of the Tibetan New Year had become by Beligatti's time a period of licence and wild revelling. The Capuchin missionaries were the first to describe it in any detail. Beligatti and two other priests, with the help of the Dalai Lama's father, secreted themselves on the latter's roof from where they could furtively watch the spectacle in the great square. Beligatti's words but hint at the scene which must have fascinated the friars:

There came forth sixty Nepalese on horseback followed by about forty *Azarra*, or pious Hindus who were rich merchants, also on horseback and clad in Chinese brocade. After these came fifty-six Musalmans of Kashmir who have large workshops in Lhasa, likewise riding, but in their ordinary attire. There followed eight laymen on horses, clad in Chinese brocade, bearing four pairs of standards or banners, each pair of a different pattern. Other horsemen came next, carrying various emblems of guilded wood to whom succeeded tambourine and trumpet bearers; and these were followed by all the governors of the different provinces, the *Deba-mi-pou*, in robes of office according to their respective ranks. After these came the *Chiokyong* in ordinary monks' robes but clean, and by way of distinction, having a red cowl and the collar turned back with skins of the marten. Next to the *Chiokyong* came all the monks

---

[1] *Ibid.*, p. 93.

of Potala in robes of yellow brocade, followed by the four Ministers of State with their staff. The Ministers of State were clad respectively in scarlet, red, green, and yellow European broadcloth. Two horses followed, richly caparisoned, bearing on their backs two huge censors of silver in which perfumes were burning, and each horse led by two religious who held it by the bridle. Then came another two horses more richly equipped than the first, having on their backs each a casket or urn of gold; in one of which I was repeatedly assured was the skin of a horse into whom Shakya-t'ubpa had once upon a time transmigrated; in the other I could not understand what was enclosed. These two were likewise led by the bridle by four handsomely attired monks. To these succeeded two horses profusely adorned, which drew the equipage of the Grand Lama, being each connected with the load by a long cord of red silk descending on both sides of the animal nearly to the ground, and which was festooned from its shoulders to the root of the tail – each horse led by two religious. After the equipage proceeded the Supreme Lama himself, bested all in cloth of gold and with his *Tscemba*, or miter, likewise of gold from the lower brim of which descended a black strap or lace resting on the tip of his nose and suspended from each temple. His horse was led by the mane by a pair of monks arrayed in yellow brocade. Astride the horse next behind that of the Grand Lama was the King, habited in pearl-coloured silk with his cap adorned with a long skin Tartar-fashion. On his left was the father of the Grand Lama clad in violet brocade. Behind these came the two sons of the King; the elder riding between the younger son (the military generalissimo) and the brother of the Grand Lama (having the same father and mother as he); and they were followed by all the Court marching in military fashion, five horsemen abreast and terminating the procession.[1]

The position of the Capuchins was a precarious one. But by May 1741 it was beginning to appear untenable. The lama clergy resented the position of prestige and favour which they enjoyed in Pholhanas's court. Beligatti recalled the final eruption which spelled the end of the Capuchin mission:

... several hundred of Buddhist priests, gathered from the different convents of Lhasa and the neighbourhood, invaded the royal palace and upbraided the King for his partiality. The latter, being terrified and dreading to meet the fate of his three predecessors, declared forthwith that the fathers had fallen from his favour; he enjoined them to preach

---

[1] *Ibid.*, pp. 95–7.

no more in Tibet . . . and at the same time he caused the converts to be searched for and had them exposed in the Chinese wooden collar; . . . the few of these who were unwilling to recite the watchword of the ancient faith he caused to be bloodily flogged.[1]

After this episode the Capuchins were objects of ridicule and abuse. They could no longer appear safely in public, much less carry out the business of their mission. It was therefore decided to reduce the mission from six to only three. Beligatti was among those selected to return. On 13 August 1742 he and two colleagues left for Patan in Nepal.

The Prefect and pioneer founder of the Capuchin mission, Orazio della Penna stayed on in Lhasa with two companions. By now he was a feeble old man with little energy to pursue his tasks in the face of continuing hostility; 'beholding themselves hedged in on every side, they decided to depart.' Pholhanas, still with a certain affection for the old missionary who had given more than two decades of his life to Tibet, promised the Capuchins that they could preach again 'on condition that they should declare the Tibetan religion to abound in goodness and perfection.' But this, of course, was unthinkable, and the last members of the Capuchin mission left Lhasa on 20 April 1745. The Lhasa mission had become Orazio della Penna's life. When it was gone, nothing further remained for him. On 20 July 1745 the broken-hearted old missionary died in Patan. It was just as well that he never lived to hear the news that Pholhanas – probably motivated by political expediency – had had the Capuchin church razed.

After thirty-eight years the Capuchins were out of Tibet. Under Beligatti and later his successor Anselmo da Ragusa, the so-called 'Tibet Mission' lingered on in Nepal until 1768 when the Gurkha revolt forced it to leave.

The missionaries had tried, but in the end failed. The successes in China and India were not to be repeated in Tibet. While the friendship of kings had permitted Christian footholds for limited periods of time, the fundamental and perhaps understandable antagonism of the Lamaist clergy prevented permanent settlement. But however futile these missions may have seemed –

---

[1] *Ibid.*, p. 98; L. Petech, *op. cit.*, p. 172.

there being no record of permanent communities of converts left behind – they at least brought to the Western world news and knowledge of this most inaccessible of lands. Their reports whetted the appetites of others whose motives were more materialistic but whose efforts would prove no more successful.

Part Two

The Merchants

6

George Bogle

The flagship *Hector* of the newly chartered East India Company dropped anchor off Surat on the west coast of India in August 1608. This was the beginning of an imperial enterprise that would change the face of Asia and reward Britain beyond all expectation. But success then seemed remote to Jack Hawkins, Master of the *Hector*, whose reception by the Moghul governor seemed anything but auspicious. Gifts brought for Emperor Jehangir were seized by the suspicious governor, while the well-entrenched Portuguese, whose intrigues may have been responsible for the attitude of the local administration, confiscated the rest of the Hector's cargo. The English ship was forced to depart, leaving Hawkins and one companion alone to seek out the Emperor while fending off the troublesome Portuguese.

Hawkins heard that two Dutch merchants in a similar predicament had just been executed by the Portuguese in Goa. Understandably he bemoaned his fate at 'remaining in a heathen country, environed with so many enemies, who daily did nothing else but plot to murder me....'[1] But the resourceful captain was eventually able to make his way to the Moghul court at Agra. While Jehangir did not grant the concessions which the Company sought, he at least extended his friendship to the Englishman – even being so kind as to provide him with an Armenian wife. The Emperor's unwillingness to grant commercial privileges was traceable to Portuguese pressure. But a toe-hold for the Company was secured.

Portuguese primacy in India was broken in 1612 when Company ships of the line decisively defeated a Portuguese naval squadron

---

[1] Philip Woodruff, *The Men Who Ruled India: The Founders*, Vol. I (London, Jonathan Cape, 1953), p. 24.

off Surat. Spared serious competition and no longer harassed by the Portuguese, the Company could begin to prosper and expand. Sir Thomas Roe established an embassy at the Moghul court and in 1618 negotiated an agreement which granted generous commercial privileges. The capture of the Persian Gulf port of Hormuz from the Portuguese in 1622 finally gave the English supremacy in the Arabian Sea and uncontested access to the sub-continent.

Domination of India dates from 1757 when Company troops, led by Robert Clive, defeated the semi-independent Moghul viceroy, Suraj-ud-Daula, at the Battle of Plassey. This engagement broke native power in Bengal, Behar and Orissa. Plassey also represented a defeat for French ambitions in India and thus had relevance to the Seven Years War, then being fought in Europe. After Plassey, Clive extracted a treaty which gave the Company all French possessions in Bengal and awarded it the lucrative right to collect the 'Emperor's revenue'. Whatever vestiges of power were to remain with native rulers, the Company *Raj* would henceforward be supreme, and foreign competition would no longer trouble English merchants in India.

Occupation of Bengal pushed the Company's domain northward to the Himalayas. No one who has seen this great barrier can be unmoved by its grandeur. Nor can anyone who has glimpsed its jagged white crest break through the mists which usually shroud it fail to wonder what lies beyond. It was perhaps inevitable that for so long only myth and legend served to describe this most inaccessible of worlds. Since Herodotus told of 'gold-digging ants' in the cloudland north of the Himalayas, the West has been tantalized by stories of Tibet's mineral riches. Some of Asia's greatest rivers wash gold-laden sand down from the Tibetan highlands as more tangible evidence of Tibet's treasure.

With no time for dreams, but acutely conscious of Tibet's fabled wealth, the Company inevitably became interested in the unknown lands north of the Himalayas. As early as 1644 correspondence with its London directors testified to the Company's interest in Tibetan borax.[1] Buying this scarce commodity

---

[1] William Foster, *The English Factories in India, 1642–45* (Oxford, Oxford University Press, 1913), p. 38.

cheaply from petty Tibetan traders who carried it on their backs over the high Himalayan passes, British traders could market it at near monopolistic prices.

Tibet also held promise as a new market for English goods. In March 1768, the Court of Directors of the East India Company pressed for an investigation of the commercial feasibility of selling English cloth in Tibet. Even more interesting was the thickly populated heartland of China which lay beyond Tibet, but which had been denied to European coastal traders by the xenophobic Manchus. The Company's directors thus urged that Tibet be considered a potential 'backdoor' to China.

The consolidation of its control over Bengal and Behar unavoidably brought the Company into contact with the Himalayan principalities. Not only did the peoples of Nepal, Sikkim, Bhutan and Assam have trade links with Tibet, but there were bonds of race and religion as well. Political relationships between the mountain states and Tibet were also important, and would play a significant role in bringing the Company in touch with Tibet.

Coincident with Company expansion in north India, was the rise of Gurkha power in Nepal under Prithvi Narayan. A hardy and aggressive hill tribe, the Gurkhas conquered their weaker neighbours in the 1760s to establish a new Nepal dynasty. The seizure of the semi-Tibetan, Buddhist Newar regions, including Kathmandu, by the Hindu Gurkhas was significant because it placed them astride an important trade route between India and Tibet. Hindu-Lamaist antagonisms, which now coloured the relationship between Nepal and Tibet, caused trade between the two countries to atrophy. This ended Company hopes that trade through Nepal could be expanded, bringing to India gold species from Tibet with which to offset an unfavourable trade balance with coastal China.

When the Newar Rajah of Patan in Nepal appealed to the English for help against the Gurkhas, the opportunity which this offered to reopen the Kathmandu route to Lhasa was difficult for the Company to resist. A column under Captain Kinloch in 1767 was sent marching through the *Terai* – the malaria-infested lowlands at the base of the Nepalese Himalayas. But, crippled by disease, Kinloch's ill-prepared expeditionary force had to withdraw before reaching Patan.

The Merchants

Again, two years later, the Company dabbled in Nepalese politics. This time a Company surgeon named James Logan was sent to establish contact with the Newar Rajah of Kathmandu, who had close relations with Tibet, and attempt to negotiate 'trade with Tibet and the western provinces of China by way of Neypall [Nepal].'[1] Logan convinced the Company that support to the Newars against the Gurkhas would ingratiate the English with Lobsang Paldan Yeshe, the Sixth Panchen Lama of Tibet – or 'Teshu Lama', as he was then more commonly known in the English speaking world[2] – and increase chances of reaching a trade agreement with him.

However plausible this plan may have seemed, it did not succeed. Kathmandu fell to the Gurkhas before the Company could respond in any useful way. Moreover, the Gurkha leader, Prithvi Narayan, so resented Company interference that he warned Tibetan leaders against further encroachments and advised the Dalai Lama to exclude English agents from Tibet just as Nepal had done.

Blocked in Nepal by the hostile Gurkhas, the Company in 1773 turned its attention to Assam and Bhutan where it hoped to find alternative routes to Tibet. The 'forward policy' toward Tibet can in part be attributed to Warren Hastings, newly appointed Governor of Bengal. When Hastings's administration began in 1772, an aggressive approach was perhaps inevitable; by nature he was an activist. From the outset he saw Company opportunities north of the Himalayas. Thus it was predictable that he would seize an opportunity to probe Tibet which grew out of a petty squabble between Himalayan princes.

The Maharajah of Cooch Behar, leader of a tiny principality between Bengal and Bhutan, was kidnapped by neighbouring Bhutanese forces led by an aggressive leader of Bhutan called the Deb Judhur. Hastings rushed a column of troops to the rescue, in

---

[1] Alastair Lamb, *Britain and Chinese Central Asia* (London, Routledge & Kegan Paul 1960), p. 7. S. C. Sarcar, 'Some Notes on the Intercourse of Bengal', *Proceedings of the Indian Historical Records Commission*, Vol. XIII, 1930, pp. 104–5.

[2] The Sixth Panchen Lama is sometimes referred to as the Third, but this latter appellation ignores the three posthumously recognized Panchen Lamas in the succession. While the title 'Teshu Lama' was in current use in India at the time above described, the spelling 'Tashi' Lama became more current in India by the late nineteenth and early twentieth century.

return for which it was understood that Cooch Behar would become a Company protectorate. There the matter might have rested but for a strong Gurkha reaction. Chronically antagonistic to the British, Prithvi Narayan now saw Hastings's action as an acute threat to his own ambitions in Bhutan. Moreover, the Deb Judhur was a close ally. The Gurkha leader complained to the Teshu Lama, also a close ally of the Deb Judhur, and urged him to demand immediate British withdrawal.

In an ingenious and poignantly worded message, the Teshu Lama did in fact appeal to Hastings. The letter, which reached Calcutta in 1774, began with an ornate greeting to the Governor General: 'Having been informed by travellers . . . of your exalted fame and reputation, my heart,' like the blossoms of Spring, abounds with satisfaction, gladness and joy. . . .' The Letter more pointedly continued:

I have been repeatedly informed that you have engaged in hostilities against the Deh Terria [his phrase for the Rajah of Bhutan] to which, it is said, the Deh's own criminal conduct in committing ravages and other outrages on your frontier gave rise. . . . As he [the Rajah of Bhutan] is of a rude and ignorant race, past times are not destitute of instances of like faults which his avarice had tempted him to commit. It is not unlikely that he has now renewed those instances and the ravages and plunder which he may have committed on the skirts of . . . Bengal and Behar have given you provocation to send your avenging army against him. . . . From a regard to our religion and customs, I request you will cease from all hostilities against him and in doing this you will confer the greatest favour and friendship upon me.[1]

The Lama's diplomatic initiative, couched as it was in conciliatory terms, seemed to provide the Company with an exceptional opportunity to establish contact with the Tibetan leader. The Lama's letter coincided with Hastings's promotion from Governor of Bengal to Governor General of all Company territory in India. Even in his first, more limited roll, Hastings had all the authority he needed to explore trans-Himalayan trade; the

---

[1] Samuel Turner, *An Account of an Embassy to the Court of the Teshoo Lama in Tibet* (London, W. Bulmer & Co, 1800), pp. ix, x.

Company had in fact specifically urged his predecessor to do so in 1768. But with the broader authority as Governor General, Hastings could negotiate on behalf of the Company with the implicit weight of the British crown behind him. The Teshu Lama's unprecedented communication gave Hastings the opening he wanted.

Five weeks after receiving the Lama's letter the Governor General informed the Company's Board in London that he had written the Tibetan leader proposing a treaty of amity and commerce. Hastings saw obvious advantage to granting clemency to the Rajah of Bhutan as requested by the Teshu Lama if by so doing he could extract a trade agreement with Tibet. And, if this in turn led to an extension of trade into Western China, the commercial possibilities were limitless. A wholly new dimension of trade would be open to the Company, heretofore kept out of interior China by the Manchus.

The Tibetan Lama's letter had been brought to Calcutta by two envoys – one a Tibetan named Padma (or Paima), the other a Hindu pilgrim, or *gossain*, named Purangir. The latter, destined to play an important role as link between Hastings and the Lama's court, presented gifts to Hastings from the Teshu Lama, which hinted at considerable trade possibilities in Tibet. Gilded leather, bearing the Czar of Russia's double-headed eagle insignia, suggested that Lhasa's bazaars regularly received Russian goods. Chinese silk confirmed the assumption that Tibet traded with China, while gold and musk were evidence of the valuable products to be found in Tibet itself.

On 4 May Hastings submitted to the Company's Council a definite proposal. The Board was asked to approve the despatch of 'an English gentleman to Tibet. . . .' This emissary would 'explore an unknown region for the purpose of discovering, in the first instance, what was the nature of its productions; as it would afterwards be, when that knowledge was obtained, to inquire what means it might be most effectively converted to advantage.'[1]

Following advice given by the Teshu Lama in his letter, Hastings frequently questioned Purangir to learn more about

---

[1] *Ibid.*, pp. xii, xiii, xiv.

Tibet. D'Anville's famous atlas, published in 1747,[1] incorporated the research of two lama surveyors, trained and despatched by Jesuit geographers in Peking. The records of the Capuchin mission in Lhasa, which are summarized in Giorgi's *Alphabetum Tibetanum* (Rome, 1762), were basic references on Tibet available to the Company. But these sources were not current, while Purangir's information obviously was. After talking with the *gossain*, Hastings could assure the Board that the information which he had been able to procure 'of the people, the country and government of Tibet gives considerable encouragement.' Presumably on the basis of Purangir's information, Hastings also felt confident in describing the Tibetans as 'a simple, well disposed people, numerous and industrious, living under a well regulated government, having considerable intercourse with other nations, particularly with the Chinese and northern Tartars, and possessing at home the principal means of commerce, gold and silver, in great abundance.'[2]

Less well understood was the political matrix of Tibet – the position of the Teshu Lama, his relationship with Lhasa and Lhasa's relationship with the Chinese. As an agent of the Teshu Lama, Purangir could not be expected to be objective or necessarily forthcoming in describing such matters. Hastings's emissary would have to find out for himself. Also unclear was the history of Tibet since the Chinese established its suzerainty.

After the invasion of Tibet and defeat of the Dzungar Mongols in 1720 – described so vividly by Desideri – the Manchus had experimented with different formulas by which to control their vassal. Having come to Tibet as 'liberator' and having posed convincingly as the protector of the child Seventh Dalai Lama, the Chinese administration was at first strong in Lhasa. This gave the Emperor leverage in Mongolia, as well, since the Lamaist population there looked to Lhasa for spiritual guidance.

Still standing in Lhasa is a stone pylon erected by the Chinese

---

[1] Map number 32 in Jean Baptiste Bourgignon d'Anville's *Nouvel Atlas de la China de la Tartarie Chinoise et du Thibet*, published in the Hague in 1737. This atlas was considered the standard work until the latter part of the nineteenth century.

[2] Markham, *Narrative of the Mission of George Bogle to Tibet and of the Journey of Thomas Manning to Lhasa* (London, Trübner & Co, 1876), p. 5.

after their occupation of Lhasa. On it is carved Emperor K'ang Hsi's 'Edict of 1720', which claims inaccurately that the Manchus had suzerain power over Tibet since 1640. Drawing unwarranted inferences from a Tibetan diplomatic mission sent to Emperor T'ai Tsung in that year, the pylon's message dated Chinese control eighty years too soon.

Also mentioned in the pylon's text is the 'patron-priest' formula – a unique relationship between the Lamaist pontiff and Chinese Emperor which provided the basis for Manchu suzerainty over Tibet, yet permitted Tibet's theocracy to exercise its own powerful influence over much of the Manchu Empire. The practical implementation of the patron-priest relationship and its different interpretation by the Tibetans and the Chinese have had much to do with determining Sino-Tibetan relations through the years.

From 1706 to 1717 Emperor K'ang Hsi relied on his ally, Latsang Khan, to keep Chinese influence paramount. Neither troops nor pro-consuls were required – although Latsang's political ineptitude did ultimately require a Chinese adviser. Following the brief interregnum of Dzungar rule from 1721 to 1723 the kingship was abolished and the Emperor found it necessary to re-establish a garrison in Lhasa. Chinese troops, not unexpectedly, proved to be an irritant to the Tibetan people, particularly since the cost of the garrison had to be borne by them. Recognizing this, K'ang Hsi's son, Yung Ch'eng, who succeeded his father as Emperor in 1722, withdrew the garrison and replaced the military governor with a Chinese civil adviser.

The power vacuum left by the Chinese military withdrawal encouraged widespread political intrigues. Ultimately civil war broke out and from 1727 to 1728 Tibet was in chaos. China was again obliged to station troops in Lhasa. The Emperor also posted in Tibet's capital two resident High Commissioners, or *Ambans*, as they were known, who watched over his interests and kept him informed. In normal circumstances they did not intervene in Tibetan affairs; but implicit in their presence was the suzerain power of the Manchu throne.

Although still a minor during the civil war, the Dalai Lama was made to bear much of the blame. For this reason, and because his presence complicated Chinese control, the young

Dalai in 1728 was sent to Litang on the Chinese border where he spent seven years in exile.

Out of the chaos of civil war emerged Phola Tegri, an exceptionally able Tibetan leader, who assumed power as head of the Council of Ministers. For eighteen years Phola Tegri ruled Tibet. Although Tibetans tended to resent his close relationship with the Chinese, he in fact managed to keep Manchu presence and influence to a minimum. Above all he provided Tibet with a sorely needed period of tranquillity. So great was his stature that in 1740 he was crowned King of Tibet by the Chinese Emperor.

In the patron-priest relationship, the Dalai Lama's power rested securely on his religious authority and influence. However much secular authority was reserved for the Manchu patron, little could be done to stifle the Dalai Lama's religious prerogatives; and implicit in many of these prerogatives was power. In a country where a quarter of the male population served as monastery monks and where a theocratic system of administration was firmly entrenched, the power of the Dalai Lama was obviously considerable.

In experimenting with formulas to ensure Tibet's vassalage, it was inevitable that the Chinese would examine ways of curtailing the power of the Dalai Lama. Exile was one method, murder another. If a Dalai Lama could be eliminated during his minority, the regent, lacking divine mandate, could more easily be controlled. Still another formula called for the creation of a counterbalancing religious rival. It was this approach which helped to bring the Panchen, or Teshu, Lama into prominence.

The Fifth Dalai Lama had originally created the position of Panchen Lama by declaring his beloved Tutor, Lobsang Ch'osgyi Gyaltsan, to be an incarnation of Dhyani Buddha Amitabha[1] – Buddha's meditative state. In thus honouring his teacher, the Great Fifth had intended that the new position complement his own more worldly activist incarnation of Buddha – the Bodhisattva Avalokitesvara.[2] The Panchen Lama was also made Abbot of the Tashilhunpo monastery near Shigatse in southern Tibet,

---

[1] Translated from the Hindi, this means 'Boundless Light'. The Tibetan title is Ö-pa-me.
[2] Translated from the Hindi, this means 'Lord of Mercy'. The Tibetan title is Chen-re-zi.

thus accounting for his appellation, Teshu or Tashi Lama. Since that time this monastery has been See of the Panchen Lama and citadel of his strength.

The Emperor saw in this Tashilhunpo Abbot a more controllable rival to the Dalai Lama. In 1728, coinciding with the Dalai Lama's exile, the Chinese sought to augment the power of the then reigning Teshu Lama. He was offered vast areas in north-central and western Tibet, which however he wisely refused, being content with more modest holdings in the vicinity of Shigatse and Tashilhunpo.

Phola Tegri's son Gyurmé Namgyal inherited Tibet's crown after his father's death in 1747. But the young king met a violent end three years later at the hands of the Chinese *Ambans* when it was discovered that he had been intriguing against them. This touched off a spate of violent street rioting in Lhasa and led to retaliatory murder of both *Ambans*. The Seventh Dalai Lama showed unexpected leadership and initiative when he stepped in at this time to restore order. A new Chinese garrison was hastily sent to Lhasa when news of the upheaval reached the Emperor. Shortly afterward the kingship was abolished, never again to reappear, and temporal authority was restored to the Dalai Lama. But the Seventh was to be the last Dalai Lama to rule Tibet for more than a century.

Following the Seventh Dalai's death in 1757, rule by Regent was to be the formula. The Eighth Dalai Lama led a contemplative life, content to let his regent run the secular administration under the watchful eyes of the Chinese *Ambans*.

In stature, the Eighth Dalai was eclipsed by the Sixth Panchen (or Teshu) Lama whose remarkable character and innate ability gained for him more regional autonomy than heretofore had been enjoyed by his earlier incarnations. This was what permitted him to take a diplomatic initiative with Hastings without recourse to Ch'ien Lung – now Emperor of China – or the Chinese *Ambans* in Lhasa. But Hastings could not know the limits of the Teshu Lama's authority when he made plans to send an emissary to Tashilunpo. Nor could he know how his action would be interpreted in Peking. The Company's embassy to Tibet would be a plunge into the unknown.

Hastings chose as his envoy George Bogle, a twenty-eight year old Scot who had joined the Company no more than five years earlier. Raised in Scotland at Daldowie on the right bank of the Clyde River, Bogle had spent a year at Edinburgh University before beginning his career as clerk in a counting house. He won an appointment to the East Indian Company at age twenty-three and arrived in Bengal soon afterwards. He reached Calcutta in the midst of the Great Bengal Famine of 1770. In a letter to his father reflecting his first impressions, Bogle described how 'whole families perished of hunger, or fed upon leaves of trees.' A million and a half people starved to death that year, which must have made a deep impression on the youthful Bogle. This was a hard initiation, but it left the young Scot with the right mixture of callousness and compassion to bear the grinding poverty of the eighteenth-century India.

Although still very junior, Bogle had the self-sufficiency which Hastings admired. As Assistant Secretary to the Board of Revenue, young Bogle had had an occasion to travel upcountry with the Governor and apparently made a good impression on him. Later he was assigned Secretary of the Select Committee where he also performed creditably. On the long trip to Tibet and during his mission at Tashilhunpo he would not be able to refer back to Fort William. Guided only by the broadest of instructions, he would have to render judgments in a strange environment and under totally unpredictable circumstances. These judgments could be crucial to the Company. Moreover the journey would not be without physical danger. There were no precedents and there would be no guide except Purangir, who was untested and whose allegiance was presumed to be with the Teshu Lama.

Hastings's instructions to Bogle were in two parts: a Letter of Appointment, dated 13 May 1774, and a more restricted document entitled, 'Private Commissions to Mr Bogle', written three days later.

The Letter of Appointment, relatively formal in style, stressed trade and commerce as the principal objectives. It informed Bogle that the 'design of [his] mission is to open a mutual and equal communications of trade between the inhabitants of Bhutan [i.e. Tibet[1]] and Bengal.' Left to his discretion was whether a Company 'Resident' should be stationed permanently

---

[1] At this time Tibet was frequently referred to as Bhot or Bhutan.

in Tibet, the guiding caveat being that unnecessary expense must be avoided. The letter also directed him to inquire into 'the nature of the road between the borders of Bengal and Lhasa, and the countries lying between; the communications between Lhasa and the neighbouring countries, their government, revenue and manners.'[1]

As a postscript Hastings informed Bogle that Mr Alexander Hamilton is appointed Assistant Surgeon of the Company to 'attend you on this deputation'. One can only surmise that Bogle found this of equal interest to the substantive body of the instruction. The congeniality and capability of his sole British companion during this lonely journey would obviously be important in the success of the mission.

The Private Commissions are revealing. Hastings's request for a live pair of *Tus* – mountain goats which produce the wonderfully soft wool from which Kashmir-type shawls are made – and for rare seed and plant samples or 'any curiosity . . . acceptable to persons of taste in England' is evidence of the Governor's imagination and enterprise.

Perhaps even more interesting is Hastings's political awareness which led him to give Bogle certain intelligence tasks. The Governor, for example, sought information on the 'countries [which] lie between Lhasa and Siberia', and the communications between them. He displayed no less interest in Lhasa's relations with China.[2] Samuel Turner, a relative of Hastings who led a subsequent mission to Tashilhunpo, recalled in his memoirs:

The contiguity of Tibet to the Western Frontier of China . . . suggested also a possibility of establishing by degrees an immediate intercourse with that empire, through the intervention of a person so revered as the Lama, and by a route not obviously liable to the same suspicions as those with which the Chinese policy had armed itself against all the consequences of a foreign access by sea.[3]

While Hastings may have been primarily concerned with commerce, a considerable interest in Tibet's foreign relations is suggested by a special memorandum addressed to Bogle in which

---

[1] Clements Markham, *op. cit.*, pp. 5, 6.   [2] *Ibid.*, pp. 8, 9.
[3] Samuel Turner, *op. cit.*, p. xiii.

he asks for '. . . any facts relative to the state of Tibet with respect to China and Tartary [Russia].' Specifically, the Governor requests information on 'a large river' which, he had been told, 'forms a boundary between China and Tibet [and] which was carefully guarded by the troops of both countries.' Hastings had also heard that 'Tibet received European commodities by way of the valley of Kashmir.' And he wanted to know 'whether Kashmir and Lesser Tibet are at present dependent on [Tibet] and whether the Dalai Lama is still a vassal to China.'

Intelligence of this nature was of understandable interest to the Company, whose security could be vitally affected by the strength and goodwill of its neighbours. And what Hastings had to know before he could commit the Company to trans-Himalayan trade was the nature of China's and Russia's political ambitions in Tibet as well as their commercial competitiveness.

The Governor's personal curiosity was boundless. But Company interests also required a broad understanding of social customs as well as political and geographic factors. What nature of man was the Tibetan? What were his mores and habits? No commercial enterpriser could dare to venture into a new land without some comprehension of its people. The young envoy was accordingly instructed to keep a diary of his observations on all subjects.

Only rarely does an envoy have instructions as wide ranging as Bogle's. More rare still is the envoy who ventures forth with no protection into a land about which so little is known. George Bogle had been selected for a unique mission which had all the ingredients of diplomacy, exploration and high adventure.

7

Road to Tashilhunpo

The route which Bogle had charted ran northward through Bengal, then cut across Cooch Behar into Bhutan. Setting out through the flat plains of Bengal in mid-May 1774 – the hottest time of the year – Bogle and Hamilton made slow progress. When not fighting dense thickets, 'formed of reeds, brushwood, long grass closely interwoven', the travellers were plagued by 'an abundance of frogs, watery insects and dank air which made it difficult even to breath.' On entering Bhutan, they had neither reliable maps to follow, nor any idea of what lay beyond. Bogle complained, 'I was equally in the dark as to the road, the climate or the people; and the imperfect account of some religious mendicants, who had travelled through it. . . .'[1]

The two travellers first encountered southern Bhutanese natives at a small village where they rested. From birdcage-like, thatched houses, perched atop hogstyes, the local inhabitants spilled into the cluttered courtyard to greet the strange visitors. The village headman and his neighbours, quite tipsy on home-made rum, tried their best to make the tired travellers welcome. Young Bogle particularly recalled a hard-drinking female pedlar who 'sojourned with him'. She had 'good features and shape, fine teeth, and Rubens' wife's eyes'. Her whole dress was 'one blanket wrapped round her, and fastened over the shoulder with a silver skewer'.[2]

On 9 June the party left the hot plains and began winding its way upwards into the foothills. They were now well beyond Company jurisdiction and could proceed only by sufferance of the Deb Rajah, or ruler, of Bhutan. As walking became more

---

[1] Clements Markham, *op. cit.*, p. 15.   [2] *Ibid.*

difficult because of the ascent, they had to take on hillsmen as porters. Bogle described the coolie labour system, which was, and still is, typical throughout the Himalayas:

The only way of transporting goods in this hilly country is by coolies; the roads are too narrow, steep and rugged for any other conveyance, and the rivers too strong and rapid for boats. . . . The carriers are pressed from among the inhabitants, receive an allowance for victuals at the pleasure of the person on whose service they are employed. . . . This is a service so well-established that the people submit to it without murmuring. Neither sex nor youth nor age exempt them from it. . . . A girl of eighteen travelled one day fifteen or eighteen miles with a burden of 70 or 75 pounds weight.

Bogle and Hamilton paused at the first pass. They stood amidst the customary cluster of wooden standards stuck in a cairn of rocks at the summit by devout Lamaist travellers – each standard flying a banner with a Tibetan prayer crudely blockprinted upon it. The two travellers looked back. Below them stretched the endless flat plains of Bengal shimmering in the heat, 'their view bounded only by the circular horizon'. Bogle mused facetiously, 'What fine, baseless fabrics might not a cosmographer build on this situation. He would discover that the sea must once have covered Bengal and washed the bottom of these mountains, which were placed as a barrier against its encroachments.'

Before continuing on Bogle paused to plant ten potatoes. The far-sighted Hastings had specified that he would do this at each rest stop so that a valuable new product might eventually be introduced into Bhutan. In fact, descendents of these potatoes appeared years later in the Lhasa bazaar.

A Tibetan messenger intercepted the party as it neared Tassisudon, Bhutan's royal capital, and delivered a bitterly disappointing letter from the Teshu Lama. Written in courtly Persian, the Lama's letter advised Bogle to abandon the trip and return to Calcutta. He noted ruefully that his country was subject to the Emperor, whose will it was that no 'Moghul, Hindustani, Patan or *Fringy*'[1] be admitted to his realm.[2] Only later would

---

[1] *Fringy* was the Tibetan word for European foreigner, used in this case to apply to an Englishman.
[2] Clements Markham, *op. cit.*, pp. 44, 45.

Bogle discover that the main obstruction was in Lhasa, not Peking. The Company's ill-starred adventure in Nepal seven years before, which had provoked the Gurkha Rajah to warn his Tibetan neighbours against the English, was apparently still remembered.

Bogle was determined to proceed. He at first hoped that Bhutan's Deb Rajah might intervene on his behalf with the Teshu Lama. He decided, therefore, to remain in Tassisudon and petition His Holiness from there rather than retrace his steps to Calcutta where he feared the expedition might bog down.

The Deb Rajah returned to Tassisudon from a trip two days after Bogle's arrival. His homecoming was heralded by the hooting of elongated Tibetan brass trumpets and other assorted noises made by castanets and fifes. Bogle recalled:

At 11:00, 30 matchlocks were fired on the road he was to pass, and the salute was repeated when he came up to them. The procession consisted of 12 led horses; 120 men dressed in red with blue solitaires; 30 matchlock men; 30 archers, 30 horses laden with cloths and other furniture ... 40 men on horseback, some of them with bushy caps; the chief *dewan* with a bushy standard; 6 musicians; the Deb Rajah on horseback, covered with a scarlet cloak, a large yellow hat like a cardinal's, a *chowra burdar* (one who carries a yak-tail fly whisk) on each side of him, and behind, a man carrying a small white silk umbrella with different coloured fringes.

As the Rajah approached, large fires were lighted by the side of the road and 'the people prostrated themselves before him'.[1]

The Deb Rajah rode straight to the palace which rose steeply, three stories from the ground. Its walls gently inclined, giving a distorted perspective when viewed from the base, which made it seem higher. The tower, entirely sheathed in gilt and ornamented with dragons, flashed in the sunlight.

Bogle's account of his first audience with the Deb Rajah superbly captures the flavour of the occasion:

If there is any satisfaction in being gazed at, I had enough of it. I dare to say there were 3,000 spectators. I was led through three courts and after climbing the two iron-plated ladders, which served for stairs in this part

---

[1] *Ibid.*, p. 24.

of the world, arrived in an ante-chamber rung round with arms. Here I waited some time before I was conducted into the presence chamber, through a dark entry and down two steps. The Rajah was seated on his throne, raised about two feet above the floor. He was dressed in the festival habit of a *gylong*, or priest, being covered with a scarlet satin cloak, and a gilded mitre on his head. A man kept twirling the umbrella over him. The pulpit was gilded, and surrounded with silver ewers and vases, and the floor was covered with carpets. His officers to the number of twelve were seated on cushions close to the wall. After making my bows, which, according to the ceremony of this country, ought to have been prostrations, and laying my presents before him, I was conducted to a cushion prepared for me in the middle of the apartment. Several copper platters with rice, butter, treacle, tea, walnuts, Kashmiri dates, apricots, cucumbers and other fruits were set before me, together with a little wooden stool. All this passed in silence. Then a man entered with a silver kettle full of buttered tea, and having poured a little into his palm and drunk it off, filled a dish for the Rajah, and went round to all his officers. After all the dishes were filled, the Deb Rajah said a grace, in which he was joined by all the company; and then he opened his mouth and spoke to me. When we had finished our tea . . . a flowered satin gown was brought me. I was dressed in it as a Khilat; a red hand-kerchief was tied round me for a girdle, and I was carried to the Rajah, who bound my head with another, and squeezing my temples, put something on my head which I afterwards found to be the image of the God, Sakya (Buddha) and muttered some prayers over me. He then tied two silk handkerchiefs together, and threw them over my shoulders. I was conducted to my cushion; we had two or three more dishes of tea, as many graces, a cup or two of whiskey, and betel-nut. I then retired.

No detail of the occasion escaped Bogle's observant eye. His description of the audience chamber is particularly vivid:

The walls of the presence chamber were hung around with Chinese landscapes mixed with their deities painted on satin. The ceiling and pillars were covered with the same devices, and at the lower end of the room, behind where I sat, there were three or four images placed in niches. Before them were censers burning with incense, and lamps with butter; little silver pagodas and urns, elephants' teeth, flowers, etc., the whole ornamented with silk, ribbons, and other gewgaws. Amongst these I must not omit to mention a solitary print of Lady Waldegrave (Maria, illegitimate daughter of Sir Edward Walpole) whom I was the means of rescuing out of the hands of these idols; for it happened to strike some of the household that she would make a pretty companion to a looking glass I had given the Deb Rajah. She was hung up on one of the pillars next to the throne, and the mirror on the other.

During a subsequent audience with the Deb Rajah Bogle discussed the Teshu Lama's letter with him. He advised Bogle to abandon the trip altogether. The young Scot's gloom at hearing this was mitigated to some extent by his suspicion that the xenophobic Rajah had his own reasons for not wanting the Company to establish relations with Tashilhunpo. For one thing, obvious commercial advantage would accrue to the Rajah if his capital could serve as half-way station and market place, permitting him to monopolize trans-Himalayan trade. Bogle would soon discover political reasons as well for the Deb Rajah's uneasiness over a relationship between the Company and the court of the Teshu Lama.

Recounting his disappointing discussion with the Deb Rajah, Bogle wrote Hastings: 'I could succeed no further than to obtain a letter from him to the Lama, which was given with so much reluctance that I am not sanguine about its good effects.' Bogle now preferred to rely on the *gossain*, Purangir. Not only did the latter have the confidence of the Teshu Lama, but since he had encouraged Hastings to send an emissary to Tashilhunpo he had some responsibility to see that the mission succeeded. With luck, the *gossain* could return within two months with a reply to Bogle's plea. In the meantime the two travellers would remain in Tassisudon.

Bhutan had long interested the Company. Since the military expedition to rescue the Maharajah of Cooch Behar, Hastings had recognized the importance of this strategically-placed principality. Having to remain in Bhutan anyway for several weeks, Bogle saw an opportunity to study this country which some in the Company believed to be a key to Tibet. His observations— both as to the strategic and military role of Bhutan—were illuminating. They were generally accepted at Fort William and, in time, became British strategic doctrine.

On the usefulness of further military action against Bhutan, Bogle had these very valid opinions to offer:

... as for keeping possession of any part of [Bhutan] if occupied ... I consider it as impracticable – unless done with the consent of the Bhutanese, which I believe will never be obtained. ... The difficulties are insurmountable, at least without a force and expense much greater than the object is worth. This does not arise from the power of the Bhutanese. Two battalions, I think, would reduce their country, but two brigades would not keep the communications open, and if that is cut off the conquest would be of no use. . . . For those reasons I am no advocate for an expedition into these countries unless the people should commence hostilitities, and then it should be done only with a view to reduce them to peace on such terms as should appear honorable and advantageous to the Company; and this would be easily effected by acting vigorously for one season.[1]

Bogle stressed again the problem of communications in commenting on the folly of military action against Nepal and Tibet. More than a century later this good advice would be ignored when an unnecessary and ill-advised invasion of Lhasa threatened to stretch Britain's imperial committments far beyond capacity. Bogle wrote Hastings: 'The objections I have made against an expedition into Bhutan hold good with respect to Nepal and Lhasa, for this sole reason, that a communication cannot be kept open; and should our troops march into these countries they must consider all communications with the low country out of the question till they return.'[2]

While direct and open trading into Bhutan, Nepal and Lhasa would, in Bogle's opinion, require more military protection than could be logistically supported, Assam presented an attractive alternative. He outlined his case:

The Bhutanese, the inhabitants of the Gurkha Rajah's country [Nepal], the natives of Lhasa, and of many other countries lying northwest of the Brahmaputra, carry on a constant trade to Assam. A settlement formed on the banks of the Brahmaputra, near the capital, would become the mart for supplying all the countries lying northwest of the Brahmaputra, as well as those countries to the eastward of that river.

Assam itself is an open country of great extent, and by all accounts well cultivated and inhabited; the road into it either by land or the Brahmaputra lies open. *The communications can always be preserved.*[3]

Bogle also noted that Assam yields a number of valuable articles for export, not least of which is gold. This led him to

---

[1] Clements Markham, *op. cit.*, pp. 57, 58.   [2] *Ibid.*, p. 60.
[3] *Ibid.*, Italics are the author's.

conclude that, 'a few months after our entering Assam, the troops might be paid and provisioned without making any demands on the Company's treasury.'

Despite the delay in gaining admittance to Tashilhunpo, Bogle was still optimistic about trade with the Teshu Lama. He wrote Hastings from Tassisudon, 'unless his dependence upon China should stand in the way, I would fain hope for some success with him.' This optimism began to appear more justified when he finally received permission to proceed on to Tibet. In a letter written to the Deb Rajah, the Teshu Lama stated that Lhasa had agreed to Hastings's emissary visiting Tashilhunpo. Purangir would meet the party near the Tibetan border and escort it to the Lama's court. Bogle's patience and stubbornness had seen him through his first test. A lesser man might have watched his mission dissolve in the bureaucracy of Company headquarters at Fort William, but Purangir perhaps deserves the greater measure of credit. From this point onward Bogle would proceed on the assumption that the *gossain*, who clearly had sold his case to the Teshu Lama, had Company interests at heart.

Bad luck continued to plague Bogle, however, as a sudden insurrection delayed his departure. A revolt by political dissidents had so unsettled the countryside that travel was out of the question.

The rebel stronghold, located a short distance from Tassisudon, was built high on a bluff. It had enormously thick walls, iron-barred doors and frequently-spaced loopholes from which archers could snipe at attackers. But new levies, hastily conscripted by the Deb Rajah, swelled the royal army to formidable proportions and made the fort untenable. Recognizing that an overwhelming force was staging against them, the rebels one night stole from their stronghold and disappeared into the countryside.

Bogle had had no choice but to wait patiently until the struggle was over. But, at least in the meantime, he had gained new insight into Bhutanese politics. This contest for power had been waged on behalf of a Bhutanese chieftain known as the Deb Judhur who had previously ruled Bhutan. Judhur had firmly allied himself with the Teshu Lama by whose support he sought to control a powerful and hostile priesthood. The priesthood, led by Lama Rimpoche, Head Lama of Bhutan, had taken issue with

Judhur over the latter's military adventures – particularly the disastrous attack on Cooch Behar which had succeeded only in provoking a retaliatory attack by Bengal Company forces. The Head Lama's followers finally overthrew Judhur and installed the current Deb Rajah in his place. Under his regime Chinese suzerainty over Bhutan had been ignored, and relations with the Teshu Lama of Tibet had badly deteriorated.

At issue, thus, was whether the clergy, calling the tune for the Deb Rajah, should continue to hold power, and whether Chinese suzerainty should be recognized. Also at issue – and of particular pertinence to Bogle – was whether the Teshu Lama, through his protegé, Deb Judhur, could once again establish his influence in Bhutan. It now became clearer to Bogle why his present host did not look with enthusiasm on a Company embassy to the Teshu Lama.

Finally, on 13 October 1774 Bogle and Hamilton left Tassi-sudon, accompanied by a Kashmiri named Mirza Settar who had joined the expedition in Rangpur as interpreter and the messenger from the Teshu Lama known as Padma. Nine days later the party reached Phari Dzong, (or Phari Fort as it is known in the English translation), 1,400 feet high on the Tibetan border.

Rising abruptly above them as they approached the town was a hill. Bogle watched a funeral procession wind its way to the summit, carrying a corpse to be thrown to the vultures. 'All manner of carnivorous scavenger birds soared above in expectation,' he noted. The town, itself, dominated by a castle built in its midst, consisted of closely packed, two storey houses, roofed with bundles of straw. Bogle complained, 'The ceilings are so low that I have more than once been indebted to the thickness of my skull; and the beams being very short, are supported by a number of posts, which are little favourable to chamber walking.' From his description of the houses one has a picture of grimy squalor. In the middle of the roof is a hole to let out the smoke which, wrote Bogle, 'departs not without making the whole room as black as a chimney'. The opening serves also to let in the light; 'the floors are full of holes and crevices, through which the women and children keep peeping'.

Now on the windswept, Tibetan plateau, the travellers felt the biting cold of late October. Like the Tibetans, they kept warm at night by burning yak-dung, which had been carefully collected from the fields and, shaped in the form of small paddies, left to dry in the sun. It made a 'cheerful and ardent fire when well kindled . . .'. The route was a bleak one – the slopes were bare, supporting only sparse tufts of withered grass. The custom of burning had through the centuries deprived the soil of the only natural fertilization which was available.

By the shore of Calo Chu Lake, some miles on, Bogle had his first lesson in Lamaist codes of hunting. Prevented by his guide, Padma, from shooting a *Kyang*, or Tibetan wild ass, the young Scot learned 'the general principle by which the [Tibetans] determined the degree of culpability in depriving an animal of life. . . .' According to the Tibetan doctrine of transmigration of the spirit, there is 'a perpetual fluctuation of life among the different animals of this world, and the spirit which now animates a man may pass after his death into a fly or an elephant.' For this reason, explained Bogle, Tibetans 'reckon . . . the life of every creature upon an equal footing, and to take it away is considered as a greater or smaller crime in proportion to the benefits which thereby accrues to mankind. . . .' The wild *Kyang* clearly contributed enough to mankind so that his life was worth sparing.

On 2 November, Purangir and several of the Teshu Lama's attendants met Bogle's group near Gyantse, one of Tibet's largest towns. Six days later they arrived at 'Desheripgay', or Dechenrubje as it is better known, where the Teshu Lama had moved his court to avoid a smallpox epidemic in the Shigatse and Tashilhunpo area. The Lama's temporary palace was small – only two stories high – but was adorned with the typical ornamented roof, found so frequently on the houses of Tibetan nobles.

The two envoys were led through the town to their own apartments where servants greeted them with 'tea, boiled rice, flour, sheep carcases and whisky'. Bogle described his room as being 'immediately above the church', where he was entertained with the 'never-ceasing noise of "cymballines and timballines" from morning to night'. Only after dark, when the gates were shut tight, could he find peace.

Soon after his arrival Bogle had his first audience with the Teshu Lama. While brief, this long-awaited encounter was important. It would set the tone of their relationship. The Lama was upon his throne formed of wood, carved and gilt, with some cushions above it. He sat cross-legged, dressed in a mitre-shaped cap of yellow broad-cloth, a yellow cloth jacket without sleeves and a satin mantle of the same colour thrown over his shoulders. On one side of him stood his physician with a bundle of perfumed sandlewood rods burning in his hand; on the other stood Solpön Chenpo, the cup-bearer. 'I was seated near him on a high stool covered with a carpet,' recalled Bogle. 'He received me with a very courteous and smiling countenance.' Servants put the Governor's presents before him, while Hastings's envoy personally delivered a letter and a costly pearl necklace from the Governor. According to the custom of the country, Bogle signified his personal greeting by giving the Lama a white scarf.[1]

After social amenities, the Teshu Lama got straight to business. Speaking in Hindustani, so that no interpreter was necessary, he referred to the earlier war between Bhutan and Cooch Behar, which had led to Company intervention and his own plea to Hastings for peace. He assigned full blame for the incident to the Deb Judhur, Bhutan's former leader. Commenting that he, himself, had disapproved greatly of Judhur's seizing the Behar Rajah and 'going to war with the *Fringies*', the Lama complained that 'the Deb would not listen to my advice'.

Bogle retraced the events and provided an eloquent justification of the Company's actions in Bhutan, claiming that there had been just cause for alarm at the Deb Judhur's aggression. 'Encouraged by their success in Behar,' the Company envoy predicted that they 'would hardly be confined, ... but [would] attempt the conquest of Rangpur tomorrow and even ... the more fertile provinces of Bengal.'

Bogle feared – probably with justification – that much of his speech had not been understood by the Teshu Lama because he had spoken Hindustani with a rich Scottish burr which he had 'inherited from his mother'. But presumably the genuinely friendly tone came through and helped convince the Lama that the Company wanted his friendship. Certainly his response was completely conciliatory; he told Bogle that the 'Deb Judhur has been turned out of his Government' and 'has fled to me', (which

---

[1] India Office Library, Commonwealth Relations Office, London, *Bogle Papers*, Mss. Eur-E, 226, Vol. 53, Document No. 267/48.

Bogle, of course, had learned in Tassisudon during the aftermath of the Deb Judhur's effort to regain power). The Lama added bluntly that Bhutan's leader had not managed the country properly and 'the *Fringies* were not pleased with him', as much as to say that Company disapproval was reason enough for his removal. Then, to establish his own peaceful motives, he stated simply that, although the Governor had reason for going to war, for his part he is 'averse to bloodshed and the Bootieas [Bhutanese] are my vassals.'[1]

Before concluding this historic first contact between Tibet and England, the Teshu Lama – always very human – succumbed to his obviously gnawing curiosity. He asked Bogle if England was near the country of the cannibals. On this ingenuous note the initial audience ended.

It was the following morning that the Teshu Lama, with astonishing candour, explained his reasons for at first having tried to stop Bogle from entering Tibet. 'I will plainly confess,' said he, 'that my reason for . . . refusing your admittance was that many people advised me against it.' The Lama confided that he had heard much of the power of the *Fringies*, that 'the Company was like a great Raj and fond of war and conquest; and as my business . . . is to pray to God, I was thus afraid to admit any Fringies into the country.'

Later, as the Lama came to know Bogle better, he would make clear that it was the Regent in Lhasa who was hostile to the idea of Company contact with Tashilhunpo. The Regent had written the Lama, transmitting to him the intelligence that two Englishmen and a great retinue of servants had arrived in Bhutan. As the English were 'predatory', the Regent strongly advised that they be refused entrance to Tibet because of the smallpox epidemic or on some other pretence. This had been the cause of his own letter to Bogle in Bhutan. But after receiving Purangir and hearing his petition on Bogle's behalf, the Lama claimed that he wrote the Regent, and in blunt terms reminded the *Gesub* that Lhasa had encouraged the Deb Judhur of Bhutan in his disastrous warlike adventures, while he, the Teshu Lama, had tried to dissuade him from invading Behar. The Lama concluded by telling the

---

[1] *Ibid.*, Document No. 271/52, 272/53.

Regent that if Lhasa persisted in trying to determine Tibet's Himalayan policy, including refusing to admit Hastings's emissary, it must bear full responsibility for the consequences.[1] Bogle also quickly learned of anti-Company machinations by Rajah Chait Singh, the disgruntled *Zemindar* of Benares, who had long been antagonistic toward Company expansion in Bengal. The Rajah's envoy to the Teshu Lama had described the English as 'a people designing and ambitious, who insinuated themselves into a country on pretences of trade, became acquainted with its situation and inhabitants, and afterwards endeavoured to become masters of it.'[2]

Bogle believed 'it most becoming the character of the English' to deal openly with this adversary. At their first meeting the plain-speaking Scot confronted the envoy directly. After a feeble attempt to shift the blame for anti-Company agitation to the envoy from Kashmir, Chait Singh's Vakil warmed to the personality of Bogle and became his good friend. The Benares envoy, in fact, helped Bogle 'to beguile a few tedious hours' at the Lama's court.[3]

Meetings between Bogle and the Lama became more frequent. Usually they met alone, although sometimes Solpön Chenpo, the Lama's 'cup-bearer', or favourite, joined them. The atmosphere was relaxed – sometimes even jocular. On the excuse that the weather had become colder, the Lama insisted that his visitors don Tibetan robes – purple and blue satin gowns lined with fox skins and trimmed at the neck and cuffs with scalloped gold lace from Russia, caps of 'flowered silk brocade, turned up with sable and crowned with a red silk tassle' and red leather jack boots.[4] The more familiar native costumes perhaps helped bridge the vast gap between the two cultures and put the Lama more at ease. This was another example of Bogle's conscious effort to adopt the customs of the country.

Conversations ranged over a wide variety of subjects. The Lama, for example, explained his own philosophy of co-existence: 'On one side of us is the Chinese Empire,' he explained. 'On

[1] Clements Markham, *op. cit.*, pp. 131, 132.
[2] *Bogle Papers, op. cit.*, Document No. 286/67.
[3] *Ibid.*, Document No. 289/69.
[4] *Ibid.*, Document No. 289/70.

another, the great Kingdom of Hindustan ... and on a third the Russian Empire.' 'As for me,' said the humble Lama, 'I am a priest – not a rajah; I know nothing about fighting. We ... do nothing but read and pray to God.'[1]

In frankly describing the politics of Tibet, the Lama made it clear that the Chinese Emperor had strong influence in Lhasa. Through the Regent, Gesub Rimpoche, whom the Emperor appointed, and the two *Ambans*, (or Chinese Residents) in Lhasa who had at their disposal a 1,000-man military guard, the Manchus controlled and guided this vassal. If the Regent governed well – that is, to the satisfaction of Peking – so much the better; if not, the Emperor 'will cut off his head', alleged the Lama.[2]

Bogle undertook to present to His Holiness an accurate description of India – one which would show the Company in a good light. Knowing full well that the image which the Lama had gained of Company-ruled Hindustan had been filtered through the eyes of wandering religious ascetics and dubious mendicants of the Himalayas, Bogle made a point of correcting the mistaken image they had created. 'These robbers, these pretended pilgrims, armed with matchlocks and swords', he said, 'have infested Bengal, burning the villages and plundering the inhabitants'. Hastings's envoy, in an effort to discredit them, pointed out that while in Tashilhunpo, 'they appear in a humble posture and with only a pilgrim's staff', in Bengal, 'they carry guns and swords'.[3]

Bogle was impressed with the Lama, finding him humble and cordial, for, although venerated as God's vice-regent through all the eastern countries of Asia, endowed with a portion of omniscience, and with many other divine attributes, he throws aside, in conversation, all the awful past of his character, accommodates himself to the weakness of mortals, endeavours to make himself loved rather than feared, and behaves with the greatest affability, particularly to strangers.'

Bogle's physical description of his host portrays a man 'about forty years of age, of low stature, and though not corpulent, rather inclined to be fat.' Bogle noted that 'his complexion is

---

[1] *Ibid.*, Document No. 291/72.   [2] *Ibid.*, Document, No. 291/72.
[3] *Ibid.*, Document No. 294/74.

fairer than that of most Tibetans, and his arms are as white as those of a European; his hair, which is jet black, is cut very short ... his eyes are small and black.' Reference to the Lama's light skin betrays the Ladakhi blood on his mother's side. It was from her also that the Lama had learned fluent Hindustani, which made direct conversation with Bogle possible. That the two got on extremely well at their first meetings is clear from Bogle's eulogistic remarks:

His disposition is open, candid, and generous. He is extremely merry and entertaining in conversations, and tells a pleasant story with a great deal of humour and action. I endeavoured to find out, in his character, those defects which are inseparable from humanity, but he is so universally beloved that I had no success and not a man could find in his heart to speak ill of him.[1]

Within a week after Bogle and Hamilton arrived, they witnessed a *durbar* – to use the Indian word for a grand audience – in which the Teshu Lama received his people *en masse*. Throngs of Tibetans flowed into town to receive the Lama's blessing as he sat under a canopy in the palace courtyard. They ranged in a huge circle around the pontiff, waiting their turn.

First came the lay folk. Everyone according to his circumstances brought some offering; one gave a horse, another a cow; some gave dried sheep's carcasses, sacks of flour, pieces of cloth, etc; and those who had nothing else presented a white Pelong handkerchief. . . . After this they advanced up to the Lama, who sat cross-legged upon a throne formed with seven cushions, and he touched their heads with his hands, or with a tassel hung from a stick, according to their rank and character.

Bogle and Hamilton were experiencing a new world – a world in which seemingly nothing was the same. Hamilton administered to the sick, which gave him some link to the familiar life he knew, but even in the universal world of medicine there was a touch of the bizarre. Mirza Settar, who had faithfully accompanied the party from Bengal, was one of the English surgeon's first patients, and a strange case he was. The simple

---

[1] *Ibid.*, ; and Clements Markham, *op. cit.*, pp. 135-8.

Kashmiri had come under the influence of a *fakir* and had accepted from him a dubious nostrum. Whatever its ingredients, the potion caused him to dance wildly 'in a manner very unbecoming his years and gravity', and roll about on the ground as a man possessed. As culmination of his mad seizure he clutched Bogle, nearly smothering him in a maudlin embrace.

Bogle urgently set about absorbing the new culture, determined to earn the Teshu Lama's confidence. His formula for successful diplomacy, described simply as follows, is classic and worthy of present-day imitation:

In order to fulfill the purpose of my commission I had to gain confidence and to conciliate good will. With this view I assumed the dress of the country, endeavoured to acquire a little of the language and manners, drank a deluge of tea and salt and butter, ate bettle . . . took snuff and smoked tobacco . . . and would never allow myself to be out of humour. . . .

A wonderful insight into the young Scot's earnestness is contained in the line, 'I sometimes consider the character not only of the English but of all people of Europe depended upon me.'[1] With this as his credo, he could scarcely fail in his mission.

Having moved quickly to establish a cordial relationship with the Lama and having dispelled much of the suspicion of the Company created by its ill-wishers, Bogle undertook to describe simply and frankly the purpose of his mission. In a word, it was 'trade'. Hastings's emissary sought not only 'a free channel of trade . . . of mutual advantage to both countries and to all the world', but he sought the Lama's assistance in securing free trade and travel through the mountain states which lie between them.

The Teshu Lama listened sympathetically, then reviewed some of the reasons for the decline in trade between Tibet and Bengal. The Deb Judhur's war with Cooch Behar had, of course, disrupted trade in that region. But the Lama assured Bogle that with Judhur's defeat and asylum in Tibet, there was no chance that he could make trouble again. More serious, perhaps, was

---

[1] Perceval Landon, *The Opening of Tibet* (New York, Doubleday, Page & Co, 1905), pp. 433, 434.

the Gurkha Rajah of Nepal, who had interfered with Himalayan trade through his country and who, even at this moment, threatened the Deb Rajah in Bhutan.

Also bothering the Teshu Lama was the fear that Lamaist traders from Tibet still ran the risk of Moslem persecution at the hands of the Moghul administrators. The excesses of the Moslem rulers in Bengal over a period of several centuries had discouraged visitors from Tibet. There had been many unfortunate incidents through the years. The Lama complained that after Bengal had been conquered by the 'Musselmen' 800 years ago, temples had been pillaged and the people plundered, sending many fleeing into the mountains to a refuge from which they never returned. But he accepted Bogle's assurances that with Company rule in Bengal, there was at last peace and security.

The Lama hinted at the real problem when he mentioned that a representative from Lhasa would soon visit him. As he wished Bogle 'to be known to all the principal people' of Tibet, he would introduce him to the Regent's agent. From this Bogle – correctly as it turned out – suspected that 'something depended on this man'. He saw plainly that the Lama, 'chose not to take any step before he had communicated with Lhasa'. In his report to Hastings, the canny Scot wrote: 'Although he [the Lama] spoke with all the zeal in the world, I confess I did not much like the thoughts of referring my business to Lhasa, where I was not present, where I was unacquainted, and where I had reason to think the ministers had entertained no favourable idea of me and my commission.'[1]

By December the smallpox epidemic in Tashilhunpo had run its course and the Teshu Lama made preparations to return to his See. On the day of departure Bogle and Hamilton were awakened early since the grand cavalcade was to leave well before sunrise. A long cloth had been stretched from the door of the palace to the horse which awaited His Holiness. Because of the penetrating pre-dawn cold he was wrapped in a fur-lined, yellow satin cloak as he gingerly mounted his stallion, assisted by two attendants who held the horse's head and two others who steadied the saddle. As the procession got under way more

---

[1] Sir Francis Younghusband, *India and Tibet* (London, John Murray, 1910), pp. 16, 17.

villagers collected. Bogle commented that 'crowds of people were assembled to see and pay their adorations to the Lama. The horsemen, however, kept them off, and they were obliged to perform their three prostrations at a great distance.'

The line of march was preceded by a horseman bearing the yellow silk standard of the Teshu Lama. Then came eight mounted kettle drummers and four mounted trumpeteers whose flourishes paced fifty mounted guardsmen trotting behind dressed in scarlet coats and yellow sheepskin bonnets. Four lamas in yellow tunics and the 'cup-bearer', or Lama's favourite, flanked the Teshu Lama himself, who was protected from the sun by a yellow satin umbrella carried on another horse by his side. Bogle and Hamilton, in places of high honour, rode immediately behind the Lama. They were followed by the Rajah of Benares, and other Hindu dignitaries visiting from India. Bringing up the rear were about a hundred horsemen of 'assorted rank and dress'.

The cavalcade stopped for two days at Teshu-tzay, the Teshu Lama's birthplace. Bogle and Hamilton, who were housed in a castle nearby, passed the time watching Tibetan dancers. Fifteen men and fifteen women – whose 'faces were washed' and who 'had an abundance of rings upon their fingers' – formed a circle with men on one side and women on the other. They danced, according to Bogle, to the accompaniment of their own singing, 'moving slowly round in a sort of half hop step, keeping time with their hands, while five men in the centre of the circle twisted round and cut capers with many strange and indescribable motions.'

Another dance performed by four or five men, 'with winged, rainbow-coloured caps who jumped and twisted about, to the lashings of cymbals and the beating of tabors.' Then a 'merry Andrew with a mask stuck over with cowries, and a clown with a large stick in his hand' amused the audience with a comic act.

On one occasion the Shigatse *Killadars*, or local governors, filed by to pay homage. Bogle noted that 'they dressed like women, except their whiskers and overgrown carcasses left no room to mistake their sex.' These strange dandies wore 'white turbans, rolled into square shapes; round turquoise earrings, about the size of watches,' and blue satin gowns.

As the procession neared Tashilhunpo, the welcoming crowds

along the road grew bigger. At each stop a large tent was pitched for the Teshu Lama, and there he dispensed his blessing on the people who filed by. Dressed in his sacredotal habit and seated on high cushions, he would administer the *chawa*, or laying on of hands. Bogle was always permitted to sit near His Holiness and watch the proceedings.

Tashilhunpo with its sprawling monastery finally came into sight. It was infinitely more imposing than the temporary See they had left behind. As the caravan approached his new home, Bogle would discover what it meant to live in a city entirely inhabited by priests. But more important, he would become a close and enduring friend of the Teshu Lama.

8

Bogle and the Teshu Lama

The return of the Teshu Lama was the occasion for a grand welcoming in Tashilhunpo. The rotund pontiff sat cross-legged on deep layers of cushions, while everyone filed by and bowed low in the traditional gesture of homage. Crowds of people – priests, Khampa tribesmen from eastern Tibet, Kalmuks from the north, governors of neighbouring fiefs, men, women and children – came to make offerings and pay obeisance to the Lama. They brought according to their station in society, 'purses of gold, talents of silver, pieces of Chinese satin, bundles of tea and fruits, dried sheep's carcasses, bags of flour and rice, small images . . . religious books, and bundles of incense.'

Bogle in his turn approached the dais, bowed and handed to His Holiness the ceremonial white scarf of greeting. The Lama exchanged pleasantries with his new friend and beckoned him to take a place of honour. The young Scot remembered being seated upon a cushion next to four lamas. Opposite him sat a Kalmuk lama, lately arrived from the Khalka Lama. The latter, whose See is in Mongolia, ranks third in the Lamaist hierarchy – after the Dalai Lama and the Teshu Lama. Also seated nearby were splendidly dressed envoys from Kashmir and ambassadors representing certain of the north Indian princes.

Tibetan butter tea was served to the dignitaries from the Lama's golden teapot. A score of young boys decked out in multi-coloured chintzes and white turbans danced 'to the music of flutes, kettledrums and bells, keeping time with hoppings and twirlings'. The programme featured religious disputations on such universal subjects as the 'immortality of the soul' and the 'unchangeable nature of sin'.

Finally an enormous banquet was served. The guests feasted

146

on Kashmir dried fruits, treacle cakes, sweatmeats, biscuits and the special delicacy, dried sheep's carcasses.

Grand spectacles of this kind were not, however, the usual fare for Hastings's envoy. Life in Namling monastery as an object of curiosity – a rare specimen on exhibit – called upon Bogle's deepest reserves of patience. He had no choice but to receive an endless procession of the curious. Their cluckings of exclamation as they gawked at Bogle's most personal effects and sampled his snuff were irritating accompaniments to a dreary, daily routine which lasted throughout the envoy's four-month stay. 'Crowds of *gylongs* [priests] used to come . . . to see me at all hours,' complained Bogle. The *Killadars* of Shigatse, curiously dressed in their feminine attire, crowded around to stare, somehow finding the sparse furnishings of his apartment unceasingly fascinating.

Bogle's quarters took some getting used to. Entering by a large red door with 'hinges of iron, cunningly gilt', one stepped into a huge room supported by nine square wooden pillars, painted red and white in such a way as to give a *trompe d'œil* effect of fluting. The floor was made of a chalky clay mixed with pebbles, which during the two decades of use had acquired a hard and smooth polish, 'not inferior to the finest variegated marble'.

Convenient to the apartment was a temple which housed eleven larger-than-life sized god images sitting cross-legged on bejeweled, copper-gilt thrones. A twelfth statue portraying the Tibetan God of War stood fiercely erect as befit his role in the pantheon. All the figures were covered with mantles and wore crowns or mitres on their heads; around their necks were price-less necklaces of coral, pearls, cornelians and agate.

To be silently surrounded by these awesome deities was en-durable, but total immersion in the animated aspects of Lama-ism proved tedious. 'Nothing but priests; nothing from morning to night but the chant of prayers and the sound of cymbals and tabors,' complained Bogle. He could keep busy and interested by studying the Tibetan language, but he was honest to admit that he found 'carrying on a broken conversation with the crowds of Tibetans who used to frequent [his] apartment . . . listless and insipid when compared with the pleasures of society.' 'Stripped of the little unmarked circumstances which amuse,' Bogle found his existence at Tashilhunpo in the main 'joyless and uninteresting'.

At least the endless streams of curious Tibetans, however tedious, provided Bogle with an opportunity to learn the customs and mores of the country. He was a conscientious chronicler of what he saw, mindful that on his return Hastings would expect an encyclopedic accounting.

Like all Western travellers to Tibet, Bogle was discouraged by the Tibetans' aversion to washing. But more understanding than most, the perceptive Scot recognized that washing was 'uncomfortable in this cold climate of Tibet'. He explained, too, that it was contrary to custom. This made it 'difficult to determine with precision the complexion of the Tibetans'. He recalled that a priest whom he knew called on him one morning while he was in the midst of shaving. He prevailed upon his visitor to try scrubbing himself with soap and water. The priest was not displeased with the new and clean face which confronted him in the mirror but the jeers and catcalls of his friends discouraged him from ever repeating the experiment.

Polyandry is a custom which has always fascinated the West. Reporting on this curious aspect of Tibetan life, which he impishly referred to as the 'women's revenge', Bogle wrote:

The elder brother marries a woman, and she becomes the wife of the whole family. They club together in matrimony as merchants do in trade. Nor is this joint concern often productive of jealousy among the partners. They are little addicted to jealousy. Disputes, indeed, sometimes arise about the children of the marriage, but they are settled either by a comparison of the features of the child with those of its several fathers, or left to the determination of the mother.

Bogle also made his contribution to earlier reported stories concerning Tibetan funeral rites. Here again, the thoughtful Scot sought rational reasons for the seemingly curious, or in this case macabre customs of Tibet. He recognized that because there was little wood in the country, most Tibetans could not afford to burn their dead as Buddhists elsewhere do. But, explained Bogle, 'they take an equally effective way of destroying them; the body is carried to a neighbouring mountain and, being cut nd beat in pieces, is left to be devoured by the wild beasts.' Bogle visited one of these 'sepulchral mounts', discovering that 'on top of this gloomy hill an aged virgin had fixed her solitary abode.'

Bogle was perhaps the first Western traveller to take careful note of Tibet's human geography. He recognized that this high plateau was a crossroads of Asia when he wrote:

Many foreign merchants, encouraged by indulgences . . . have settled in Tibet. The natives of Kashmir who, like the Jews in Europe or the Armenians in the Turkish empire, scatter themselves over the eastern kingdoms of Asia. . . . Their agents, stationed on the coast of Coromandel, in Bengal, Benares, Nepal and Kashmir, furnish them with the commodities of these different countries, which they dispose of in Tibet, or forward to their associates in Seling [Sining] . . . The *gosains*, or trading pilgrims of India, resort hither in great numbers. Their humble deportment and holy character, heightened by the merit of distant pilgrimages, their accounts of unknown countries and remote regions, and, above all, their professions of high veneration for the Lama, procure them not only a ready admittance, but great favour. . . . The Kalmuks who, with their wives and families, annually repair in numerous tribes to pay their devotions at the Lama's shrines, bring their camels loaded with furs and other Siberian goods.

A diversion which occasionally relieved the tedium of the day was 'Kalmuk chess'. The Kalmuks were inveterate chess players. Each player invariably had two or three of his companions standing behind him. They would 'lay their great bare heads together, canvassing and consulting about every move.' Bogle boasted that he used to 'beat them hollow' by assembling a similar Tartar brain trust to help him.

Then there were the ubiquitous fortune tellers. Bogle commented that 'a man skilled in palmistry, or a company of gypsies would have a world of business in these parts; for . . . the Tibetans have great faith in fortune telling.' Hamilton, as a doctor, was somehow expected to be adept at this art. That he was not came as a great disappointment.

Few envoys have felt the burden of explaining and describing their homeland as keenly as Bogle. Nor have many diplomats had so much ground to cover. He set himself the astonishing task of writing from memory a complete history of Europe. To appease the Lama's insatiable curiosity, Bogle also dredged the depths of his memory to describe the customs and manners of eighteenth-century Europe. This was a story of wayside inns, stage coaches, highwaymen, duels and all that went with this colourful period. To give the inquiring Lama some feel for the English language Bogle recited Gray's *Elegy in a Country Churchyard*. He also answered searching questions on the Christian religion, going deeply enough into this subject to sketch the doctrinal differences between Protestantism and Catholicism.

Bogle had to imagine himself a Tibetan and note down things which would interest the Teshu Lama. That he succeeded can be judged by the fact that his ingenious work survived for more than a century in Tibet and served as their standard text on Europe. All official views and judgment on the far away world of the *Fringies* very likely were moulded by the Young Scot's words regardless of how Europe might change through the years.

While this project and his studies kept him occupied, Bogle's real satisfaction came from his talks with the Teshu Lama. His mission, of course, depended on a prospering of this relationship. But he was genuinely drawn to the Lama and found him of 'cheerful and affable temper, with a great curiosity and very intelligent.' Bogle's words describe a wise and judicious leader:

... his views are liberal and enlarged, and he wishes, as every man wishes, to extend his consequence. From his pacific character, and from the turn of his mind, naturally gentle and humane, he is averse to war and bloodshed, and in all quarrels, endeavours by his mediation to bring about reconciliation. In conversation he is plain and candid, using no flattery or compliments himself, and receiving them badly if made to him. He is charitable and is universally beloved and venerated, not only by the Tibetans, but by the Kalmuks and by a great part of the Chinese.

One important influence on Bogle's relationship with the Teshu Lama must certainly have been his marriage to a woman described as the Pontiff's 'sister'. Unfortunately, this fascinating aspect of Bogle's life is not well documented. The date of the marriage is not even recorded. All references to his Tibetan wife were deleted when his papers were edited. But, in the excellent book, *A Short History of Tibet*,[1] H. E. Richardson, the Government of India's Resident in Lhasa from 1936–1940 and again from India's independence to 1950, brings out this little known fact.

---

[1] H. E. Richardson, *A Short History of Tibet* (New York, E. P. Dutton & Co, Inc, 1962).

Two daughters born to the Bogles were raised and educated in Scotland. Both married Scots and, according to Richardson, proud descendents are alive today.[1]

Bogle's narrative gives few details of the Teshu Lama's family. The Lama's sister-in-law – wife of his brother – seems to be more interesting than most. Her marriage was a curious interlude in a life otherwise devoted to religion. Chum Chusho, as she was known, is described as a 'cheerful widow of about 45 with a ruddy complexion and the remains of having once been handsome.' She had been a nun in her younger days, but upon meeting the Lama's brother, a priest, 'they happened somehow to form such a connection together as put an end to their state of celibacy.' This obviously disturbed the Teshu Lama, who refused to see his brother for many years. After the wayward priest died, Chum Cusho resumed her vows as a nun and was ever after 'as merry as a cricket'.

Bogle's report also describes a daughter of Chum Chusho's husband by an earlier liaison. This twenty-six or twenty-seven year old maiden was believed to be an incarnation of the divine consort of Chenrezi, and as such ranked just after the Teshu Lama himself in the Lamaist hierarchy of Tibet. As Abbess of Samding monastery on Lake Yamdok Tso, north of Shigatse, this illustrious female bearing the awesome title, 'Thunderbolt Sow', (Dorje Phagmo), has through the ages in her earlier incarnations wielded great influence. To Bogle, however, she seemed a sickly person, afflicted with a 'languor and melancholy' caused by the joyless life she led.[2] Hamilton had the responsibility of treating her melancholy – a not too onerous task judging by Bogle's slyly dropped comment that he paid her daily visits.

The hard realities confronting Bogle became apparent when he received two representatives of the Regent who came to see him from Lhasa. As Bogle had feared, this delegation was essentially antagonistic to the concept of a Company presence in Tibet. However persuasive Bogle may have been, there remained China's shadow in the background. Pretending that their Regent, Gesub Rimpoche, would do 'everything in his power to help',

---

[1] *Ibid.*, p. 65. [2] Clements Markham, *op. cit.*, pp. 105, 108, 109.

the envoys made it clear that Tibet was subject to the Emperor. Bogle grumbled helplessly to Hastings that 'this is a stumbling block which crosses me in all my paths.'

The Teshu Lama later confirmed the Scot's fears, explaining that 'Gesub's apprehension of the English arose not only from himself, but also from his dread of giving offence to the Chinese, to whose empire the country is subject; and that he wished to receive an answer from the court at Peking.'

The relationship between the Teshu Lama and the Chinese on one hand and the Regent on the other was delicately balanced. Bogle summed it up:

The influence of the Teshu Lama proceeds chiefly from the veneration that is paid to his character and the weight of his abilities. The Emperors of China, being of Tartar extraction, profess the religion of the Lamas and reverence them as the head of their faith, and the present monarch undertakes no expedition without consulting Teshu Lama[1]. . . .

Bogle added that although the Gesub Rimpoche, as Regent, was jealous of the Lama's influence, he was nonetheless 'obliged to pay attention to the Pontiff's advice'. So long as the Dalai Lama had not reached his majority, supreme religious authority was lodged in the Teshu Lama who thus could not be ignored. But in the case of this particular Lama, his prestige was greatly increased by his very exceptional abilities.

Yet with all his prestige and despite the fact he was located far from the watchful eyes of the *Ambans* in Lhasa, the Lama could not ignore the Emperor. For one thing, the Chinese maintained a 1,000-man garrison in Lhasa, which, theoretically at least, could be deployed against Tashilhunpo. If that did not suffice, an expeditionary army could always be sent from the Middle Kingdom to deal with the recalcitrant Lama. One such army was, in fact, then deployed in eastern Tibet to fight dissident Khamba tribesmen. But perhaps more important than the coercive strength of the Chinese army was the recognition that the Emperor's protection, particularly in the face of a currently aggressive Nepal, was a fair price to pay for the suzerain's long leash. As Bogle admitted, 'internal government . . . is committed

---

[1] Clements Markham, *op. cit.*, p. 196.

entirely to natives . . . no tribute is extracted, and the people of Tibet, except at Lhasa, hardly feel the weight of a foreign yoke.'[1]

Bogle asked the two emissaries to carry a letter to the Regent. But even this form of petition was discouraged. While the Lhasa agents had no objection to a brief note, thanking the Regent for the presents he had sent, they refused to take any letter in which Bogle discussed trade. The envoy's exasperation was met only by the evasive response that 'much conversation was not the custom of this country'.

The Lama professed to feel as badly as Bogle did about the Regent's rebuff. He said the people from Lhasa were 'little men and knew no better'. The only real hope he could hold out was the fact that the child-Dalai would come of age within two years, at which time the Regent would no longer be in a position to obstruct trade. He did, however, offer to draft for Bogle's signature a letter to Gesub Rimpoche. Written in proper Tibetan idiom, the letter was brief and, presumably because of the warning of the two emissaries, touched but gently on matters of trade.

Bogle was understandably upset that he was not allowed to go on to Lhasa where he could plead his case in person. He rejected the Regent's alternative offer permitting a native servant to visit Tibet's capital in his place. This he did partly in principle but mainly because he wanted to dramatize the fact that his only interest was to foster trade relations – not to conduct a reconnaissance of the country. 'To tell the truth,' wrote Bogle, 'I had restrained my curiosity merely to counteract the idea of my having come to examine and pry into the country.' He was throughout extremely careful to hide from view his political and geographic investigations, lest they be misconstrued – even by the Teshu Lama – as a sign of imperial interest in Tibet. As Bogle put it:

I considered the Company could have no interest in this country but that of commerce, and that to know a number of outlandish names and to correct the geography of Tibet – although a matter of great curiosity and extremely interesting – was of no use to my constituents . . . and that to

---

[1] *Ibid.*, p. 195.

this I might be sacrificing objects of far greater importance, and exciting that jealousy which had hitherto so cruelly thwarted me in all my negotiations.

This is a good rejoinder to charges made by some historians and geographers many years later – particularly the famous Swedish explorer, Sven Hedin – that Bogle had ignored geographic research while in Tibet.[1] It is true that the 'pundits', or native explorers used in Tibet by the British a hundred years later, were by contrast with Bogle more thorough and ingenious geographers. But by this later date British interests were predominately strategic and urgently required such details. Moreover, the pundits' missions were undertaken clandestinely, while Bogle's mission was an open, diplomatic one. He could not take chances which would jeopardize his all-important relationship with the Teshu Lama. It was through the latter that Bogle must attempt to establish trade relations between Tibet and Bengal. Furthermore, China, itself, could possibly be reached with the Lama's help. The stakes were too high for any incautious act.

The careful and uncompromisingly honest approach, as shrewdly calculated by Bogle, did win the Teshu Lama's confidence. And, as it turned out, the Pontiff volunteered to have his scholars write for Bogle a comprehensive report on the laws and customs of the country. This made furtive probes by Bogle even less necessary. He also offered Bogle a detailed map of Tibet which was eagerly accepted. For information to satisfy Hastings's interest in Tibet's foreign relations, Bogle could elicit much through the normal course of his many conversations with the friendly Lama.

With regard to foreign affairs, of particular interest were the predatory attacks by Nepal's Gurkha Rajah against the princely state of Sikkim, or Demo Dzong, as the Teshu Lama insisted on calling it. The Gurkha Rajah had written the Teshu Lama and the Regent in a hostile vein. Recounting his many victories, the Rajah boasted that he was a Rajput of warrior heritage and would not shirk from war against Tibet if provoked. He specifically

---

[1] Sven Hedin, *Trans-Himalaya*, Vol. III (London, Macmillan & Co, 1910), p. 135.

sought to establish trading posts at Kuti and Kerant on the Tibet-Nepal border, where Tibetan merchants might purchase commodities of his country and Bengal. Finally, the Rajah exhorted the Tibetans to avoid all connections with the *Fringies* and Moghuls.

Prophetically, Bogle warned the Lama during a long conversation in late December that Gurkha ambitions were a threat also to Tibet. If they succeeded in the conquest of Demo Dzong, they would then attack Phari Dzong in Bhutan; next would come Tibet. Bogle voiced his concern that 'the Gurkha Rajah, after having ... made himself master of all Nepal, after having subdued Bijapur and Murung, and after having at length attacked the territories of Demo Dzong – a vassal of Lhasa – should be considered by Gesub Rimpoche ... as more to be trusted than the English, who had never attempted to extend the boundaries of Bengal. ...' Bogle added, 'I confess I saw nothing more likely to make the Gurkha Rajah desist from his war with Demo Dzong ... than the knowledge of a connection between the government of this country and that of Bengal.'[1]

By early March, however, rumours of the Gurkha Rajah's death had reached Tashilhunpo and were soon thereafter confirmed. The Rajah's three wives and six concubines in the traditional Hindu *suttee* ceremony leapt on their master's funeral pyre and went to a flaming death. Singh Pertab inherited the Nepalese throne, and Tibet as well as the East India Company could then hope for a less aggressive policy in Nepal. The Teshu Lama, possibly influenced by Bogle, wrote the new ruler urging that his country be opened to trade.

The role of Russia in Tibet, which would one day provoke British troops to occupy Lhasa, was even at this early date important. Hastings had shown remarkable intuition when he included Tibet's relationship with its distant Tartar neighbours among the subjects to be investigated by Bogle. The Teshu Lama's concern with the Russian problem, more specifically Russian-Chinese hostilities, was exemplified during a mid-March meeting with Hastings's envoy when the Lama recounted an incident in which a Russian Tartar tribe had gone over to the

---

[1] Clements Markham, *op. cit.*, pp. 150, 151.

Chinese. As a consequence of this defection, the Russians had sent a series of four ambassadors to China to demand the return of their vassals. Each in succession had been imprisoned by the Emperor, with the results that Russian-Chinese relations had seriously deteriorated.

The tartar tribe referred to was the Torgut branch of the Eleut people. The Lamaist Torguts, originally inhabiting the Koko Nor region north-east of Tibet, had been driven out of their homelands in 1616 by the eastern Mongols. Under the loose suzerainty of Russia, they wandered through the steppes of Russian Central Asia, finally settling along the Volga River. There they were harassed by hostile neighbours. An estimated two-thirds of the original 400,000 tribesmen were killed in battle or died of the hardships they were forced to endure.

In 1770 a Torgut leader, named Tsebek Dorje, conspired to revolt against his suzerain, Czarina Elizabeth, and secretly made plans to lead the troubled tribe back to the protection of the Manchu Emperor, Ch'ien-lung. As a result, a quarter of a million Torguts began their epic move to the east in early 1771. As the tribe painfully crossed frozen tundra, foraging for food as they went, they were pursued by the Czarina's Cossacks and harassed by hostile tribes whose lands they crossed. Heavy snows killed the livestock and engulfed exhausted stragglers. The daily funeral ceremonies of fallen Torguts added to the pall of despair which hung over the helpless nomads.

Summer followed winter and the decimated Torgut horsemen continued to fight their way east, beating off the marauding Bashkirs and Kirkhiz who harassed them now in the unrelenting heat of the steppes. Reaching the banks of Lake Balkash, the pitiful remnant plunged waist-deep into the water to drink and refresh themselves, only to be ambushed by more Bashkir swordsmen laying in wait. The water was stained red with the victims' blood. A total massacre was prevented only because Chinese cavalrymen providently arrived to rout the assailants and rescue survivors. On crossing the Ili River, the remnant of the once-powerful Torguts had reached at last the 'Celestial' Empire. In seven harrowing months an entire people had fled 2,400 miles while under continual harassment. Recognizing the political value to be derived from the return of the Torguts, Emperor Chien-lung gave to the exhausted tribesmen land, grain and livestock. With their return, he could finally boast that he now ruled all the Mongols. For the occasion he erected a plaque on the banks of the Ili which included the following passage: 'Now the hour has struck when, without fear of exaggeration, one can say that all the races of Mongolia have surrendered to our great dynasty. . . .'[1]

The Russians were not easily reconciled to the loss of their vassals and were bitter at the Emperor's gloatings. The Teshu Lama, who feared war between his two giant neighbours, welcomed Bogle's views. With a wider perspective than his host's, the young Scot could describe other important facets to the problem. He pointed out that since the Russians were at war with the Turks, they were unlikely to consider war simultaneously with China. 'But,' warned Bogle, 'as soon as they had made peace with the Sultan . . . I have no doubt of their resentment of the conduct of the Chinese.'[2] He portrayed Catherine the Great as an able ruler, and described the Russian people as 'very hardy and warlike'. He predicted that should the Russians decide to attack China, the Emperor's troops would be no match for them.

The Lama's reply revealed his opinion of his suzerain: while former Chinese emperors would, in his opinion, realize this danger, the present Manchu ruler 'was too violent and fond of war to listen to advice.'[3] Moreover, he was still angry that the Russians had provided refuge to the Dzungar Mongols after the latter had been driven from Tibet by Chinese forces. Gloomily the Teshu Lama predicted that 'things must now take their course . . . no representations of his or of his friend, the Lama of Peking, could prevent a war.'[4]

The Lama asked Bogle if the King of England had influence on the Russian Empress. The Scot replied honestly that George III had more influence at the Russian court than any other prince of Europe, but the two kingdoms 'were separated at a great distance from one another'. Even so, the Lama appeared to find some comfort in this, exclaiming: 'in the event of a war between Russia

---

[1] Sven Hedin, *Jehol, City of Emperors* (New York, E. P. Dutton & Co, 1933), Chapter 3.
[2] Clements Markham, *op. cit.*, pp. 169, 160.
[3] *Ibid.*, p. 160.   [4] *Ibid.*

and China, I may perhaps be able, through means of the Company, to do something toward bringing about peace. And that,' he added, 'is the business of us Lamas.'[1]

Another indication that the possibility of a Sino-Russian war was taken seriously in Lhasa was a remark made by the representative of the Regent who visited Bogle in Tashilhunpo. Bogle was specifically warned by him not to make any reference to the Russians in his letter to the Regent. 'If I said . . . anything about the Kalmuks, that might bring trouble on the country or on the Gesub,' recalled Bogle, 'they would not carry [the letter].' 'I confess,' the Scot added, 'I was much struck with the answer.'

It does not seem to have occurred to Bogle that his visit to Lhasa was opposed out of fear that it could be interpreted by the Russians as a sign of growing Chinese-English amity, and cause a worsening of the already strained Sino-Russian relations. One theory attributes Bogle's failure to reach Lhasa, at least in part, to the Tibetan Regent's conviction that it would provoke outright Russian intervention.[2]

While the Teshu Lama himself does not seem to have anticipated a direct Russian attack against Tibet, he was genuinely concerned by the indirect affects of a Sino-Russian war. And it is not illogical to suppose that the Regent, who ruled under the watchful eyes of the Chinese *Ambans* and who was necessarily responsive to the Emperor, saw the Company presence in Tibet as a gratuitous influence in the deterioration of China-Russian relations. If Bogle did not speculate along these lines he can probably be excused on the grounds that he knew so little about Russian influence in Chinese Central Asia. And, anyway, this issue was secondary to the more obvious one: the Manchus did not want English competition in Tibet.

A Byzantine plot of intrigue and provocation, referred to as the 'Chowdry Affair',[3] illustrates the lengths to which the Regent was willing to go to discredit Bogle. Not long after the latter arrived in Tashilhunpo a Himalayan hillsman, calling himself

---

[1] *Ibid.*, p. 166.

[2] Wei Kuo Lee, *Tibet in Modern World Politics, 1744–1922* (New York, 1931), p. 16; and Taraknath Das, *British Expansion in Tibet* (Calcutta, 1929), p. 4.

[3] *Bogle Papers, op. cit.*, 23rd unnumbered page.

Chowdry presented himself, claiming to represent the Regent. The Gesub had made Chowdry his envoy to the Company with instructions to accompany Bogle on the latter's return trip to Calcutta – or so claimed Chowdry.

This, of course, struck Bogle as exceedingly odd. In the first place, the Lama had never mentioned Chowdry and seemed unaware of his overture. And, even more suspicious, the Regent's two representatives, who had visited with Bogle but one day before, made no reference to any such person. In fact, the scarcely concealed antagonism of the two representatives seemed completely inconsistent with Chowdry's friendly approach. Bogle responded politely but cautiously. He told his visitor, 'it was the custom with the English to deal plainly and openly,' and that he 'could do nothing without mentioning it to the Lama.' This he did on the earliest occasion.

Bogle for a moment wondered if this had been a wise approach to take. 'A man more artful than myself, knowing how little cordiality there was between Gesub and the Lama, might perhaps have carried on his negotiations with Chowdry without communicating them to the Lama.' But, rationalized Bogle, 'I must own that in my small experience through life I have always found candour and plain dealing to be the best policy and I had no notion of running the risk of forfeiting the confidence of one who I had every reason to believe was well disposed towards me.'[1]

When Bogle next saw the Lama the latter, still much perturbed, decided to write Gesub for an explanation. The Regent replied ingenuously, disclaiming anything but the most casual contact with Chowdry. Moreover, as proof of his sincerity he gave instructions that the 'imposter' be returned to Lhasa for punishment.

Bogle saw nothing more of the shadowy Chowdry until about a week before leaving Tashilhunpo. The canny Scot on this occasion extracted from him a disjointed but wholly unconvincing explanation, which made it apparent that the Regent had been guilty of a crude provocation. Having heard also that Chowdry had received from the Regent a generous reward,

---

[1] *Ibid.*

Bogle could safely conclude that, 'being jealous of my visit to the Lama and desirous to know my errand, Gesub had employed Chowdry to sound me.' Then, reasoned Bogle, when the approach had been reported to the Teshu Lama, Gesub 'disclaimed any connection with him and summoned him to Lhasa on the pretence of punishing him.'

The Teshu Lama's messenger to Lhasa, who had carried the letter from Bogle to the Regent, returned in late April. The Regent had been seriously ill – so ill that the Chinese *Ambans* consulted conjurors for advice. The *Ambans* despatched messengers to Peking bearing the worrying news of the Regent's ill health. During one crisis they had the Lamaist extreme unction performed, so hopeless did it seem. But after spending several days in a coma, the indestructible Regent rallied and, according to the messenger's report, was completely out of danger.

However significant this news may have been to the monks of Tashilhunpo or to the Teshu Lama, whose own power position was compromised by the Regent's antagonism, the messenger brought nothing to encourage Bogle in his trade objectives. Hastings's envoy was forced to conclude that permission for Company men to trade in Tibet was out of the question. He wrote the Governor that the attitude of the Lhasa administration was distinctly hostile to the idea, and, for that matter, there was no chance that the Bhutanese or Nepalese would provide safe transit for English traders. But, he observed, there was no reason why trade conducted by Asian agents could not prosper. Since Bengal commodities sold in Tibet were generally paid for in gold, the channel through which the trade was conducted did not greatly matter.

Before Tibetans or other hillsmen could be encouraged to appear at the Bengal markets, they had to be disabused of existing prejudices. They must be convinced that the Company *Raj*, unlike its Moghul predecessor, would not oppress Buddhist/ Lamaist worshippers. Buddhist contacts between Bengal and Tibet – dormant since the twelfth century – and toleration of Buddhist rites should be encouraged so that a suitably hospitable atmosphere could be created to help stimulate commercial intercourse between the two countries.

A scheme close to the Teshu Lama's heart to establish a

Lamaist monastery near Calcutta on the banks of the sacred Ganges would be a move in the right direction and this was encouraged by Bogle.[1] The trusted Purangir would, of course, be the Lama's agent for this project. In the meantime the Teshu Lama was also encouraged to send high ranking monks to Bengal from where they could make pilgrimages to Buddhist shrines such as Bodh Gaya.[2] Bogle, who stimulated the Lama to make these kinds of plans, was convinced that the existence of a Lamaist temple on the Ganges would serve to overcome the Tibetan prejudice against the hot and humid Bengal delta. He also believed that 'the fondness of the Tibetans for everything strange or curious, strengthened by religion, will probably lead many others to undertake so meritorious a journey; and these pilgrimages, like the Hadj at Mecca, may in time open a considerable mart for the commodities of Bengal.'[3]

In early April, shortly before Bogle's departure, the Teshu Lama urged his friend to ask for any particular favours which struck his fancy. Bogle seized the opportunity to acquire certain exotic animals which had intrigued Hastings. The musk goat was an example of the kind of creature which the Governor felt might have commercial value. It could perhaps be reared in the Indian Himalayas and its precious scent added to the Company's exports. The rugged Yak, too, might prove to be a worthy beast of burden in North India's highlands just as it is in Tibet.

Bogle tried to satisfy other requirements which the intellectually curious Hastings had given him. For example, he took advantage of his new friendship with the Teshu Lama to gather data on early comet sightings. The Lama promised to inquire of Peking for Chinese astronomical records going back '20,000 years', and forward his findings to Calcutta.

A few days before Bogle left, the critical question of English trade with China through Tibet came up in conversation. The Teshu Lama was astonished to learn that a country as powerful as England had had no contact with Peking. Only one Englishman, a physician in the service of the Russian Czar, had ever

---

[1] *Ibid.*, p. 2.   [2] *Ibid.*, p. 11.
[3] Clements Markham, *op. cit.*, p. 198.

been admitted to the imperial capital and this had been some fifty years ago. Bogle made very clear his Company's eagerness to rectify this situation and appealed to His Holiness to use his good offices to help. The Lama did, in fact, promise to do what he could by working through the Lama of Peking. But, he held out no great hopes of success. 'Whether I shall be able to carry this out or not, I cannot say,' admitted the Lama. He was frankly pessimistic. However much he would genuinely like to 'open a connection between the [English] and the Emperor of China,' there remained the inevitable problem of Lhasa. As the Lama pointed out, 'Gesub was before and will now be again a little man; it would serve no purpose to work through him.'[1]

Another question which had to be settled before Bogle left concerned future contact. With his usual candour the Teshu Lama told the envoy, 'I will be plain with you; I wish the Governor would not at present send [to Tibet] an Englishman.' He explained: 'you know what difficulties I had about your coming into the country and how I had to struggle with the jealousy of Gesub Rimpoche and the people of Lhasa. Even now, they are uneasy at my having kept you with me so long . . . Gesub looks upon you so much as come to spy.' Reiterating his hope that Tibet's government would pass into the hands of the Dalai Lama when the latter reached his majority, the Lama promised that at that time, 'I will inform the Governor and he may send an Englishman to me and to the Dalai Lama.' In the meantime, he added, 'I wish . . . that the Governor would send [to me] a Hindu.'[2]

Departures are always difficult when friends are concerned, and it could truly be said that by now Bogle and the Teshu Lama were close friends. Their relationship clearly transcended the official. The saddened Lama promised to 'pray to heaven' for Bogle and, as the envoy recalled, 'he spoke . . . in a manner and with a look very different from the studied and formal compliments of Hindustan.' Bogle for his part admitted: 'I never could reconcile myself to taking a last leave of anybody, and what from the Lama's pleasant and amiable character, what from the

[1] *Bogle Papers, op. cit.*, p. 15. [2] *Ibid.*, pp. 13, 14.

many favours and civilities he had shown me, I could not help being particularly affected.'[1]

As a parting ritual the Lama threw a white scarf about Bogle's neck and put his hand upon Bogle's head. This was the last they would ever see of each other.

---

[1] *Ibid.*, p. 19.

9
Death of Bogle

Bogle returned from Tibet as he had come, by way of Bhutan. Convinced that Bhutan's capital, Tassisudon, would one day become a centre of commerce, Hastings had written his emissary instructing him 'to open a communication of trade with Tassisudon, and through that place to Lhasa . . .'. The young envoy thus tried once more to negotiate a trade agreement with the Deb Rajah. The suspicious Rajah, however, was not to be easily convinced. The advantages of trade did not seem worth the danger implicit in permitting *Fringies* a free run of his kingdom. For that matter, the Company's new relationship with the Tibetan Lama was, in itself, enough to worry and antagonize Bhutan's ruler.

Although Bogle had been unable to extract trade agreements from either Tibet or Bhutan, his mission was nevertheless a success. He had made a friend of the Teshu Lama and had earned his trust. The Tibetan Pontiff now realistically viewed the Company as a counterweight to Gurkha power in the Himalayas – in much the same way the Company hoped that the Teshu Lama would keep the Bhutanese in check. But an important part of the Lama's motivation stemmed from his confidence in Bogle. Thanks to this unique relationship, the Company could entertain hopes that the Teshu Lama would eventually admit English traders to Tibet and use his influence in Peking to open long-denied trade doors to China. This latter, in fact, was the real prize which seemed tantalizingly within reach. If more English manufactured goods could be sold to China and if a greater quantity of gold specie could be imported from Tibet, the imbalance of China trade, caused by large English tea imports, could be corrected. However unrealistic or at least premature this dream may have been, it excited Hastings whose hopes hung on Bogle's friendship with the Teshu Lama.

Bogle's report touched on Tibet's fabled gold. The emissary also listed musk, yaktails, salt and wool as potential imports from Tibet. Strangely he didn't include borax, which was by then known to be abundant in Tibet. Broadcloth, spices, tobacco and rice were mentioned as commodities which could be traded against these Tibetan products. Most promising of all was the insatiable market for tea in Tibet.

Bogle earnestly believed that India could replace China as Tibet's principle trading partner. The route to Tibet from China through Sining was long and difficult as compared with the trans-Himalayan route from India. What Hastings's envoy apparently had not realized, however, was that Sino-Tibetan trade was an integral part of the traditional tribute system and could not easily be replaced. Tribute from the Dalai and Teshu Lamas – incense, bronze, religious objects, amber, rosaries – was exchanged in China for gold plate ware, satin cloth and animal skins provided by the Emperor. But despite this politico-economic fact of life, there was no question but what Tibetan-Indian trade, if unrestricted, could multiply many times over and richly reward the Company.

Evidence of growing Russian-Tibetan trade promised still more interesting possibilities. Lamaist Kalmuks and Buriat Mongols mixed pilgrimage with trade to bring to the Tibetan markets such varied commodities as Russian furs, hides, fresh-water pearls, brocades and camels. Could Tibet also be a back door to the steppes, tundras and forests of Central Asia – to the riches which must surely exist there? While Cossack adventurers in the vanguard of Russian pioneers had already reached the borderlands of the Manchu Empire, the contest for Central Asia was still very much open. Tibet was a key.

Since Bogle had been gone, however, changes had taken place in Calcutta. In October 1774 Hastings had been made Governor General – the first Company officer to be granted this title, which carried with it authority over all Company holdings in India. But his actual power had been circumscribed. A new governing council, established by the Regulating Act of 1773, was antagonistic to Hastings and consistently opposed his Tibet policy. Council members Philip Francis, General Clavering and Colonel

Monson were particularly obstructionist and missed no opportunity to oppose the Governor General's program. Not until late 1776, when Monson's death deprived this fraction of its majority, did Hastings regain his full power. In the meantime any extension of Company activity into Tibet was blocked. Francis made clear that his 'expectations of commercial advantages to be derived from a communication with Tibet [were] by no means so sanguine as those expressed by the Governor General.'[1]

The temporary eclipse of Hastings affected Bogle's position as well. He was deprived of high appointment because of a veto cast by a member of the Francis clique. A bonus purse of 15,000 rupees awarded for his accomplishments in Tibet, while appreciated by Bogle and timely in saving his family estate in Scotland, was small compensation for his failure to advance. In a letter to his brother, Bogle sadly observed, 'The factions in Calcutta render society, beyond the circle of one's intimate friends, very unpleasant. . . .' He quite frankly assessed his own career in terms of Hastings's position. 'As Mr Hastings had always patronized me,' he wrote his father, 'my success depends in a great measure upon his fate.'[2]

Relieved at last of Francis's obstructionism, Hastings again looked northward. Company revenues had been disappointing. The lure of Himalayan trade and the prospect that it could make up the Company's deficit were still strong. Bogle's conclusions had been reinforced by Hamilton, who took subsequent trips to Bhutan in 1775 and 1777. Hastings, therefore, felt justified in noting for the record on 19 April 1779 that new channels of commerce had to be opened to compensate for the drain of money out of Bengal.[3] Hastings at the same time instructed Bogle to make another trip to Bhutan and Tibet for the purpose of 'cultivating and improving the good understanding subsisting between the chiefs of those countries and the Government, and to endeavour to establish a free and lasting intercourse of trade

---

[1] Indian National Archives, Bengal Public Consultation, No. 7, 19 April 1779.
[2] *Bogle Papers, op. cit.*; and Clements Markham, *op. cit.*, pp. cxlvii, cxlviii.
[3] Sarkar, S. C., 'Some Notes of the Intercourse of Bengal with Northern Countries in the Second Half of the Eighteenth Century', *Proc. Indian Historical Records Commission*, Vol. XIII, 1930, p. 121.

with the Kingdom of Tibet and the other states to the northward of Bengal.'[1]

Hastings felt the time was ripe to exploit Bogle's relationship with the Teshu Lama, and in turn the latter's relationship with the Chinese Emperor, to secure permission for an English mission in Peking. The Governor General summed it up when he wrote: 'In so new and remote a search we can only propose to adventure for possibilities; the attempt may be crowned with the most splendid and susbstantial success, or it may terminate in the mere gratification of useless curiosity, but the hazard is small. . . .' Bogle was specifically requested to 'endeavour by means of the Lamas of Tibet to open a communication with the Court of Peking.'[2]

A second journey to Tibet had to be postponed, however, when news reached Calcutta that the Teshu Lama was leaving imminently on the long march to the Chinese court to pay rare homage to the Emperor. One must assume that the aggressive new empire south of the Himalayas, which had already engaged Bhutan in battle and had had the effrontery to send an emissary to Tashilhunpo, was a source of serious concern to the Manchus. The 'Celestial' realm could ill-afford to face simultaneously the pressures of both Imperial Russia and the East India Company. Clearly it was time to curb any proclivities for independent foreign action which the Teshu Lama might have.

Emperor Chien-lung had repeatedly invited the Lama to visit him. Despite his apprehension over rising Company influence in southern Tibet, the Emperor had very much in mind his Mongol vassals whose spiritual guide was then the Teshu Lama; if the latter appeared at the Chinese court, this would strengthen his influence over them. Each time the Lama found an excuse not to accept; he was busy with religious affairs or apprehensive about the smallpox epidemic then rampaging throughout China. The truth of the matter was he did not want to be placed in a position where he would be vulnerable to Chinese pressure. Nor did he want to run the risk of forced detention – a possibility which

[1] Clements Markham, *op. cit.*, p. cli.
[2] Alastair Lamb, *Britain and Chinese Central Asia* (London, Routledge & Kegan Paul, 1960), p. 16.

could not be ignored, and one which had abundant historical precedent.

Finally, in 1779 the Lama found he could no longer refuse. The occasion was to be the celebration of the Emperor's seventieth birthday. In a disarming and flattering letter the 'Sun of Heaven' wrote: 'My age is now . . . 70 years and the only blessing I can enjoy before I quit this life will be to see you.'[1] The Emperor pointed out that he had already spent vast sums to erect facilities along the route from Tibet's border to Peking so that the Lama's journey would be comfortable and safe. Moreover, he wrote to influential Tibetans, asking them to use their power to persuade their Pontiff.

The Teshu Lama accepted the imperial invitation with grave forebodings however. He confided to his closest friends that instinct warned him he would not return.

Bogle saw in the Lama's visit an opportunity to go himself to Peking. Possibly a permanent embassy could be established to conduct relations with the 'Forbidden City'. But at least he could negotiate certain outstanding problems which had arisen between the Manchu court and the Company. In a brief memorandum he outlined his plan.

Pointing out that Chinese merchants owed English coastal traders between a million and a half and two million pounds sterling, Bogle saw his proposed mission as an opportunity to collect these long-outstanding debts. Implicit in the Scot's plan was the hope that his friend, the Teshu Lama, would intercede on his behalf with the Emperor. Bogle recalled that the Tibetan pontiff had promised to speak in favour of Tibetan-Indian trade at Chien-lung's court and try to secure for him a passport permitting travel to Peking. Bogle assumed that the Lama would welcome his presence during the forthcoming trip so that a personal introduction to the Emperor could be made.

The Company estimated that the grand entourage would leave Tashilhunpo in October. Assuming the arduous journey would take approximately eight months, His Holiness would arrive at the Chinese court sometime in May 1780. Bogle planned to travel overland with the entourage or, if this proved im-

---

[1] Samuel Turner, *op. cit.*, pp. 456, 457.

possible, by sea to Canton from whence he would proceed inland to meet the Lama in Peking. In the latter case, Purangir, who was to accompany the Teshu Lama, would detach himself from the entourage and meet Bogle in Canton, visa in hand, and escort him to the capital.

Bogle – perhaps naively optimistic – believed that if he reached Peking he would 'be in a situation to urge any points at the court ... with the greatest advantage.' 'Even if I should be disappointed,' he added, 'I don't think it is possible for me to fail in procuring a channel of communication with the Court of Peking and get some person stationed at Canton through whom representations can be made.'[1]

Large pearls and coral, exotic birds and Arabian horses would be included in Bogle's baggage. If agreement with the Emperor proved impossible, these intended presents would instead be sold on the spot for rich profit. For all his diplomatic acumen, Bogle was a merchant – the balance sheet could not be ignored.

The Teshu Lama with an escort of 5,000 troops actually did not reach the Emperor's summer palace at Jehol until 20 August 1780. Heavy snows had forced the party to winter at the Kumbun monastery near Koko Nor, believed by the Tibetans to be the birthplace of Tsong Khapa, Tibet's fourteenth-century Buddhist reformer. It was here that Purangir caught up with the Teshu Lama's party. The *gosain's* account of the long journey, the Lama's grand entrance to the summer palace at Jehol and the conversations with the Emperor there are virtually all that history has to go on.

Purangir's account of the historic first meeting, which took place shortly after the Lama's arrival on 25 August 1780, does not bear out Chinese historical records claiming that the Teshu Lama humbled himself before the Emperor. The Lama did not *kow tow*, or prostrate himself in the classic attitude of vassalage but, according to the *gosain*, met the Emperor forty paces from the throne and there shook hands with him. Seated on deep cushions, they talked for an hour. On taking his leave the Lama was presented with '100,000 *illeung* of silver and many pieces of

---

[1] *Bogle Papers*, Mss Eur-E 226, Vol. 34. Copy of a memorandum by Bogle about his proposed trip to Peking, August 1779, 3rd and 4th pages.

curious silks, some strings of pearls, and other curiosities of China'.[1]

On the fourth day the Teshu Lama raised the subject of the English with the Emperor. Purangir recalled the gist of the Lama's words:

In the country of Hindustan, which lies on the borders of my country, there resides a great prince, or ruler, for whom I have the greatest friendship. I wish you should know and regard him also; and if you will write him a letter of friendship, and receive his in return, it will afford me great pleasure, as I wish you should be known to each other, and that a friendly communication should, in future, subsist between you.[2]

Purangir's understandable desire to tell the English what they wished to hear and, at the same time, posthumously cast the best possible light on the Lama's actions have raised some question as to the accuracy of his testimony. But in broad outline his comments are probably true. Certainly, contemporary Company records give no hint of doubt at the time. Remarks made by the Lama's brother, Chungpa Hutukhtu[3] and his cup-bearer, Solpön Chenpo[4] also tend to confirm that the late Lama did speak to the Emperor on the Company's behalf even if he probably did not go so far as to ask that Bogle be invited to Peking.[5]

Purangir claimed that the Emperor responded to the Lama's statements on a conciliatory note, saying that the Lama's request was a small one and that anything else he desired would be granted. But Ch'ien-lung's line of questioning, which followed hard on this statement, suggests that he was anything but happy with the thought of a closer relation between his Tibetan vassal and India. He wanted to know, for example, the extent of Governor Hastings's realm and the size of his army. He was clearly measuring the Lama's new friend as an adversary, not as a friend.

As autumn approached, the Emperor and his holy guest left Jehol for Peking. In the capital the Lama was housed in the

1 Samuel Turner, *op. cit.*, pp. 461, 462, Appendix iv.
2 *Ibid.*, Appendix iv, p. 463.
3 Referred to by Bogle as 'Chanzo Cusho'.
4 Spelled by Bogle as 'Sopon Chumbo'. Samuel Turner spelled it 'Choomboo'.
5 Samuel Turner, *op. cit.*, pp. 449–52, 455.

Yellow Palace, a magnificent villa, built originally by Emperor Shun-chih for the Fifth Dalai Lama's visit. Here the Teshu Lama received the nobility and prominent personages of Peking. The Manchus were, for the most part, Buddhist. Regardless of the motives which the Emperor may have had for inviting the Teshu Lama, the court took full advantage of his presence to seek spiritual inspiration. For those who were not Buddhists he had at least great curiosity value. Many, therefore, flocked to his audiences.

Purangir was a good witness of the pageantry and protocol which marked the Teshu Lama's stay in Peking. Making allowances for his proclivity to embroider the facts, his account is valuable. It provided the Company with first-hand intelligence on the court of Ch'ien-lung, revealing amongst other things the court's veneration of the Tibetan Lama. When the *gosain* later was questioned in Calcutta he recalled:

When any of the princes or immediate relations of the Emperor's were presented, they were all received by the Lama without moving from where he sat, but they were distinguished by his laying bare hands upon their heads whilst he repeated a short prayer. The Nobility, or men of the second rank, when introduced, went through the like ceremony except that the Lama wrapt a piece of clean silk round his hand and in that manner rested it on their heads whilst he repeated the blessing; and for those of inferior note, a piece of consecrated wool of about a yard long was substituted. . . .[1]

A special protocol was devised to enable the Lama to administer to the Emperor's womenfolk. He sat self-consciously on a makeshift dais opposite the door to the women's quarters. A yellow gauze screen was hung over the door so that when the Emperor's favourite women appeared, they could see the Lama without his being able to see them clearly. As each appeared he spoke a blessing, 'all the time bending his head forward and turning his eyes directly towards the ground to avoid the possibility of beholding the women.'[2] The Empress, of course, merited special consideration. Ch'ien-lung personally escorted

---

[1] Samuel Turner, *op. cit.*, pp. 464, 465.   [2] *Ibid.*, p. 466.

the Lama to her private apartments where prayers and meditation took place for nearly half an hour. The veil was dispensed with; presumably her exalted position gave her the privilege of being looked at by the holy Lama.

An idea of the lavishness of the arrangements made for the Teshu Lama is seen in the description given by Lama Solpön Chenpo, the Teshu Lama's cup-bearer, who accompanied his master to Peking. He described newly erected figures of a gigantic size, representing the signs of the zodiac. 'Each figure, as the sun entered its corresponding sign, became a fountain of water which continued to play until its passage to the next.' He recalled also that 'the Emperor had ordered a ship to be constructed on a large lake and armed with guns to resemble a first rate man-of-war. The guns were discharged on board this ship to give them an idea of a sea engagement.'[1]

Once again the question of Company relations came up in the conversations between the Emperor and the Teshu Lama – or so alleged Purangir who claims to have been within earshot. The *gosain* described an informal exchange which took place following religious devotions at one of Peking's Buddhist temples. His Holiness reminded his host of their earlier conversation about Hastings, 'Prince of Hindustan'. He reiterated his wish that the Emperor should know him and 'hold friendly intercourse with him also, by writing to him and receiving his friendly answers'. Ch'ien-lung, in what can hardly be accepted as a genuine ex-expression of cooperation, promised to correspond with Hastings. To convince the Lama of his sincerity, he would 'cause a letter to be immediately written to the Governor, in such terms as the Lama would dictate.'[2]

No such letter was ever written and, assuming for the moment that Purangir's memory is accurate, it is doubtful that the Emperor had any intention of accommodating his vassal. One can speculate that Purangir exaggerated the Emperor's words to please his English friends and make the Teshu Lama appear cooperative with them.

The facts were never to be revealed since the Teshu Lama suddenly died in Peking of the dread smallpox. Our chronicler of

---

[1] *Ibid.*, p. 291.   [2] *Ibid.*, p. 468.

this tragic episode is again Purangir: 'One evening the cold was so great and the snow fell so heavy that the Lama was prevented ...from returning to his own house; he slept at Cheengeea Gooroo's [Changkya Hutukhtu, the Grand Lama of Peking] and in the morning they visited the Emperor together, after which they retired to their respective habitation.' Then, recalls the *gosain*, 'within an hour ... he complained of a violent headache and in less than an hour more he was seized with a most violent fever, which continued very severe until about the same hour next day when his disorder was discovered to be the smallpox.'[1] The Emperor rushed to his side. He took the Lama's hand in his and 'for a considerable time did not cease to encourage him with the most soothing and affectionate language. ...'[2] Then, curiously, Ch'ien-lung ordered several large paintings, portraying human figures in almost every stage of smallpox, to be hung up in the room before the dying Lama – presumably for curative purposes.

Death came four days later. With his brother and six or seven attendants including Purangir by his side, the stricken Lama murmured that he found 'his disorder so much more than he could support that he considered their prayers as the only comfort he could enjoy.'[3]

Within a short time he breathed his last and, in so doing, set rumours flying across Tibet that Emperor Ch'ien-lung had murdered him.

The Lama's brother, the Karmapa Lama of Shigatse, was among those Tibetans who suspected a plot by Ch'ien-lung to install a regime more responsive to the Chinese. Fearing that the Teshu Lama's death was a forerunner to further outrages against the family, he fled Tibet for Nepal. This only heightened speculation of foul play among Tibetans who are traditionally prone to suspect Chinese motives anyway.[4]

It is unlikely, however, that the Emperor induced the fatal smallpox or had the unfortunate Lama killed in any other way. At least, there is no significant evidence which points to murder. It is true, of course, that the Teshu Lama's death benefited the

---

[1] *Ibid.*, p. 469.   [2] *Ibid.*   [3] *Ibid.*, p. 470.
[4] C. B. Diskalkar, 'Tibetan-Nepalese War, 1788–1793', *Journal of the Bihar and Orissa Research Society*, Vol. XIX, 1933, No. 12, p. 380.

Chinese; power in Tibet reverted to Lhasa where the Dalai Lama and his Regent were more responsive to the Chinese *Ambans* than the Teshu Lama had been. But, certainly, to have the Lama killed in the midst of a state visit, with the whole Buddhist Lamaist world looking on, would seem politically inept. The Emperor could not afford to alienate the still-worrisome Mongols who considered the Teshu Lama their spiritual leader.

However secretly pleased the Emperor may have been, he exhibited publicly every mark of grief and regret. He arranged what must be one of the longest, most costly funeral processions in history to bear the Lama's body back to Tashilhunpo. The Emperor, to use his own words, 'was filled with the most poignant grief', and his eyes were bathed in tears.[1] He wrote the Dalai Lama, 'I have given directions . . . for making a shrine of gold.' With a thousand holy men attending him he later officiated at a ceremony in which the Lama's coffin was placed within the finished shrine. This, in turn, was placed within a richly-wrought copper casing. After three months of mourning and when the weather conditions for travel were best, the funeral procession set out for Tibet. An honour guard of a thousand men escorted the casket to the outskirts of the city where two hundred of the Emperor's finest horsemen joined the cavalcade to mount guard throughout the seven-month journey.

The Lama's untimely death caused Bogle to abandon his plans to visit Peking. It is very unlikely that the Emperor would have granted him permission anyway. Nothing in Purangir's account suggests that the Teshu Lama had made any effort to acquire a visa for Bogle. If the Teshu Lama actually did explain his contact with Hastings to the Emperor, it was probably not to seek his imperial blessing for it, but rather to threaten obliquely that the new empire to the south could be used as a counter balance to Chinese power in Tibet. Moreover, it is unlikely that the Emperor would have seriously considered admitting a Company mission to Peking. To have encouraged Bogle to visit the 'Forbidden City' while the Teshu Lama was a state guest would have been to advertise the growing friendship between the Lama and the Company, and this was not in Ch'ien-lung's best interest.

---

[1] Samuel Turner, *op. cit.*, p. 447.

There is no clearer expression of Emperor Ch'ien-lung's attitude toward English trade than that which was included in an arrogant letter he wrote to King George III on the occasion of England's first mission to the Manchu court in 1793, led by Lord Macartney. Just thirteen years after the Teshu Lama spoke before the Emperor on behalf of the Company the 'Son of Heaven' wrote the British monarch:

As to your entreaty to send one of your nationals to be accredited to my Celestial Court and to be in control of your country's trade with China, this request is contrary to all usage of my dynasty and cannot be entertained. Hitherto, all European nations, including your own country's barbarian merchants, have carried on this trade with Our Celestial Empire at Canton. Such has been the procedure for many years, although Our Celestial Empire possesses all things in prolific abundance and lacks no product within its own borders. There was therefore no need to import the manufactures of outside barbarians in exchange for our own produce. But as the tea, silk and porcelain which the Celestial Empire produces are absolute necessities to European nations and to yourselves, we have permitted, as a signal mark of favour that foreign *hongs* [Chinese business associations] should be established at Canton, so that your wants might be supplied and your country thus participate in our beneficence.[1]

It is unlikely that Ch'ien-lung's attitude toward foreign trade and the English changed between 1781 and 1793.

Bogle, in the meantime, had been appointed Collector at Rangpur, a Bengal border outpost on the route to Bhutan, which served as a trade mart where English, Tibetan and Bhutanese products could be exchanged. His dream of a Company presence in Tibet died with the Teshu Lama. After hearing of the Lama's death, Bogle wrote his brother: 'I shall regret the absence of my friend the Teshoo Lama, for whom I have a hearty liking, and should be happy again to have his fat hand on my head.'

The young Scot's enthusiasm for native trade was, however, still high. He wrote from Rangpur of 'schemes and projects for introducing new articles of commerce through Bhutan'. While he complained of the 'narrow-minded jealousy of the Bhutanese', he felt that he was warranted in making this effort.

---

[1] *Ibid.*, pp. 108, 109.

In 1781 Hastings appointed Bogle to a new 'Committee of Revenue' in Calcutta, which gave him authority over all collection activities in the provinces. His star was rising. Even without the Teshu Lama's friendship and the unique position this had given him, he was moving rapidly. But suddenly and tragically, at the young age of thirty-four Bogle became ill and died. With his death, the Company lost one of its most able officers. Tibet lost a sincere and good friend.

10

Samuel Turner

The deaths of the Teshu Lama and Bogle threatened Hastings's Tibet policy. The Company was deprived of a unique relationship, which might have led to an early extension of trade across the Himalayas and perhaps even a Company presence in Tibet. Yet, despite this set back, the aggressive Governor General was determined to pursue his objective. He was encouraged by cordial letters from the late Lama's court, which Purangir delivered in 1782.

Chungpa Hutukhtu,[1] brother of the deceased Sixth Lama and now Regent of Tashilhunpo, wrote Hastings thanking him for his past kindnesses and endorsing his late brother's request that a Lamaist sanctuary for Tibetan pilgrims and traders be built near Calcutta on the banks of the holy Ganges. Solpön Chenpo,[2] 'cup-bearer', or Chief Steward, to the late Lama, also sent his greetings and expressed the hope that Hastings would 'honour him with his favour'.

Tidings that a new incarnation of the Teshu Lama had been officially located arrived soon afterwards. The discovery of the seventh incarnation[3] provided Hastings with a perfect excuse to send a new envoy to Tashilhunpo. Samuel Turner, a relative of the Governor General's and a respected young lieutenant in the army of the East India Company, was chosen to convey Company respects to the new Pontiff. With him would travel Lieutenant

---

[1] Samuel Turner, who led a second mission to Tashilhunpo in 1783, referred to the Lama's brother as 'Changoo Cooshoo Punjun Irtinnee Neimoheim, Regent of Tashilhunpo'.

[2] Turner referred to the cup-bearer as 'Soopoon Choomboo, Mirkin Chassa Lama, Minister of the Teshu Lama'.

[3] He is sometimes referred to as the Fourth Teshu or Panchen Lama, but when this is the case the first three posthumously named Panchen Lamas are not counted.

Samuel Davis to map and sketch the still-strange lands of Himalaya, and Dr Robert Saunders to provide the inevitably important medical services during the long and hazardous journey. Of course, the indispensible Purangir would accompany them as guide and mentor. Their itinerary would take them in the footsteps of Bogle; first to Bhutan where Turner would try once more to reach a trade arrangement with the Deb Rajah, then to Tashilhunpo for similar talks with the new Regent.

The Company was not overly optimistic. If Bogle, with his close personal relationship with the late Lama, had not been able to overcome Lhasa's resistance to direct Company trade, Turner could scarcely do better dealing with a regent of as yet uncertain power. Hastings himself admitted that he expected 'no great things from Turner's Embassy'. He would be content with additional intelligence from Tibet which 'will at least satisfy [his] curiosity.'[1]

In late April or early May 1783 – and Turner unexplainably did not record a precise date – the mission set out from Calcutta. The route was by now familiar: across the plains of Plassey, 'ever memorable by the brilliant and decisive victory of Lord Clive,'[2] on to Moorshedabad and Rangpur, then across the plains of Calamatty. The party next crossed the Durlay River and entered the princely state of Cooch Behar.

Turner is generous in his commentary and relives his journey leisurely through his sprightly narrative. On reaching the northern borders of Cooch Behar he pauses to take notice of a cluster of wild pineapples. These, he notes, must be distant descendants of the first pineapple to be introduced into India. Portuguese missionaries imported the first of these exotic fruits to ingratiate themselves with Emperor Akbar. The pioneer stock, which was nurtured carefully in the garden of a certain Murteza Zeman in Delhi, flourished wonderfully. During the reign of Emperor Augangzeb an obscure Moghul commander, while pacifying the Cooch Behar region, cultivated the sweet fruit so that he might find relief from the drab monotony of Bengali

---

[1] Alastair Lamb, *Britain and Chinese Central Asia* (London, Routledge & Kegan Paul, 1960), p. 18, footnote 1, quoting *Warren Hastings's Letters to Sir John Macpherson*, edited by H. Dodwell (London 1927) p. 189.

[2] Samuel Turner, *op. cit.*, p. 4.

food. At least this was as plausible as any theory to explain Turner's discovery since, as he points out, no Bengali 'could for a moment entertain the idea of their torpid apathy being roused to transplant from even so short a distance this elegant luxury.'

The party entered the fort of Chichacotta on the frontier of Bhutan on 11 May. Here is the site of the battle between Company troops and Bhutanese raiders in 1772 – an event which resulted in the Teshu Lama's appeal for peace to Hastings and Bogle's pioneering expedition to Tashilhunpo. The Bhutanese had defended the primitive stockade with sabre, bow and much obstinacy, but succumbed in the end to the superior power of English firelocks and cannon.

Turner's party began its ascent into the hills just before reaching the town of Buxadewar. The hills were 'clothed to their summits with trees, dark and deep glens . . . and the tops of the highest mountains, lost in the clouds.' It was a scene of extraordinary magnificence and sublimity. 'As the road winds round the hills, it sometimes becomes a narrow ledge, hanging over depths which no eye can reach,' and, adds Turner, 'were not the horror of the scene in some degree softened by the trees and climbing plants, which line the precipices, the passenger would find it impossible to advance.'[1]

Reaching a plateau, possibly thirty miles wide, they found themselves choking on fumes rising from the luxuriant vegetation. This phenomenon, described by many Himalayan travellers has been variously explained. Turner attributed the noxious exhalations to 'a multitude of springs whose gases are collected and confined by these almost impervious woods'. He blamed these gases for the deaths of Captain Jones and many of his troops as they marched against the Bhutanese in 1772.

As the party approached Buxadewar they were met by a herald sounding a trumpet and five mountain nymphs 'with jetty flowing tresses'. No traveller could be weary after such a welcome. But the wretched hut assigned them for the night soon spoiled the effect.

Turner called on the Governor, or *Soobah* as he is locally known, and exchanged compliments. To win over this suspicious

---

[1] Samuel Turner, *op. cit.*, p. 20.

official, he presented him with a small telescope. The *Soobah* immediately caught in his sights an old programme for Bell's British Theatre, which revealed a magnified picture of the luxuriant leading lady of a long-forgotten play. With whoops of joy and astonishment the Governor shouted; 'How small about the waist and what a vast circumference below.'[1]

Turner and his party took part in a colourful religious cere-mony to mark their arrival in Bhutan. They marched solemnly in procession to a nearby hilltop where the ritual was to be held. Seven beautiful maidens with their long tresses hanging loose danced by, chanting an eerie song as they went. The *Soobah*, 'dressed in a vest of blue satin with gold embroidery and a garnet-coloured shawl', marched prominently in front, while two priests brought up the rear. At the summit stood a row of priests beating tabors and cymbals before a vast altar. Another priest blew on an instrument made from the shin bone of a man while two trumpeteers bleated a mournful dirge on other macabre instruments.

The ceremony began with the chanting of priests to the accompaniment of tabors, trumpets and cymbals. Turner was given one end of a large white scarf to hold while a priest held the other as they both approached the altar. The scarf was then released by Turner on signal and the priest waved it over the smoke from burning candles. The girls advanced, still dancing, and the ceremony came to a climax and sudden end with 'loud exclamations by all'.[2] The deity had been properly invoked to assure Turner full protection and a prosperous journey.

On arrival in Bhutan's summer capital of Tassisudon, Turner was told that the Deb Rajah was so immersed in religious ceremonies and meditation that he could not immediately receive him. The envoy suspected this to be a protocol posture – a petty 'plan concerted to magnify the importance and piety of their chief.'[3]

On 3 June the Rajah finally consented to receive his foreign visitors. They were ushered into his presence with great pomp. Sitting cross-legged and sunk deep into a pile of cushions, Bhutan's ruler presided over an ornate throne room of blue and

---

[1] *Ibid.*, p. 30.   [2] *Ibid.*, pp. 32–5.   [3] *Ibid.*, p. 65.

vermillion caked with gilded ornamentation. The walls were covered with portraits 'wrought in silk, of some champions of their faith, as stiff and formal as any heroes that ever appeared in tapestry'.[1] In this august setting Hastings's envoy greeted the once troublesome ruler whose goodwill would be necessary if the Company were to have unrestricted access to Tibet by the most practical route.

For nearly a month Turner and his companions passed the time at Tassisudon, waiting for the Teshu Lama to respond to their petition and send them permission to proceed. They explored the long valley and acquainted themselves with the customs of this little known civilization about which Bogle had commented only briefly. During the delay Turner found several occasions to talk with the Deb Rajah whom he found progressively more friendly. Because of Bhutan's strategic position, Turner's cultivation of the Deb Rajah was not without point; and in the course of these audiences the English officer was able to learn much about this isolated mountain kingdom, which lay astride the main route to Tibet.

As had been the case with Bogle before him, Turner found himself unexpectedly a witness to a rebel uprising. The 'Soompoom of Wandipore', a disgruntled chieftain allied with other dissidents, stormed the Rajah's winter palace at Punakha in a rash act of rebellion. His forces then marched on Tassisudon. Turner watched fascinated from his window as the local citizenry mobilized for the defence of their capital.

As the insurgents appeared on the crest of a hill overlooking the town, the Rajah's bowmen advanced to meet them. Before Turner's very eyes the battle for Tassisudon unfolded. A sudden clanging of bells signalled attack as loyalist troops sallied forth from the palace, shouting savagely and brandishing their arms. The rebels came on with equal belligerence. Turner could see 'both parties endeavouring to keep themselves as much as possible under cover, availing themselves of all irregularities in the ground, and now and then making a random shot with bow or matchlock.' Saunders was pressed into duty to treat the wounded, while Turner tried to commission several long-unused

---

[1] *Ibid.*, p. 67.

cannon. These ancient relics, it turned out, were beyond repair. Turner was forced to conclude that 'the greatest mischief to be apprehended from this ordnance [would be] to the person who applied the match.'[1]

On the following day it was noon before the battle was rejoined. Each warrior with 'stout heart and full stomach, issued forth to battle, having raised his courage and his spirits by an ample meal and copious draughts of *chang* [Tibetan beer].' An irregular, slow discharge of musketry took place with the Rajah's forces steadily gaining ground. Finally, recalled Turner, 'the rebels were obliged to resort . . . to pelting their adversaries with stones.' Soon afterward a truce parley took place in which the rebels were forced to make terms. Being permitted to withdraw, the defeated warriors left in a 'confused crowd' toward the south. Thus ended the Battle of Tassisudon.

Turner's characterization of the Bhutanese combat style puts in good perspective this short but furious engagement: 'A Booteea, in the moment of his highest exultation, forgets not his personal safety, but is most careful to guard against the danger of missile weapons; he is one instant jumping and twirling himself about, brandishing his sword and shield with an air of defiance, and with a wild and savage shout apparently challenging attack: the next moment, if a gun be pointed, he shrinks into concealment.'[2] He gave the Bhutanese credit, however, for being basically a strong and courageous race, attributing 'their feeble mode of attack' to their lack of discipline; 'to their not fighting in compact files or platoons; and to their constant distrust of each other. . . .'[3]

While the Rajah and his forces marched forth from Tassisudon to mop up a few remaining pockets of insurgency, Turner and his party visited the Rajah's castle of Wandipore. This is considered one of Bhutan's most consecrated places, and the Deb Rajah made it a point to reside there part of each year. From Wandipore they travelled to Punakha, the Rajah's winter residence and his favourite seat. While not admitted inside to see the rich furnishing, they could admire the magnificent gardens and fruit orchards surrounding the palace.

---

[1] *Ibid.*, pp. 113, 114.　　[2] *Ibid.*, p. 116.　　[3] *Ibid.*, p. 118.

Plate 2 The Great Magnificence of Prester John, Lord of India and Ethiopia. Frontispiece to a once popular poem on Prester John

Plate 3   The Observatory at Peking during Grueber's service with Adam Schall

Plate 4   Tartars of Koko Nor, by Grueber

Plate 5 The
Castle of Putala,
from a sketch by
Grueber

Plate 6   Courtiers in Tibet, from a sketch by Grueber

Plate 7   Common Dress in Tibet, from a sketch by Grueber

Plate 8   Donna Juliana Diaz da Costa

Plate 9   A 'Pundit's' sketch of the Potala, the residence of the Dalai Lama
at Lhasa

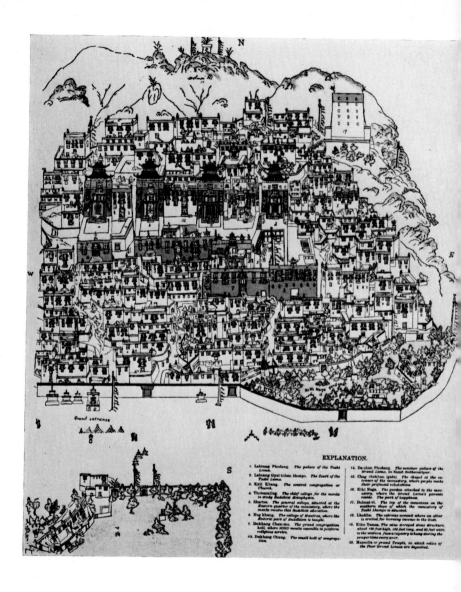

Plate 10 A 'Pundit's' sketch of the Grand Monastery of Tashilhunpo

Plate 11 *above* Sarat Chandra
Das crossing the Donkhya
Pass of the Himalayas

Plate 12 *right* George Bogle

Plate 13   The Emperor K'ang-Hsi of China in his old age, a woodblock by the author

Plate 14   A Tibetan type bridge which Captain Turner crossed *en route* to Bhutan and Tibet

Plate 15   The Palace of Tassisudon in Bhutan

Plate 16 The valley near Tassisudon with a procession of the religious going to their ablutions

Plate 17   The Palace of Punakha in Bhutan

Plate 18   The Castle of Wandipore (Bhutan)

Plate 19   The Mausoleum of Teshoo Lama (Tashilhunpo)

Plate 20   The Dwelling of Tessaling Lama, with the religious Edifice
styled Kugopea (Tibet, near Tashilhunpo)

Plate 21 The Residence of Lam' Ghassatoo (near Tassisudon, Bhutan)

Plate 22   The Yak of Tartary

FR. HUC DRESSED IN CHINESE COSTUME

Plate 23   Abbé Huc in Chinese costume

BENDER ON HORSEBACK.

Plate 24 Manchu Archer, drawing by Abbé Huc

Plate 25   'Pundit' Nain Singh of the Survey of India

Plate 26 *left*
'Pundit' Kintup

Plate 27 *below*
Immediately before
the fight at the wall
erected by the
Tibetans just north
of Tuna

Plate 28   Sir Francis Younghusband

Returning from their excursion, Turner and Saunders set about keeping themselves busy in the capital. A waggish side of Turner is revealed as he describes how, to pass the time, he would administer mild electric shocks to incredulous courtiers with a home-made battery device. He recalls 'after the first . . . exclamation of astonishment, there never failed to ensue among them a hearty laugh; each being delighted at the idea of what he supposed the other felt.'[1] The Rajah, himself, derived great delight by calling in his favourites to be 'electrified' in his presence. He would rock with joy as he observed their astonished reactions.

Bull fights were a favourite diversion at Tassisudon. One was staged for Turner's benefit toward the end of his stay. Led into a ring with stout ropes, two bulls were released on opposite sides of an arena. 'The moment they felt their liberty, they tore up the turf with their horns, elevated the spines of their backs, and appeared animated with the strongest symptoms of rage.' Turner added: 'They did not at the first instance rush together; but turning sideways, eyed each other askance, all the while making a slow circular advance, until a very small distance divided them: they then turned opposing a full front, and ran impetuously, their heads meeting together with an astonishing concussion.' With horns now entangled, they struggled like wrestlers, 'the ground yielding to their heels as they pressed their brows, and alternatively retreated and pushed forwards in the conflict.' When the contest clearly favoured one bull, the weaker was driven away by attendants armed with bludgeons while the victor was 'conducted to his stall, highly indignant and full of wrath'.[2]

Finally a representative of the Tashilhunpo Regent arrived. After much discussion he permitted Turner and one companion to proceed on to Tibet. He would permit no more than two Englishmen to enter the Teshu Lama's See, however, on the curious grounds that this had been the size of Bogle's party. A slave to precedent, the Regent presumably did not want to encourage a trend toward larger Company missions. Forced to leave Davis behind, Turner was understandably irked; he was

---

[1] *Ibid.*, p. 152.   [2] *Ibid.*, pp. 160, 161.

moved to comment: 'it is extraordinary what absurdities and prejudices I had to combat.'

Hastings's envoy left Tassisudon in the midst of the *Monlam*, or New Year festival, during which Virtue, as symbolized by the Goddess Durga, battles the geniis of Vice. An effigy of Durga in combat with the forces of evil was exhibited 'amidst a most gaudy group of evil genii ...' The young lieutenant recalled the grotesque symbols of evil that exhibited themselves in the form of 'elephants, horses, apes and a most frightful figure environed with snakes'.[1]

Turner, Saunders and, of course, Purangir began the second phase of their journey on 8 September. It took them nearly two weeks to travel from Tassisudon to Tashilhunpo. On arrival the two Englishmen, according to a very sensible custom of the land, were left alone to rest. Waiting for them in their quarters were messages of welcome from both the late Lama's brother and his cup-bearer. Also there were, of course, the inevitable ceremonial white scarfs of greeting. But on the first day, at least, they were spared the other tiring protocols of the monastery.

An audience with the Regent was scheduled for the following day. Turner and Saunders entered the presence chamber which had been previously described by Bogle. The Governor General's letter of greeting, ornamented with a string of pearls, was delivered into the Regent's hands. Turner delivered a brief presentation speech, conveying the Governor's good wishes and congratulations for 'the joyful tidings of the [Teshu] Lama's reappearance in the world'. In response, the Regent assured Turner that the new incarnation, being one with his predecessor, held the same views towards Hastings. The Regent, in speaking of the Lama's bodily death in Peking, assured Turner that before being struck down by smallpox the late Lama had 'begun to open his mind to the Emperor of China' on the subject of the English.[2]

The infant Teshu Lama was at this time about to be moved from the place of discovery to the Terpaling monastery, a day's journey from Tashilhunpo. The accompanying ceremonies,

---

[1] *Ibid.*, pp. 162, 163.   [2] *Ibid.*, p. 239.

scheduled for 27 September, promised to be colourful. 'No mark of respect, no pomp or parade [would be] omitted, which, in their ideas, could possibly ... add dignity and splendour to the solemn ceremony.' The Chinese Emperor had assigned a large detachment of troops to escort the infant Lama, and any Tibetan of any importance would attend the 'moving throne', or cavalcade, bearing the Lama to his new home.

Understandably, Turner was eager to be present at such a memorable spectacle. He sent Purangir to petition the Regent while he sought out, himself, the cup-bearer to inquire into the possibilities of being invited. Unfortunately, the response was negative. From the cup-bearer he learned of the 'great anxiety under which the Tashilhunpo Regent and himself had laboured' in arranging for this second Company mission to Tashilhunpo. Attendance of Englishmen at such a ceremony would be going too far. The influence of the Chinese Emperor was strong in Tibet and the Chinese *Ambans* in Lhasa were zealous in protecting his influence. Moreover, spies of the Manchu court kept the Emperor intimately informed of anything which threatened the 'Celestial Realm'. The Regent was frank in admitting that he was afraid of giving offence to the Chinese. The Regent was frank, too, in admitting that his relationship with the Chinese was a precarious one.

By watching the official retinue as it returned to Tashilhunpo, Turner could, however, see something of the colourful costuming and pageantry of the occasion. The Tashilhunpo Regent, escorted by two or three hundred horsemen, was more immediately surrounded by a select party of the principal officers of state. He wore a 'yellow satin robe, lined with sable fur and fastened with a girdle round the waist; a garnet-coloured shawl mantle, partially covering his satin robe, according to their fashion, passed round the body and its end was gathered up to rest upon the left shoulder, leaving the right arm at liberty.' Covering his head was a round mitre, covered with a yellow glassy lacquer that glittered in the sun. He was shod in red bulgar boots which gripped his mount's stirrups. The horse, itself, was decorated 'with large crimson tassels and other splendid trappings while a number of bells, suspended to a collar that hung around his neck, jingled as he moved along the slow and solemn pace; the body of the horse, from the multitude of cowtails that hung on both sides, could scarcely be seen. . . .'¹

The other members of the entourage could be distinguished by their dress. The more humble ranking officers wore yellow or red dresses and round hats with flowing tassels of scarlet silk. The most extraordinary hats were those worn by the Kalmuks. They 'were of vast dimensions – not less than two feet in diameter – with shallow crowns, but monstrous brims; the whole covered with long locks of wool matted together.'² There were Hindu *gosains*, decked out in their national robes and turbans; Mongols from the Persian borders, and other assorted emissaries from lands far away.

While the new Teshu Lama was beginning his official life it was appropriate that Turner pay respects to the tomb of the previous incarnation. The young Englishman's visit to the Sixth Lama's mausoleum near Tashilhunpo was the last act in an important episode of English-Tibetan relations.

The grand mausoleum stood in a courtyard ringed with a vermillion and gilt colonnade, painted with mythological figures of gigantic proportions. On entering, Turner saw two paintings of enormous size, depicting 'with hideous countenances' in vivid blue and scarlet colours, incarnations of Tibet's version of Kali, the bloodthirsty Hindu Goddess. In the centre of the colonnade was a gate, opposite which stood the portico of the mausoleum. Under the portico sat a priest whose duty it was to pray eternally and keep alive a sacred fire that burned before the shrine.

The tall doors to the mausoleum were also painted vermillion and embossed with huge gilded knobs. They 'made the whole fabric ring, as their pivots grated within the sockets and their massy sides came with strong concussion against the walls.'³ Within was a pyramid, which covered the coffin of pure gold, wrought in Peking at the command of Emperor Ch'ien-lung and used to carry the Lama's remains back to Tashilhunpo.

Turner described a gold effigy of the late Lama, sitting in an attitude of devotion within the concave of a large shell. 'The Image,' adds Turner, 'is represented sitting upon cushions, and has the drapery of a yellow satin mantle, negligently flowing

---

¹ *Ibid.*, pp. 250, 251.   ² *Ibid.*, p. 251.   ³ *Ibid.*, p. 260.

over the lower part, whilst a cap resembling a mitre covers the head.' 'Round the borders of the canopy were suspended the various rosaries of the richest gems used by the Lama during his life; they consisted of pearls, emeralds, rubies, sapphires, coral, amber, crystal, lapis lazuli. . . .'
The sides of the pyramid were encased with plates of solid silver.

About breast-high from the base of the pyramid was one step considerably deeper than the rest, in front of which were represented two lions rampant carved in relief; and between them was placed a human figure with eyes extravagantly large and prominent; his countenance was expressive of the most anxious agitation, and his person thrown into strange contortions; his hands were applied to a stringed instrument called a cittaur.[1]

On the right side of the pyramid was another life-size image of the Lama, placed in a pulpit covered with a canopy of silk. Here His Holiness was represented in a devout attitude of study, holding a book before him. Turner observed:

on an altar covered with a white cloth were spread about the common objects of daily oblation; such as fruits and flowers, with various kinds of corn and oil. Intermixed among the offerings were seen at the same time, several lamps burning, which, being considered as sacred fire, are never permitted to go out; the smoke arising from these, and from a multitude of odoriferous tapers, filled the surrounding space and strongly perfumed the air.[2]

*

The Tibetan view of the rest of the world was understandably limited. China, naturally, was relatively well-known – the trade routes well-travelled and the government well represented by the *Ambans*. Less well-known was India. While Hindu pilgrim traders brought some news, centuries of Moghul rule and intolerance had discouraged Tibetans from crossing the Himalayas into India. As for the world beyond, almost nothing was known.

---

[1] *Ibid.*, p. 262. [2] *Ibid.*, p. 263.

Earlier Jesuit missionaries were doubtless responsible for some of the meagre facts of Europe which had found their way to Tibet. But Bogle, as will be recalled, had left behind the most definitive history and description of Europe. Aside from these sources, Tibet depended on the rare wanderer – usually a religious ascetic who ventured further than he had intended – to bring news and knowledge of the *Fringies*.

The Tashilhunpo Regent exhibited a lively interest in geography and made the most of Turner's stay to satisfy his curiosity. He plied Turner with searching questions. How could it be, for example, that far to the north the sun never set for half of the year and never rose for the other half? Like the late Teshu Lama, the Regent was also interested in the political problem posed by Russia. He knew that the Empress of Russia some years earlier had sent ambassadors laden with presents to the 'Taranout Lama' of Mongolia.[1] He showed Turner a Russian Bible which the Mongolian Lama had forwarded to Tashilhunpo with a plea for advice on how Russian overtures should be met. The late pontiff counselled caution but condoned limited trade. While Turner was in Tashilhunpo, a large party of Kalmuk traders, in fact, arrived from more than 1,000 miles away, bringing as an offering to the Lama a string of Mongolian horses, and a great quantity of furs and hides.

The Regent understandably asked many questions about the British Empire – its extent, military might, and wealth. He was particularly interested in the recent war, 'which, by unhappily interrupting the general intercourse of nations, had augmented prices and occasioned a scarcity of every article of foreign trade.' Turner described the causes of the war between England and America. He also tried to give a clear idea of the circumstances which led to war with France, a war 'which had involved the Carnatic in confusion, interrupted the communications between India and Europe, and covered the seas with hostile fleets.'[2]

While admiring the bold spirit of English enterprise, the Regent could not understand why so many Englishmen were willing to leave their country for the 'inclement climates and

---

[1] This refers to the Grand Lama of Urga in Mongolia.
[2] Samuel Turner, *op. cit.*, p. 276.

rude, inhospitable men' of other lands. There must be some de-
fect in England to account for the large number of expatriates
living permanently in India. Turner's defence of English
colonialism is a classic and must surely have stirred the puzzled
Regent with its fervour and conviction, if not with its logic. The
Company envoy, feeling the broader responsibility of empire,
expounded:

In order to account for that restlessness of disposition, which disperses
my countrymen over the whole surface of the globe, I was led to
expatiate at some length on the system of education prevailing amongst
us. This, I told him, was calculated perpetually to awaken genius and
call forth peculiar talents, which might otherwise have rested for ever in
a torpid state, unexerted and unknown; but which, when once roused
and improved, would not suffer their possessors to sit down in listless
and inglorious inactivity. Hence it was that numerous branches of
respectable families, prompted by curiosity, not less than by a desire of
wealth, spread themselves over every region of the universe. I added
that our Sovereign, reknowned for his love of science, and encouragement of useful research, had at various times, commanded ships to be
fitted out at an immense expense for the purpose of visiting unknown
regions and navigating distant seas. . . . In these voyages, lands had been
discovered and nations explored, of which neither history nor tradition
supplied the slightest information; and navigators, by publishing to the
world their observations and their accounts of these newly discovered
countries, had communicated much curious and important knowledge.[1]

As one of his nation's explorers, whose duty it was to help
solve the riddles of the still-unknown lands, Turner tried to
elicit geographic details of Tibet and its northern neighbours.
This was not easy. Perhaps explaining why Bogle's geographic
information had been so meagre, Turner found the Tibetans
generally confused and ignorant about their own land. But he
was able at least to learn something of the two great rivers which
drain southern Tibet.

The Ganges and the Tsangpo, he noted, are 'nearly related in
their birth as well as . . . in their termination.' Their source was
then believed to be Lake Manasarovar in south-western Tibet.

---

[1] *Ibid.*, pp. 277, 278.

(This belief was successfully challenged in 1907 when the distinguished Swedish explorer, Sven Hedin, conclusively located the
true source of the Tsangpo east of Manasarovar, while the source
of the Ganges was discovered to be further south.) He was also
told that the Tsangpo, which flows eastward from its source,
leaves Tibet and cuts through the Himalayas into Assam from
whence it enters the eastern boundary of Bengal in its search for
the sea. Several decades would pass, however, before the
Tsangpo's actual route into Assam could be traced and it could
be proven that the Tsangpo was identical with the Brahmaputra.

The Ganges, [noted Turner] by a different course seeks the milder
climate and more productive plains of Hindustan; no sooner disengaging
itself from the embarrassment of mountains . . . after having . . . quitted
Hurdewar, than it is met by the adoration of suppliant tribes and
receives the homage of the bordering nations as it flows along, fertilizing
the lands it washes, enriching their inhabitants, and bearing the wealth
of India in its arms.[1]

Turner probed history for clues of an ancient nation believed
to have once been located along the shores of Lake Baikal, and
from which 'the learning, arts and sciences of India, and even of
Europe, were supposed to have derived'. But any memory of the
original Aryan civilization was 'buried in deepest oblivion'. The
environs of Baikal, even to the most learned Tibetan, meant only
Tartar nomads, undistinguished by any superior culture.

The Tibetans held interesting theories to account for the
Mongols' aversion to fixed dwellings. This prejudice, they
believed, may have had its foundation in their dread of earth-
quakes, so frequent in that part of the world. Or perhaps they
found themselves forced to move frequently and quickly to
escape the calamitous effects of smallpox which regularly swept
the Central Asian steppes.

Turner was fascinated by Tibet's religion and the influence it
exerted on Tibet's culture. He was particularly interested in its
ritual music. Like the missionaries before him who saw in
Lamaist ritual an earlier Nestorian influence, Turner noted much
in common between the music of the Tibetan Lamaist service

---

[1] *Ibid.*, p. 300.

and that of a Roman Catholic mass, despite the great difference in the instruments used. The Tibetan instruments were of enormous size:

trumpets six feet long; drums stretched over copper cauldrons . . . gongs made of thin hammered bell metal and capable of producing a surprising sound; cymbals, hautboys; and a double drum, shallow, but of great circumference, mounted on a tall slender pedestal, which the performer turns with great facility, striking either side with a long, curved iron, as the piece requires a higher or lower tone: these together with the human tibia and sea conch . . . composed for the most part their religious band.[1]

When joined in unison and accompanied by a chorus of two or three hundred men, this weird assemblage of instruments 'managed with varying modulation, from the lowest and softest cadence to the loudest swell, [to produce] an effect extremely grand.'

Tashilhunpo, a city of priests, provided an unexcelled view of monastic life in Tibet. Turner could see at first hand a way of life in which over a quarter of the Tibetan male population devoted themselves to the celibate life of religion. Tibet was then perhaps the most complete theocracy the world had ever known. Turner described the nation as 'divided into two distinct and separate classes, those who carry on the business of the world, and those who hold intercourse with heaven.'[2] As 'Vice Regent of God' – mediator between mortals and the Supreme – the Head Lama of Tibet, immaculate, immortal, omnipresent and omniscient, ruled from the summit. Below him was a vast theocratic hierarchy with a graduation of priests, ranging in rank from the young novitiates to the most venerated incarnations of Buddha.

Youths intended for the priestly class entered the monasteries at about eight or nine years of age to study and prepare themselves for a lifetime of monastic duty. At age fifteen they were usually admitted to the order of *tohba*, the first step in their religious class. On passing a qualifying examination they then became *gylongs*, or common lamas. Only then were they eligible for appointment to a supervisory role in some monastery where

---

[1] *Ibid.*, pp. 307, 308.   [2] *Ibid.*, p. 312.

they must 'confine themselves to the austere practices of the cloister'.[1]

Turner added his observations on Tibetan death rituals to those made by Western visitors before him, going over much the same ground. He described in the usual gory detail how the average Tibetan, upon death, is carried to a nearby hilltop, disjointed and left as prey for ravens, kites and other carnivorous birds. His description of the annual October ceremony for the dead is, however, relatively more original:

... as soon as the evening drew on and it became dark, a general illumination was displayed upon the summits of all the buildings in the monastery; the tops also of the houses upon the plain, as well as in the most distant villages, scattered among the clusters of willows, were in the same manner lighted up with lamps, exhibiting all together a brilliant and splendid spectacle. The darkness of the night, the profound tranquillity and silence, interrupted only by the deep and slowly-repeated tones of the bowbut, trumpet, gong and cymbal, at different intervals; the tolling of bells and the loud monotonous repetition of sentences of prayer, sometimes heard when the instruments were silent; were all so calculated by their solemnity, to produce serious reflection, that I really believe no human ceremony could possibly have been contrived more effectively to impress the mind with sentiments of awe.[2]

Soon after the Regent returned to Tashilhunpo following a month's journey to western Tibet, Turner had another audience with him. Since it was already November and the English mission would have to leave soon if it were to avoid the heavy winter snows which block the Himalayan passes, the Regent presented him with farewell gifts and a letter of greetings for Hastings. He addressed Turner affectionately, saying: 'though a separation is about to take place between us, our friendship will not cease to exist.'[3] Using the infancy of the Seventh Teshu Lama as an excuse, the Regent regretted his inability to conclude any formal agreements with the Company. But on a note of hope he bid farewell, saying: 'be not cast down; when he shall come of age ... all will be well.'[4] In the meantime, he promised that Indian merchants trading in Tibet would be protected.

---

[1] *Ibid.* [2] *Ibid.*, p. 319. [3] *Ibid.*, p. 328. [4] *Ibid.*, p. 328.

Perhaps as an indication of Turner's success in establishing warm personal relations with the Regent, the latter had made arrangements for the young Englishman to be received by the infant Teshu Lama at Terpaling monastery *en route* home. This, in fact, would be the climax of the journey.

Turner found the eighteen-month old child seated solemnly on a mound of silk cushions roughly four feet high. Flanked by his mother and father, the infant lama looked with obvious interest at the strangely dressed foreigners. Scarfs were exchanged with the Lama's parents while gifts of bright pearls and coral from Hastings were laid before the wide-eyed child. The Lama's father commented that 'the Teshu Lama had awoke very early, before the English gentlemen were arrived and he could not sleep.'

Turner was completely enchanted by the child and amazed with his apparent perception. The English envoy observed, for example, that the Lama's eyes were scarcely ever turned from him. When the guests' tea cups were empty the child appeared uneasy. Then 'he took out some burnt sugar out of a golden cup containing some confectionary and, stretching out his arm, made a motion to his attendants to give them to me.'[1] The holy child was totally attentive as Turner solemnly spoke his own and Hastings's greetings. Occasionally he would nod knowingly as though he understood perfectly what Turner was saying. Turner recalled, 'while unable to speak, the child made the most expressive signs and conducted himself with astonishing dignity and decorum.'

The Lama's father, Gyap, spoke most candidly with Turner. Still unused to the fact that the Teshu Lama had chosen his family to be born into, the Tibetan seemed genuinely anxious for the Company's friendship. A long-standing antagonism on the part of the Chinese *Ambans* and Lhasan nobility had caused him to leave his native city of Lhasa and make his residence in Tashilhunpo well before his child had been discovered to be the new incarnation. Gyap's new position of prominence made him still more uneasy. He described the Lhasan establishment as a group of 'crafty, designing men ... black at heart'. The vehemence of his condemnation made Turner counsel patience. The

---

[1] *Ibid.*, p. 334.

Englishman's parting advice was to 'wait the event of time; when Teshu Lama should be fixed in power.'[1]

Time, however, would not work either to the advantage of the young Teshu Lama or the East India Company. War between Tibet and the Gurkhas of Nepal would change the Himalayan power equation and bring to India's borders the power of the Manchus.

---

[1] *Ibid.*, p. 341.

11

The Closing of Tibet

Turner was the last Company man to enter Tibet. As so often happens the currents of history began to rush too swiftly for the orderly plans of man. The sudden emergence in the 1760s of a unified Nepalese state, imbued at birth with an aggressive, expansionist spirit confronted Tibet with a new and dangerous problem. Nepal owed its nationhood to Prithvi Narayan Shah, a Rajput prince who was able to weld together several of the petty Himalayan principalities. But this extraordinary leader was not content to confine his ambitions to the southern slopes of the Himalayas; the riches of southern Tibet were too tempting to be ignored. As a result, however, he provoked the Manchus and brought to his own borders and those of British India the strength of China. Before the end of the century China would have bound Tibet in vassalage to the 'Celestial Realm' and blocked all Company plans for trade expansion. Hastings's dream, so promising in the 70s, would be but a memory by the 90s.

Hastings had viewed Nepal as a convenient route to Tibet, just as he had hoped Tibet, in turn, would prove a gateway to China. Prithvi Narayan interfered with these concepts. His militant, Hindu hillsmen could with little difficulty block access to the Nepalese Himalayas and the Tibetan highlands beyond. The Company, therefore, viewed with dismay the prospect of losing 'benefits arising from the former intercourse....'[1]

When the Rajah of Patan called for help to support his fellow Newar rajahs against Gurkha insurgents, it had not been difficult to justify sending a small force of Company troops to Nepal.

---

[1] The India Office Library, Commonwealth Relations Office, London, Hodgson MSS, Vol. 1.

Unhappily the expedition failed; the force under Captain Kinloch was at the start inadequate, and the toll taken by disease in the fever-ridden foothills of Nepal enfeebled it so that it never saw action against the enemy. For that matter, by 1770 the Newar princes were beyond saving; the new rulers were solidly entrenched in Kathmandu.

The Hindu Gurkhas were religiously and racially incompatible with the Lamaist Tibetans. The subjection of the Buddhist Newar states and the severing of their traditionally close Tibetan ties thus inevitably resulted in an abrupt decline in trans-Himalayan intercourse. Not only did Prithvi Narayan Shah close Nepal's northern passes, but he sought to prevent Company contacts of any kind with the Tibetans lest he find himself outflanked. Nepal's new ruler, soon after coming to power, wrote the Dalai Lama to advise him against allowing English agents or goods to enter Tibet.

The death of Prithvi Narayan in 1771 did not change the character of Gurkha rule or slow its momentum. In 1775 his successor invaded the small princely enclave of Sikkim which separated Nepal from Bhutan. Tibet offered assistance to the threatened Sikkimese and supported them in the ensuing truce conference. Already annoyed by Tibet's role in Bhutanese politics and the Teshu Lama's cordial reception of Bogle in 1774, the Gurkha ruler even more deeply resented this interference in Sikkimese affairs.

Another source of friction between Nepal and Tibet arose over trade and currency matters. Since the sixteenth century Newari rajahs in Nepal had provided minting facilities for Tibet's coinage. It will be recalled that Desideri described how silver bullion, brought to Tibet by the Chinese during their invasion in 1720, found its way to Nepal for minting. By debasing the currency with metal alloys, the Nepalese rajahs had grown rich. The practice of offering adulterated coinage in exchange for pure bullion continued uninterrupted. One estimate placed Nepal's yearly profit at 100,000 rupees – an impressive sum for the times.[1]

When Prithvi Narayan came to power he tried to introduce a new coinage into Tibet, but was rebuffed by the suspicious

---

[1] William Kirkpatrick, *An Account of the Kingdom of Nepaul* (London, 1811), p. 211.

Tibetans who had by this time lost faith in the purity of Nepalese coinage. Despite repeated attempts by the Nepalese to convince the Tibetans that the new coinage would be worth more than the old, Lhasa stubbornly refused to accept it. Deprived of Nepal's traditional minting profits, the Gurkhas treated Tibet's refusal as provocation, and this very soon provided a useful excuse for aggression. The basic motive which lay behind Nepal's threatening stance, however, was avarice. Within tempting reach were the riches of Shigatse and Tashilhunpo, which had been left untouched by the earlier Mongol invasions of Tibet.

On being informed of the Sixth Teshu Lama's death in Peking, a younger brother known as Shamarpa Hutukhtu,[1] or more commonly as the Karmapa Lama, fled Tashilhunpo and found asylum in Nepal. He believed that his brother had met an unnatural death at the hands of the Chinese, and feared that he and other members of the family would be similarly disposed of. It eventually became obvious, of course, that this was not the case; but in the meantime the oldest brother had assumed power as Regent of Tashilhunpo and taken custody of the immense riches which went with the office. In vain the Karmapa Lama complained that he had been denied his fair share of the inheritance. He knew, though, that it would be unwise to return to Tashilhunpo from his Nepal refuge to press this claim. As a priest of the Red Hat sect, he could not expect to enjoy a safe, much less privileged, position in Tibet under the new Regent who was, by definition, a senior lama of the rival Yellow Hat church. The Regent had indeed assumed exclusive custody of the vast Tashilhunpo treasure and had made it clear that he would not share it with his renegade younger brother. It is natural to suppose that the Karmapa Lama, who saw in his Gurkha hosts his only chance to regain this inheritance, excited them with exaggerated tales of Tashilhunpo's riches.

The Gurkhas contrived a plot in which the Karmapa Lama was declared a hostage whose freedom could be bought only by a Tibetan promise to negotiate a new trade and currency agreement. If satisfaction were not received, Nepal would occupy the Tibetan border districts of Nyanang, Rongshar and Kyirong.

---

[1] 'Sharmapa Hutukhtu' is a title which literally means an 'Incarnation of the Red Cap sect of Lamaism'. His true name was Shamar Trulku.

Although the Karmapa Lama personally requested the Dalai Lama to accept the Nepalese demand and thus 'free him', it must be assumed that the renegade lama was, in fact, a willing accomplice in the plot. At least this was Lhasa's point of view. Tibet's formal reply stated that the Karmapa Lama had gone to Nepal of his own accord and could thus not be considered a hostage. The letter underscored its point with the homily, 'knowing how to shoot, [he] bought the bow.'[1] While the Tibetan Government expressed a willingness to make a few minor trade and currency concessions, it refused to take part in the proposed conference, particularly in view of the crude pressure which had been brought to bear.

Making good Kathmandu's threat, 5,000 Gurkha troops invaded Tibet in 1788. The six-year old Teshu Lama was bustled off to safety in Lhasa while the Regent frantically requested assistance from the East India Company. In the meantime a ragged Tibetan army moved toward the enemy to defend Tashilhunpo, and the Chinese set in train a larger expeditionary force with which to defend its vassal.

An advance contingent of the Chinese army reached Shigatse in good time but its commander, Shen T'ai-tu, in a fit of caution, refused to advance. An account of Shen's cowardly performance, recorded by a member of the Tibetan assembly, who had been assigned as liaison officer to the Chinese force, provides flavour to the ignominious episode:

Shen T'ai-tu spent five days at Shigatse, making a number of petty excuses for delaying the advance. . . . Shen told me that if we advance without waiting for the main body of the Imperial Army to catch up, we would be inviting defeat and disgrace. If we remained at Shigatse until the main army joined us, our total number would be too great for the resources of the town. . . . I received the impression that the officer wanted to avoid a fight. . . . Shen T'ai-tu then openly asked me if there was no way we could negotiate with the Gurkhas. . . .[2]

Hastings had felt obliged to resign in January 1785 – a victim of political harassment in England and vicious fighting within the

---

[1] Tsepon W. D. Shakabpa, *Tibet, A Political History* (New Haven, Yale University Press, 1967), pp. 157, 158.
[2] *Ibid.*, p. 159.

Company. After a brief interim in which John Macpherson acted as Governor General, Lord Charles Cornwallis assumed charge. Having recently returned from Yorktown where he had surrendered British forces to end the American Revolutionary War, this illustrious commander assumed his new duties in February 1786. He was instructed to devote himself principally to the many pressing problems within India itself. While he endorsed Hastings's Tibetan trade objectives and felt, just as keenly as Hastings, the Company's need for Tibet's gold bullion, his main focus was internal. He could recognize the practical obstacles which faced the Company in trying to breach the Himalayan wall. Perhaps for this reason he was no more than correct to two Tibetan emissaries[1] from Tashilhunpo who arrived in December 1788, bearing an urgent request for help from the Regent.

They delivered a letter from the Teshu Lama – obviously drafted by his Regent – which pleaded for assistance against the Gurkhas. The letter's real significance, however, lay in its candidly expressed fear of China. The Regent's explicit rationale for requesting British military help was to make unnecessary a Chinese expeditionary force, which would pose a greater threat to Tibet's independence than the Nepalese. Only by quickly reaching a negotiated peace could the Regent hold back an Imperial army, which had already been requested by the *Ambans* in Lhasa.

With astonishing candour the Tashilhunpo Regent admitted that his communication with the Company could be very compromising. If this indiscretion were discovered by the Chinese, he felt it would most certainly bring 'ruin and destruction' upon him.

This was the very kind of political situation which Hastings had dreamed of. He would have reasoned that by aiding Tibet in its time of need, the Company would secure a position of paramountcy throughout Trans-Himalaya, and Tibet would continue to serve as a protective buffer area between India and China. At the same time, Nepal would be brought to heel and,

---

[1] The emissaries were Mohamed Rejeeb and Mohamed Walli, two Moslem clerics from Kashmir.

being outflanked, would have no choice but to accept English domination of Himalaya.

Cornwallis, however, was not Hastings, nor were the times the same. The new Governor General had the benefit of Hastings's experience; gradually it had become obvious that Chinese influence in Tibet was strong enough to prevent English trade penetration. After a two-month delay Cornwallis replied negatively; English military intervention was out of the question. First it would be too costly; secondly, the Company had no cause to attack Nepal; and thirdly, British sea trade with China was too important to risk alienating the Emperor by such an act of aggression. The General concluded with the suggestion that the 'Teshu Lama [meaning, of course, the Regent] should inform the Chinese Emperor of the close friendship existing between the Company and Tashilhunpo so that secrecy would no longer be necessary.'[1]

While Cornwallis may not have believed that the Tibetans could influence the Chinese, he must at least have considered them a useful means of bringing to the Emperor's attention the advantages of a friendly British presence on Tibet's troublesome southern border. The *quid quo pro* for Company protection of Tibet's exposed southern flank could, reasoned the Governor General, be permission to establish a trade mission in the 'Forbidden City' itself.

Cornwallis's negative response did not imply a lessening of Company interest in Tibet; as recently as March 1788 the London directors had reiterated to Cornwallis their view that Tibet trade would be to the great advantage of Bengal 'by a regular importation of bullion and [by] the encouragement of the manufacturers of Great Britain. . . .' But the practical problems of sending an expeditionary force into Nepal were overwhelming. The lessons of Kinloch's disastrous experience in 1767 were remembered all too well. Moreover, Cornwallis had his hands full in India itself where Company finances were in a precarious state and Marathra insurrection in the south was worrisome. He could ill-afford a campaign of doubtful benefit, which, for that matter, could fail

---

[1] D. B. Disalkar, 'The Tibeto-Nepalese War, 1788–1793', *Journal of the Bihar and Orissa Research Society*, Vol. XIX (Patna, 1933), pp. 367–9.

altogether. The open door to Tibet was too heavy a price to pay for Nepalese and Chinese enmity. Wisdom dictated a policy of strict neutrality. But, as it turned out, Cornwallis could not convince either side that he was neutral.

Unable to defend themselves – even with the aid of the advance units of a Chinese army – and without hope of receiving Company support, the Tibetans sued for peace in early 1789. This decision was taken mainly on the advice of Sakya monastery monks and the anti-Chinese father of the young Teshu Lama. The Lama's father, like the Regent, believed that a negotiated peace with Nepal was preferable to the occupation of southern Tibet by a large Chinese army of occupation.

The Gurkhas agreed to withdraw when Tibetan negotiators accepted a compromise adjustment of the outstanding coinage and trade problems, and promised to pay an annual tribute to Nepal of 300 Tibetan silver ingots. Two Chinese representatives at the truce conference endorsed these terms on the important condition that the Gurkhas send a mission to Peking with a token tribute offering. This would save Chinese face by giving the illusion that the Emperor's army had been victorious. Face was, in fact, saved for the moment in 1791 when a train of tired elephants and an equally tired Nepalese orchestra were presented to Emperor Ch'ien-lung in Peking by the promised tribute mission.

When the Emperor came to realize that his generals had disgraced themselves and China by suing for peace, he became predictably angry. In Lhasa, too, there was much discontent over the peace terms. The Regent of the Dalai Lama, (not to be confused with the Tashilhunpo Regent who represented the Teshu Lama) was so enraged by what he considered a humiliating treaty that during a *kashag*, or parliamentary, debate he threw a bowl of barley flour over the front benchers. Still furious, he refused to pay Nepal the agreed-upon tribute. Lhasan authorities righteously claimed that the Dalai Lama, during the Regent's absence in China, had never agreed to the peace terms. Quite obviously the Regent was also opposed to these terms. He was heard to shout in parliament that if the Nepalese wanted their tribute they would have to come and get it themselves. He recognized that the surrender by Tibetan and Chinese forces in the face of the Gurkha attack had been premature. It had been a cowardly act and he was understandably incensed. Yet there were dark rumours abroad that the Regent secretly favoured Nepalese attacks against Tashilhunpo in the hope that this rival of Lhasa might once and for all be eliminated.

While feigning willingness to renegotiate the humiliating tribute agreement, the Nepalese secretly plotted a new attack against the Tibetans. On the excuse that the latter had defaulted on their tribute payments, but more likely because the glittering treasure of Tashilhunpo still tempted the Gurkha warriors, Nepal once again invaded southern Tibet. News of the invasion reached Lhasa in mid-1791 and became known in Peking shortly thereafter – even as unhappy Nepalese tribute bearers waited on the Emperor. By October, 18,000 Gurkhas had reached Shigatse and stormed Tashilhunpo monastery, carrying off Tibet's greatest remaining treasure – the religious and tribute offerings of many centuries.

The Chinese *Amban*, Pao-t'ai, made plans to have both the Teshu Lama and Dalai Lama removed to the north for safe-keeping. So panic-stricken were the Tibetans when this alarming news leaked out, that the Dalai Lama was forced to address his people and assure them that he had no intention of fleeing. But even this did not stop frantic preparations by Lhasan nobles to save themselves and their riches from the Gurkhas' horde.

Chinese records suggest disdainfully that the Tashilhunpo monks abandoned their monastery to the enemy without a struggle. Blamed for this was the 'advice' of an inanimate goddess image. If, however, the Tashilhunpo lamas sought advice at all, it was more probably from the nearby Abbess, Dorje Phagmo – the 'Thunderbolt Sow' – who ranked third within Tibet's Lamaist hierarchy. It is perhaps understandable that the 'Thunderbolt Sow', being a practical woman, saw no point for needless bloodshed in the face of the overwhelmingly powerful Gurkha army.

News of the invasion shocked Peking. One of the Chinese officials, who had been a party to the earlier abortive truce settlement, felt he had suffered such loss of face that he committed suicide by drowning himself. The Emperor vowed he would crush the Gurkhas, once and for all. His army, already poised on the Tibetan border as a result of the first Gurkha invasion, was 18,000-strong. Under the command of Fu K'ang-an, a brilliant campaigner who boasted a blood relationship with Ch'ien-lung, the Imperial force was made up of Daghor horsemen from the Manchurian-Mongolian border, rugged mountaineers from western Szechuan, hard-riding cavalry from Koko Nor and new Tibetan recruits from eastern Tibet. Marching rapidly to the southern Tibet front by two routes – the Sining-Koko Nor route from the north, and the Szechuan-Tachienlu route from the east, the Chinese force engaged the enemy in mid-winter 1792.

The Gurkhas had already been forced back to Shekar and Dzongka by Tibetan troops, but when the full force of the Imperial army struck, the Nepalese reeled in defeat and began a long, painful retreat. Unable to anticipate that a force so large could have moved so rapidly over such difficult terrain, the Gurkhas were caught completely by surprise. The astonished Gurkhas, heavily burdened by their loot, were shattered in a series of battles as the Chinese pursued them into Nepal. Simultaneously, the east flank of Nepal was harassed by Sikkimese troops who had been encouraged by the Tibetans to launch a simultaneous attack.

The Rajah, in the meantime, was faced with a terrified Kathmandu populace, which expected the capital to fall to the revengeful Chinese and Tibetans. Quickly forgetting his traditional animosity toward the English, the Gurkha leader hastily signed a trade agreement with the Company, embodying the features which Calcutta had wanted for so long. While there was nothing written into the agreement calling for military assistance, it is possible that the Company's local agent in Kathmandu[1] held out hope that the British would rescue Nepal. At least by agreeing to the Company's trade requests, the Rajah could hope that this might be the case.

The next step of desperation was, in fact, a Nepalese plea for military aid. The Rajah twice petitioned Cornwallis. In the first letter, which reached Calcutta on 22 August 1792, he specifically asked for ten cannon and ten officers to instruct the Gurkhas in their use. Then, only a few weeks later, a second letter urgently

[1] The Company agent in Kathmandu was Abdul Kadir Khan who reported to the Company Resident in Beneres, Jonathan Duncan.

requested two battalions of European troops plus two battalions of native sepoys and an arsenal of guns.

The Company agent in Kathmandu independently confirmed the seriousness of the situation. The Chinese and Tibetans were by then only a ten-day march from the Nepalese capital. So precarious was the Rajah's position that he had had the Royal Treasury evacuated and was, himself, on the verge of fleeing. Clearly it was too late for help – even if the Company had been inclined to offer it.

Cornwallis replied to the Gurkha Rajah, explaining that it was Company policy not to interfere in the disputes of others. He frankly admitted that Company coastal trade with China was too valuable to risk by sending a relief force to Kathmandu. All he could offer was his good offices for mediation. The Governor General also replied to a letter he had received from the Dalai Lama through the Teshu Lama and Purangir, warning the Company against helping the Nepalese. Cornwallis reassured the Dalai Lama that his policy was one of neutrality, but informed him that he intended sending a mediator to Kathmandu.

This could only have raised new suspicions or at least puzzlement on the part of the Dalai Lama since by this time a peace agreement had been concluded and final terms extracted from the defeated Nepalese. It must also have appeared to be a less than forthcoming response to the Chinese, whose commanding general, Fu K'ang-an, had on 31 March 1792 asked for English help to meet Nepalese aggression.

Hastings's mediator, Captain William Kirkpatrick of the Bengal infantry learned of the end of the war only after he arrived in Kathmandu. The Gurkhas had been decisively beaten in a final battle which took place twenty miles from Nepal's capital. According to the peace terms, the Gurkhas returned to the Tibetans the spoils of Tashilhunpo and handed over the followers of the, by now deceased, Karmapa Lama. The currency and trade problems were adjusted and the Nepalese agreed to send a tribute mission to Peking every five years with a token offering of respect in the form of elephants, peacock plumes and rhinocerous horns. In so doing, Nepal technically became a 'dependent' nation in much the same category as Korea, Siam and Burma – or at least this was the viewpoint adopted by the Manchus. Thankful that the campaign could be ended before the

winter snows closed the passes between Nepal and Tibet and cut
off necessary supplies, the Chinese withdrew from Nepal.

Even after news of the peace settlement reached Cornwallis,
he was not ready to recall Kirkpatrick. The Governor General
instead sent his envoy new instructions urging him to conduct
new trade negotiations. Under the circumstances this was
patently impractical. The Kirkpatrick mission proved particularly unfortunate as it served to stir up Chinese suspicions. Coinciding as it did with the first British mission to Peking headed
by Lord Macartney, Kirkpatrick's unexplainable presence in
Kathmandu was particularly unfortunate.

Members of the Macartney Mission, long before they had
heard of the events in Nepal, sensed Chinese hostility. Gradually
it became clear that Peking suspected England of aiding the
Gurkhas in the Nepal-Tibet war. Macartney, while still in the
dark as to the actual events and without realizing Kirkpatrick
was in Kathmandu, was mystified when in Peking he suffered a
studied rudeness on the part of Fu K'ang-an, newly arrived from
his triumph in Nepal. While the basic xenophobia of the Chinese
certainly lay behind the failure of the Macartney Mission,
Macartney, at least, was convinced that Company actions in
Nepal were the cause of his difficulties.

Cornwallis's refusal to help Nepal was resented by the defeated Gurkha Rajah. The treaty with Nepal regarding trade
with Tibet was never implemented and the Rajah's reaction to
Kirkpatrick was something less than enthusiastic. This was
hardly the time to talk trade.

Tibet's reaction too, could only have been cool. The Teshu
Lama did write a polite letter to Cornwallis, pointing out that
events had moved beyond mediation since Nepal in defeat had
become a vassal of the Manchus. He urged that they continue
their correspondence, but it is significant that the Company
never heard from him again. That which the Teshu Lama's
Regent had feared had come to pass; a large Chinese presence in
Tibet seriously compromised Tibet's independence. An effort
had been made in Lhasa to rid Tibet of the Chinese occupation
army, and the Tibetan people, by posters and demonstrations,
had made clear their animosity towards the Chinese even as
the war was being fought; but Chinese control of Tibet was now a
fact.

The *Ambans* were promoted to the same rank as Chinese provincial Governors General; memorials, or petitions, to the Emperor must now go through them. Henceforward all official correspondence abroad would also be read and approved by the *Ambans*. Moreover, Chinese troops were garrisoned at Shigatse and Dingri. In 1793 the Chinese deployed troops to Phari on the Indian border. Turner, who recognized this as a move to stop the trading pilgrims from trafficking with Tibet, was spurred to write, 'a most violent prejudice prevails even against the Hindu *gosains*.'

Somehow symbolic of the total break between India and Tibet was the death of Purangir in 1795. This valiant and able envoy, who did more than anyone to bring about close relations between the Company and Tibet, was murdered in his monastery by robbers. The intruders mistakenly believed he had secreted Tibetan valuables there. Purangir's monastery, the sanctuary near Calcutta for Tibetan traders which the Sixth Teshu Lama had ordered built as a symbol of closer relations between Tibet and Bengal, thereafter withered through disuse and neglect.

Tibet would be closed to Westerners for a long time to come. It was now truly the 'forbidden land'. Open exploration, much less trade, was out of the question. As the needs of empire grew, a new technique of clandestine probes by native explorers would lift a little the curtain of secrecy surrounding Tibet that protected it from the prying eyes and covetous intrigues of foreign 'barbarians'. But no Englishman would succeed in reaching Lhasa for well over a century – no Englishman, that is, except one.

Part Three
Entr'acte

12

Thomas Manning

It is somehow satisfying to know that the first Englishman to reach Lhasa wandered there on his own, having made no serious preparations for the hazardous journey. With neither support nor encouragement from any source whatsoever, Thomas Manning tripped gaily to Tibet. His credentials consisted of nothing more than a dubious claim to being a medical practitioner and several bottles of fine cherry brandy. His staff consisted of one disagreeable Chinese servant who was equally ill-prepared for the rigours of the Himalayas.

Born in 1772, the second son of the Reverend William Manning of Norfolk, Thomas began life as a sickly child whose precarious state of health kept him from school. A succession of tutors nonetheless crammed him full of the classics so that he could be admitted to Cambridge University. He concentrated on mathematics at Caius College and eventually published a rather remarkable text on algebra. For all his brilliance, however, he never received a degree: a strong repugnance to 'oaths and tests' prevented him from receiving the academic recognition which could easily have been his.

While still at Cambridge Manning became deeply interested in China. After college he went to France where he devoted himself to a serious study of the Chinese language until the outbreak of war in 1803. Only because of the esteem in which his scholarship was held by French orientalists was he permitted to leave the continent after hostilities broke out. Napoleon, himself, signed his pass – a favour for which the eccentric Manning would much later find occasion to thank him in person during a curious visit to St Helena.

We are indebted to the nineteenth-century British Tibetan scholar, Clements Markham, for salvaging Manning's journal and editing it for publication.[1] A highly personal narrative which reveals more about Manning than Tibet, it is a subjective account of an English eccentric's experiences – short on fact and long on trivia. As it is filled with whimsical observations and flights of fancy, only occasionally is one able to catch glimpses of what would have been memorable experiences for any orthodox explorer. But even though Manning wrote no very useful description of this little-explored cranny of the globe, he at least left a delightfully odd reminiscence which must be preserved for its uniqueness, if for no other reason.

From Cambridge days, Manning remained a close friend of Charles Lamb. Markham found some thirty-three letters which that illustrious author had sent to Manning over the years, and he made generous reference to them in his book. Thanks to Lamb, we know that since undergraduate days Manning harboured romantic dreams of visiting Central Asia. As early as 1803 Lamb, who clerked at East India House in London from 1792 to 1825, begged the unorthodox scholar: 'get the idea of visiting Independent Tartary out of your head.' Lamb blamed Manning's incurable wanderlust on the reading of Chaucer and accused his friend of having been misled by 'foolish stories about Cambusean and the ring, and the horse of brass.' 'Believe me,' wrote Lamb, 'there are no such things. 'Tis all the poets invention. A horse of brass never flew and a king's daughter never talked with birds.' With what seemed to be genuine concern for his friend's balance, Lamb pleaded with him, 'read no more books of voyages.' 'Pray try and cure yourself,' he urged, and avoid the 'fiend' of travel.[2]

Manning would not be dissuaded from his enterprise. He secured an appointment to the East India Company in 1806, and arrived at Canton the following year to begin a three-year assignment to the English factory. He set for himself ambitious objectives to acquire

a view of China; its manners; the actual degree of happiness the people enjoy; their sentiments and opinions so far as they influence life, their

---

[1] Clements Markham, *Narratives of the Mission of George Bogle to Tibet and of the Journey of Thomas Manning to Lhasa* (London, Trübner & Co, 1876).
[2] *Ibid.*, p. clvi.

literature; their history, the causes of their stability and vast popula-
tions; their minor arts and contrivances; what there might be in China
worthy to serve as a model for imitation, and what to serve as a beacon
to avoid.

Although disapproving of Manning's travel lust, Lamb continued
to correspond faithfully with his 'old adventuring friend' who
had gone to 'wander among the Tartars'.

The xenophobic Chinese would not suffer the foreign 'barbarians' to intrude beyond the coastal trading stations. Manning
could thus see little past the door of the English factory in which
he worked. If he was to accomplish his ambitious mission of
inquiry he must find some better vantage point than Canton.
He inveigled the Company's Seclect Committee at Canton to
write Lord Minto, Governor General of India, requesting his
permission to probe China's underbelly from the direction of
India. The letter explained: 'The object of this gentleman's visit
to China has been to qualify himself by studying the Chinese
language and customs, to explore the country . . . but finding his
ultimate views impracticable from this quarter, he proceeds to
Calcutta, and will personally explain his future plans.' The
Seclect Committee added: 'As we consider Mr Manning eminently qualified for the task he has undertaken, we anxiously
hope your Lordship will not consider it improper to afford Mr
Manning every practicable assistance in the prosecution of his
plans, and this we beg to solicit in his behalf.'[1]

The Governor General permitted Manning to enter Bengal,
but clearly he had no interest in his project, if indeed he ever
gave him time to explain it. Manning was socially active in
Calcutta where he was remembered for wearing a fancy dress,
which he claimed was that of a 'Tartar gentleman', but he was
not taken seriously by the official community.[2] There was something ridiculous about his broad English face and full flowing
beard, which looked 'as little like a Tartar as any son of Adam'.

The Company cannot be blamed for its attitude toward
Manning. Who could believe this eccentric visitor, for all his
linguistic accomplishments, would ever reach Lhasa; and if he

[1] *Ibid.*, p. 12.
[2] H. T. Princep, *Tibet Tartary and Mongolia* (London, 1852, 2nd edition).

did, how could he be expected to carry on any significant discussions with the Tibetans? But Manning, understandably enough, was miffed. He scrawled in his journal: 'I cannot help explaining in my mind (as I often do) what fools the Company are to give me no commission, no authority, no instructions; what use are their embassies when their ambassador cannot speak to a soul and can only make ordinary phrases pass through a stupid interpreter?'

The English community was quite oblivious to the start of Manning's remarkable journey when in early September 1811 he made his way to the Bhutan frontier. Accompanied by his *munshi*, or Chinese servant, whom he had brought from Canton, Manning arrived at a place called Cantalbari (or Kathal-bari), sixty-three miles north of Rangpur, on the first leg of what would be a very long stroll to Lhasa. This was a 'wretched, pigsty of a place' which revolted Manning and inspired him to push on rather than spend the night as he had originally planned to do.

The journals of Himalayan travellers are customarily filled with heroic prose to describe the perils and hardships of crossing the world's most formidable mountain barrier. Those blazing new trails usually include meticulous topographical details, permitting map-makers to fill in those vast voids which trouble them so. Manning's journal, however, had its own style: there was no tedious geographic intelligence – hardly any intelligence at all – to inform the experts, and no effort to dramatize what was, after all, a perfectly simple outing in the hills of Himalaya. There was instead a running account – uphill and downdale – of the petty occurrences of each day. A favourite subject was his aggravating *munshi* who seemed to delight in unsettling him. Manning's words are self-revealing if not very helpful in describing nineteenth-century Tibet:

October 16: At night I found that my Chinese servant had changed our silver spoons into pewter. I told him I would not go on till I got my spoons. Now the *chaprassi* (porter) . . . is a partner in iniquity. . . . At last my slave went and returned with one silver and one pewter again. I swore I would have the other, or go back myself and speak to the magistrate. This frightened my rascal; he sent the slave again and he brought back the other. It was not the value but the example. I am in bad, bad hands.

October 18: We are now come on about six miles. The Chinaman is as cross as the devil and will not speak. We are lodged in a loft, open shed-like, but snuggish place to sleep in. Snowfall in sight. Charming weather – strange sensation coming along: warm and comfortable. Horse walking in a lane between two stone walls. The snow! Where am I? How can I be come here? Not a soul to speak to! I wept almost through excess of sensation not from grief. A spaniel would be better company than my Chinese servant.

October 19: I found out at night why my servant was cross. He fell off his horse and thought I took no notice of it.

October 21: Arrived Pari Jong [Phari Dzong]. I was lodged at a strange place, but so are the natives. Two magistrates came to look at us and ask questions. I took them for idle fellows and paid no respect to them.

October 23: I went to visit the religious resident at Pari Jong. They cheated me . . . all cheats.

October 27: The Chinaman was cross again. Says I: 'Was that a bird at the magistrate's that flapped so loud?' Answer: 'What signifies whether it was a bird or not?' These are the answers I get. He is always discontented and grumbling. . . .[1]

The coincidental arrival of a Chinese general at Phari Dzong gave Manning a rare opportunity to ingratiate himself with the establishment and petition for approval to proceed on to Lhasa. But it was cherry brandy that turned the trick. The English traveller makes an entry in his log dated 1 November: 'I gave him two bottles of cherry brandy and a wine glass. . . . He was very civil and promised to write immediately to the Lhasa Mandarin [*Amban*] for permission for me to proceed.'[2]

Manning's alleged proficiency in medicine also appealed to the Chinese general whose escort force was badly in need of medical attention. The English traveller apparently held clinic in Phari Dzong since he notes: 'The soldiers describe their complaints, but concealed their origin – supposing perhaps that I, as a physician, can find them out.'[3]

---

[1] Clements Markham, *op. cit.*, pp. 215, 216.
[2] *Ibid.*, p. 217.   [3] *Ibid.*, p. 218.

Manning's credentials as physician were suspect, to say the least. But, however inadequate his training, he did not suffer from any lack of self confidence: 'My medicines do wonderfully well, and the patients are very grateful. They have petitioned for me to go with the Mandarin tomorrow toward Giansu [Gyantse] and not to have the misery of staying here for an answer from Lhasa.' Hearing that several patients awaited him in Gyantse, Manning cheerfully exclaims, '*Tout Mieux*', but in the next moment he sighs that his doctoring is 'a great trouble'.[1]

On 5 November Manning noted in his journal: 'We left Pari Jong early in the morning . . . bitter frost . . . no wine to drink, as it must be heated first.' But despite this deprivation they mounted their horses and 'scampered over the plain'. It was somewhere between Phari Dzong and Gyantse that it must have occurred to Manning that clothing appropriate for Calcutta and the humid Huglie delta would never do in the cutting winds of the high Tibetan plateau. He admitted: 'I was not sufficiently clothed and had to borrow a heavy cloak from one of the soldiers in the General's escort.'

Geographers who later searched Manning's manuscript in vain for useful topographic details may have found some small satisfaction in a passing reference to a 'lake or sea' on which our odd traveller longed to show his 'skating skill'. This was un-doubtedly the Lake Calo Chu seen by Bogle. Manning also re-called passing some hot springs just as Bogle and Turner had before him,[2] thus his route could be traced with some accuracy. But of more interest to this gentleman traveller at the time were the 'many fine, fat, wild ducks' he saw. Obviously referring to Tibet's funeral customs, Manning quipped: 'The people of Tibet eat no birds . . . on the contrary they let the birds eat them.'[3]

The subject of wild fowl again crept into his log; he observed that he had seen the *hayta*, or *weety peety*, 'a strange appearance in the air, strongly resembling the flight of innumerable birds'. This natural phenomenon, he explained, was the result of 'conflict between the extreme cold and the burning heat of the sun'.[4]

---

[1] *Ibid.*, p. 218.　　[2] Samuel Turner, *op. cit.*, p. 220.
[3] Clements Markham, *op. cit.*, p. 220.　　[4] *Ibid.*, p. 222.

After a trying day of travel in which a runaway horse nearly threw him into a 'fearful bog', Manning could finally rest in a small village where he was lodged overnight with a Tibetan family. He recalled that 'several women and girls came in . . . undressed themselves . . . and spread their beds, long after I was laid down and quiet.' He admitted that 'now and then' he took 'an impertinent peek', but 'could discern nothing for the smoke from the yak-butter lamps'.[1]

The trials of the road were many, and as Manning approached Gyantse he could take pride in the fact that not since Turner had any Englishman penetrated so deeply into Tibet. But any sense of achievement or reflections on glory which might have occurred to Manning were crowded out by secret chagrin and the need to perform an urgent ceremony. 'I was so eaten up by little insects, which I shall not name,' he wrote, 'that I was compelled to set aside shame, and sitting down on a terrace buttress in the sunshine, dismiss as many of my retinue as I could get sight of. I suffered a good deal from these little insects whose society I was not used to.'[2]

Gyantse impressed Manning as being a 'large town, half situated on a hill and half at the foot.' He noted that 'there is an abundance of water flowing about it, which they do not seem to know how to keep off the road. There is not a blade of anything green to be seen, but there are corn fields around and a few trees. . . .' There must have been many other details about this major town in Tibet which Manning could have recorded had he been interested. But instead he takes the occasion to compose an essay on British sartorial mores in India. While an odd diversion from his account of travel through Tibet, it is a perceptive piece and in its own amusing way paints a truer picture of the Englishman in Asia than many more serious efforts have been able to do:

The warmth and thickness of a European cloth coat is not so great an evil, though evil enough in a hot climate, as the tightness of his clothing, which occasions throbbing, and a stifling sensation of heat and sweat, and probably may be very injurious to the health. He will deny, I know by experience, that his clothes are inconvenient, but his natural efforts to relieve himself betray the contrary. When he comes home in the

---

[1] *Ibid.*, p. 223.   [2] *Ibid.*, p. 225.

evening, though he is not going to bed for an hour or two, does he not take off his neck cloth and unbutton his breeches' knees with a pleasing inarticulate expression, denoting that he is somewhat relieved that his blood has room to circulate. As I, myself, have used both kinds of clothing, the European and Chinese, in hot climates, I can with confidence assert the difference in comfort, particularly while sitting still, is very great indeed, and in favour of the Chinese dress. . . .

Women in Europe, if there be a bush or branch in the way, or other mere nothing of an impediment, or if anyone stamps on their robe, or only the foot of a chair, betray a slight uneasiness, and often give vent to some expression of discontent. I have often, when dressing in long slight robes, caught myself in a similar state of mind, and using similar actions and expression, and have observed to my companions that now I understood thoroughly what the evil was that women often seem to make so much of and men so slight of. . . . It seems to me not refining too much to say that this habitual fear of entanglement, and the facility with which the dress can be laid hold of tend to take off from a man's boldness. . . .

The inconvenience which a European suffers from his dress in India he attributes to the climate; or if he does not allow that a cloth coat is hot, yet he says 'for gentlemen to meet in society without cloth coats would be highly improper. . . .' He adds, 'The natives would not respect us in any other dress,' as if it was the cut of a European's coat which held the natives in subjection, and not the Europeans.

The natives respect the Europeans in spite of their dress, for their vigour of body and mind. I am persuaded they would honour them more if their dress was less monstrous. . . .[1]

Manning's own wardrobe was at odds with his philosophy. To brave the frigid wastelands of Tibet he carried with him only 'eight grasscloth gowns and two gauze gowns, and a few light drawers'. Finally succumbing to the Chinese General's advice, Manning augmented his drawing room wardrobe in Gyantse. Through the courtesy of a military tailor he had made an 'ample, coursish, red woollen cloth robe with fur cuffs', lined with sheepskin. He also bought sheepskin stockings and Chinese boots so that he was able to keep his feet 'cosy, whatever weather might ensue'.[2]

The General, whom Manning accused of being 'no better than

---

[1] *Ibid.*, p. 229.   [2] *Ibid.*, p. 240.

an old woman' was nonetheless his sponsor and key to his success. He obviously had taken a liking to Manning and because of this the English traveller was permitted to go on to Lhasa. 'He was greatly taken with my beard,' recalled Manning, and 'seemed as if he never could sufficiently admire it.' Preening himself happily, Manning noted in his journal: 'When I had combed my beard and adjusted it properly, and he saw its tapering shape descending in one undivided lock, he again expressed his admiration, and declared he never had seen one nearly so handsome.' The eccentric Englishman fluttered on: 'The General likewise approved of my countenance and manner: he pretended to skill in physiognomy and fortune-telling; he foretold very great things of me.'[1]

The General, it seemed, was fond of music as well as tapering beards, and was 'no bad performer'. An evening's musicale in Gyantse was Manning's reward for taking an interest in his talents:

I took an opportunity one day, while he was smoking his pipe in my courtyard, of introducing the subject [of music] and paying my court to him by requesting the favour of hearing his music. This brought me an invitation to take an evening repast and wine with him, which was just what I liked. He gave a very pretty concert. . . . He performed alternatively on several instruments, and with considerable taste. Two of the soldiers acted a musical scene from a drama, while he accompanied them on the Chinese guitar. . . . The Chinese music, though rather meager to a European, has its beauties, and has like most other national music, its peculiar expression, of which our musical notation, which we vainly imagine so perfect, conveys no idea whatever. The General insisted on my giving him a specimen of European music on the Chinese flute. I was not acquainted with the fingering of that instrument, but I managed to produce something which he politely praised. He made me play several times, always making polite remarks. . . . I tried a few country dances, but perceived that that quick kind of music was not very gratifying to their ears.[2]

While the state of the medical profession in the early nineteenth century left much to be desired, Manning's credentials obviously left even more. Manning – obviously a biased judge –

---

[1] *Ibid.*, p. 229.   [2] *Ibid.*, p. 236.

recalls: 'I had great success with my medicines. I had so many patients now, both indoors and outdoors, that my time was fully occupied.' But his techniques make one wonder if Tibet was the better for his visit. Manning 'cured' the fevers of one Chinese patient and his wife with opium, Fowler's solution of arsenic and 'a few papers of bark'. This Chinese gentleman's mother-in-law who was suffering from the 'complaint of old age', was at the same time 'cheered up with a little physic'.[1]

Manning thought himself particularly successful in treating coughs, indigestion, and disorders of the eyes. 'Numbers of the monks,' he wrote, 'are afflicted with indigestion and disorders of the alimentary canal, occasioned . . . by feeding principally on parched barley flour.' Eye disorders were common in Tibet and, Manning thought, were attributable 'to the cold winds and to remaining too long in the temples, or perhaps to the salt they use.'

It was with some foreboding that Manning set off for Lhasa. He had learned from the official who delivered his permit to proceed – a drunk, described quaintly by Manning as a 'pot-valiant' – that the *Amban* in Lhasa was the same Chinese official who had been disgraced at Canton for his mismanagement of affairs at the time of the East India Company's expedition to Macao. His attitude toward Englishmen was thus assumed to be something less than friendly. Moreover, he was reputed to be a man of a particularly suspicious temper who could be expected to 'give us all the trouble in his power'. Manning wrote: 'I was sorely afraid lest the Tatar Mandarin [*Amban*] recollect having seen my face at Canton.' But the lure of Lhasa overcame any qualms the English traveller had, and off he strolled again on the final leg of the journey.

The most memorable experience *en route* to Lhasa was obviously the crossing of the Brahmaputra. Only Manning's own words can do justice to his remarkable behaviour during the ride across the swift-running river:

The reminiscences occasioned by the motion of the boat brought on a fit of European activity. I could not sit still, but must climb about, seat myself in various postures on the parapet, and lean over. The master of

---

[1] *Ibid.*, p. 232.

the boat was alarmed and sent a steady hand to hold me tight. I pointed to the ornamented prow of the boat, and assured them that I could sit there with perfect safety, and to prove to them how commodiously I was seated, bent my head and body down outside of the boat to the water's edge; but finding, by their renewed instances for me to desist, that I made them uneasy, I went back to my place and seated myself quietly. As the boat drew near shore, I meditated jumping out, but was pulled back by the immense weight of my clothes and clumsiness of my boots. I was afraid of jumping short and having the laugh against me.[1]

Manning's first impressions of Lhasa are a refreshing effort to convey something besides the state of his own psyche. Perhaps the Potala, presiding majestically over the town, inspired him as earlier scenes of the bleak Tibetan countryside had not. In fairness to Manning, it must be admitted that the only record of his trip was his diary – a very personal document indeed – and he never presumes to have recorded his observations with an eye to eventual publication. This, at least, lends a spontaneity and frankness which otherwise might be lacking.

Of the Potala, Manning wrote:

. . . the palace of the Grand Lama presented itself to our view. It seemed close at hand, but taking an eye observation upon the change of certain angles as I advanced, eighty or a hundred paces, I sagaciously informed my *munshi* that it was still four or five miles off. As we approached I perceived that under the palace at one side lay a considerable extent of marshy land. This brought to mind the Pope, Rome and what I had read of the Pontine Marshes. We passed under a large gateway whose gilded ornaments at top were so ill-fixed that some leaned one way and some another, and reduced the whole to the rock appearance of castles and turrets in pastry work. The road here, as it winds past the palace, is royally broad; it is level and free from stones, and combined with the view of the lofty towering palace, which forms a majestic mountain of building, has a magnificent effect. . . . My eye almost perpetually fixed on the palace, and roving over its parts, the disposition of which being irregular, eluded my attempts at analysis. As a whole, it seemed perfect enough. . . .[2]

Upon closer inspection the city of Lhasa passed less well. Manning described it critically as having 'nothing pleasing in its

[1] *Ibid.*, p. 251.   [2] *Ibid.*, p. 255.

appearance'. 'If the palace had exceeded my expectations,' he wrote, 'the town as far fell short of them. The habitations are begrimed with smut and dirt. The avenues are full of dogs, some growling and gnawing bits of hide which lie about in profusion and emit a charnal house smell; others limping and looking livid; others ulcerated; others starving and dying, and pecked at by the ravens, some dead and preyed upon.' 'In short,' concluded Manning, 'everything seems mean and gloomy and excited the idea of something unreal – even the mirth and laughter of the inhabitants, I thought dreamy and ghostly.'[1]

Protocol demanded that Manning first present himself to the Chinese *Amban*. Still concerned that this official might recognize him from Canton days, the nervous traveller wore Chinese spectacles to disguise his appearance, and he followed his servants advice not to speak Chinese lest he excite the Resident's suspicions. 'Coming into their [the *Amban*'s and his staff's] presence,' recalled Manning, 'I for the first time in my life performed the ceremony of *ketese* [kowtow].' 'My *munshi* was afraid I should dislike the ceremony; he knew how adverse the Europeans are to bending, but,' confessed Manning, 'I had no objection whatever in so much that, on the contrary, I was always asking when I could *ketese* or kneel; and if there was an option between one *ketese* and three, I generally chose to give three.' As it turned out there was no danger of the Tartar Mandarin recognizing Manning. 'The old dog was purblind and would not see many inches beyond his nose.'

The grand climax of Manning's remarkable journey to Lhasa was his audience with the Dalai Lama. The event took place on 17 December 1811, shortly after his arrival in Tibet's capital. Chatty as ever, the eccentric Englishman listed the various gifts he had brought to present to His Holiness. They were but trifles, he explained: 'I had a pair of good brass candlesticks which I had cleaned and furbished up and into them I put two wax candles to make a show.' Manning confided: 'To speak the truth, these candlesticks belonged to the East India Company; they were what were lent me for my use at Canton, and upon leaving that place I had honestly left them to be returned to the stores.' But,

---

[1] *Ibid.*

it seems, Manning's Chinese servant mailed them on to him in India by mistake.

The presents also included Nanking tea, English broadcloth, twenty 'new, bright dollars', and a bottle of 'genuine Smith's lavender water'. With these offerings he marched to the Potala – the first Englishman ever to be received in Lamaism's Holy See. The child-Ninth Dalai Lama must have been curious about this incongruous representative of his powerful neighbour to the south. It is unfortunate that there is no Tibetan record of the historic encounter. We do, however, have Manning's own account:

We rode to the foot of the mountain on which the palace is built, or out of which, rather, it seems to grow; but having ascended a few paces to a platform, were obliged to dismount. From here to the hall where the Grand Lama receives is a long and tedious ascent. It consists of about four hundred steps, partly stone steps in the rocky mountain, and the rest ladder steps from storey to storey in the palace. Besides this, from interval to intervals along the mountain, wherever the ascent is easy, there are stretches interspersed, where the path continues for several paces together without steps. At length we arrived at the large platform roof, off which is built the house or hall of reception. There we rested awhile, arranged the presents, and conferred with the Lama's Chinese interpreter. . . .

The *Timu-fu* [Regent] was in the hall with the Grand Lama. I was not informed of this until I entered, which occasioned me some confusion. I did not know how much ceremony to go through with one before I began with the other. I made the due obeisance, touching the ground three times with my head to the Grand Lama and once to the *Timu-fu*. I presented my gifts, delivering the coin with a handsome silk scarf with my own hands into the hands of the Grand Lama and the *Timu-fu*. While I was *ketesing*, the awkward servants contrived to let fall and break the bottle of lavender water. Of course, I seemed not to observe it, though the odiferous stream flowed close to me, and I could not help seeing it with the corner of my eye as I bowed down my head. Having delivered the scarf to the Grand Lama, I took off my hat, and humbly gave him my clean-shaved head to lay his hands upon. . . .

The Lama's beautiful and interesting face and manner engrossed almost all my attention. He was at that time about seven years old, had the simple unaffected manners of a well-educated, princely child. His face was, I thought, poetically and affectingly beautiful. He was of a gay and cheerful disposition; his beautiful mouth perpetually unbending into a graceful smile, which illuminated his whole countenance.

Sometimes, particularly when he had looked at me, his smile almost approached to a gentle laugh. No doubt my grim beard and spectacles somewhat excited his risibility, though I have afterwards, at the New Year's festival, seen him smile and unbend freely, while sitting myself unobserved in a corner, and watching his reception of various persons, and the notice he took of the strange variety of surrounding objects. He had not been seated long before he put questions to us which we rose to receive and answer. He addressed himself in the Tibet tongue to the Chinese interpreter; the Chinese interpreter to my *munshi*, my *munshi* to me in Latin. I gave answer in Latin which was converted and conveyed back in the same manner. I had been long accustomed to speak Latin with my *munshi*. There was no sentiment or shade of sentiment we could not exchange. Thus the route was circuitous, the communication was quick, and the questions and answers delivered with an accuracy which I have reason to believe seldom happens in Asia when interpreters are employed.

The Lama put the usual questions of urbanity. He inquired whether I had not met with molestations and difficulties on the road; to which I promptly returned the proper answer. I said I had had troubles, but now that I had the happiness of being in his presence, they were amply compensated. I thought of them no more. I could see that this answer pleased both the Lama and his household people. They thus found that I was not a mere rustic, but had some tincture of civility in me. They motioned to my servant . . . and we withdrew.[1]

It had obviously been a moving experience for Manning. He rhapsodized:

I was extremely affected by this interview with the Lama. I could have wept through strangeness of sensation. I was absorbed in reflection when I got home. I wrote this memorandum: 'This day I saluted the Grand Lama! Beautiful youth. Face poetically affecting – could have wept. Very happy to have seen him and his blessed smile. Hope often to see him again.'[2]

Manning gained some insight into the political undercurrents of the day. Through one of his patients, an influential Chinese official whom he referred to as the 'Mad Mandarin', Manning came to learn of a serious schism between the Tibetans and Chinese, not to mention bickering amongst the top Chinese representatives in Lhasa as well.

---

[1] *Ibid.*, pp. 265, 266.   [2] *Ibid.*, p. 266.

The death of the Eighth Dalai Lama in 1804 had stimulated popular sentiment against the Manchu suzerain. A political faction in Lhasa, which had earlier conducted pamphlet attacks against the Manchus, now openly protested to the Regent[1] against the Chinese presence in Lhasa. This faction accused certain Tibetan officials of collaborating with the Chinese and demanded the permanent withdrawal of the *Ambans*. As a result of these agitations, anti-Chinese disorders broke out in Tibet. So serious did they become that the Manchu Emperor, Chia-ch'ing, sent two special emissaries to Lhasa to investigate.

While the investigation was being conducted, ominous rumours spread throughout Lhasa further inflaming the people. Demonstrations were held and certain Tibetans were publicly accused of collaborating with the *Ambans* and stealing from the treasury. So angry did the mobs become and so hostile were the people in opposition to the Chinese that the Regent was forced to deploy Tibetan troops to protect the *Ambans*.

Sharp disagreements broke out among the Chinese investigators culminating in their replacement by two new officials sent to Lhasa in 1805. The new inquiries resulted in the recall of the *Amban* in disgrace.

Presumably Manning was referring to these episodes when he wrote that a special Chinese commission, which included the 'Mad Mandarin', the 'Tartar Mandarin', or Chief *Amban*, and a lesser *Amban* referred to as the 'Honest Mandarin', took part in an investigation of the anti-Chinese riots. The 'Honest Mandarin' was so called by Manning because he refused to accept bribes offered by the others to suppress evidence suggesting that Chinese maladministration had provoked the riots. As a result he was made to bear the blame so that the others could, themselves, escape censure. It is likely that it was Manning's 'Honest Mandarin' who was recalled in disgrace. Manning's own knowledge of these dark doings came from the ravings of his patient, the 'Mad Mandarin', whom he hints was driven mad to begin with because of a sense of guilt for the part he played in the plot to implicate his more honest colleague.

When first attending his patient, Manning 'found him not a

---

[1] Tenpai Gonpo Kundeling.

little insane, but good humoured'. 'He was uncombed, unwashed, beslimed with his own spittle and dirt,' added Manning. The Englishman's motives were clear enough: 'If I could make a cure of him,' wrote Manning, 'it would be nothing to ask him to get me admitted to Peking.'

Complications arose when the Chief *Amban* – Manning' so-called 'Tartar Mandarin' – began to take umbrage at his close relationship with the sick Mandarin. The *Amban* obviously, and with good reason, feared that Manning would learn too much through the ravings of his patient. In fact, the Mad Mandarin 'in his mad fits, confessed the bribes he had taken, mentioned the sum and offered to restore it.'[1]

Manning's patient at one point seemed to get better – 'he was more composed and his eyes were less wild'. But the *Amban's* displeasure at the relationship was growing. Manning by now had to visit his patient 'by stealth – stepping into another near house first to inquire if any of the Tartar's spies were about the premises.' Finally, however, Manning was denied access to the Mad Mandarin altogether. The pathetic soul gradually grew worse and soon died – greatly relieving, no doubt, the *Amban's* apprehensions.

Manning's observations on the Chinese position in Tibet, however scanty, is not without perception:

It is very bad policy thus perpetually to send men of bad character to govern Tibet. It no doubt displeases the Grand Lama and Tibetans in general, and tends to prevent their affections from settling in favour of the Chinese government. I cannot help thinking, from what I have seen and heard, that they would view the Chinese influence in Tibet over-thrown without many emotions of regret; especially if the rulers under the new influence were to treat the Grand Lama with respect, for this is a point in which these haughty mandarins are somewhat deficient, to the no small dissatisfaction of the good people of Lhasa.[2]

Practising medicine, while a chore, had its compensations – at least when Manning's patients were pretty Tibetan ladies. One girl, in particular, 'was still young, plump and rather handsome, and her face was washed clean'. Her attendants all the while 'stood

---

[1] Clements Markham, *op. cit.*, p. 267.   [2] *Ibid.*, p. 274.

tittering and giggling about'. Two other young lady patients also livened up the young Englishman's practice when they visited his clinic with their mother. He recalled, 'I could not find out that there was anything the matter with them except super-abundance of health and spirits.' 'It was so long since I had seen female charms of this order,' he wrote, 'that feeling their pulses rather disordered my own.'[1]

A brief entry in Manning's journal reveals that he was not always successful. One patient – the Grand Lama's own Tibetan physician, no less – called complaining of a 'stiff neck and back . . . a swelling in his knee and general debility of body and mind.' Manning gave him 'a Spanish fly blister' and an 'oily mixture for an inward complaint', and advised him 'to drink a small quantity of wine every day'. The entry concludes cryptically with the phrase, 'he died'.[2]

It would be unfair to Manning's reputation as explorer if it were not noted that he had at least made a gesture in the direction of science:

I had a small sextant with me, and an excellent time piece watch, and I much wished, now the sky remained clear and cloudless, to take a few observations; but the aperture of my window was too small and I was too subject to interruption. Our lodging had indeed a commodious flat roof, where I could have taken them easily enough; but it would have been madness in me to suffer anyone to see me looking at the heavens through an astronomical instrument. I might perhaps in the night time have observed some of the stars without being observed myself, but it was hazardous. Besides I was now very ill with acute rheumatism. . . . There was nothing I could do for geography that would compensate the risk I must run.[3]

Manning and his servant were under steady surveillance throughout their stay in Lhasa. The ever-suspicious Chinese were predictably wary of their visitor. The 'Tartar Mandarin' detested the Europeans, noted Manning. They were 'the cause of his personal misfortunes'. 'He frequently betrayed his apprehensions to me,' noted Manning – 'sometimes he said I was a missionary and at other times a spy.' The *Amban* reasoned: 'These Europeans are very formidable; now one man has come to spy

---

[1] *Ibid.*, p. 285.   [2] *Ibid.*, p. 287.   [3] *Ibid.*, p. 283.

the country – he will inform others – numbers will come, and at last he will be taking the country from us.' And making matters worse, a fantastically brilliant comet, which had appeared over Lhasa, was somehow linked to Manning's arrival and considered a harbinger of evil.

The crescendo of rumour and suspicion reached alarming proportions – at least in Manning's mind. He related with obvious horror a story which had reached his ears that he and his servant were to be 'examined by torture'. While the *Amban* clearly found the English intruder a worry, it is unlikely that he plotted violence against him; but this was not clear to the agitated Englishman who frankly acknowledged his timidity. He was, in fact, inspired to write a very subjective little essay, which he honestly entitled; 'Daydream of Terror'. Manning was no lion, perhaps, but one can nevertheless find grounds for sympathy with this lonely wanderer in a strange land. He could have been killed or incarcerated without George III knowing or caring about it. He had no credentials, no backing and no protection. There are times when cherry brandy is not enough. If Manning had a particular horror of torture, he is not alone in the world in this phobia. And, for that matter, it is more refreshing to hear the confessions of one who knows he is a coward than the boastings of a false hero. The following lines which appeared in his journal should touch a sensitive chord within all pioneers who have ventured into new worlds for the first time:

I never could, even in idea, make up my mind to submit to an execution with firmness and manliness. . . . I put myself in imagination into the situation of the prisoner accused; I suppose myself innocent; I look around; I have no resource, no refuge; instruments of torture, instruments of execution are brought by florid, high-cheeked, busy, grinning, dull-hearted men; no plea avails; no kind judge to take my part, as in England, but on the contrary, because I am accused, I am presumed guilty.

I am before evil-minded men, void of conscience, who proceed according to the forms, and violate the spirit of justice. . . . If one is before a generous-minded man, who is wantonly exercising his power, one may appeal to what is noble in his nature, and excite a flame that will dissipate his malice and dark suspicions; but these evil-minded men, who are outwardly perfect politeness, and inwardly are perfect selfishness, have no touchwood in their heart; nothing for the spark to catch hold of; one may as well strike fire against the barren sand, as appeal to their hearts. This friendlessness, this nothingness of the prisoner, is what sickens me to think of. I had rather be eaten up by a tiger than fall into such a situation and be condemned. . . . I have often striven to rectify my sensations, often, often, at Lhasa; but the associations are too strong to be thoroughly disengaged, though I hope and believe I can go far to master them as to be able to submit to any fate without acting like a coward.[1]

However intense his fears, Manning remained throughout a staunch Christian gentleman who would never compromise with the 'heathen' in matters of religion – even to save his neck. For example, he refused to twirl Tibetan prayer cylinders. While a conformist in certain ways, he admitted he was most obstinate in others: he would 'sooner die than swerve a tittle'. Toward the end of his stay in Lhasa, Manning visited a large Lamaist temple and, consistent with his principles, refused to perform the rituals of obeisance expected of Tibetans. This fact was noted and indirectly brought to his attention through his servant. Manning commented sarcastically: 'No doubt my *munshi* made out the best account he could for me to the Mandarin's people! How delicate his conscience was! So anxious to damn my soul in order to shelter his own carcase!'

Manning may have been unfair in this accusation. When he left Lhasa on 19 April his servant was not allowed to accompany him. And one can assume that the *munshi*'s treatment thereafter was less than friendly. He can't really be blamed for turning state's evidence, knowing that as a Chinese he would be at the mercy of the *Amban* long after his master had safely left Tibet.

By June 1812 Manning had returned to Calcutta none the worse for wear. He summed up his experiences in a letter to a friend: 'having lived for some time on terms of good fellowship with the lamas and made arrangements for penetration further into those unknown regions, the Emperor of China sent for my head; but as I preferred to retain it on my shoulders, I had made the best of my way back rather than go on. . . .'[2] Still determined to see the inside of China, Manning returned to the Company factory at Canton. His long absence in the Orient provoked Charles

---

[1] *Ibid.*, pp. 278, 279.   [2] *Ibid.*, p. 14.

Lamb to write him a Christmas letter in 1815, saying: 'Still in China! Down with idols – Ching-chang-fo and all his foolish priesthood. Come out of Babylon, O' my friend!'[1]

Manning's chance to penetrate the Celestial Realm finally came in 1817 when he was chosen to accompany Lord Amherst's embassy to Peking as interpreter. The Ambassador at first objected to his odd countryman's long beard, but he compromised in the end: Manning could keep his beard if he would dispense with his long Chinese gowns.

A profile of Manning by Sir John Davis of Amherst's Mission is revealing:

I knew Manning well, and liked him much. His eccentricities were quite harmless, and concerned only himself personally. His beard was merely continued from his first adoption of it previous to his journey to Lhasa and gratified his natural indolence. . . . He was seldom serious, and did not often argue any matter gravely, but in a tone of banter in which he humorously maintained the most monstrous paradoxes. . . . He did everything in his own odd and eccentric way. Being one day roused by a strange shouting, I went out and discovered it was Manning, who, wishing to cross the water and finding nobody who would attend to him, commenced a series of howls like a dog, supplemented by execrations derived from the Chinese vernacular. This led our attendant Mandarins very naturally to infer that he was mad and they lost no time in conveying him over the river to the other side, which was all he wanted.[2]

The last years of Manning's life were lived out at Bexley in England where he roamed about a cottage bare of furnishings save for his Chinese books. His beard by now was milky white and extended luxuriantly to his waist. On 2 May 1840 at the age of sixty-eight, Lhasa's English discoverer died of a paralytic stroke. One may criticize him in retrospect for not leaving behind more serious observations of Tibet's capital and long-awaited geographic data on this most unknown spot in the world. But one cannot take from him the credit of reaching the cloistered citadel of Lamaism with only his own wit and eccentric charm to help him. In whatever Nirvana is reserved for explorers of Tibet, he can feel just a little bit superior to those many others who could never quite reach this goal.

---

[1] *Ibid.*, p. 15.   [2] *Ibid.*, p. 16.

13
Abbé Huc

Two French Lazarist priests, Evarist Huc and Joseph Gabet, walked through the gates of Lhasa one day in January 1846 to become the first missionaries to see Tibet's capital since the expulsion of the Capuchins a century before. They were not allowed to establish a church as the Capuchins had done, nor were they even permitted to stay very long. From the point of view of the Church their mission was a failure; but as explorers of the northern approaches to Lhasa – roughly the route followed by Grueber in 1661 – they had accomplished a remarkable feat. The story Huc told when he returned was immensely entertaining, but it took years and the corroborating evidence of later explorers to convince the sceptics that it was essentially true. Huc's talent for titillating his readers with lively accounts of his adventures offended traditional scholars, trained to be suspicious of any embroidery on stark fact and unwilling to keep an open mind when it came to the bizarre. It was not until their fellow countryman, Prince Henry Philip of Orleans, an accomplished Tibet explorer himself, defended Huc in 1893[1] that the Lazarist's account of his journey became more or less accepted in responsible academic circles. It is, in fact, Huc's unique chronicle, reminiscent perhaps of Rubruck's style, which sets him apart from the other evangelists who visited Tibet. At least, not since Desideri had so much detail been recorded in so entertaining a fashion. Here was an individualist in the best tradition whose devotion to cause, however strong, never interfered with his human urge to meet the unbelievers on their own terms and accept what he felt was valid in their culture.

---

[1] Calman Levy, *Le P. Huc et ses Critiques* (Paris, 1893).

Both Huc and Gabet had prepared themselves well for the long journey ahead. Among the Mongols bordering north China, they found ample opportunities to examine the same Lamaist ritual which they would find in Tibet. Finally, confident that they could defeat the adversary through force of religious disputation, Huc and Gabet set out from Heishui in eastern Mongolia on their long march to Tibet in August 1844. They wore the yellow robes and mitres of the local lamas, and adopted the ways of the nomads so as to reach them through the common ground of custom.

The route chosen by the two Lazarists led them through cheerless plains which sloped away from the southern Kinghan Mountains. Once richly forested, this region had been stripped bare in the mid-seventeenth century by Chinese marauders. Since that time fierce winds churned the barren desert into awesome sand storms known as 'black burans'. And occasionally hailstorms hurled about stones of ice weighing up to two pounds. The only sanctuaries from such tantrums of nature were the *serais*, spaced infrequently along the desert route. These were large adobe inns where travellers could find warmth, food and companionship. Wayfarers huddled together around *khangs*, or long table-like platforms, under which hot air was circulated from charcoal stoves. They smoked together far into the night with the kind of comraderie universally found among travellers.

Huc enjoyed these occasions and, being a warm-hearted extrovert, found no difficulty entering into the banter of the simple Mongol travellers. Sly efforts at evangelism, however, never found their mark, nor was he so unwise as to press the attack. Passing efforts to extol the virtues of Christianity or argue religious doctrine with the Mongol lamas were effectively met by shrugs of non-comprehension or cryptic references to 'the West', i.e. Tibet, the fountainhead of the only 'true doctrine'.

The inquisitive natives found it difficult to classify the two French missionaries. Fortunately they were not mistaken for 'sea devils', as the English coastal traders were then known by the Chinese, because their hair was not red and their eyes were not blue. But just what kind of stranger they had in their midst was never clear to the insular Tartars. Nor did it particularly matter since the warm, outgoing personality of Abbé Huc and his willingness to share their simple life and endure with them the dangers of the road won them over.

Brigandage was the greatest danger which faced the travellers. Huc and Gabet frequently had to join with the others in defending the *serais* where they rested from attacking robber-tribesmen. In larger centres guarded accommodation was available but the cost of such quarters went up accordingly so that the professional militia in residence could be paid.

The long and often tedious marches gave Abbés Huc and Gabet abundant opportunities to watch the primitive priesthood of the plains administer to the nomads. Huc described an exorcism ceremony in which a demon of sickness was cast out from an ailing Tibetan before their very eyes. The ceremonies began as the local lamas congregated in the tent of the patient. Prayers were chanted continuously for a week. Around an effigy to the indisposed person the lamas swirled in an orgy of chants, incantations and prayers calculated to make the evil spirit uneasy. The climax came when the Chief Lama set fire to the effigy and had it flung far out onto the desert. The therapy was in this case eminently successful. Relatives of the sick man all converged on him with congratulations: they formed a noisy procession to accompany him to a nearby tent where he was left to regain his strength. Within a few days he was completely cured!

The Chinese frontier town of Dolon Nor, the first major town on their route, was a disagreeable place. The streets were narrow and clogged with mud and offal. Low class Chinese traders preyed on the simple and gullible Tartars. Pawnshops, overflowing with shoddy collateral, told a story of shameless Chinese exploitation. But this was Mongolia; Chinese influence would become progressively less as the two travellers moved westward away from the heart of the Empire.

Among the Ordos-Tartars on the highroad to Koko Nor, the French Abbé learned from passing pilgrims details of an astounding rite allegedly performed periodically at the Rache-Tchurin monastery. That Huc seemed to accept such tales of the supernatural as true may suggest a credulous mind. But certainly he can't be blamed for sharing a good story with his readers. Here is Huc, the story teller, at his best:

When the appointed day is come, the multitude of pilgrims assemble in the great court of the Lamasery, where an altar is raised in front of the Temple-gate. At length the Boktè appears. He advances gravely, amid the acclamations of the crowd, seats himself upon the altar, and takes from his girdle a large knife which he places upon his knees. At his feet, numerous Lamas, ranged in a circle, commence the terrible invocations of this frightful ceremony. As the recitation of the prayers proceeds, you see the Boktè trembling in every limb, and gradually working himself up into phrenetic convulsions. The Lamas themselves become excited: their voices are raised: their song observes no order, and at least becomes a mere confusion of yelling and outcry. Then the Boktè suddenly throws aside the scarf which envelopes him, unfastens his girdle, and seizing the sacred knife, slits open his stomach, in one long cut. While the blood flows in every direction, the multitude prostrate themselves before the terrible spectacle, and the enthusiast is interrogated about all sorts of hidden things, as to future events, as to the destiny of certain personages. The replies of the Boktè to all these questions are regarded by everybody as oracles.

When the devout curiosity of the numerous pilgrims is satisfied, the Lamas resume, but now calmly and gravely, the recitation of their prayers. The Boktè takes, in his right hand, blood from his wound, raises it to his mouth, breathes thrice upon it, and then throws it into the air, with loud cries. He next passes his hand rapidly over his wound, closes it, and everything after a while resumes its pristine condition, no trace remaining of the diabolical operation, except extreme prostration. The Boktè once more rolls his scarf around him, recites in a low voice a short prayer; then all is over, and the multitude disperse, with the exception of a few of the especially devout, who remain to contemplate and to adore the blood-stained altar which the Saint has quitted.[1]

Between Kuk Khoto and Koko Nor flowed the great Yellow River. It was in spate when the two travellers reached it and proved to be a formidable obstacle. Its rampaging waters overflowed the plains on either bank, making the crossing time-consuming and hazardous. But once safely across, Huc and Gabet encountered no major difficulties along the route to Sining. In the more intensively cultivated areas there was a tendency for the road to lose itself in a maze of garden plots, but in most

---

[1] E. Huc, *Souvenirs of a Journey through Tartary, Tibet and China* (Peking, Lazarist Press, 1931), Vol. I, pp. 268, 269.

stretches of this well-trod Central Asian trade route the travellers experienced no problems. Kumbun Monastery, near lake Koko Nor on the eastern border of ethnic Tibet, seemed a good place for Huc and Gabet to break their journey and devote several weeks to the further study of Lamaism. Here also seemed a challenging place to preach the gospel. If they could succeed in this holy sanctuary of Lamaism, perhaps a permanent mission could be established.

It was near Kumbun that Tsong Khapa, Tibet's great fourteenth-century Buddhist reformer, had been born. Since then pilgrims from all over Tibet and Mongolia have flocked here to pay reverend homage to the founder of the *Gelugpa*, or 'Yellow Hat', sect of Lamaism.

Under the colourful tutelage of one 'Sandara the Bearded', a charming extrovert of a lama, the two priests learned much of the history and folklore of Lamaism at Kumbun. The story of Tsong Khapa's birth for example, is not only a momentous event in Tibetan history, but it provides an accurate glimpse of life in the barren mountains of Amdo. Huc's account of this epic doubtless reflects long conversations with the irrepressible Sandara and because of this, his version of Tsong Khapa's birth may differ from more orthodox versions. Nevertheless, the story as told by Huc is as charming as it is interesting and deserves to be repeated:

... toward the middle of the fourteenth century of our era, a shepherd of the land of Amdo, named Lombo-Moke, had set up his black tent at the foot of a mountain, near the entrance to a deep ravine, through which, over a rocky bed, meandered an abundant stream. Lombo-Moke shared with his wife, Chingtsa-Tsio, the cares of pastoral life. They possessed no numerous flocks; some twenty goats and a few *sarligues*, or long-haired cattle, constituted all their wealth. For many years they had lived alone and childless in these wild solitudes. Each day Lombo-Moke led his animals to the neighbouring pastures while Chingtsa-Tsio, remaining alone in her tent, occupied herself with the various preparations of milk, or with weaving after the manner of the women of Amdo, a coarse linen with the long hair of the *sarligues*.

One day, Chingtsa-Tsio, having descended to the bottom of the ravine to draw water, experienced faintness and fell senseless on a large stone which bore inscribed on it various characters in honour of the Buddha. When Chingtsa-Tsio came to herself, she felt a pain in the side, and at once comprehended that the fall had rendered her fruitful. In the year of the Fire-hen (1357) nine months after this mysterious event, she brought into the world a son, whom Lombo-Moke named Tsong Khapa, from the appellation of the mountain at whose feet his tent had stood for several years past. The marvellous child had, at his birth, a white beard and his face wore an air of extraordinary majesty.[1]

When three years old the divinely-conceived child resolved he would renounce the world, much as Buddha had done, and to devote his life to religion. His mother shaved his head in the manner of a lama and threw his long, flowing locks outside their tent. 'From this hair, there forthwith sprung a tree, the wood of which dispensed an exquisite perfume around, and each leaf of which bore, engraved on its surface, a character in the sacred language of Tibet.'[2]

Tsong Khapa retreated from the world, leaving even his parents, and spent the next period of his life on the summit of the wildest mountains in profound meditation and prayer. It was at this time that 'a lama from one of the most remote regions of the West', visited the land of Ando. According to Lamaist tradition the stranger from the West was unique in his appearance, and, wrote Huc: 'People especially remarked on his great nose, and his eyes that gleamed with a supernatural fire.'[3] Overwhelmed with the sanctity of the stranger, Tsong Khapa prostrated himself at his feet and begged to have the opportunity to study with him. The stranger for his part, was no less impressed with the piety and wisdom of Tsong Khapa and was determined to become his disciple. Together they studied and worshipped until the stranger, 'having initiated his pupil in all the doctrines recognized by the most reknowned saints of the West,' died on a stone slab, high on a mountain.

Huc, like so many of his predecessors, was struck with the similarities in Christian and Buddhist ritual. Not only was there the account of Tsong Khapa's immaculate conception and other reflections of the Christian story in legends of the Great Reformer's youth, but there were 'the service with double choirs, the psalmody, the exorcisms, the censer . . . the benediction

[1] E. Huc, *Souvenirs of a Journey through Tartary, Tibet and China*, Vol. II, pp. 91, 92.
[2] *Ibid.*   [3] *Ibid.*, p. 93.

given by the Lamas by extending the right hand over the heads
of the faithful; the chaplet, ecclesiastical celibacy,' to name but a
few. Huc was convinced that these similarities could be traced to
early Christian influences.

Being familiar with the history of Mongol missions to the
Pope in medieval times, Huc postulated that the 'barbarians . . .
must have been struck with the pomp and splendour of the
ceremonies of Catholic worship and must have carried back with
them into the desert enduring memories of what they had seen.'
John of Monte-Corvino, first Archbishop of Peking in 1307, had
organized a choir of Mongol monks and practised them daily in
the ceremonies of the Catholic faith. Surely it was reasonable to
assume that his influence must also have been felt far and wide.
Huc asks: 'May it not be reasonably inferred that this stranger
with the great nose was an European, one of those Catholic
missionaries who at the precise period penetrated in such numbers into Upper Asia?' The good Abbé pointed out that on more
than one occasion the resident lamas at Kumbun commented
upon 'the singularity of our features'. saying that 'we were of the
same land with the Master of Tsong Khapa'.[1] It would indeed
seem plausible that some of the ritual, the superficial attributes
of reform Buddhism as introduced by Tsong Khapa, were inspired by the teachings of early Catholic missionaries.

Kumbun means 'ten thousand images' and refers to the
famous tree which, it is said, sprang from Tsong Khapa's hair
and whose leaves thereafter were inscribed by Tibetan characters
with religious significance. Huc and Gabet were understandably
eager to find out whether this phenomenon did, in fact, exist.
Here is the evidence presented by Abbé Huc who staunchly
defends it as the truth:

At the foot of the mountain on which the Lamasery stands, and not far
from the principle Buddhist temple, is a great square enclosure
formed by brick walls. Upon entering this we were able to examine at
leisure the marvellous tree, some of the branches of which had already
manifested themselves above the wall. Our eyes were first directed
with earnest curiosity to the leaves, and we were filled with an absolute

[1] *Ibid.*, pp. 96–8.

consternation of astonishment at finding that, in point of fact, there were upon each of the leaves well-formed Tibetan characters, all of a green colour, some darker, some lighter than the leaf itself.[1]

Huc confessed that his first impression was one of suspicion, but 'after a minute examination of every detail', he could discover no evidence of deception. Even when he removed a piece of old bark, the young bark under it 'exhibits the indistinct outlines of characters in a germinating state, and what is very singular, these new characters are not infrequently different from those which they replace.'[2]

Huc may have been ingenuous in his ready acceptance of Tibetan mysteries. But he sought to report objectively the beliefs of the Tibetans, graciously refraining from scoffing at their validity. For example, he describes as fact the Tibetan belief that the mortal remains of Tsong Khapa – as well preserved in death as in life – lie unsupported a few inches above the floor of his crypt in the lamasery of Kaldan near Lhasa.

In commenting on the state of Tibet's medical science, Huc also concedes all benefit of doubt. He admits generously that they 'may ... be in possession of very important secrets, which science alone is capable of explaining, but which very possibly science itself may never discover.' The Abbé suppresses any derisive thoughts which may have run through his mind when, in coldly clinical terms, he describes the Tibetan method of urinalysis. Tibetan physicians, it seems, 'attach extreme importance to the inspection of the patient's water,' whatever the complaint. 'They examine it with the most minute attention, and take the greatest heed to all the changes undergone by its colour; they whip it from time to time, with a wooden spatula, and they put it up to the ear to ascertain how much noise it makes; for in their view, a patient's water is mute or silent according to his state of health.'[3]

Kumbun was the site of a much-revered Faculty of Medicine, noted for its advanced herbology. Every year in early September the learned lamas of Kumbun's medical college trekked to the nearby valley of Chogortan to collect medicinal herbs. Once

---

[1] *Ibid.*, pp. 99, 100.   [2] *Ibid.*   [3] *Ibid.*, p. 156.

there, encamped in tents sheltered by the great trees of the Chogortan monastery, they went forth each morning to search in the mountains for plants having exceptional curative powers. 'Before sunset, the Lama physicians returned, ladened with faggots of branches and piles of plants and grasses.' Abbé Huc wrote that he and Gabet 'were often obliged to escort in person those who had special charge of the aromatic plants; for our camels, which attracted by the odour, always put themselves in pursuit of these personages, would otherwise . . . without the smallest scruple, have devoured those precious samples destined for the relief of suffering humanity.'[1]

The harvesting of herbs lasted eight days. Five additional days were devoted to the selection and classification of the various items collected. Then on the fourteenth day the product was distributed – a small part going to each student, while the bulk of the harvest was retained by the Faculty of Medicine. After being thoroughly dried back at Kumbun, the herbs were reduced to powder and divided into small doses, neatly enveloped in red paper and labelled with Tibetan characters. The Abbé notes disapprovingly that 'the pilgrims who visit Kumbun buy these remedies at exhorbitant prices.' He adds: 'The Tartar-Mongols never return home without an ample supply of them, having an unlimited confidence in whatever emanates from Kumbun, even though the very same roots and grasses grow in abundance in their own lands.'[2]

Clearly fascinated by Tibetan medicine, Huc has this to say in general about the profession:

The Tibetan physicians are as empirical as those of other countries – possibly somewhat more so. They assign to the human frame four hundred and forty maladies, nothing more nor less. The books, which the lamas of the Faculty of Medicine are obliged to study and learn by heart, treat of four hundred and forty maladies, indicating their characteristics, the means of identifying them, and the manner of combating them. These books are a hotch-potch of aphorisms, more or less obscure, and of a host of special recipes.[3]

The missionaries' stay at Kumbun came to an end when they refused to don lamas' robes. Somehow, to do so would symbolize

---

[1] *Ibid.*, pp. 154, 155.   [2] *Ibid.*, p. 157.   [3] *Ibid.*, p. 156.

compromise with the unbeliever – perhaps this was anticipated when the Monastery had insisted on their guests conforming to their customs in clothing. It would not be strange if the monks had grown weary of their religious disputation and eager to see them on their way.

Having endured eighteen months of hard travel, Huc and Gabet on 29 June 1846 finally reached Lhasa where they would endure severe 'moral sufferings' at the hands of the 'infidel population' before retracing their steps to China. In Tibet's holy capital they found modest lodging in the uppermost rooms of a large Tibetan house. To reach their accommodation they had to climb twenty-six rickety steps without railing, so steep and narrow that they were forced to mount with both hands and feet. Their room was lighted by a slit of a window and a small round hole in the ceiling. The purpose of the hole was to permit the smoke from their faggot-burning stove to escape; but it also provided an entrance for the wind, rain and snow which most of the time swept the cold Tibetan plateau. But, as the travel-hardened Huc remarked: 'Those who have followed the nomadic life are not deterred by such trifles.'[1]

A small closet off the main room served as kitchen and pantry. The missionaries' loyal servant, Samdadchiemba, who had suffered with them the rigours of the Mongolian and Tibetan deserts as cameleer, now became cook and steward. He cooked on a large brick stove, and kept in order the sparse furnishings which consisted of two goatskins spread on the floor, two saddles, some old shoes, two dilapidated trunks, three ragged robes and ragged bed rolls stacked in the corner.

Huc recorded with admirable detail his observations of the city. 'The principle streets of Lhasa are broad, well laid out and tolerably clean,' he wrote, but 'the suburbs are revoltingly filthy'. The houses in the city were for the most part large and handsome, built 'some with stone, some with brick and some with mud'. Huc noticed that in one of the outlying districts the houses were made from the horns of oxen and sheep. 'These singular constructions,' he remarked, 'are of extreme solidity.' 'The horns of the oxen being smooth and white, and those of the

---

[1] *Ibid.*, p. 216.

sheep, on the contrary, rough and black . . . are susceptible of infinite combinations and are arranged accordingly in all sorts of fantastic designs.'[1]

No description can convey an accurate impression of Lhasa without featuring the Potala, which dominates the scene. Huc, like all other travellers to the See of Lamaism, stood in awe of this towering structure. He wrote:

The palace of the Talé-Lama merits, in every respect, the celebrity which it enjoys throughout the world. North of the town . . . there rises a rugged mountain of slight elevations and of conical form, which, amid the plain, resembles an islet on the bosom of a lake. Upon this grand pedestal, the work of nature, the adorers of the Talé-Lama have raised the magnificent palace wherein their Living Divinity resides in the flesh.

Huc noted that the palace 'is an aggregation of several temples, of various size and decoration'. The central structure overlooks the rest and culminates in a dome 'entirely covered with plates of gold'.

The secondary palaces grouped around the great temple serve as residences for the lamas, 'whose continual occupation is to serve and do honour to the living Buddha'. Huc observed that 'two fine avenues of magnificent trees lead from Lhasa to the Buddha-la [Potala] and there you always find crowds of foreign pilgrims, telling the beads of their long Buddhist chaplets; and lamas of the court, attired in rich costume and mounted on horses splendidly caparisoned. The Potala inspires a strange silence in which religious meditations . . . occupy all men's minds.'[2]

In contrast is the city, itself. Here, 'all is excitement, and noise, and pushing . . . every single soul in the place being ardently occupied in the grand business of buying and selling.' Commerce and religious devotion attracted to Tibet's capital an infinite number and variety of strangers so that 'the streets, always crowded with pilgrims and traders, present a marvellous variety of physiognomies, costumes, and languages.'[3]

Huc's description of the Tibetan man portrays a colourful person:

---

[1] *Ibid.*, p. 217.   [2] *Ibid.*, p. 219.   [3] *Ibid.*

The Tibetans are of the middle height; and combine, with the agility and suppleness of the Chinese, the force and vigour of the Tartars. Gymnastic exercises of all sorts and dancing are very popular with them, and their movements are cadenced and easy. As they walk about, they are always humming some psalm or popular song; generosity and frankness enter largely into their character; brave in war, they face death fearlessly; they are as religious as the Tartars, but not so credulous. Cleanliness is of small estimation among them; but this does not prevent them from being very fond of display and rich sumptuous clothing.

The Tibetans do not shave the head, but let the hair flow over their shoulders, contenting themselves with clipping it every now and then, with the scissors. The dandies of Lhasa, indeed, have of late years adopted the custom of braiding their hair in the Chinese fashion, decorating the tresses with jewellery, precious stones and coral. The ordinary head-dress is a blue cap, with a broad border of black velvet surmounted with a red tuft; on high days and holidays, they wear a great red hat, in form not unlike the Basque barret-cap, only larger and decorated at the rim with long, thick fringe. A full robe fastened on the right side with four hooks, and girded round the waist by a red sash, red or purple cloth boots, complete the simple, yet graceful costume of the Tibetan men. Suspended from the sash is a green taffeta bag, containing their inseparable wooden cups, and two small purses, of an oval form and richly embroidered, which contain nothing at all, being designed merely for ornament.[1]

The ladies, too, were colourfully dressed but disfigured by an incredible toilet custom which required them to smear their faces 'with a sort of black, glutinous varnish, not unlike currant jelly'. The origin of the practice, according to Huc's research, can be found some 200 years before when Tibetan women flaunted their natural beauty so appealingly that even the rigid discipline of the monasteries began to break down. In order to arrest the libertinism which was infecting the country, the King published an edict prohibiting women from appearing in public without the heavy varnish calculated to mask their beauty and make them less tempting. 'And,' exclaims Huc, 'the women have blackened themselves furiously and uglified themselves fearfully down to the present time.' But as time passed, the anti-cosmetic motivation was replaced by a religious one: 'women

---

[1] *Ibid.*, pp. 219, 220.

who daub themselves most disgustingly being reputed the most pious.'[1]

The proper Huc could only comment ruefully that, however black the women's faces are painted, 'there is lamentable licentiousness amongst them'. 'Christianity alone can redeem the pagan nations from the shameful vices in which they wallow.' But even Huc, with all his asceticism, had to admit that in Tibet 'there is less corruption than in other pagan countries' and that the women at least enjoy a great freedom 'instead of vegetating, prisoners in the depths of their houses'.[2]

Huc took pains to investigate the foreign community in Lhasa. He described the 'Pebouns', or Indians from the south slopes of the Himalayas in Bhutan, as being the most numerous of the foreigners. Of slight frame, 'their features are rounder than those of the Tibetans; their complexion very dark, the eyes small, black and roguish; the forehead is marked with a dark, cherry coloured spot.' Dressed in a uniform pink robe and small felt skull cap, they ply their trade as jewellers and metal-workers in the Lhasa bazaar. It is thanks to the Pebouns that Lhasa's splendid gilt temple roofs were built. Their workshops and laboratories are nearly underground, being entered by a 'low, narrow, opening, down three or four steps'. Over the doors of their quarters are invariably painted a red globe and white crescent meant to symbolize the sun and moon.

The *Katchi*, or Kashmiri Moslems, are the second largest minority group in Lhasa. Distinguished by their turbans and luxuriant beards, they stride about town with a certain air of superiority. They originally came to Tibet from Kashmir several centuries before to escape the despotism of a particularly notorious ruler, but, having prospered as merchants, they elected to stay. They are the only class permitted to travel to India and thus have a monopoly on the lucrative trade between the two countries. In Calcutta they trade Chinese silks and Russian linen for knives, scissors, cutlery and British cotton goods. They also serve a useful function by bringing back news of the English Empire for the benefit of apprehensive officials in Lhasa.

The Kashmir merchants described the English to Huc as 'the most cunning people in the world; little by little they are

---

[1] *Ibid.*, p. 221.   [2] *Ibid.*, p. 224.

acquiring possession of all the countries of India, but it is always rather by strategem than by open force.' 'Instead of overthrowing the authorities,' recounted Huc, 'they cleverly manage to get them on their side, to enlist them in their interest.' The English position is best described by an old Kashmiri saying: "The world is Allah's, the land the Pashas', but it is the Company that rules.'[1]

Huc and Gabet were received in Lhasa with much suspicion. The Regent surrounded them with spies who clumsily pretended to be traders. The government's agents would loiter in their quarters, subjecting them to inane questioning. Finally, realizing that this line of approach was getting nowhere, the Regent sent for the two missionaries and their servant, Samdadchiemba, so that he might interview them in person.

Sitting cross-legged on a thick cushion covered with a tiger-skin, the Regent gazed at his foreign visitors for a long while in silence. He turned his head alternately to the right and left, smiling quizzically. Finally, breaking the silence, Abbé Huc spoke up in French, saying: 'this gentleman seems a good fellow: our affair will go on very well.'

Since neither the Regent nor anyone in his entourage could understand this strange tongue, Huc was asked to translate his remarks. On hearing the Abbé's sentiments, the Regent quipped merrily that in truth he was not kindly, but very ill-natured. Nonetheless the right note had been struck and henceforward the missionaries got on well with their interrogator.

Less pleasant was their encounter with the Chinese *Amban*. This imperious mandarin, named Kishan, was most objectionable. He had previously crossed swords with the 'foreign devils', when, as Governor General, he faced the British in Canton at the outset of the 'Opium War' during the spring of 1840. Thus, he was in no mood to extend undue cordiality to the foreigners who now stood before him. During the 'Opium War' it had been Kishan's misfortune to be made scapegoat for British successes. Although he had, in fact, quite accurately alerted his Emperor to the power of the British opponent with its steamship fleet[2] and

---

[1] *Ibid.*, p. 230.

[2] When British steamships appeared off Canton in 1840, Kishan wrote the Emperor: 'They [the British] can fly across the water without wind or tide, with the current against them.' (Henry McAleavy, *The Modern History of China*, New York, Praeger, 1967, p. 49.)

powerful cannon and, otherwise handled the situation as well as could be expected, he was made to bear the brunt of the Emperor's frustration. Eventually, however, the unhappy Kishan was rehabilitated and posted to Lhasa where Huc and Gabet were thus destined to bear the full force of his bitterness toward all 'foreign devils'.

Kishan attempted, among other things, to extract from Huc and Gabet information about their Chinese associates back in Peking. When the two abbés refused to compromise their friends and converts in China, the *Amban* angrily smote the table with his fist in frustration. He then turned on Samdad-chiemba and proceeded to villify him for embracing the religion of the foreign 'barbarians'. The poor servant, quivering with each new volley of questions, staunchly defended his faith.

After their ordeal with the *Amban*, Huc and Gabet were again summoned by the Regent. It was late at night when the latter, quite alone, tried to comfort the distraught missionaries. He recognized their predicament and meant to convey to them his own personal sympathy. He meant also to warn them that the Chinese *Amban* suspected them of being foreign spies intent upon mapping the vassal lands of his Emperor.

It turned out that the Regent, too, had some fear that the two Abbés were, in fact, plotting a route through which a foreign army would march on Tibet. Until their personal effects could be searched for surveying equipment, the Regent – however friendly his instincts were – felt obliged to keep them confined as 'guests' of the palace.

Lodged in a cubicle furnished only with two hard benches, Huc and Gabet tried to get much-needed sleep despite the visits of curious Tibetans. Huc recalled: 'In all those eyes staring at us there was neither sympathy nor ill-will; they simply expressed vapid curiosity . . . we represented merely a kind of zoological phenomenon.'[1]

In the morning the two missionaries and their servant were taken back to their own quarters in town where they were asked to submit all their effects to inspection. The Regent personally attended this ceremony. He seated himself squarely in the

[1] E. Huc, *op. cit.*, Vol. II, p. 267.

middle of the room on a gilded chair as the two missionaries spread all their possessions on the floor. When this ordeal was over the Regent jovially observed that he had never really thought them dangerous to begin with. Relieved that no surveying instruments had been found, he brought forth a golden seal which he applied to all the missionaries' bags in preparation for still another inspection in the presence of the *Amban*.

Huc gives a good picture of the wonderment with which the Chinese and Tibetans at the *Amban's* court greeted each new object brought forth from their bags:

We took out the contents, one after another, and displayed them on a large table. First came some French and Latin volumes, then some Chinese and Tartar books, church linen, ornaments, sacred vases, rosaries, crosses, medals, and a magnificent collection of lithographs. All the spectators were lost in contemplation of this small European museum. They opened large eyes, touched each other with the elbow, and smacked their tongues in token of admiration. . . . The faces of all brightened up, and they seemed entirely to forget that we were suspected and dangerous people. The Tibetans put out their tongues and scratched their ears at us; and the Chinese made us the most sentimental bows. Our bag of medals especially attracted attention, and it seemed to be anticipated that, before we left the court, we should make a large distribution of their dazzling gold pieces.[1]

The greatest success of all was a microscope which Abbé Huc had in his possession. The *Amban* had some notion of what this instrument was, and assuming the airs of a very superior person, he undertook to explain it to the others.

Huc and Gabet had passed the test. No surveying instruments or maps of their own drawing had been found. They were guiltless. What maps they did possess – printed maps of Asia and the world – served to fascinate the Regent. He thought it nothing less than miraculous to have his country spread out before him, although he found the distance between Lhasa and Calcutta distressingly short.

Now that they had been accepted, the two missionaries arranged a small chapel. Out of curiosity the Tibetans at first flocked to the church and filed through in a seemingly endless

---

[1] *Ibid.*, p. 273.

procession. A few seemed genuinely interested in the new faith taught by the two priests. But like the Jesuits and Capuchins before them, Huc and Gabet were more intent upon making conversions at the top. As Huc wrote frankly: 'Whilst we were making efforts to spread the evangelical seed amongst the population of Lhasa, we did not neglect the endeavour to sow the divine seed also in the very palace of the Regent.'[1]

Almost every evening the two missionaries visited with the Regent who seemed to enjoy religious disputation. There seemed to be much similarity in their respective doctrines; only the Lamaist doctrines of the origin of the world and the transmigration of souls prevented the Regent from accepting Christianity. Or, at least, this was how Huc consoled himself after failing to bring the Regent into the fold.

The Regent and Huc found much else to talk about. The Regent was eager to learn about France and quick to be impressed. He asked detailed questions about all aspects of life in the missionaries' homeland. He was understandably amazed with Huc's description of Daguerre's new camera and with the astronomical instruments with which to search the heavens. There were also the aerial ships and railway trains to describe – or try to describe. The astonished Regent could only waggle his head at such miracles. Nothing in the world of science, however, dumbfounded the Regent as much as Huc's microscope – particularly after the missionary had cajoled the Regent into producing a louse plucked from his person for inspection under the lense. The rat-sized monster which the Regent then saw through the viewer caused him to recoil in terror and hide his face in his hands.

The *Amban* also found fascinating Huc's tales of the outside world, even though he had had some exposure to Western ways in China. He had heard all about Queen Victoria and how her husband was kept virtually locked up in the palace gardens. Huc, a French nationalist to the core, did nothing to disabuse the anti-British Kishan of this curious misconception. 'In France,' he said smugly, 'the women are in the gardens and the men in the State.'[2]

---

[1] *Ibid.*, p. 282.   [2] *Ibid.*, p. 287.

Huc and Gabet were eager to meet the child-Dalai Lama, and had been promised an audience at the Potala by the Regent. But the sudden outbreak of a smallpox epidemic caused the plans to be abandoned. Tibet's Pontiff could not be exposed to anyone who could conceivably infect him.

Not a year goes by but that this scourge strikes Tibet. So feared is it that the families of those stricken are banished from the towns to eke out an existence on fruit and berries in the mountains; or, as is more likely, to become the prey of wild beasts. Huc was quick to see the evangelical leverage which would be his if only he could import smallpox vaccine. 'The missionary who should be fortunate enough to endow the Tibetans with so invaluable a blessing, would assuredly acquire over their minds an influence capable of competing with that of the Tale [Dalai] Lama himself,' wrote Huc. Quite carried away by this scheme, he added: 'The introduction of vaccination into Tibet by the missionaries would, not improbably, be the signal of the downfall of Lamaism, and permit the establishment of the Christian religion among these infidel tribes.'[1] Here, finally could be the Christian miracle which Kublai Khan had invited five centuries before as he compared the merits of Christianity and Buddhism in his search for a new state religion.

Huc and Gabet had been in Lhasa but two months when the *Amban*, the ever-antagonistic Kishan, took steps to expel them. The bitterly disappointed missionaries blamed the abrupt end of their mission on Kishan's fear that their influence constituted a threat to China's suzerainty. Huc wrote: 'Christianity and the French name excited too forcibly the sympathy of the people of Lhasa, that the preachers of the religion of the Lord of Heaven should be driven from Lhasa.'[2]

The Regent protested to the *Amban*, but was peremptorily told: 'You Tibetans do not comprehend the gravity of this matter . . . If they [Huc and Gabet] remain long at Lhasa, they will spellbind you. You will not be able to keep from adopting their belief and then the Talé Lama is undone.'[3] According to Huc, the question of their continued presence had at length provoked such a quarrel between the Regent and the *Amban* that a

---

[1] *Ibid.*, p. 295.   [2] *Ibid.*, p. 304.   [3] *Ibid.*, p. 307.

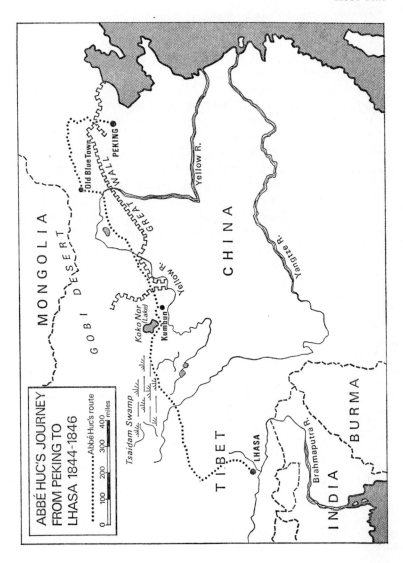

ABBÉ HUC'S JOURNEY
FROM PEKING TO
LHASA 1844-1846

.... Abbé Huc's route

0 100 200 300 400
miles

MONGOLIA

GOBI DESERT

Old Blue Town

PEKING

GREAT WALL

Yellow R.

CHINA

Koko Nor (Lake)

Kumbun

Yellow R.

Yangtze R.

Tsaidam Swamp

TIBET

LHASA

Brahmaputra R.

BURMA

INDIA

political crisis of major proportions was shaping up. 'For fear of compromising the Regent, and of becoming perhaps the cause of lamentable dissensions between China and Tibet,' Huc and Gabet decided to leave.

While the Regent was sad and a little embarrassed by the two missionaries' decision, Kishan was obviously relieved. As the Emperor's representative, responsible for protecting China's paramountcy in Tibet, he could tolerate no other foreign influence in Lhasa. Kishan provided Huc and Gabet with horses and an escort. He even entrusted to them a considerable treasure which he wanted safely transported to the borders of China. The return trip was a long and arduous one. In crossing the last range before entering China, the exhausted missionaries were nearly buried in the snow. But in June 1846, three months after leaving Lhasa they were safely back in China.

Never again would a Christian mission in Lhasa be attempted. The next Westerners to reach Tibet's capital would carry the standard of empire rather than the cross of Christ, and Tibet would lose its tranquil isolation to become a victim of big power politics.

Part Four

The Imperialists

14

The Pundits

As the Himalayas became better known it was inevitable that the still-uncharted Tibetan plateau stretching far beyond would take its place as an object of further exploration. Hastings's dream of profit – Tibet's fabled gold and new markets for trade – had, if anything, become even more tantalizing as this elusive goal became more remote. But in the wake of the 1857 Sepoy Rebellion, imperial imperatives replaced narrower Company interests: after 1858, India was not only a prized possession, but also a serious responsibility for the Crown. Its defence demanded close attention to the great land border to the north and intelligence on what lay beyond.

In the years to come, British policy in the sub-continent would be obsessed with frontiers. The 'buffer' concept or, as Lord Curzon would later define it, the frontier in depth, would dominate British strategic thinking. The conflict with the warlike Gurkhas in 1814–16 was a sharp reminder that native enemies could threaten India's northern borders. But as the century advanced it became apparent that Russia posed the real threat and that the contest would have ramifications far beyond India. The eastward expanding empire of the Czar must invariably exert pressure on India just as it had on China. Collision seemed possible anywhere from eastern Persia through Tibet, but the trans-Himalayan regions of eastern Turkestan and Tibet were unique since here all three empires met to present a particularly complicated and explosive situation. It was important that these regions be explored and charted.

One of the great names of early nineteenth-century trans-Himalayan exploration is Thomas Moorcroft. The exploits of this Indian civil servant provided the first accurate topographical data on the jagged mountain wall which forms the sub-continent's northern and north-western natural boundaries. In 1812 Moorcroft and Hyder Jung Hearsey, the natural son of a Bengal infantry officer, explored the Kumaon approaches to the Himalayas on the west flank of Nepal. Disguised as native *fakirs*, they made their way across the Himalayan range into western Tibet to become the first Englishmen to see holy Mount Kailas and the sacred lakes, Manasarovar and Rakas-Tal, which mirror its impressive peak. Recrossing the Kumaon district on their way home, the two explorers were captured on orders of Nepalese authorities and grossly mistreated. Only a fortuitous encounter with two sympathetic and influential Bhutia Rawat brothers, Bir Singh and Deb Singh, saved them from a more serious fate. The Singh brothers intervened to obtain the prisoners' release and thus began a relationship with the British which would span two generations: their sons were destined to become two of India's most ingenious native explorers and would carry on the work of the early British explorers.

Later Moorcroft and a Company geologist named George Trebeck devoted five years to the exploration of Ladakh and Baltistan, north-west of Ladakh. They probably did their best work in exploring the high Karakorums and are credited with discovering the Karakorum Pass linking Ladakh and Eastern Turkestan. But their long range reconnaissance of western Turkestan is what they are best but sadly remembered for. In August 1825 Moorcroft met his end mysteriously some 200 miles south of Bokhara. Trebeck, whose letter carried this melancholy news, died himself before he could tell the complete story – if indeed he ever knew it. It is probable that the unfortunate Moorcroft was robbed and murdered by local tribesmen. A fanciful report that he had not died, but instead had made his way secretly to Lhasa and lived there in disguise for twelve years, can probably be dismissed as imaginative conjecture on the part of Abbé Huc who first reported this story. Huc based his intriguing but almost certainly fallacious conclusions on an account given him by a Tibetan whom he met in Lhasa who had either worked for Moorcroft in Bokhara, himself, or had robbed the real servant of letters written by Moorcroft.[1]

---

[1] E. Huc, *op. cit.*, Vol. II, p. 298.

The British acquired the Kumaon-Garhwal region as a result of the Treaty of Segauli, which ended the two-year war with Nepal in 1816. This region was thereafter open for exploration. The first to take advantage of this situation were John Hodgson and James Herbert. Others associated with early exploration of Kumaon and the area north and north-east of Simla were the brothers Alexander and J. G. Gerard. G. W. Traill, who served as Commissioner of Kumaon from 1817 to 1835 and whose name was given to one of the high passes along the Himalayan watershed, also deserves credit for his original exploration in this region.

Lieutenant Henry Strachey of the 66th regiment of the Bengal Native Infantry was perhaps the best known British officer to follow Moorcroft in the exploration of western Tibet beyond Kumaon. Like Moorcroft, Strachey was intrigued by Lake Manasarovar and Mount Kailas, those unique holy places which attract Hindu and Buddhist pilgrims alike. On catching his first glimpse of Kailas in October 1846, he described this snow-capped Asian Olympus as being 'remarkable for the deep purple-blue colour of their lower rocky parts'. He added extravagantly: 'The beauty of this novel scene appeared to me to surpass anything that I had seen on the south side of the Himalaya.'

In 1845 Lieutenant Richard Strachey covered much the same ground as his brother Henry. Accompanied by J. E. Winterbottom, Richard Strachey set out to settle a long-standing topographical argument as to whether or not there was a water link between Lakes Manasarovar and Rakas-Tal. This point was critical in determining whether Rakas-Tal, from which the Sutlej River begins its flow, or Manasarovar is the ultimate source of this great river. Moorcroft, who had not seen any channel between the lakes, erroneously gave to Rakas-Tal the distinction of being the true source of the Sutlej. Henry Strachey recognized, however, that most of the time the water level of both lakes was high enough to cause a river to flow between them. He had, himself, seen 'a large stream, 100 feet wide and three feet deep, running rapidly from east to west through a well defined channel' and correctly concluded that it must join the two lakes.[1]

---

[1] Sven Hedin, *Trans-Himalaya*, Vol. III, p. 221.

Richard Strachey confirmed his brother's earlier findings when he saw from a rise on the isthmus between Manasarovar and Rakas-Tal the same stream. The Strachey brothers, having actually seen the channel, must therefore be given credit for claiming Manasarovar as the ultimate source of the Sutlej. It had been Moorcroft's bad luck to reach the lakes during a dry spell when the channel was dry.[1]

The death of the Punjab leader, Ranjit Singh, and the Sikh wars which followed focused attention on Hindu Jammu, Moslem Kashmir and Lamaist Ladakh, all buffer areas which lay astride the western approaches to Tibet. Here had traditionally been the trijunction of Asia's greatest religions and would soon bring together in dangerous proximity three empires – Russian, British and Chinese. Henry Strachey figured prominently in explorations of this critical area. He worked closely with Alexander Cunningham, a Special Commissioner for Punjab Himalaya, in examining the frontier between the British controlled districts and those ruled by the Dogra Chief of Jammu, Gulab Singh. It was during these explorations that Henry Strachey discovered the great Siachen glacier in the Karakorums and otherwise made many valuable contributions to the fund of topographical data on which the Kashmir part of the Survey of India would be based.

The 'Great Trigonometrical Survey of India', which resulted in an accurate mapping of the sub-continent, owes much of its success to Sir George Everest. This remarkable geographer, who began his career in India as an artillery cadet in 1806, became Superintendent of the Survey in 1823 and rose to Surveyor General of India seven years later. He designed a system of stations and triangulations oriented to an arc of the meridian which he plotted from Cape Comorin at the extreme southern tip of India to a station called Banog in the farthest Himalayas. Everest's system was perhaps most dramatically applied in the

---

[1] The geographers Saint-Martin and Klapoth tried to prove that Tieffenthaler and Anquetil de Perron had solved the problem in 1784 – twenty-eight years before Moorcroft's visit to Manasarovar. Tieffenthaler's map, while correct, was drawn on the basis of an assumption not then proven. If Saint-Martin and Klapoth's thesis is accepted, then according to the same reasoning, first credit must go to Manchu Emperor K'ang Hsi's topographers whose even earlier maps also showed the two lakes connected. Presumably this too had been based on hearsay evidence.

Himalayas where the precise heights of all the major peaks were accurately calculated. By 1862 the Survey of India could boast that a survey of the greatest range in the world had been completed. One peak of 29,028 feet stood out as highest in the world and was appropriately named Everest in commemoration of the man whose genius had made its measurement possible.

The survey of Kashmir was entrusted to T. C. Montgomerie, an engineer in the Bengal Army. He personally conducted much of the tedious reconnaissance which eventually enabled the Survey of India to locate and measure some thirty-two peaks of the Karakorum range bordering Kashmir and Ladakh. Nineteen of them were over 25,000 feet, including Everest's nearest rival, K-2, which was measured at 28,250 feet.

It was at a meeting in London of the Geographical Society held in 1888 that it was proposed that K-2 be named Godwin-Austin after one of Montgomerie's assistants who had played a leading role in locating this peak. This suggestion was never officially adopted, however, mainly because there were many who felt that it was presumptuous to rename Himalayan mountain peaks after Western discoverers when in fact these peaks had been long since discovered and named by the indigenous people. As a result, the native names or surveying code numbers have been generally used by Western geographers to identify the peaks of the Himalayas.

By 1864 the frontier surveys west of Nepal were completed. Uncharted and unknown, however, were the lands to the north. Closed to foreign travel in 1792, Tibet was still the enigma which it had always been to the West. Almost equally unknown and hidden from view by the Karakorums was Eastern Turkestan which borders Kashmir, Ladakh and Tibet to the north. Here, more than geographic curiosity was involved: defence of the subcontinent required knowledge of the northern approaches to it.

The vast empty spaces of Central Asia were inexorably being filled by Russian expansion. Cossack freebooters ranged further and further eastward, while Russian settlers followed in their wake. In 1864 Czarist policy was enunciated when the Imperial Chancellor, Prince Gorchakov, was most explicit in stating that the safety of Russia's frontier required the complete absorption of the western Turkestan khanates within the empire.

Tashkent fell to the Russians in 1864 and was annexed within a year. It was then only a matter of time before Samarkand, Bokhara, Khokand, Merve and Pendjdeh would follow. Well before the end of the century Russian power would reach the Pamirs and it was then inevitable, given the climate of the times, that forward reconnaissance would be conducted by Russia and Britain beyond their lines of control in the rarified air of the Hindu Kush, Pamirs and Karakorums. At stake in the 'Great Game', as this contest of intrigue came to be known, were the frontiers of empire. Kipling captured the flavour in his novel, *Kim*, but the true story of the 'Great Game', no less exciting, remains for the most part buried in long-forgotten archives.

The Russian Empire had earlier expanded eastward, inevitably colliding with the western borders of Manchu China. Of particular importance to India was the Treaty of Tarbagatai in 1860 and a supplemental protocol signed in 1864, which re-aligned China's western borders in favour of Russia and brought Russia to the gates of eastern Turkestan. British military strategists could reason that not only was Russia in position to move southward into the sub-continent across Afghanistan and over the Hindu Kush and through the Khyber Pass, but it now had the option to take a more easterly invasion route through Eastern Turkestan, by-passing Afghanistan altogether. This latter route could either lead southward through Karakorum passes into Baltistan and Ladakh, or run farther east along the traditional caravan route from Kashgar to Gartok, which crossed the Aksai Chin desert and followed the western edge of Tibet to the Himalayan passes leading into Kumaon and India proper. Thus it was now more urgent than ever that the Government of India know the topography of western Tibet and Turkestan.

The problem was access. It was no longer feasible for British officers to explore Tibet and Turkestan. However dashing and romantic the idea of disguised Englishmen ranging deep into Central Asia may have seemed, the risks were excessive. Moorcroft's death had been a tragic lesson. Moreover, there were political objections against Englishmen entering areas claimed and jealously guarded by China. Tibet was definitely closed and no disguise worn by an Englishman could deceive the alert and suspicious Tibetans. A new approach had to be devised.

It was Montgomerie who found a solution. This ingenious

officer, working in close partnership with General J. T. Walker, set about organizing a unique school to train native explorers, popularly called 'pundits', in clandestine survey techniques. It was planned that these indigenous agents, when fully trained could travel undetected and serve as the eyes and ears of empire beyond the Himalayas.

In 1863 Montgomerie selected the first two students, cousins named Nain Singh and Mani Singh, and began their course of training at Dehra Dun hill station near Simla. They were the sons of the two Bhutias who had been so helpful to Moorcroft and Hearsey in their Kamaon survey of 1812, and were considered completely reliable. The course of training, which lasted two years, was exceptionally thorough. The students were taught the use of the sextant and compass, they were drilled in navigational astronomy and techniques for calculating altitude. The missions would be secret so they were instructed in clandestine methods. Their luggage had secret compartments, their clothes hidden pockets. Tibetan prayer wheels were loaded with rolls of blank paper on which cryptic notes could be scribbled. They were taught to transcribe their notes into verse and memorize them as they memorized Buddhist prayers – by constant recitation as they walked. Prayer beads were used as counting markers: one to be dropped for every so many steps taken during the journey. Their walk had to be perfected so that each stride would be uniform in measuring distances. They were rigorously drilled in assuming false identities as itinerant merchants or pious pilgrims. To protect their true identities, they were referred to by cryptonym – usually two initials assigned to them by Montgomerie.

Nain Singh, the more famous of the two, set out on his inaugural mission in March 1865, travelling by way of Nepal. At the Tibetan frontier town of Kyirong he was turned back by a suspicious governor who found his story unconvincing. The disappointed pundit returned to Kathmandu where he changed his disguise to that of a Ladakh merchant – pigtail and all. This time he was successful and passed through Kyirong without detection. He joined a trading caravan which took him to Tadum monastery; here he fell in with a legitimate Ladakh trader who befriended him. Together they walked to Shigatse where they visited the nearby Tashilhunpo monastery, See of the Teshu Lama.

The Teshu, or Panchen Lama, then a lad of eleven, received the disguised pundit while surrounded by the inevitable red and saffron-robed lamas whose bare heads kept bobbing down so that the child Lama could pat them reverently. Not since Turner's visit to Tashilhunpo in 1781 had a servant of the British been in attendance at the court of the Teshu Lama, although, of course the Lama had no way of suspecting that it was a British agent who now sipped tea with him.

Singh arrived in Lhasa on 10 January 1866 and immediately set about his secret survey. He carried out his tasks faithfully during the weeks he remained in Tibet's capital: he made sixteen thermometer readings each day for a fortnight, and twenty solar and stellar observations which enabled him to plot the exact location of Lhasa for the first time in history. By noting the boiling point of water he was also able to establish with reasonable accuracy Lhasa's altitude at 11,699 feet above sea level.

The pundit's existence in Lhasa was a precarious one. Early in his stay two Kashmiris saw through his disguise, but for their own reasons they kept their secret to themselves. The uneasy pundit also had found that he was in Lhasa at the same time as the Governor of Kyirong. This official, who had suspected him at the frontier, fortunately did not see him again in Lhasa, but fear of a chance encounter kept the wary pundit off the streets.

The return trip took Nain Singh as far west as Lake Manasarovar before he turned southward to cross the Himalayas into India. This first sortie by one of Montgomerie's graduates had been a success. In all, 1,200 miles had been covered, route surveys had been made between Kathmandu and Tadum and from Lhasa to Manasarovar along the main east-west trail to Gartok. Moreover the Tsangpo had been charted from its source to its junction with the Kyi Chu tributary near Lhasa. The pundit's findings permitted Montgomerie to calculate the approximate discharge of the Tsangpo after being joined by the Kyi Chu. By comparing this flow with that of the Brahmaputra in Assam a convincing circumstantial case could be made that the two rivers were the same.

Nain Singh's next mission was to explore western Tibet and the upper Indus Valley. The pundit was instructed to plot the location of Gartok, Tibet's largest western city, and – most intriguing of all – to investigate the fabled Tibetan gold fields at Thok Jalung, east of Rudok in western Tibet.

From earliest times Tibet was believed to be rich in gold. In what was probably Europe's first historical reference to Tibet, Herodotus mentions a desert north of India where 'great ants in size somewhat less than dogs, but bigger than foxes' throw up sand heaps full of gold as they burrow. But a tribe which 'dwells northward of all the rest of the Indians . . . more warlike than any of the other tribes' sends forth its men to steal it. When the Indians reach the gold, 'they fill their bags with sand and ride away at their best speed'. The ants, according to Herodotus, then 'rush forth in pursuit'. The great Greek historian concludes: 'If it were not . . . that the Indians get a start while the ants are mustering, not a single gold-gatherer would escape.'[1]

During the period of Nain Singh's explorations Ladakh gold was still referred to locally as 'ant gold', and some natives commonly believed that the surface gold which they found was the product of ants' labour. The origin of this obviously ancient myth is obscured by time, but it is tempting to speculate that the marauding Indians described by Herodotus actually saw Tibetan gold diggers crouching on the ground shrouded in their great black yak-skin capes to keep out the chilling winds. From a distance this could have looked like ants burrowing in the ground. Adding to the effect may have been the antelope horns, which the primitive miners used to scratch for gold; and the fierce black mastiffs, which traditionally guard Tibetan encampments, were from a distance perhaps mistaken for pursuing ants by the panic-stricken raiders of Herodotus's time.

Gold was not extracted from Tibet in greater quantity probably because of religious taboos against digging deep to find the precious metal. Many Tibetans are to this day convinced that to extract gold from beneath the ground is to make the ground infertile. This taboo can be traced to a belief that Padma Sambhava (or Urgyen), the Indian teacher credited with introducing Tantric Buddhism to Tibet in the ninth century, endowed

---

[1] Manuel Komroff (ed.), *The History of Herodotus* (New York, Tudor Publishing Co, 1956), pp. 184, 185.

Tibet's soil with gold in the first place. If it is disturbed, Tibetans fear that his displeasure will be shown by hail or rain storms which wash away their crops.[1]

British interest in Tibetan gold began early. Warren Hastings found tantalizing a present of gold sent him by the Teshu Lama in 1775, and had a sample of it promptly assayed in England.[2] It will be recalled that Bogle and Turner were instructed by the Governor General to investigate the commercial feasibility of importing Tibetan gold ore in quantity. Turner wrote in his report: 'The first in this list [of valuable ores] is deservedly gold: they find it in large quantities and frequently pure.'[3] So it is not surprising that Montgomerie placed the Thok-Jalung fields high among his priorities. Not only could Tibetan gold help Indian trade balances, but from a strategic point of view this valuable commodity might prove tempting to the Russians.

In May 1867 Nain Singh set out for Thok-Jalung, walking northward from Musoorie. With two companions he crossed into Tibet through the 18,570-foot Mana Pass. Chinese border guards searched their baggage with more than usual thoroughness but could find nothing. The next settlement they came upon was a Tibetan encampment located on a tributary of the Indus. The headman, with surprising shrewdness, spotted the travellers for what they were. Only with bribery would he let them proceed. One of Nain Singh's companions, either ill or frightened, dropped out of the expedition at this point, while the other according to prior design struck out on his own for another sector. Alone, Singh climbed the Chomorang Pass to make the long descent on the other side to the gold fields.

After three days of blinding blizzards Nain Singh reached his goal. Thok-Jalung was a bleak and desolate plain, 16,000 feet high, dotted by black yak-hair tents. Strewn about aimlessly were bales of fine wool for shawl making, tea boxes and strings of dried beans. The gold was extracted from shallow trenches dug in the alluvial soil by primitive hydraulic methods: streams,

---

[1] Sir Charles Bell, *The People of Tibet* (Oxford, 1928), pp. 110, 111.
[2] Alastair Lamb, *Britain and Chinese Central Asia* (London, Routledge & Kegan Paul, 1960), p. 14, from Indian National Archives, General Letter to Court, dated 15 January 1776.
[3] Samuel Turner, *op. cit.*, pp. 404, 405.

diverted from the nearby hills, were channelled through the trenches to wash the soil from the gold.

The headman – a lama judging by his dress – lounged in his tent, alternatively sipping *chang* and sucking at his silver-mounted hooka, or water pipe. Crouched as sentinel before his tent was a giant black mastiff emitting low rumbles from his deep, white-thatched chest as Nain Singh approached. The headman viewed the approaching pundit with undisguised suspicion. He carefully inspected the traveller's box, noting that it was a bit too luxurious, but happily failed to come upon the secret compartments which hid the surveying instruments. With the keen intuition which made him one of Montgomerie's most resourceful agents, Nain Singh assuaged the headman's suspicions with reassuring remarks and a gift of coral ornaments for his wife.[1]

Nain Singh stayed long enough to bring back a report of the gold fields which was thorough and useful. Although the surface gold of Thok Jalung would be gone by the end of the nineteenth century, these desolate fields at the time of the pundit's visit were still producing well for Tibet and China. The yield was good and the quality high. (Singh saw one nugget which was fully two pounds in weight.) The details brought back by him did much to keep the Company dreams of Tibet's mineral wealth alive and contributed to a later flurry of excitement in European banking circles over the possibilities of systematically exploiting Tibet's gold reserves.[2]

Another pundit whose contribution to empire would be recognized and remembered by a grateful Government of India was Rai Bahadur Kishen Singh Milamwal, better known by his cryptonym, Krishna, or sometimes by his code initials, A-K. This extraordinary agent distinguished himself by his secret explorations in the northern districts of central Tibet.

Kishen Singh and four assistants disguised as drivers and menials set out in the autumn of 1872, hoping to work their way as far north as Koko Nor, near the Chinese border. The mission aborted when they were attacked and robbed at Lake Tengri (Tengri Nor). Forced to return to Lhasa to resupply themselves,

---

[1] Sir Thomas Holdich, *op. cit.*, pp. 240–3.
[2] Government of India Library, Commonwealth Relations Office, London, Home Correspondence – India, Volume 182, No. 1021, Tibetan Gold, 'Gold Mines in Tibet'.

the pathetic little band reached Tibet's capital on the verge of starvation on 9 March 1873. After regaining their strength they returned to India to report their unavoidable failure to complete the mission.

Kishen Singh set out again in 1878 to explore the north, central and southern districts east of the meridian of Lhasa. On 5 September he arrived in Lhasa, intending to spend a year learning Mongolian so that he could travel in Mongolia in the course of his northern explorations. Life in Lhasa was interesting and he absorbed much of the customs and practices of the Tibetans. Like Beligatti, nearly 150 years earlier, Kishen Singh was fascinated by Tibetan religious celebrations – particularly the New Year, or *Monlam* ceremony in which the gods and goddesses gather in Lhasa. 'During this period,' he wrote, 'the city is governed by lamas of the Daibung Gomba [Drepung Monastery] whose will becomes the supreme law for the time being: they inflict arbitrary punishment for trifling offences.'

Another festival called Chongju Saiwant is held during the month following *Monlam*. 'During this festival,' recalled Kishen Singh, 'a Tibetan of a certain tribe is summoned by the Lama; his face is coloured half black and half white and a leather coat is put on him; and he is immediately turned out of the city and ordered to go to Chetang via Samye, where he resides for the year.' At Samye he is obliged to remain for seven days and to sleep at night in a solitary room in the monastery called the Gate of Death, which is 'filled with skins of huge serpents and wild animals . . . all calculated to excite feelings of terror in the individual.' During his seven-day stay he exercises despotic authority, often capriciously, much to the despair of the lamas.[1]

Kishen Singh left Lhasa in September 1879 with a caravan made up of Tibetan and Mongolian traders who moved cautiously northward through bandit-infested country. On one occasion some 300 Golok tribesmen did attack but were finally beaten off. By the spring of 1880 the pundit had arrived at the Mongolian encampment of Yembi in the Tsaidam district. Here Kishen

---

[1] The India Library, Commonwealth Relations Office, London, W/2189, J. B. N. Hennessey, 'Report on the Explorations in Great Tibet and Mongolia made by A-K in 1879–1882', Dehra Dun, 1884.

Singh's luck deserted him: first his servant robbed him of all his precious supplies, then the Governor would not permit him to continue his journey. Suspecting him of being a spy, this official forced him to remain in Sachu, north of the Humboldt Range, in semi-custody. Seven months elapsed before he was permitted to leave, and then only because an influential lama whom Kishen Singh had met earlier in his journey vouched for him and agreed to include him in his caravan as servant. This journey, not of his planning, took him south again.

Kishen Singh wandered hundreds of miles through Kham province in eastern Tibet, visiting most of the principal towns. In Batang on the eastern border of Kham the now-impoverished and weary pundit was taken in by French missionaries. Desperately needing their assistance and supplies, he confided his true mission for the Indian Government to them. With his supplies replenished, Kishen Singh struck south-west from Batang. He crossed the Atak Gangla range and pushed westward along the southern watershed of the upper Salween River. Bypassing Lhasa, he followed the Tsangpo westward to Khamba Pass where he turned south into India. In early 1882, four years after he had started, Kishen Singh returned to home base at Dehra Dun. The wealth of new information which he brought and the satisfaction he found in his pioneering exploits compensated for his fatigue. The pundits were no ordinary men.

For sheer stamina and dogged devotion to duty the exploits of Kintup – or K.P., as he was cryptically referred to in Survey of India reports – are difficult to match. Teamed with a Mongolian Lama whose servant he pretended to be, Kintup began his remarkable odyssey in 1880. The mission assigned them was to explore the Tsangpo and discover if, as suspected, it was the father of the Brahmaputra. By measuring the waterflow of the Dihang River as it left the Himalayas and debouched on to the Assam plains to join other tributaries of the Brahmaputra, Captain Harman of the Survey of India had earlier been able to hypothesize that only the Tsangpo could provide this volume of water. But the need remained to prove conclusively this thesis. Moreover, details of how the Tsangpo dropped from a height of almost 10,000 feet above sea level to the 500-foot level of the Dihang extension of the Brahmaputra intrigued Survey geographers. There was an unexplored distance of only about 120 miles to be accounted for. Did the Tsangpo drop precipitously in what could be the world's most awesome falls, or were there a series of rapids which brought the racing waters out of the Himalayas onto the Assam plains. Efforts to probe northward along the Dihang spur to trace its source had always been frustrated by the hostile hill tribes of Assam. If this intriguing mystery was to be solved, it must be as a result of exploration down the Tsangpo on the Tibetan side of the mountains. In the event it proved impossible to follow the Tsangpo through its Himalayan chasm, Kintup was equipped with a drill and small metal tubes which he was instructed to implant in logs of wood and send floating down the Tsangpo in the expectation that their later discovery in the Brahmaputra would constitute conclusive proof that the two rivers were one.

Kintup and his ostensible Mongolian master successfully reached Gyala in Tibet across from where a tributary of the Tsangpo descends in a series of cascades amidst dank caves and overhanging rock ledges. Lurking beneath one such cave was believed to be a benevolent demon called Shingje Chögye. In fact, this mythical demon's image is painted on a rock behind a small waterfall.

The explorers pushed on but were forced to halt at the lamasery of Pemaköchung where the trail became impassable. In an effort to find a new approach, which would permit them to continue their journey, the travellers entered a totally unknown region called Po Me. At a town named Tongkyuk Dzong the Mongolian lama, apparently discouraged and altogether sick of the hazardous enterprise he had allowed himself to be sent on, deserted his partner. But even worse, he sold Kintup to a leading personage of Tongkyuk Dzong as slave. The dismayed pundit had no choice but to work as domestic servant for his new master. Only after seven months of this drudgery was he able to contrive a means of escape.

Totally committed to his mission, Kintup resisted any temptations he may have felt to return to India and safety by the quickest route. Instead he again struck out to follow the Tsangpo downstream. After several false starts he succeeded in rejoining the river at a place called Dorjiyu Dzong. His exhilaration at again catching up with the twisting and tumbling quarry which he was determined to track was, however, short-lived.

Agents of his master caught up with him at Marpung and took him into custody.

With considerable resourcefulness, Kintup sought an audience with the Head Lama of Marpung. Falling at the lama's feet, the distraught pundit explained that he was but a humble pilgrim who had been treacherously sold into slavery by his travelling companion. Overcome with compassion, the Head Lama bought Kintup for fifty rupees and himself kept him as a slave for four and a half months. At least the pundit now had a benevolent master who even granted him leave to make a pilgrimage down river to the holy mountain, called Kondü Potrang. On this excuse Kintup was able, at last, to mark and prepare for launching some fifty logs. Recognizing that he must alert the Survey before sending his logs on their long journey, Kintup appealed to his permissive master to grant him leave to visit the holy places in Lhasa; only by returning to Tibet's capital could he get a message back to India, informing his principals of the precise date on which he intended to release the logs so that they could watch for them as they floated down the Brahmaputra.

Kintup dutifully returned to his master and served him nine months longer so that he would be close to his cache of banded logs and able to despatch them when the specified date arrived. It is a measure of the man that he resisted the temptation to flee to India from Lhasa when he had the opportunity to do so. By returning to the Marpung monastery to complete his mission, he risked bondage for life.

The Head Lama was so impressed with Kintup's apparent piety that he freed him. Unable to follow the Tsangpo further and having sent off the marked logs, Kintup returned to India by way of Lhasa, arriving in 1884 – four years after he had set out on his mission. On his return he found to his intense disappointment that his message from Lhasa had never reached India so that his logs must have drifted unnoticed into the Bay of Bengal. Worse still, he found that his detailed report on the Tsangpo and his account of his own adventures was received with scepticism by many in the Survey of India. Only later were Kintup's accomplishments given the full credit they deserved, but by then he had disappeared from sight.[1]

---

[1] F. M. Bailey, *China, Tibet, Assam* (London, 1945), pp. 9–16.

Marathon journeys of this sort were then not uncommon. Nain Singh, Kishen Singh and Kintup were outstanding examples of the long range reconnaissance agents used by the British, but they were by no means unique. The techniques perfected by the Survey of India combined with the skill and incredible endurance of the pundits produced a mass of information on the heretofore uncharted wastelands of the Tibetan plateau.

The journeys of the pundits had to be planned with utmost secrecy since the Tibetans had learned of their techniques and took increasing precautions to prevent their infiltration. The technical skills demanded of these agents were sophisticated. In one of his reports Kishen Singh described a typical procedure. With his prismatic compass he would fix on some prominent distant terrestial object due south of his station. Knowing the magnetic meridian he could measure the altitude of the object with unerring accuracy. To eliminate any chance of error, he would then check his computations by stellar readings.[1]

Probably the most tedious of the pundits' tasks – one demanding exceptional self discipline and accuracy – was the linear measurement of the route. It was not uncommon for the pundits to range 2,000 to 3,000 miles in a single mission over tortuous terrain, counting each step along the way. Not only did they have to compensate for irregular terrain features such as rocks, precipitous slopes, streams, etc., but they were forced to improvise new techniques when faced with unusual situations. Kishen Singh recalled an occasion when a caravan leader insisted that everyone ride horseback so as to speed their journey through robber-infested territory. The pundit 'set at once to work counting the beast's paces ... in this way he reckoned his distances for nearly 230 miles.' The geographic analyst at Dehra Dun commented admiringly that the results did 'credit alike to the explorer's ingenuity and the horse's equability of pace.'[2]

Montgomerie fell ill, a casualty of his years of exertions in India. By now a full colonel, he was forced to return to England in 1876. He died less than a year later at the age of forty-seven. No better memorial exists than the accomplishments of his

---

[1] J. B. N. Hennessy, *op. cit.*, p. 6.   [2] *Ibid.*

students. Their reports, frequently bearing Montgomerie's name as compiler, were the stuff of empire.

The momentum of the programme and the high calibre of his successors enabled the Great Trigonometrical Survey of India to carry on with increasing efficiency after Montgomerie's death. But as knowledge of Tibet's geography increased, so did a more general curiosity about this strange and still remote country. It was need for a more comprehensive understanding of Tibet that encouraged a scholarly Bengali schoolmaster named Sarat Chandra Das to devote his life to the study of Tibet. This exceptional person, generally believed to have been the prototype of Babu Hurree Chunder Mookerjee in Kipling's *Kim*, was a new kind of pundit – one who could provide a political dimension to the trans-Himalayan surveys of the British.

Das began his government career in 1874 as headmaster of the Bhutia Boarding School in Darjeeling. This unique experiment in education had as its more obvious object the education of the Tibetan or semi-Tibetan boys living in the Darjeeling-Sikkim border region. Recognizing the connections between Bhutias, or Tibetans, living on the Indian side of the border and some of the prominent families of Tibet, the Government of Bengal saw in this programme a means to improve relations with Tibet. Unmentioned, however, was the intention of the British to identify and select from the Bhutia school the more outstanding students for training as pundits at Dehra Dun. In this way there could be assured a continuing supply of qualified surveyors, ethnically identical to the people of Tibet with whom they must blend unnoticed.

Das was joined by Ugyen-Gyatso, a respected Tibetan lama from Sikkim, whose ostensible responsibility it was to instruct the Bhutia students in Tibetan language, literature and religious studies, but who secretly would serve from time to time as a surveying agent inside Tibet. Das plunged into Tibetan studies, fascinated by the little known civilization to the north. The 'Babu', as the Bengali pundit was known, was determined to travel in Tibet and see at first hand this country which now so thoroughly absorbed his interest. In 1878 he openly petitioned the Teshu (Panchen) Lama for permission to visit Tashilhunpo and the Dalai Lama's Regent for approval to visit Lhasa. It is not surprising that he received no reply from Tibet's capital where

Chinese influence continued to be strong. But the Teshu Lama, showing something of the same independence he had in his earlier incarnation when he was a friend of Bogle's, responded favourably.

Careful preparations for the journey were made. While Das was to concentrate on the social, religious, economic and political facets of contemporary Tibet, Ugyen would conduct a detailed geographical survey of the route, and otherwise bear the scientific burden of the journey. Although still employed by the Bengal Educational Department, both pundits were seconded to the Survey of India for training. Das was given secret instructions by Nain Singh while Ugyen was more intensively schooled in surveying techniques by Colonel Tanner of the Survey.[1]

The Teshu Lama's First Minister was host to the two travellers for the six months they stayed in Tashilhunpo. During this time the Babu had an unequalled opportunity to examine the rare monastery library, and was able to bring back with him an invaluable collection of Tibetan books – those thick sheafs of handwritten text, sandwiched between two ornately carved wooden boards which served as covers. He was also able to establish a close personal relationship with the First Minister whose fascination with the West was equal to his own interest in Tibet.

Das was received by the Teshu Lama, whom he described as being 'twenty-six years of age, of a spare frame and middling stature', with 'a remarkably broad forehead and large eyes, slightly oblique'. The Babu recalled that his expression, although highly intelligent, was not engaging, and lacked 'that sympathy and dignity so conspicuous in the Minister's countenance'. The old monks of Tashilhunpo informed Das that 'unlike his predecessor, the present Grand Lama was more feared than liked, on account of his cold and self-reliant spirit'. He was 'strict in the observance of ceremonies and in the administration of justice, and slow to forgive.'[2]

Encouraged by his first visit and still determined to reach Lhasa, the Bengali schoolmaster made plans for a second trip to Tibet. After a year of intense study and research, Das and Ugyen

---

[1] Sir Thomas Holdich, *op. cit.*, p. 247.
[2] Sarat Chandra Das, *Narrative of a Journey to Lhasa* (Calcutta, 1885), p. 76.

again set out for Tashilhunpo in November 1881. Early on 9 December the two weary travellers once again came within sight of the fort at Shigatse, just beyond which lay the monastery of Tashilhunpo. Das recalled his own 'high spirits' despite the cold wind that chilled them to the bone, but commented that Ugyen 'was ill and fretted fearfully'.[1] Sir Thomas Holditch, who dealt with Ugyen while serving as an officer of the Survey of India, explained in his excellent book, *Tibet, The Mysterious*: 'The Lama [Ugyen] was the harassed and hard-working surveyor; the Babu, the light-hearted observer.'[2] But, however much the Survey of India owed to Ugyen for his back-breaking technical surveys, the broad brush portraits of Tibetan life and political intelligence brought back by Das were, in their way, equally valuable. Not since Turner had the Government of India so benefited from an observer who was articulate, perceptive and truly scholarly in his approach.

Das had taken great pains to travel discreetly. From the beginning he had intended to find an opportunity to go on to Lhasa if he possibly could and didn't want his chances spoiled by unwanted publicity. He followed a circuitous route to avoid the usually travelled paths. In Tashilhunpo he lived simply and quietly, staying with the chief Tantric lama whose friendship he had made on his previous journey. Another reason for not calling attention to himself was the presence of the Chinese *Ambans* and their retinue in Shigatse where they were making their annual formal visit to the Teshu Lama. There was already tension in the town because of certain incidents caused by the overbearing attitude assumed by the Chinese officials, and the Babu recognized that his own presence could be used as an excuse by the Chinese to exert additional pressure on the Tibetans.

Das's description of the pomp and posturing of the *Ambans* provides the best possible insight into the Chinese position in Tibet at this point in history. From the roof of a friend's house Das observed and noted in the following words the parade of the *Ambans* on the occasion of the anniversary of the Chinese Emperor's accession to the throne:

---

[1] *Ibid.*, p. 57.
[2] Sir Thomas Holdich, *op. cit.*, p. 250.

Flag-bearers and a mounted troop came first, then Tibetan officials. . . .
The Chinese were conspicuous by their pigtails and petticoats and,
though very well-dressed, were all black and of villainous appearance,
greatly contrasting with the respectable Tibetan gentry, which forced
me to think that they were all recruited from low-class people from
western China; and the Tung-chen told me that these men were noted
in Tibet for their dissipated and licentious habits.

Some men carried boards about two feet square, on which were
written the *Ambans'* titles and his commissions to supreme authority
over the whole of Tibet. . . . There were about three hundred dignitaries and gentlemen of the provinces of U and Tsang, besides the followers and retainers of the *Ambans*. The *Ambans'* sedan chairs were
carried by eight Chinese soldiers to each, and some fifty Tibetan soldiers
helped to drag them with long cords attached to the bars of the chairs.
After paying homage at the sacred chapels and tombs of the departed
saints, the procession came out of the monastery by the eastern gate,
and, headed by the *Shape* Bora, marched across the market place
towards Kun-Khyab-ling. First came the officers of state, then followed
the paymaster's party, then the Chinese officials, followed by the
Chief *Amban* in his state chair. . . . Throughout the march the Tibetans
occupied a subordinate position, and the Chinese displayed their
superiority in every possible way. Though the crowd had reason to
fear a whipping from the Chinese, who ran on all sides, they did not
suffer from the *Ambans'* guard. The junior *Amban*, as he followed on
horseback, seemed pleased to see the heavily chained prisoners, the
recently punished headmen groaning under the weight of their
cangues. His sedan chair was carried by the same number of soldiers as
that of the senior *Amban*, and his retinue and followers resembled his.
Then came the other *shapes* [ministers] with their respective retinues.
The guards were all armed with Chinese matchlocks and long spears.
Following them came the captains and lieutenants of the army, with a
hundred men; and behind these marched the yellow and blacked-
turbaned officers of Labrang and the Djong.[1]

While in Tashilhunpo Das met a prominent and imposing
lady of Lhasa who as wife of a Tibetan minister, bore the title
'Lhacham'. His friendship with this influential person provided
the opportunity he had been hoping for since he was able to
attach himself to her party travelling to Lhasa and later enjoy
her patronage there. Soon after they started news arrived that a

[1] S. C. Das, *Narrative of a Journey to Lhasa* (Calcutta, 1885), pp. 80–2.

smallpox epidemic was spreading rapidly throughout central Tibet from Lhasa where it had already taken a serious toll of lives. This alarmed the Lhacham who was at the moment staying in a house where five of the inhabitants had already gone down with the dread disease. Her concern was further heightened when Das, himself, became seriously ill with a high fever and racking cough. She, therefore, set out for Lhasa immediately without her companion.

Unable to travel, Das had to stay behind at the Samding monastery near Yamdok Lake. The Lhachan left him in the care of two 'skillful physicians' of the monastery and gave him a letter of introduction to the Head Lama – an attractive twenty-six year old woman, the Abbess 'Thunderbolt Sow' – considered to be an incarnation of the divine consort of the God, Chenrezi.

Her youthfulness belied an illustrious and long career stretching over many incarnations. According to the Babu's version of the Tibetan legend, there once lived a horrible monster called Mantrankaru who terrorized the world. With all nature of demons, goblins and evil spirits at his command, he conquered not only the world, but the 'eight planets, twenty-four constellations, the eight Nagas and the Gods'. With the coming of Buddha, it was ordained that the great God, Chenrezi, and his divine consort Dolma would conquer this menace. Taking the form of a disembodied horse's neck, known as Tamdrin, Chenrezi neighed three times while his consort, transformed into a sow known as Dorje Phagmo, grunted five times. Mantrankaru and his wife were so terrified by this display of the Gods' displeasure that they lay 'prostrate at the feet of the two divinities'.[1]

The Thunderbolt Sow again figured prominently in Tibetan history in 1716 when the Dzungar Mongols invaded the country. By refusing to obey a command to appear before the Mongol commander she provoked the invaders to raze the walls of Samding monastery. Once inside the Dzungars found only eighty pigs and eighty sows 'grunting in the congregation hall under the lead of a big sow'. Terrified by this eerie phenomenon, the Mongols spared the monastery, whereupon the porcine inhabitants changed back into human lamas and nuns under the

---

[1] *Ibid.*, p. 186.

saintly Dorje Phagmo. Thereafter Samding enjoyed immunity from the alien conquerors.[1]

Thanks to the Lhacham's letters of introduction, the Thunderbolt Sow was the soul of hospitality. She told the Babu's fortune, reassuring him that while his illness was serious, it was not fatal. She also dispensed several sacred pills made from the particles of the Kashyapa Buddha's relics, and prescribed a series of religious rituals calculated to cure the most intransigent of maladies. She encouraged the monastery physicians to have certain healing rites performed by the learned lamas of Samding. The genii, for example, were propitiated to ensure peaceful dreams. Death was deceived by a sacrificial offering of an image of Das to the Lord of Death, while the Lord of Life was appeased by a ritual called 'life-saving charity' in which 500 fish from a neighbouring fisherman's catch were released back into the lake. Finally, the stricken pundit was fed a potion which seemed to consist of saffron and rhubarb.

Das at last recovered, either because of or despite the solicitude of the Thunderbolt Sow and her physicians. While convalescing, he was permitted to explore Samding monastery, wandering the endless corridors and rummaging through the many musty chambers. In the upper stories he came upon images of demons and genii so horrible that they were 'always kept veiled'. He visited a mausoleum of the former incarnations of Dorje Phagmo where he marvelled at silver statues encrusted with priceless jewels. The Babu learned that the waters of nearby Demons' Lake (Dumo Tso) were kept from overflowing and inundating the country only by the spiritual influence of the Thunderbolt Sow.

A final audience with Her Holiness was memorable for another propitiation ceremony during which she sprinkled saffron water on Das with the end of a peacock feather. The Babu – rather disappointingly – could register only annoyance since he feared the sacred shower would cause him to 'catch a cold'!

In the course of his audience she expressed her concern for the pundit's good health, and as a last parting act of charity before he left to continue his journey to Lhasa, she thrust upon him three

---

[1] *Ibid.*

more sacred pills to spur his complete recovery. Finally taking his leave of the Thunderbolt Sow, he remembered her admiringly as a woman with 'long tresses, an agreeable face and dignified manners'.

It was 4:00 p.m. on 30 May when Das at last reached his goal and entered the western gate of Lhasa. The trip had been a difficult one and he still felt weak from his debilitating illness. 'My head,' he recalled, 'drooped with fatigue, my eyes were hidden by dark goggles....' Townfolk commented as he passed; 'Look! there comes another sick man; smallpox has affected his eyes – the city is full of them.' His very disreputableness perhaps accounts for the failure of the town authorities to inspect him more closely and made it possible for him to enter the forbidden city without being detected.

Gaining admittance to the Jokhang, or sacred shrine of Buddha, one of Lhasa's major landmarks, Das watched monks from the nearby monasteries prostrate themselves before a statue of Buddha in observance of the holiest day of the year. The scholarly pundit also managed to visit most other places of interest in Lhasa during his brief stay. His curiosity drove him to every corner of the city, heedless of the smallpox that infected the city, with the result that he amassed a phenomenal amount of information which he meticulously recorded.

A high point in the Babu's stay was his audience with the Dalai Lama arranged by his patroness, the Lhacham. The thirteenth incarnation of the Dalai had been selected differently from his predecessors. It had been for many years the custom of the Regent and his ministers to select a new High Lama by drawing from a golden vessel one of several slips of paper bearing the names of eligible children. But in 1875, following the death of the Twelfth Dalai Lama, the Regent and a college of ranking incarnate lamas, in a departure from tradition, consulted the State Oracle at Ne-chung. The Oracle declared that the true incarnation could only be discovered by a monk of purest morals – specifically by a saintly lama of the Ganden monastery known as the Shar-tse Khampo. Duly appointed to the task, the Ganden Lama, on the advice of the Oracle, visited a village south-east of Lhasa where a vision came to him. Voices told him to wait on the banks of a nearby lake for further revelations. This he did and while in deep meditation he saw emerge for a

moment from the crystal surface of the water the image of a child
Grand Lama seated in his mother's lap. Only a few days later the
monk stopped by chance in a village in the province of Tag-po at
the house of a respectable and wealthy family. Here to his astonishment he saw in real life the child whose image he had seen in
the Madonna vision rising from the lake. The Regent was immediately notified and the college of senior lamas assembled to
administer the several tests to prove a true incarnation. The
child's actions and responses satisfied the lamas and he was
installed in the Potala as the Thirteenth Dalai Lama.[1]

Das described the new Dalai as 'a child of eight with a bright
and fair complexion and rosy cheeks'. The pundit observed that
'a yellow mitre covered his head, and its pendent lappets hid his
ears: a yellow mantle draped his person, and he sat cross-legged
with joined palms.' The audience began with a ceremonial
serving of tea followed by grace. 'After this,' Das recalled, 'the
Solpön Chenpo put a golden dish full of rice before the Dalai
Lama . . . His Holiness, in a low, indistinct tone, chanted a hymn
which was repeated by the assembled lamas in deep, grave
tones.'[2] The seance was concluded when a venerable man rose
and delivered a short address, reciting the many acts of mercy
the Dalai Lama had vouchsafed Tibet.

Das likened the Dalai Lama's position to that of the Pope in
the Christian world. As the incarnation of Chenrezi, the Dalai
Lama is Buddha's Vice-Regent, incarnate, on earth and protector

---

[1] Sir Charles Bell's version of this phenomenon, which appeared in his authoritative book, *Portrait of the Dalai Lama* (London, 1946), p. 41, is similar to that which Das
brought back but differs in a few details. This well known Tibetan expert who
served for many years as British political representative in Tibet and who was a
close friend of the adult Thirteenth Dalai Lama wrote:

Armed with the pronouncements of the oracles, a high lama of the austere Gyü
Monastery in Lhasa, attended by several doctors of divinity, was sent to look for a
vision. . . . the 'Wheel of Religion' [Lake] did not fail him. A wind arose – those
tempestuous Tibetan winds are never far away – and dispersed the snow, leaving
the ice clear before the lama, who was observing it from a neighbouring hill. Then
he looked into it, as into a glass, and saw an image of the house and the land round it.
He also saw a peach-tree in flower, several months out of the season for peach blos-
som. That night in a dream he saw a vision of the young Dalai Lama, then somewhat
less than two years old, in a woman's arms. A few days later he came to the house
seen in the lake and found the child in the arms of his mother, and the face of the
boy was unmistakably that seen in the dream.
[2] S. C. Das, *Narrative of a Journey to Lhasa*, pp. 221–3.

of Tibet. He never dies, but when displeased with the sinfulness of the world, he retires to the 'western abode of bliss', leaving his mortal remains on earth. When born again in the body of a child, he makes known his holy heritage by various unmistakable signs.

So long as the Dalai Lama was a minor, the government would be headed by a Regent, or *'Desi'* who had been elected by the Council of Ministers and confirmed by the State Oracle. Only upon coming of age would the Dalai receive the seals of office, both spiritual and temporal, permitting him to assume power. And if he followed the pattern of several past incarnations, he would somehow never reach his majority, thus sparing the Chinese a rival to their authority.

At the time Das visited Lhasa, the Regent was assisted by a *Chasag*, or Vice-Regent, whose appointment was specifically approved by the Emperor of China. This powerful figure, whose title literally means 'strainer of the tea', had to pass on any government petition before it would reach the Regent. The Council of Ministers was composed of four lay officials and one lama, each of whom was appointed for life and known by the title, *Shape* or *Kalon*. The Council met daily in the *Kashag*, or Council Hall, and transacted political, judicial and administrative business of the government. 'The ministers,' according to Das, 'sat cross-legged on thick cushions placed on raised seats, with a bowl of tea on a little table in front of each of them.'[1]

Das described the *Amban* as a very influential figure. While he theoretically had no authority in the internal administration of the country, his position as head of the Tibetan Army gave him, in fact, considerable power. Additionally, he had the authority to settle political differences between the various states of Tibet and the central government in Lhasa. Aiding him was an assistant *Amban*, who probably also kept an eye on him for the ever-distrustful Emperor. Actually the authority of the *Ambans* was on the wane at the time Das visited Lhasa. One indication of this was the independent way the Tibetans set about locating the thirteenth incarnation. As is apparent, the previous system in which names were drawn from a golden urn, provided the Chinese with a more manageable way to rig the selection.

[1] *Ibid.*, p. 231.

Certainly, none of the names in the urn had been unacceptable to the Chinese.

The pundit had little good to say of the *Ambans*. They were 'the terror of the Tibetans, who abhor them from the depth of their hearts.' When on tour in the provinces, 'provisions, conveyances, and all sorts of labours are forcibly extracted from the poor villagers, who are deprived of their ponies and yaks, which, owing to the merciless treatment of the *Ambans*' numerous retainers, die in numbers on the road.'[1] Das accused the *Ambans* of sowing distrust of the British and Russians among the Tibetans. Taking advantage of a Tibetan legend in which the Panchen Lama is supposed to retire forever one day to 'Shambala', the Utopian city of the Buddhists, the Chinese *Ambans* spread the prediction that when this day comes the English and Russians would intervene and destroy Lamaism.[2]

Das accurately dated Tibetan antagonism toward Europeans from 1792 when it was commonly, though erroneously, believed that the British aided the Gurkhas against Tibet. He recognized that increased Chinese influence in Tibet following the Gurkha War played an important part in forming this attitude. Aside from wanting to protect its political paramountcy, the Chinese sought to preserve a favoured trade position. They were all too aware that Peking was an eight- to ten-month journey from Lhasa while the markets of India were but a few weeks' journey away. Without excluding British and Indian trade, the Chinese could not, in the long run, hope to compete.

British frontier policy also played a part in Tibet's attitude toward India. Typical of the kind of incident which fed Tibetan suspicions was one in which a former minister of Sikkim fled to Tibet, claiming knowledge of British plots against Tibet. Having fallen into disfavour with the British over mistreatment of two British officials, Hooker and Campbell, the soured official alleged that it had been their intention to enter Tibet for purposes of spying. The renegade minister added that he, personally, had refused a proposition from the British in which he would be grandly rewarded for supplying information on Tibet. Only his diplomatic skill, he asserted, had foiled this scheme.

---

[1] *Ibid.*, p. 231. [2] *Ibid.*, pp. 239, 240.

Das's assessment of Tibetan suspicions was more accurate than he knew. Ironically, it was the eventual revelation of his own secret mission to Lhasa which exacerbated these suspicions and seriously compromised any possibility of Tibet-India rapprochement. While the pundit had successfully remained in Lhasa without detection for two weeks – leaving when he did only because of the worsening smallpox epidemic – his secret mission to Lhasa was soon thereafter given unfortunate publicity in India. The Tibetans were outraged and severely punished those known to have aided him. The Tibetans were determined to prevent other non-believers from duping them as Das had done.

At the root of Tibet's policy of foreign exclusion was probably fear that Lamaism would be undermined by foreign influences. Recognizing this, Imperial Russia with considerable shrewdness or sheer luck devised a way of penetration which took full advantage of Tibet's religious preoccupation.

15

Russian Reconnaissance

As Russians pressed further into far Asia it was inevitable they would become curious about the remote, unknown lands beyond the Kun Lun range. Imperial ambition, and the relentless urge to explore would lure the more adventurous across the arid wastelands of Eastern Turkestan and over this great mountain barrier to the high plateau of northern Tibet. But if Englishmen, whose bases in India were relatively close, had been unable to penetrate Lhasa, it is understandable that Russian explorers found Tibet's capital even more difficult to reach. Distance and terrain were the enemies. They conspired with hostile tribes to keep the uninvited from coming close to Tibet's holy citadel. But Russian explorers, like their British counterparts, distinguished themselves nonetheless by their stamina, daring and scientific skill even though their goal eluded them. They amassed a wealth of valuable geographic information on the areas which they were able to reach, and brought to Europe for the first time accurate and comprehensive knowledge of these forgotten corners of Central Asia.

The giant of Russian Central Asian exploration was Nicholas Mikhailovich Prjevalski. His four expeditions to Eastern Turkestan and northern Tibet during the 1870s and 1880s added enormously to the West's store of geographic knowledge. He was the first modern traveller to explore the Lop Nor region in Turkestan, which decades later would become a Chinese nuclear test site to threaten a world which bore no resemblance to the one Prjevalski knew. He was also the first Western traveller in modern times to delineate the Kun Lun mountain system which forms the outer barrier of northern Tibet, and to explore the sources of the Yellow River.

Prjevalski's first expedition set out from St Petersburg in the

278

autumn of 1870. The Russian explorer enjoyed discreet backing by the Czar who equipped him with a small Cossack guard. While genuinely prodded by scientific curiosity, there was no question but what Prjevalski, in return, considered the interests of empire in planning his itinerary. The Russian party spent its first year in south-west Mongolia. By early 1872 it had reached Koko Nor. Then, like the missionary travellers before him, Prjevalski moved southward across the salty plains of Tsaidam into Tibet. But he could advance no further than the Di-chu River in northern Tibet since crossing was difficult and he knew that his camels were unsuited to the mountainous region beyond.

Although Prjevalski explored the Lop Nor region again in 1876, it was another three years before he once more entered Tibet. This latter expedition – his third – was perhaps the most successful. With the inevitable Cossack escort he travelled from Semi-palatinsk to Barkul at the eastern end of the Tien-Shan range; then across the north-western face of the Nan Shan mountain complex. Indulging in the controversial Western custom of christening newly discovered geographic landmarks, Prjevalski renamed one of the ranges he crossed after Alexander von Humboldt, the early nineteenth-century German geographer whose studies had contributed much to an understanding of Tibetan geography. Working his way southward over a series of lesser ridges, Prjevalski again reached the Di-chu River in Tibet. This time he was prepared to make the crossing and, once safely across, he began the long march toward Lhasa.

Success must have seemed near to the Russian explorer who had for so long dreamed of entering Tibet's forbidden city. But word of his approach caused great consternation in the capital and set in motion a frantic effort to stop him. Rumours raced through Lhasa that the Russians intended to kidnap the Dalai Lama. Suspicions, long seeded by the Chinese *Ambans*, that Christian 'barbarians' would try to destroy Lamaism, infected the people as exaggerated tales of an imminent Russian invasion spread throughout the country.

A Tibetan militia was hastily mustered and warnings were sent northward along the route of the 'invaders'. Tibetans were exhorted to deny the foreigners provisions and harass them in every other possible way. Prjevalski's party was finally detained at Nagchu, only 170 miles from its goal. The town authorities notified Lhasa of its quarry; as could be expected, instructions were received by return courier to eject the intruders from the country. Thus, after eighteen months of hard travel, the bitterly disappointed explorers were forced to retrace their steps without as much as a distant glimpse of the Potala.

In November 1883, Prjevalski mustered a new party of twenty-one men for his fourth assault on Tibet. The Russians crossed the Gobi Desert by the same route which Prjevalski had followed before. The month's journey across Mongolia's ocean of shifting sand was marked by good weather. Colourful sunsets, created by the dust cast high in the atmosphere by Krakatoa's cataclysmic volcanic eruption in the Sunda straight off Java, provided spectacular finales to each long day's march.

In early January the party rested near the town of Din-Yuan-ing. Here Prjevalski encountered a German named Grezel, who worked as purchasing agent for a British trading company.[1] The Russian explorer must have suspected this camel hair and wool buyer of being a political agent for the British – a player of the Great Game. His presence in so remote a village served as a reminder that British interests, like Russian, demanded reconnaissance far beyond their line of control.

Prjevalski moved forward, following the track through southern Alashan to the borders of Kan-su. Skirting the towering palisades of the Alashan range, the versatile Russian meticulously recorded all that he saw. Bird fanciers are indebted to him for his discovery of *Accentor Koslowi*, a new breed which he named after his travelling companion, Captain Kozlov. He took stellar sightings when the clouds of dust which floated above them cleared sufficiently, and made careful topographical surveys during the daylight hours.

The Russians' route from Baian-Bulak crossed a southern reach of the Tingri shifting sands, climbed the Burkhan-Buddha range and wound its way slowly toward the great lakes which are the sources of the Hwant-ho or Yellow River. This great waterway, so vital to the life of China, rises in the eastern slope of the Baian-Kara-Ula range.[2] Known as the Altyn Gol, the

---

[1] Royal Geographic Society Supplement, Vol. III, Part I, p. 4 (London, 1890).
[2] *Ibid.*, p. 6.

parent stream flows a hundred miles to the north-east before it loses itself in a vast marsh, known by the Mongols as *Odontala*, or 'Starry Steppe', because of the myriads of sparkling springs which bubble to its surface. The spring waters break out of *Odontala* in two main streams which eventually meet to form the Saloma River. It is this junction where the Mongols and the Chinese believe the great Yellow River to be born. A cairn atop an 800-foot ridge overlooking the merging streams serves as a shrine where sacrifices are offered to the spirits of the 'Great River'. Every year a high-ranking provincial official, flanked by a retinue of Mongol and Tibetan noblemen, mounted the hill to read a prayer, invoking the help of deities to ensure a plentiful flow of water. So important was this ceremony that the Chinese Emperor personally signed the prayer which was delivered.

Prjevalski, the first serious and systematic explorer in this region since one of Kublai Khan's lieutenants searched for the sources of the Yellow River in 1280, followed the Saloma until it debouched into Tsaring Nor. The outflow from this lake runs into another lake, equally large, known as Oring Nor. Both serve as reservoirs regulating the vital water supply for the northern plains of China. Prjevalski, of course, could not resist renaming these two inland seas: Tsaring Nor became 'Russian Lake' while Oring Nor became 'Expedition Lake'. And to commemorate a victory over a band of marauding Tangut bandits, Prjevalski waggishly renamed the river which linked the two lakes, 'Robbers' River'. It is interesting that the Russian explorer, using modern surveying methods, located these lakes precisely where d'Anville placed them on his famous 1733 map of Tibet.

Stopped again by the Di-chu River, Prjevalski returned to the Tsaidam region where he reconnoitered a road said by the Mongols to have been formerly used by merchants travelling from Sining to Lop Nor. He discovered and described at some length, a valley in which fierce gales perpetually scoured the desert floor. Appropriately named the 'Valley of the Winds' by Prjevalski, this depression runs for 150 miles between the Chaman Tag range to the north and the Akka Tag range to the south. Veering northward the Russian party crossed the Amban Ashkan Pass and once again surveyed the Lop Nor and Tarim River areas before arriving home in October 1885.

This had been a valuable expedition although perhaps not as

successful as Prjevalski's third. With him travelled two companions, Lieutenants Peter Kozlov and V. I. Roborovsky, who led memorable expeditions of their own after Prjevalski's death. Also in the party was a Buriat Mongol known as Aguan Dorjiev, whose presence was scarcely, if at all, noted by the geographers who honoured Prjevalski. Perhaps only because this anonymous Buriat interpreter was included in a frontispiece group photo with other members of the expedition which was published in 1888[1] was his relationship with the great explorer remembered. But he was destined to emerge from obscurity and would ultimately play a critical role in Tibet's future. Within two decades Aguan Dorjiev,[2] agent of the Czar, would in fact provoke the British to assault Lhasa in a last and later regretted spasm of imperial thrust. His influence on the Dalai Lama would first subtly, then blatantly, guide the political fortunes of Tibet at the expense of Curzon's dreams. His shadowy activities, while undoubtedly exaggerated by an exasperated Government of India, would nonetheless score significant points in the Great Game. If Lhasa shunned English non-believers because it feared that they were intent upon destroying Lamaism, it embraced this Lamaist Buriat who somehow convinced the Dalai Lama that the Russian Czar was a Buddhist at heart.

Dorjiev's early career is obscure. Born near Lake Baikal, he was by nationality a Russian. This would prove important in his motivation and would enable him to serve his Czar faithfully for most of his adult life. But as a Buriat Mongol he also had a commitment to his religion and it was this which gave him his strength in the world of Lamaism. Unlike Montgomerie's Hindu pundits, Dorjiev did not have to pretend – or rely on disguises – to enter the citadel of Lamaism.

---

[1] N. M. Prjevalski, *The Fourth Journey in Central Asia of N. M. Prjevalski* (St Petersburg 1888).

[2] Variants of the name are Dorjieff, Dorji, Dorshieff, Dorzhievy, Dogiew, Dorjew, etc. The Buriat, on at least one occasion in India, used the alias, Akohwan Darjilikoff. One Tibetan name used by Dorjiev was Ghomang Lobzang. (P. Landon, *The Opening of Tibet*, New York, 1905, p. 22.) Ekai Kawaguchi, the Japanese Buddhist traveller to Lhasa in 1900, referred to Dorjiev by the Tibetan appellations, Ngaku-wang Dorje and Khende Chega. The German Tibetologist, W. A. Unkring, considered the Buriat's correct Tibetan name to be Nag-dhan Dorje, or 'The Gifted Orator, Thunderbolt'.

However often the Tibetans have had to defend themselves from predatory Mongol tribes, they have a common religious bond which links them. The Grand Lama of Urga ranks third, just after the Panchen Lama, in Lamaist hierarchy, and traditionally many Mongols study in Tibetan monasteries. Dorjiev, who is believed to have taken his earlier Buddhist studies at Ganden monastery near Urga, thus quite naturally moved to Tibet for more advanced theological study. He entered Drepung, or 'Rice Heap' monastery near Lhasa. But sometime before this he became an agent of the Russian Government.

It is difficult to date the beginning of Dorjiev's secret career. Possibly he was recruited by Russian intelligence when he joined Prjevalski's fourth expedition in 1884. The German explorer, Wilhelm Filchner, who took a particular interest in this subterranean aspect of Tibetan history, was convinced that the Buriat monk had joined the Russian service by 1885.[1] This is plausible since it was then that he began his new life in Drepung. Dorjiev rose rapidly in the priesthood. Either by good fortune or connivance, he was appointed 'Work-washing Abbot', with the prestigious duties of tutoring the young Dalai Lama who had just come of age. This position, given its curious title because the incumbent is called upon to sprinkle saffron-scented water throughout the Dalai's sacred quarters in the Potala in a symbolic cleansing rite, provided rare propinquity with His Holiness. As tutor and companion, the Buriat monk's influence on Tibet's Pontiff grew rapidly. The Japanese Buddhist monk, Ekai Kawaguchi, who spent two years in Lhasa disguised as a Chinese lama (1900-1902), could testify that Dorjiev through sheer theological brilliance so outshone the other members of the Dalai's entourage that he became the most powerful of the young Pontiff's advisers. The observant Kawaguchi was aware, however, that Dorjiev sought to ingratiate himself for a very specific purpose. The Buriat 'omitted no pains to win the heart of his little pupil' so that the latter 'was naturally led to hold him in the greatest estimation and affection.'[2]

---

[1] Wilhelm Filchner, 'A Story of Struggle and Intrigue in Central Asia', *Journal of the Central Asia Society*, 1927-28, p. 359. (This is a summary of Filchner's *Sturm Uber Asien*, Berlin, 1924.)

[2] Ekai Kawaguchi, *Three Years in Tibet* (Benares & London, 1909), p. 496.

Dorjiev made no secret of his Russian sympathies but he took care not to step out of character as a Lamaist monk. He avoided the tell-tale clues which usually betray a secret advocate of foreign interests. There was no talk of trade rights nor did he resort to other blandishments reminiscent of Curzon's heavy hand. Dorjiev was well aware of the Dalai's dread of foreign exploitation. He knew, for example, the Pontiff's suspicion of Curzon's intentions. He had seen a letter to the Maharajah of Sikkim, which accused the British of being 'well practiced in . . . political wiles' and wishing 'to overreach us' under the guise of 'establishing communications'.[1]

Dorjiev would not make these same mistakes. With a deft hand the Buriat insinuated his influence through the medium of religion. He treated the Dalai Lama not as chief of state but as God-king. If the Dalai Lama's court came to believe that the British agent, Sarat Chandra Das, had penetrated Lhasa to 'rob Tibet of her Buddhism',[2] it was equally convinced that Dorjiev genuinely meant to spread their faith – to extend their Pontiff's religious realm to include the vast empire of the Czar.

Kawaguchi reported that Dorjiev had authored a pamphlet in Lhasa which quoted ancient folklore in an effort to prove that the Czar was in fact a reincarnation of Tsong Khapa, the revered founder of the Yellow Hat sect. This near-deity, credited with introducing a reform Buddhism to Tibet, would, according to legend, reappear to rule from a capital called Chang Shambhala, far to the north. Since an early Tibetan prophet had projected this great Buddhist centre some 3,000 miles north-west of Bhudda's Indian birthplace, Dorjiev could plausibly claim it was in Russia. Even more outrageously he would allege that the Czar was a latter-day embodiment of the great Founder.[3] Kawaguchi admitted that he had never actually seen this pamphlet himself, but claimed on good authority that it existed. As he put it, Dorjiev's 'artful scheme has been crowned with great success, for today almost every Tibetan blindly believes in the ingenious story concocted by the Mongolian priest, and holds

---

[1] Sir Charles Bell, *Portrait of the Dalai Lama* (London, 1946), p. 62.
[2] Ekai Kawaguchi, *op. cit.*, p. 224.   [3] *Ibid.*, p. 498, 499, 500.

that the Czar will sooner or later subdue the whole world and found a gigantic Buddhist empire.'[1]

If the Japanese monk was guilty of some exaggeration, he was nonetheless accurate in so far as the Buriat propagandist did seem to have convinced the Dalai Lama that the Russian Czar was about to become a Buddhist. Sir Charles Bell, Indian civil servant, who years later was to become a close friend and adviser of the Thirteenth Dalai Lama, recalled in his authoritative book, *Portrait of the Dalai Lama*, that Dorjiev 'appears to have told the Dalai Lama that . . . since there are close contacts with Mongolia, more and more Russians were adopting Buddhism in its Tibetan form, and even the Tsar himself was likely to embrace it.'[2]

Dorjiev was also able to give the Dalai Lama very practical reasons for encouraging closer relations with Imperial Russia. By 1895 – the year in which the young Dalai reached his majority – it could be convincingly argued that Chinese and British influence could best be counteracted by Russian power. Russia's image had been a good one. Russian traders were Asians and many were Buddhists as well. Russian Mongols entered the Tibetan priesthood, living exemplary lives in Tibetan monasteries. These were all arguments which Dorjiev could and did use to good effect. But from a coldly analytical point of view the Buriat monk could point out that only Russia among the big powers was able to compete with Britain and China in the Central Asian arena of politics and defend Tibet from the imperialist designs of either.

The problem of Tibet's defences became acute in 1892 when Nepal again posed a threat. A disagreement over the rate of exchange between Tibetan salt and Nepalese rice revived the traditional enmity which for so long underlay relations between the two neighbours. By 1895 the dispute had provoked a Chinese reaction reminiscent of that caused by the earlier Tibet-Nepal crises of the 1870s and 1880s. But this time the Tibetans, who for the first time in many years had a ruling Dalai Lama rather than a pro-Chinese Regent, assumed a more independent attitude and

---

[1] *Ibid.*, p. 500.
[2] Sir Charles Bell, *Portrait of the Dalai Lama* (London, 1946), p. 62.

resisted Chinese advice to sue for terms with the Nepalese. The Tibetan Government felt that it must now look to its own defences rather than depend on its unhelpful suzerain. As a result the Dalai Lama had built in 1896 an arsenal capable of manufacturing modern rifles.

From the perspective of the British it was easy to exaggerate the Russian threat to Tibet at the turn of the century. Yet there was evidence which could not be ignored that the Czar indeed planned to extend his empire to include the high plateau. There were persuasive voices in St Petersburg which stirred His Imperial Majesty's imagination with dreams of Asian conquest. Prjevalski's explorations had popularized the idea of Russian supremacy over Asia. While still Crown Prince, Nicholas had toured the Far East accompanied by Prince Uktomskii who fervently believed that 'people of various races feel drawn to us [Russians] and ours by blood, tradition and by idea.' He assured Nicholas that 'this great and mysterious Orient is ready to become ours.'[1]

One of the more persuasive voices belonged to Dr P. A. Badmaev who advised the Russian Foreign Ministry on Mongol affairs for nearly two decades. Badmaev, a fellow Buriat and friend of Dorjiev, was also a court physician. This gave him access to the royal ear without the tempering filter of the more cautious Foreign Ministry. He could speak directly to the Emperor and persuade him that the Dalai Lama was the key to Mongolia. According to Witte, the Czar's influential Minister of Finance who long espoused economic expansion in the Far East, Badmaev was responsible for an imaginative scheme to ignite a mass uprising of the Tibetans and Mongols against the Chinese. Czar Alexander III was interested enough in this heady dream to promise Badmaev two million rubles with which to pay Buriat agitators who would excite the Tibetans and Mongols to revolt.[2]

Badmaev's influence continued undiminished when Nicholas replaced his father on the Russian throne and, if anything, the

---

[1] George A. Lensen (ed.), *Russia's Eastward Expansion* (Englewood Cliffs, N.J., Prentice Hall, 1964), Chapter 22, 'The Ideology of Russian Expansion', by Andrew Malozemoff, pp. 92, 93.

[2] A. Yarmolinsky (ed. and translator), *Memoirs of Count Witte* (London, 1952), p. 86.

grandiose plans for Central Asian expansion became even more ambitious. The fine hand of Badmaev seems to have been behind the visit to Lhasa of Menkujinov and Ulanov, two Buriat emissaries to the Dalai Lama, which was reported by the Russian press in 1894. Dorjiev, too, must have played a role in the secret discussions which took place in the Potala. Just what transpired has never been fully revealed, although subsequent events provided certain clues. There surely must have been some connection between this meeting and a vague, third-hand rumour reported in 1895 by the British Legation in Peking. Quoting as ultimate source the assistant to the Chinese *Amban* in Tibet, British Minister O'Connor wrote: 'Some time ago some Russian officers had been in communication with the Tibetan authorities . . . and impressed upon them the importance of maintaining friendly relations with the Russians who alone were able to protect them against the ambitious designs of the English who evidently coveted possession of Tibet.'[1]

In the summer of 1898 a Tibetan enthusiast in Darjeeling named Paul Möwis wrote an intriguing article[2] for the *Simla News* in which he claimed to have learned of a second Russian mission to Lhasa during the winter of 1898–99. The leader, he alleged, was Baranoff, a Russian officer who had once been secretary to Prjevalski. This article may have helped stimulate Curzon for on the next day he wrote Lord Hamilton, Secretary of State for India: 'There seems little doubt that Russian agents and possibly even someone of Russian origin have been at Lhasa, and I believe that the Tibetan Government is coming to the conclusion that it will have to make friends with one or another of the two great powers.' The Viceroy added: 'In as much as we have no hostile designs against Tibet, as we are in a position to give them something on the frontier to which they attach great importance and we none; and as the relations that we desire to establish with them are almost exclusively those of trade, I do not think it ought to be impossible if I could get into communications

[1] Alastair Lamb, 'Some Notes on Russian Intrigue in Tibet', *Journal of The Royal Central Asia Society*, January 1959; from FO 228 1186, O'Connor to Viceroy, 4 June 1895.
[2] India Office Library, Commonwealth Relations Office, London, FO 17 1407, India to Bengal, 24 May 1899 in I.O. to F.O., 22 November 1899.

with the Tibetan Government to come to terms.'[1] Curzon
would soon discover that this would not be easily accomplished.
The British had no Dorjiev in the Potala to plead their case, and
even if they had, he could not have moved fast enough to catch
up with the nimble Dorjiev.

On 22 October 1900, the British Foreign Office received in its
diplomatic bag a despatch from Her Majesty's Chargé d'Affaires
in St Petersburg. Hardinge enclosed a clipping from the 15
October edition of the *Journal de Saint Petersbourg*, which described briefly the reception by the Czar on 30 September of
'Aharamba Agyan Dorjief', described as 'First Tsanit Hamba'[2] to
the Dalai Lama of Tibet.[3] This was interesting news indeed.
When did this mysterious Buriat arrive in Russia and what really
was his mission? All the British Embassy could report was what
appeared in this single obscure announcement. The audience
took place in the Livadia Palace at the Black Sea resort of Yalta.
Hardinge confessed that he had not been able 'to procure any
precise information with regard to this person or to the mission
on which he is supposed to have come to Russia.'[4] He had not, for
one thing, learned that Dorjiev bore a private letter from the
Dalai Lama to the Czar.

When news of Dorjiev's appearance in Russia reached Calcutta,
Curzon went on record minimizing its importance. The strong-
willed Viceroy, still confident that his own plans to establish contact with the Dalai Lama would succeed, could not yet believe
that his adversary in the Great Game was outscoring him. He
wrote Hamilton on 18 November 1900: 'We are inclined here to
think that the Tibetan Mission to the Czar is a fraud and does not
come from Lhasa at all ... that the Tibetan lamas have so far overcome their incurable suspicion of all things European as to send
an open mission to Europe seems to be most unlikely.' Revealing
the serious inadequacies of the British assessment of the situation,
Curzon added: 'Tibet is, I think, much more likely in reality to
look to us for protection than to look to Russia, and I cherish a

---

[1] *Ibid.*, Private Correspondence, India, Pt II, Vol. XIII, Curzon to Hamilton, 24
May 1899.
[2] 'Tsanit Hamba' may be a garble of Tsa Nyi Kenpo, Dorjiev's Tibetan title.
[3] *Papers Relating to Tibet, 1904*, London, Cmd 1920, No. 31, p. 113.
[4] *Ibid.*

secret hope that the communications which I am trying to open with the Dalai Lama may inaugurate some sort of relations between us.'[1]

What Curzon would not discover for several months was that Dorjiev, en route to Russia in May or June 1900, passed through Darjeeling. He had stayed at a Buddhist monastery whose head had been specifically briefed and paid to report on travellers from Tibet. Moreover, while Dorjiev was there the eminent Tibetan scholar and pundit, Sarat Chandra Das, had unknowingly met with him. In response to a specific query Das had, in fact, telegraphed Calcutta on 14 November 1900 that 'if any mission had been sent from Lhasa, he would have heard regarding it.'[2]

Lord Curzon would hear much more of Dorjiev and finally discover the role of this enigmatic Buriat in twisting the lion's tail.

---

[1] India Office Library, London, Private Correspondence, India, Pt II, Vol. XVIII, Curzon to Hamilton, 18 November 1900.

[2] India Office Library, London, FO 17 1506, telegram Bengal to India, 14 November 1900 in I.O. to F.O., 1 July 1901.

16

Agents of the Czar

The British had become accustomed to dealing with Tibet through Peking: China was the suzerain power and as such controlled Tibet's external affairs. Moreover, Britain had been understandably reluctant to jeopardize its valuable coastal trade with China by any gesture toward Tibet which might alienate Peking. But it was obvious that such attention to propriety had not yielded results. Indicative of the Manchu's attitude toward the British in the mid-nineteenth century was their refusal to even discuss the demarcation of the Ladakh-Tibet boundary as proposed by the Government of India in 1846. Thirty years later, however, China's closed door in Tibet was opened a crack and this gave the British grounds for cautious hope. A single clause in the Chefoo Convention of 1876 between China and Britain permitted British exploratory missions to cross Tibet. This seemed to be a significant concession and, if interpreted liberally, could provide the British with the opening they wanted.

When in 1885 the Government of India attempted to test the Chefoo Convention, the realities of China's supposedly suzerain position in Tibet began to emerge. Specific approval was sought in Peking for Colman Macaulay of the Bengal provincial government to lead a mission to Lhasa. Permission was denied by the Chinese on the grounds of 'international consideration'. Macaulay was obliged to abandon the project. But the truth of the matter was obvious: the xenophobic Tibetans had refused to accept the British mission. An irate Tibetan government had gone so far as to muster its primitive army in the Chumbi Valley to stop Macaulay with flintlocks if need be. Certainly there was nothing China would or could do to force the Tibetans to accept the mission. However slow the British may have been in facing up to reality it was now at least clear that China's suzerain authority was more theoretical than real. Not only had the Thirteenth Dalai Lama come of age and assumed his traditional powers and prerogatives, but Peking's ability to resist Tibetan autonomy was severely diminished.

China's prestige had been seriously weakened by the humiliating defeat at the hands of the Japanese in 1895; no longer could the Manchus pretend to be the undisputed leaders of far Asia. But well before this, China's authority in Lhasa had been minimal. Peking's inability to prevent Tibet's violation of Sikkim territory in 1886 was a significant indication of the true situation. A Tibetan force had at that time moved into Sikkim from the Chumbi Valley and occupied a small area in the vicinity of Natong on the southern slope of the Himalayas. Since Lhasa had never recognized Sikkim as having any legal connection with the Government of India – to the contrary it was considered a vassal of Tibet – it could be argued that Tibet's action was not an act of provocation. But the British considered it so and after a year of patient waiting sent an ultimatum to the Dalai Lama. When this was ignored a small British force was sent to Sikkim where, after a brief skirmish, it drove the intruders across the border back into Tibet.

This incident alarmed the Chinese who feared that the British might take advantage of the situation to extract a bilateral settlement of the Sikkim border problem with Tibet. Rather than compromise its suzerain position, Peking agreed to negotiate with the British to determine the status of Sikkim and to define British trade rights in Tibet. The results were embodied in the Anglo-Chinese Convention of 1890 and the Tibetan Trade Regulations of 1893. This suited the British admirably. As Foreign Minister Lansdowne wrote: 'We shall probably before long be engaged in other and far more important negotiations respecting the Pamirs in which our interests and those of China will be in many respects identical.'[1] Britain obviously found it useful to keep its relations with the Chinese intact rather than see Russia benefit from serious tensions between them.

It soon became apparent that the Chinese could not impose

---

[1] India Office Library, London, FO 17 1168, Ind For Letter No. 134, 4 July 1893 in I.O. to F.O., 10 August 1893.

the terms of the Anglo-Chinese Convention and the Tibetan Trade Regulations on Tibet. Moreover, by negotiating with the Chinese for recognition of the Government of India's rights in Sikkim, the British had in effect acknowledged and supported Chinese sovereignty when it no longer existed and thus made even more remote any chance of Tibetan acceptance.

Curzon, who became Viceroy in 1899, realized pragmatically that if Britain's trade rights in Tibet, granted by the Chinese, were to have any meaning, there must be direct communications with the Dalai Lama so that his cooperation and goodwill could be secured. In describing the Chinese authority in Lhasa as 'an admitted farce', the British Viceroy was acknowledging that the Dalai Lama, not the Chinese, had the upper hand there. More basically, Curzon believed that China's defeat by the Japanese called for a reappraisal of Britain's Tibet policy. No longer should the myth of Chinese control over Tibet inhibit Britain from taking whatever steps were necessary to keep Tibet from falling under Russian influence.

Curzon's approach to Tibet was based on his conviction that Britain would ultimately have to defend the sub-continent from Russian aggression. In commenting on Russian ambitions, he wrote in 1901: 'As a student of Russian aspirations and methods for fifteen years, I assert with confidence – what I do not think any of her own statesmen would deny – that her ultimate ambition is the dominion of Asia. . . . Each morsel but whets her appetite for more, and inflames the passion for pan-Asiatic domination.'[1] Tibet unhappily seemed to be one of those morsels for which the Czar hungered. Bengal itself might even be gobbled up next. Curzon saw Tibet, like Afghanistan, as a buffer necessary to keep the Russians at a safe distance. If China could not or would not ensure this, then through direct negotiations and personal diplomacy with the Dalai Lama he would do so. 'I do not think it ought to be impossible,' he wrote '[to] get into communications with the Tibetan Government to come to terms.'[2]

The problem was to find a suitable emissary who would carry

---

[1] India Office Library, London, Letters from India, Vol. 139, No. 1376, Minute by Lord Curzon on Russian Ambitions in East Persia, dated 28 October 1890.
[2] *Ibid.*, Private Correspondence, India Pt II, Vol. XIII, Curzon to Hamilton, 24 May 1899.

a letter from the Viceroy to the Dalai Lama. Brief consideration was given to using a half-caste Chinese adviser to the Government of Burma, but it turned out that he was simply 'too fat' for the rigours of travel in Tibet. Another candidate was Chirang Palgez, the Ladakhi lama who traditionally headed the 'Lapchak' triennial tribute mission to the Dalai Lama from Leh. This approach had much to commend it: Ladakh was close to the Tibetan trade centre of Gartok, yet remote from Lhasa. Palgez, however, suffered from 'over-imbibing' – to put it delicately – and for this reason did not seem suitable.

Before abandoning the western approach altogether an effort was made to send a letter from the Viceroy to the Dalai Lama by way of the two governors, or *Garpons*, of Gartok. Captain R. L. Kennion, Assistant to the Resident in Kashmir, volunteered to make the journey to Gartok and to establish contact with the governors for this purpose. It was also recognized that Kennion, once in Gartok, could alternatively seek out the leader, or *Chapba*, of a triennial trading mission from Lhasa which was about to return to Tibet's capital from Gartok. As a merchant, he might be sympathetic to British trade aspirations and agree to carry a letter from Curzon to the Dalai Lama.

Sarat Chandra Das drafted for the Viceroy a letter suitably couched for the Dalai Lama's benefit. It was friendly and conciliatory. It assured His Holiness that the British simply wanted to 'facilitate trade . . . and to foster that direct and friendly intercourse which should subsist between neighbours'.[1] The Dalai was urged to send a responsible emissary to Calcutta where further conversations could take place.

Kennion was stopped by the Tibetans before he reached Gartok. Although the *Garpons* had promised to forward Curzon's letter to Lhasa, they returned it to Kennion several months later, claiming that Lhasa had refused to accept it. Within a month the governors had changed their story and now wrote that they had never forwarded the letter to Lhasa. The seals were broken and Kennion, at least, was convinced that officials in Lhasa had in fact received and read Curzon's message. By claiming that it had never reached Tibet's capital, the Dalai Lama could avoid the

[1] *Papers Relating to Tibet, 1904* (London, 1904), pp. 120, 121.

onus of having rejected it. Curzon, however, did not accept this analysis. He preferred to believe that his message had never got through so that he was still justified in searching for a suitable envoy to deliver his letter.

Kazi Ugyen,[1] Bhutan's Minister stationed in Darjeeling, was an obvious possibility. He had visited Lhasa in 1898 and upon his return had been cooperative in reporting on his trip to John Claude White, British Political Officer in Sikkim. Ugyen's testimony at that time hinted that the Dalai Lama, whom he claimed to have seen, was dissatisfied with Chinese suzerainty and desired to have closer relations with India. In a general sort of way it appeared that His Holiness had suggested to Kazi that he convey this to the British.[2] A year later the Bhutanese Minister, or *Vakil*, was persuaded to follow up this overture with a letter to the Dalai Lama reflecting Curzon's hope of establishing closer relations with Tibet. But in December 1899 Curzon wrote Lord George Hamilton, Secretary of State, admitting that the Dalai Lama did not respond 'for fear of the Chinese *Amban*'. Kazi Ugyen wrote the Dalai Lama again in December 1899. This time the tone of the letter was significantly stronger: 'should the Viceroy in Calcutta lose patience, it will not end well for you.' But this more threatening letter had no more success than the one before.

In June 1901 Kazi Ugyen was commissioned by the Dalai Lama to escort to Lhasa a curious cargo consisting of two elephants, two peacocks and a leopard. It seemed significant that Kazi had been selected for this assignment. It suggested that the Bhutanese *Vakil* still enjoyed the Dalai Lama's confidence. And perhaps – at least Curzon could hope – it was a signal that the Dalai wanted this opportunity to hold substantive conversations with Kazi Ugyen about the British. Whatever the case, Curzon was determined to take the rare occasion of the Vakil's trip to send a revised letter to the Dalai Lama. This version of the Viceroy's

---

[1] Kazi Ugyen was grandfather of Jigme Dorje, Prime Minister of Bhutan, who was assassinated on 5 April 1964.

[2] *Royal Central Asia Society Journal*, Jul/Oct 1964, Vol. LI, Parts III, IV, p. 302: from Foreign Department Secret E Proceedings, August 1899, No. 56. Letter from Chief Secretary, Bengal, 23 January 1899 containing a 'note' by Kazi Ugyen on his visit to Lhasa.

message was peremptory in tone. He warned the Dalai Lama that if his current attitude persisted, Great Britain '. . . must reserve their right to take such steps as may seem . . . necessary' to see that the Convention of 1890 and the Trade Regulations of 1893 were properly observed.

This letter too was rejected with the seals intact. On his return to Calcutta in October 1901, Kazi Ugyen claimed that the Dalai Lama excused himself by alleging that tradition forbade him from accepting messages from foreigners like the British. It is still a matter of scholarly dispute whether Ugyen was telling the truth. There was gossip in the Darjeeling bazaar that he had not delivered the letter personally to the Dalai Lama as instructed and – even worse – had revealed the substance of his mission to certain Tibetan ministers. But Sir Charles Bell, author of *Portrait of the Dalai Lama* and friend of the Thirteenth Lama in later years, accepted at face value Ugyen's version of what happened in Lhasa and seems to have thought highly of the Bhutanese *Vakil*. Certainly Ugyen never ceased to protest his own innocence. Curzon, however, frustrated by his inability to establish contact with the Dalai Lama, was convinced that he had been betrayed by Kazi Ugyen. To have believed otherwise would have been tantamount to admitting that his tactics of trying to force the Dalai Lama to enter into a diplomatic dia-logue had been wrong. The strong-willed Viceroy wrote Lord George Hamilton:

You will remember me telling you, some time ago, when we were discussing what should be done after getting into communications with the Dalai Lama that the opening of communications, not their prosecu-tion or their sequel, was the course. This has been borne out by the experience of the Bhutanese envoy, Ugyen Kazi, whom we sent up, or rather entrusted with the last letter from me. He alleges that he handed it to the Dalai Lama himself, and that the latter refused to take it. Accordingly he brought it back with the seal intact. I do not believe that the man ever saw the Dalai Lama or handed the letter to him. On the contrary, I believe him to be a liar and in all probability, a paid Tibetan spy.[1]

---

[1] India Office Library, London, Private Correspondence, India, Pt II, Vol. XXI, Curzon to Hamilton, 5 November 1901.

Curzon's inability to correspond with the Dalai Lama was galling enough, but the Viceroy's fury and frustration reached new heights when news arrived that the mysterious Dorjiev had made a second trip to Russia during the summer of 1901, and was rumoured to have brought to Russia friendly letters from the Dalai Lama. Dr Badmaev simultaneously announced from St Petersburg that the Tibetans were now seeking Russian guarantees of assistance in the event of aggression.

The British Consul General in Odessa forwarded a clipping from *Odessa Novosti* dated 12 June 1901 mentioning Dorjiev's brief visit to that city while en route to St Petersburg. Describing it as an 'Extraordinary Mission' with diplomatic significance, the article hinted that Dorjiev's object was to strengthen Tibet-Russian relations. *Odessa Novosti* also revealed that Dorjiev would, among other things, raise the matter of establishing in St Petersburg a permanent Tibetan Mission.

The Russian newspaper, *Novoi Vremya*, editorialized: 'A rapprochement with Russia must seem to him [the Dalai Lama] the most natural step, as Russia is the only power able to frustrate the intrigues of Great Britain.' Lamsdorff, the Russian Foreign Minister, however, debunked this sort of conjecture and assured the British Embassy that the conclusions drawn by certain Russian newspapers were 'ridiculous and utterly unfounded'. He added that Dorjiev's object was simply to collect donations for his religious order from the numerous Buddhists in the Russian Empire.[1]

Yet when Dorjiev was received by the Czar on 23 June at the Grand Palace at Peterhof, he was described in the *Messager Official* as the 'Envoy Extraordinary' from the Dalai Lama. When an agitated British Embassy complained again, Lamsdorff uncomfortably replied that the mission was of the same character as those sent by the Pope to the faithful abroad. These reassurances were not convincing in London and the British Ambassador in St Petersburg on instructions informed Lamsdorff that 'His Majesty's Government would ... not regard with indifference any proceedings that might have a tendency to disturb the existing status in Tibet.' This, however, only provoked

[1] *Papers Relating to Tibet, 1904* (London, 1904), p. 166.

Lamsdorff to repeat starchily that Dorjiev's mission was 'chiefly concerned with matters of religion, and had no political or diplomatic object or character'.[1]

Had Whitehall then realized that the Dalai Lama himself had seriously considered visiting St Petersburg, its concern would have been even greater. Dorjiev's neatly tailored description of Tibet's place in the *real politik* of Asia had convinced the Dalai Lama that only Russia would defend him from almost certain British invasion. The Buriat stressed the impotence of China, Tibet's natural protector, and argued plausibly that to protect itself from British coastal pressures, China would ultimately sacrifice Tibet to Great Britain as a sop. So close was the Dalai Lama to making an unprecedented journey to Russia that he had already sent to St Petersburg the sacred cushion on which he would sit in audience with the Czar, and an exquisite *codex aureus* as a present for His Majesty. The Tsong-du, or Tibetan National Council, had intervened, however, and made it clear that the Dalai Lama had exceeded his authority in even entertaining such an idea. The Tibetan Pontiff had had to be satisfied with sending a personal envoy to accompany Dorjiev on his second trip. It had been the high-ranking abbot named Tsannyid who returned with the Russian proposal that a prince of the royal house and Cossack guard take up residence in Lhasa in a somewhat ambiguous status – a sort of paraplenipotentiary – to promote friendly relations between Russia and Tibet.[2]

Curzon was now seriously troubled by the mysterious Dorjiev. He wrote Hamilton on 11 September 1901:

I am afraid it cannot be said that the Tibetan Mission to Russia only represents monasteries in the north of Tibet. On the contrary, the head of the mission [Dorjiev], though originally a Russian Mongolian subject, has been resident in Lhasa for many years, and is no doubt familiar with the priestly junta who rule in that place. I do not myself believe that he is upon a mission, or that he conveys a formal message from the Dalai Lama to the Tsar, but that he will go back with such a mission and such

[1] Sir Francis Younghusband, *op. cit.*, p. 70.
[2] Percival Landon, *The Opening of Tibet* (New York, 1905), pp. 23, 24.

a message. I have not the slightest doubt whatever, that, whether the rational attitude of the Tibetan Government is thereby affected or not, the result must in any case be unfavourable to ourselves.[1]

News of the second Dorjiev mission to Russia provoked Curzon to launch a serious investigation. What the dismayed Viceroy discovered did nothing to lighten his worries nor give him confidence in the Bengal Government's handling of border intelligence. Belatedly it was discovered that in April 1901, Dorjiev and three companions had for the second time passed through India – this time to Bombay from where they embarked by ship to Singapore. From Singapore the party made its way to Peking – then overland via the Trans-Siberian and Trans-Caspian railways to Odessa. The Viceroy admitted to Hamilton that he was 'very much exercised over the question of Tibet', and complained about the Bengal Government's intelligence failure. He wrote: 'So utterly have they [Government of Bengal] failed in the discharge of this particular duty, that we now learn that two Tibetan missions that visited the Tsar at Livadia last year and again this, left Lhasa, crossed the British border – passed in one case through Darjeeling and in the other through Segowlie [via Nepal] – traversed India by rail and took ship from Indian ports without the slightest inkling on the part of the Bengal Government or its agents that any such persons had been in their midst.'[2] He later described this as 'one of the most eloquent results of handing over political functions to local governments which have no aptitude, no taste, no experience and no men for the job.'[3]

Curzon was determined to take Tibetan affairs into his own Viceregal hands rather than rely on the obviously inadequate Bengal Government. Any vestige of a soft policy toward Tibet had now disappeared from Curzon's thinking. He wrote:

I am not certain [but what] . . . I shall not require to adopt some such policy towards Tibet as Tibet adopts toward ourselves; in other words we might have to prevent any Tibetan subject or caravan from crossing

---

[1] India Office Library, London, Private Correspondence, India, Pt II, Vol. XXI, Curzon to Hamilton, 11 September 1901.
[2] *Ibid.*, Vol. XX, Curzon to Hamilton, 10 July 1901.
[3] *Ibid.*, Vol. XXI, Curzon to Hamilton, 5 November 1901.

our frontier . . . it would be giving the Tibetans tit for tat, and it would, I expect, bring them more promptly to their knees than any other proposal.[1]

It was at this time that Curzon began to believe that since the Dalai Lama would not correspond with him, the British should send a mission to Lhasa to obtain satisfaction. Although he assured Hamilton in July 1901 that such ideas had 'hardly yet taken shape in my mind', it was obvious that the Viceroy was veering closer to grapeshot diplomacy.[2]

Much had been rumoured about Russian arms aid to Tibet during the tense days following the turn of the century. As usual the Bengal Government's Tibet watchers had little to go on beyond frontier rumours. It wasn't until years later that a German orientalist named Wilhelm Filchner claimed to have the details of this episode in Russo-Tibet relations. In a book entitled *Storm Over Asia: Experiences of Secret Diplomatic Agents* (Berling, 1924), which purported to be the story of Russian-Tibetan intrigues, Filchner named a Mongol lama called Zerempil as one of Russia's prime instruments in Lhasa. Zerempil had studied under Dorjiev at the Ganden monastery near Urga and had then been recruited by the Russian intelligence service and trained by the India Section of the General Staff in St Petersburg. After various secret missions in the Pamirs and along the Northwest Frontier, he entered the Tibet scene in 1901 when he was picked by Colonel Orlov (alias Bogdanovitch) of the Russian General Staff to lead one of two caravans of arms being secretly shipped to Lhasa.[3] This project was presumably the result of an arrangement negotiated with Dorjiev during his first trip to Russia.

Filchner's narrative, which is somewhat sensational in nature and thus considered suspect by most scholars, describes in considerable detail the arms caravans. The larger of the two, consisting of 200 camels loaded with rifles, was conducted by Orlov himself, under cover of a 'scientific expedition'. It marched from Urga through the Gobi desert, Tsaidam, and Tong La to enter

---

[1] *Ibid.*, Vol. XX, Curzon to Hamilton, 10 July 1901.
[2] *Ibid.*, 31 July 1901.   [3] W. Filchner, *op. cit.*, p. 359.

Lhasa early in December 1901.[1] The second caravan, under Zerempil's leadership and allegedly guarded by twenty Cossacks, consisted of 55 horses and 200 yaks laden with rifles and ammunition. It travelled from Urga by way of Koko Nor, arriving in Lhasa in November 1902. Zerempil's next task was to construct a small gun factory in Lhasa to manufacture Martini Henry rifles for the Tibetan army.

While these particular details were not known to Curzon, some inkling of what was occurring in Lhasa reached the Indian Government from Sarat Chandra Das who regularly corresponded with Ekai Kawaguchi, the Japanese Buddhist who lived in Lhasa in disguise from 1900 to 1902. Judging by the wealth of detail which appeared in his book *Three Years in Tibet*,[2] published a few years later, Kawaguchi was a remarkably well-informed observer. He was probably a Japanese intelligence agent, whose country's interest in Tibet was based on its fear of growing Russian power on the Asian mainland and derived from the assumption that this high plateau represented a vulnerable back door to China.

Approximately two months after Dorjiev's return from Russia (*circa* February 1902) Kawaguchi personally observed 'two hundred camels, fully loaded, arrive from the north-east'. He recalled with some precision that 'the load consisted of small boxes, two packed on each camel.' Although the drivers of the caravan were reticent about discussing the cargo with Kawaguchi, the curious Japanese elicited the story from a loose-tongued Tibetan official within a day or two.[3] Kawaguchi later even found the opportunity of inspecting one of the guns.

Kawaguchi was also the source of the only information to reach the Western world concerning Dorjiev's activities in Lhasa. Upon returning from Russia, the mysterious Buriat appeared suddenly affluent and generous. He presented to the Dalai Lama a full set of episcopal robes given by the Czar, himself. Whatever symbolic significance this strange gift was meant to have, it was an awesome thing for Tibet's pontiff. Dorjiev, according to Kawaguchi, was particularly generous toward

---

[1] P. Mehra, 'Tibet and Russian Intrigue', *Journal of the Royal Central Asia Society*, January 1958, p. 36.
[2] Ekai Kawaguchi, *op. cit.*   [3] *Ibid.*, pp. 505, 506.

Shata, Tibet's Senior Minister. Playing on the Minister's anti-British bias and general venality, Dorjiev was able to enlist him as a secret ally by a liberal disbursement of Russian-supplied gold.

By the end of 1902 the accumulated evidence pointing to secret Russia-China collaboration could no longer be ignored. Weakened by the Sino-Japanese War, China was in no position to oppose growing Russian influence along its Central Asian borders. And agreement on Tibet would have the advantage to China of keeping the aggressive Curzon from moving on Tibet. Russia's aggressive designs on Tibet were entirely consistent with its *Drang Nach Osten* – or so it seemed to the British in India. There were indeed a growing number of *Vostochniki*, or Easterners, in Russia who had convinced themselves that all of Asia was Russia's natural sphere of influence. If the European powers were justified in carving up Africa, wasn't it just as natural for Russia to absorb the Far East? In 1883 V. P. Vasil'ev, a noted Russian orientalist, insisted that Russia must advance toward the east to liberate peoples oppressed by the 'tyranny of internecine strife and impotency', and a few years later the Russian philosopher, Vladimir Solov'ev preached that it was Russia's duty to defend Europe against the 'yellow power'. At the time of Dorjiev's first arrival in Russia, the influential paper, *Novoe Vremya* (17 November 1901), was stirred to echo this philosophy and apply it to Tibet:

Present events in China are quite sufficient to explain this attempt on the part of Tibet to seek a rapprochement with Russia, if such it really be. It is only natural considering the actual state of the Chinese Government that Tibet would seek Russia's protection. Russia has gained such renown by her peoples of Central Asia, who like Bokhara, have fallen under her power or appealed to her protection, that it would be perfectly natural if not only Tibet, but all the other regions of Northern and Western China, contiguous with the Russian dominions, were to begin to take steps to obtain peace and tranquillity under the aegis of the Czar.[1]

---

[1] Alastair Lamb, *Britain and Chinese Central Asia* (London, 1960); from India Office Library, Home Correspondence, India, Vol. 191, No. 2486.

While philosophers cloaked the strategic designs of the empire with ideological robes, Russia's General Staff saw Tibet much as Curzon saw it – the eastern wing of a vital buffer zone between the two expanding empires. The problem arose because each believed that this buffer should be its own particular fief. If Russia was convinced that a friendly and controlled Tibet was necessary to protect Russian paramountcy in Sinkiang and in the Pamirs, Curzon was equally certain that a Tibet responsive to Great Britain was necessary to protect the Himalayan dependencies which served as guardian fortresses for India itself.

A parallel situation existed in Afghanistan where still another agonizing Afghan war was yet to take place to determine in whose sphere of influence this important keystone of the long buffer zone would be. North-east Persia, the extreme western wing of the zone, was likewise a region of tension between the two great powers.

Viewed against this background, there were various bits and pieces of specific evidence which pointed to a secret Sino-Russian accord on Tibet, and this seemed ominous indeed. In February 1902, rumours of an understanding between St Petersburg and Peking were heard from Nepal. The British representative in Nepal reported a fantastic story in which the Maharajah Chandra Shamsher Jang of Nepal, quoting a Tibetan lama, alleged that British pressure on the Tibetan frontier had provoked China, Tibet, Bhutan and Ladakh to band together and seek Russian assistance in the event of a British attack on Tibet. As an earnest promise of Russia's intentions three Russian engineers were even now supervising the construction of a weapon factory in Lhasa.[1] The purpose of the Lama's conversation with the Maharajah was to invite Nepal to join this defensive alliance. The Chinese reformer, Kang Yu-wei, living in exile in Darjeeling, reported in May that a secret treaty had been signed between Russia and China. And if this source seemed dubious, confirmation of a sort came from the British Legation in Peking when in August, Sir Ernest Satow, British Minister, passed on press reports telling a story very similar to Kang Yu-wei's. While Satow

---

[1] Alastair Lamb, *Britain and Chinese Central Asia* (London, 1960), p. 267; from India Office Library, FO 17 1745, Colonel Pears to India, 13 January 1902 in I.O. to F.O., 24 February 1902.

was appropriately sceptical, he did point out that there had been solid indications that China was interested in coming to some agreement on Tibet.[1]

Captain Parr, China's customs officer at Yatung on the Sikkim-Tibet border, had information from supposedly good sources confirming the existence of a secret treaty proposal and describing it as a document of eleven articles. In this Russia promised to support the integrity and internal security of China in return for a recognition by China of Russian rights in Tibet. China would continue to have its commercial interests in Tibet, and have the right to post consular representatives there. Chinese goods would continue to enter Tibet duty-free or with only light duties. By the terms of the alleged agreement Russia would be permitted to station government representatives in Tibet, but they would be pledged to show consideration toward the local population: they must neither oppress the people nor impose Christianity on them. Both countries agreed to participate jointly in mining and railway enterprises in Tibet.[2]

Satow in Peking reported similar terms which he had gleaned from an article in the *China Times* of 18 July 1902. The inclusion of a twelfth clause in which Russia agreed to respect sacred places during the 'construction of a rail line', revealed St Petersburg's plan to link Tibet with the Trans-Siberian rail system. As Bogle observed more than a century earlier, there could be no defence of Tibet without adequate supply arteries. Satow had doubts that the draft treaty – if such existed – had yet been signed, but he seemed to have no doubts that 'some sort of *pourparlers* of an unofficial kind have taken place'.[3]

Satow was heard from again in October 1902. Jung Lu, trusted adviser of the Empress Dowager, was reported to have impressed his personal seal on the secret draft agreement with the Russians. According to one of Jung Lu's agents, who actually showed the agreement to an informant of the British Legation, the Russians would be awarded a privileged role in China proper, and Peking

---

[1] *Ibid.*, FO 17 1745, Sir Ernest Satow, Telegram No. 230 of 2 August 1902.

[2] Alastair Lamb, *Britain and Chinese Central Asia* (London, 1960), p. 269; from India Office Library, FO 17 1745, White to India, 20 August 1902 in I.O. to F.O., 16 September 1902.

[3] *Ibid.*, FO 17 1745, Sir Ernest Satow, No. 217 of 5 August 1902.

would recognize the border regions of Mongolia, Sinkiang and Tibet as being in the Russian sphere of influence. According to this startling document, Russia in return would also help China suppress internal uprisings. Jung Lu, acting in effect as a secret agent of the Czar, promised to secure the Empress Dowager's endorsement of the principal points of the agreement if Russia in exchange for his efforts would protect him against punishment for the prominent role he had played in inciting the Boxer uprisings.[1]

Hardinge, the British Chargé d'Affaires in St Petersburg, added a new dimension to the mystery in November 1902 with a report from a secret, but reliable source, alleging an agreement between Russia and the Dalai Lama. According to this agreement, Buriat Lamaists in Russia would be permitted to station an official representative in Lhasa. The person selected for this latter post would be none other than Badmaev.[2] Shortly after Hardinge's information had been received, Satow passed on a copy of a telegram, alleged to have been sent to Jung Lu in Peking by one of the *Ambans* in Lhasa, which revealed that the Dalai Lama had given permission for a Russian officer and a mining engineer to establish themselves in Lhasa, complete with Cossack guard detachment.[3]

The role which gold played in Russia's policy toward Tibet was for some reason overlooked or suppressed in the record. British official sources, such as the so-called 'Blue Books'[4] on Tibet, ignored the subject altogether. Perhaps Whitehall simply felt that it introduced an unnecessarily complicating factor. In 1899 Rothschild banking interests, which had gotten wind of Russian plans, were not, however, so willing to ignore them. Through an agent named Miller they sought permission from the India Office to preempt and exploit Tibetan gold. Miller argued that Sven Hedin, the Swedish explorer, had secretly contracted with the Russian government to survey known gold fields

---

[1] Alastair Lamb, *Britain and Chinese Central Asia* (London, 1960), p. 270; from India Office Library, FO 17 1745, Sir Ernest Satow, No. 289, Confidential, 8 October 1902.

[2] *Ibid.*, FO 17 1746, Younghusband to India, 3 June 1903, in I.O. to F.O., 8 July 1903.

[3] *Ibid.*, FO 17 1745, Sir Ernest Satow, Telegram No. 361 of 20 November 1902.

[4] Known officially as *Papers Relating to Tibet*, published in 1910 by His Majesty's Stationery Office.

on his next expedition to Tibet. Thus, as first step to beat the Russians, Miller proposed employing the respected Englishman, Sir Thomas Holdich, late of the Survey of India, to head a British expedition to Tibet. Should gold in commercial quantities be located, the British Government would, according to Rothschild's plan, be called upon to extract a mining concession from China.

The India Office, always alert for commercial opportunity, was reasonably sympathetic to Miller's scheme. Gold had interested the East India Company from the earliest days and the more recent survey of western Tibet's Thok Jalung fields by the pundit, Nain Singh, had refired this interest. But Curzon, probably realizing the many complications, was less than enthusiastic and managed to have the project killed.[1]

It was never proved that Sven Hedin acted as an agent for the Russians, either for purposes of gold exploration or for any other reason. But there was other evidence that Russia was interested in Tibetan gold. A certain Russian named von Groot, who managed Russian gold mining operations in Mongolia, was reported in November 1902 to have petitioned the Chinese for a concession to extend the Trans-Siberian rail line into Tibet so as to enable Tibetan gold to be exported economically. In this connection it is interesting that the British Embassy in St Petersburg described von Groot less than a year later (October 1903) as the 'chief organizer of Russian influence in Mongolia and Tibet'.[2]

More explicit evidence of Russia's mineral interest in Tibet appeared in the 26 March 1903 edition of the *North China Herald*. The story described an eight-point treaty with Tibet and China which gave Russia extensive mining rights in Tibet. By the terms of this treaty China would receive a ten per cent royalty on all profits, and reserved the right to be consulted on all Russian Mining operations.[3] The essence of this information had also reached the British from secret sources in the Chinese Government, which added that a party of five Russians had gone from China to Lhasa to negotiate the agreement, and had in fact

---

[1] Alastair Lamb, *Britain and Chinese Central Asia*, pp. 355–7.
[2] *Ibid.*, p. 273; from India Office Library, FO 17 1746, Spring Rice, No. 335 of 15 October 1903.
[3] *Ibid.*, Indian Foreign Letter No. 88 of 2 July 1903 in I.O. to F.O.

reached an agreement in Lhasa with the Chinese *Amban* in February 1903.

By late November 1902, the accumulating evidence of secret collaboration between Russia and China on the subject of Tibet had convinced Curzon that British interests were gravely in jeopardy. In a private letter to Hamilton the Viceroy wrote: 'I am myself a firm believer in the existence of a secret understanding, if not a secret treaty between Russia and China about Tibet: and as I have before said, I regard it as a duty to frustrate this little game while there is yet time.' Analysing the problem further, Curzon added: 'My impression is that the Russians have told the Chinese on no account to negotiate with us, or to allow us to come to close quarters with the Tibetans, for the results of such proceedings must be greater intercourse between India and Tibet, if not an improved treaty.'[1]

Curzon was already beginning to formulate his plan and in the same letter he sketched it out informally for Hamilton: 'My idea . . . is that we should let the Chinese and Tibetans play the game of procrastination for some little time longer, and should then say . . . as it is clear that they do not mean business, that we propose to send a mission up to Lhasa to negotiate a new treaty in the spring [1903] . . . I would inform China and Tibet that it was going, and go it should. It would be accompanied by a sufficient force to ensure its safety.'[2]

The concept of a mission to Lhasa was opposed by many in London whose objections are well documented. But the story of British initiatives in Tibet for the next two years is the story of Curzon riding rough-shod over domestic opposition. The 'forward thruster' would have his way – for better or for worse.

---

[1] India Office Library, London; FO 17 1745, extract from private letters from Lord Curzon on 13 November 1902, with a minute by Lord Lansdowne.
[2] *Ibid.*

Francis Younghusband

Chinese suzerainty over Tibet, in Curzon's opinion, was a 'constitutional myth', which had created a yawning vacuum to tempt the Czar. If this continued, it would, he felt, permit Russia 'to come down to the big mountain and . . . begin intriguing with Nepal'. While few seriously believed that Russia coveted India itself, many feared a dangerous erosion of British prestige if Russia were permitted to reach the Himalayas. In practical terms this latter possibility meant that the British border dependencies might gravitate to Russia rather than Britain for protection. And, if the Sepoy Mutiny had taught any lesson, Indians themselves could not be trusted to remain loyal to the British Raj, particularly if a rival were to show up its weakness and beckon from the frontier.

Curzon had become convinced that the only way to keep Russia from persisting in Tibetan adventures and to dissuade Tibetans from heeding Russia's blandishments was to apply direct pressure. The failing Manchus had already revealed their impotence in Tibet, and the Dalai Lama's unwillingness to enter into a dialogue with Curzon clearly ruled out a local diplomatic solution. The state of Russo-British relations, aggravated as they were by tension along their contiguous Asian spheres of influence, made early agreement even more unlikely.

Curzon's tactical plan, first proposed in February 1902, called for gradually increasing pressure on the Sikkim-Tibet frontier. First the Tibetans must be evicted from the contested sliver of border territory north of Giaogong, which had been previously seized and occupied by Tibetan troops. If Lhasa still refused to accept the boundary delimitation agreed upon in the Anglo-Chinese Convention of 1890 or concede British trading rights as specified in the 1876 Chefoo Convention, also signed with China,

British forces would have to consider occupying Tibet's Chumbi Valley. The Viceroy actually felt that there was little hope in achieving any meaningful agreement with the Tibetans through local border negotiations: only in Lhasa itself could a settlement be reached. But it was impolitic to go this far yet in pleading his case with London where caution was still the rule of Indian colonial policy.

The India Office approved the occupation of Giaogong which had a defensible legal basis, but predictably withheld from the aggressive Curzon authority to push on further. In June 1902, John Claude White, the Viceroy's Political Officer in Sikkim, with a small force of 150 troops removed with ease a few Tibetans quietly grazing their livestock near Giaogong oblivious to their role in the Great Game. China was miffed that Whitehall had not seen fit to inform them of this move. To save some face Peking named two commissioners to meet with White. Even though they never actually appeared, China had made its point – albeit feebly.

Curzon, who had long since written off China as a power in Tibet, was inclined to be cavalier in considering Peking's rights and interests in its supposed vassal. The India Office was more cautious and correct; it still saw China – even a weak China – as a necessary deterrent to increasing Russian influence. At a minimum it was important to prevent China from being used by Russia to extend its influence into Tibet as would be the case if the rumoured treaty negotiations between them came to fruition. Consideration for China's territorial rights was, in fact, an important reason for the Home Government's reluctance to invade the Chumbi Valley.

Another and more compelling reason, however, was fear that the occupation of the Chumbi Valley would bring the Tibetans no nearer to the conference table, yet would gratuitously provide Russia with an excuse for even bolder action in Tibet – or elsewhere along the edges of Britain's Asian Empire. The India Office was inclined to suspect that Curzon, who must also have realized that a Chumbi expedition would only stiffen Tibetan intransigence, cynically sought this excuse to justify an advance to Lhasa. Certainly, British forces could not meekly withdraw simply on the basis of being snubbed in the Chumbi Valley. Once having entered Tibetan territory, the only option would be to go on. This, in turn, would lead to impossible military com-mitments, undesirable at that time in view of requirements for the Boer War in South Africa. Perhaps more serious was the likelihood that a British presence in Lhasa would provoke serious Russian counteraction in Afghanistan or eastern Persia, threatening India's North-west Frontier.

The India Office in London tried unsuccessfully to convince Curzon of the merits of an alternative to his strategy of direct pressure on Tibet. This was the so-called 'Lee-Warner Plan' to use Nepal as a 'cat's paw'. Kathmandu, whose relations with Lhasa were not of the best, would be encouraged to attack Tibet. Justification would be the terms of the 1856 Tibeto-Nepal Treaty since Russian influence in Tibet could be construed as a threat to Nepal. But the strong-willed Viceroy would have none of it. Exasperated with the Home Government's timidity and unrealism, he forcefully made his views known in a definitive despatch dated 8 January 1903.[1] Curzon's thesis was that the spectre of Russian pre-eminence in Tibet demanded a new approach to that problem – one not inhibited by the myth of Chinese suzerainty. Britain would inform Peking that talks with Tibet would begin in early 1903, but would insist that they be held in Lhasa rather than on the border. The talks would include the whole question of British-Tibet relations, not just the Sikkim border problem, and would conclude with agreement that a permanent British representative with military escort be stationed in Lhasa. Trade would be discussed, but as a purely secondary issue: Russia was the main problem, and no settle-ment could be acceptable without an elimination of the Russian presence in Lhasa.

Prime Minister Balfour still feared that a British mission in Lhasa would be viewed around the world as a blatant infringe-ment of the integrity of China. He preferred to try first a recom-mendation by Lansdowne to negotiate with Russia in the hope that a declaration of disinterest in Tibet could be extracted from the Czarist Government. Curzon's proposal, however brilliantly articulated, was still too dynamic for the Cabinet. Whitehall would not yet permit the Viceroy to go beyond negotiation

---

[1] India Office Library, London, FO 17 1745, Indian Foreign Letter of 8 January 1903.

with an accredited Tibetan representative on the Sikkim-Tibet border while Lansdowne, in the meantime, proceeded to seek satisfaction in talks with Russia's Ambassador Benckendorff in London.

As might have been foreseen, conversations with the Russians simply provided the latter with an opportunity to complain about British moves toward Tibet. For every rumour of Russian action with which Lansdowne could confront Benckendorff, the Russian diplomat could cite with equally plausible evidence examples of British provocation. Lansdowne did wheedle out of Benckendorff acknowledgment that the British, as a power contiguous with Tibet sharing a common frontier, was entitled to insist by force, if necessary, that Tibet respect its treaty obligations. But St Petersburg could never bring itself to endorse its envoy's admissions. Lansdowne also complained that St Petersburg would not respond with a categoric yes or no when specifically asked 'whether there was or not a secret agreement between Russia and Tibet'.[1] Russia, in fact, assumed a somewhat threatening stance, claiming that it 'could not remain indifferent to any serious disturbance of the *status quo*' in Tibet. If one occurred, Russia 'might be obliged to take measures elsewhere'.

London was forced to rely solely on Benckendorff's very tentative and unendorsed views – tenuous grounds indeed – hoping for Russian acquiescence to Britain's Tibet policy as it unfolded in action. Far from meeting face to face on the Russian threat to Tibet, Lansdowne had been intimidated into falling back to the pallid and unconvincing issues of frontier trade and frontier delimitation, and making the most of them to justify Britain's posture in Tibet.

Curzon, whose views were asked on 14 April, was neither pleased nor appeased. He wrote testily to Hamilton on 8 January; 'If you ask me whether Benckendorff's apparently categorical reply denying Russian activity in Lhasa removed my suspicions, I say emphatically no.' The Viceroy felt that while British *démarches* may have warned off Russia for the moment, the Czar would not simply pursue his goals in Lhasa in a more

---

[1] *Papers Relating to Tibet, 1904* (London, His Majesty's Stationery Office, 1904), p. 187, Lansdowne to Scott, 24 March 1903.

discreet manner. This made it all the more urgent that Britain
place a mission in Lhasa to observe what was really going on.
But rather than clash head on with the British Cabinet's opposition to such a mission, the Viceroy contented himself with re-
opening border negotiations in the hope that these would show
the folly of treating with Tibetans anywhere short of Lhasa, and
would eventually justify a mission to Lhasa.

Curzon proposed that negotiations be held with China and
Tibet at Khamba Dzong, the closest Tibetan town north of
Giaogong. In attendance must be Chinese and Tibetan envoys of
sufficient rank to make the talks meaningful. The Viceroy felt
keenly that if the Chinese and Tibetans failed to appear, the
British envoy, equipped for this contingency with an armed
escort, should move on to Shigatse or Gyantse in the hope that
this gesture would bring the Tibetans to the conference table.

It is likely that Hamilton saw through Curzon's scheme, recognizing that the Viceroy intended to assert political influence
in Tibet under the guise of extended trade operations – 'a gross
exploitation and distortion of Britain's treaty relations with
China for a purpose which went well beyond the original intent
of the treaties.' But there was little he could do about it.
Curzon's tactic of letting events argue his case while drawing the
British inexorably closer to a confrontation with Tibet from
which they could not withdraw was difficult to cope with.
London agreed to Curzon's plan for talks at Khamba Dzong but
forbade him to advance beyond this point without seeking a full
review of the whole question. This gave Curzon the small opening he needed. He now at least realized that despite the Home
Government's concern for Russia's sensibilities, it was willing, if
need be, to enter Tibetan territory with a military force.
Whether such a force was allowed to march twenty-five miles or
two hundred and twenty-five miles was a matter of degree, not
principle. The aggressive Viceroy had won a point and could
conclude that the Home Government, despite Russia, had in
spirit if not in word, accepted the need for extending a British
presence to Tibet, and in the final analysis would sanction a
deeper thrust if the Kamba Dzong negotiations failed.

Curzon now needed the right man – someone on whom he
could rely to press every advantage. The man he chose, Major
Francis Edward Younghusband of the King's Dragoon Guards,

fitted the bill perfectly. A 'forward thruster', of Curzon's own cut, Younghusband would prove to be an aggressive player of the Great Game who would through force of arms outscore the nimble Dorjiev, even if he could not outwit him.

Younghusband began his military career in Meerut after passing out at Sandhurst. But cantonment life on the hot plains of India held few rewards for the serious-minded cavalryman. He found more to his liking the exciting world of the North-west Frontier where he was posted after two years in Meerut. Lonely patrols in the mountains beyond Kohat fired him as polo and parade grounds could never do. He loved the Great Game, the intrigue and drama of fencing with the Russians over sky-high passes into Afghanistan. Younghusband was an adventurer at heart, a searcher of new lands. He was also of the rare breed who intuitively understood the primitive politics of the frontier. He was one of those who could and did on more than one occasion wade alone into a camp of hostile hillsmen to argue them out of precipitous action.

In 1886 Younghusband dexterously managed a trip to Manchuria. Then, ignoring orders to return straightway to India, he travelled overland along the edges of the crumbling Manchu Empire in a remarkable journey to explore Inner Mongolia and Sinkiang before returning home by way of the Karakorums and Kashmir. In 1889 Younghusband was assigned to the Foreign Department at Simla. He was chosen for a reconnaissance mission to the remote Kingdom of Hunza where Russian intrigues made the Government of India uneasy. While on long-range patrol in the Pamirs he would encounter from time to time Russian opposite numbers. Captain Grombtchevski, for example, whom he met in some obscure corner of the Pamirs, introduced himself and cheerfully boasted of his government's intention of one day invading India. In another episode in the Great Game, Younghusband came on a Colonel Yonov. This Russian officer who had the advantage of a strong Cossack escort cordially entertained Younghusband before placing him under arrest and evicting him from the region. The incident provoked a stiff protest to the Russians from Whitehall and earned for Younghusband a certain notoriety. The Viceroy was full of praise and made a note of this young officer who bore the standard of empire so courageously.

In 1893 Younghusband was posted as Political Agent in Chitral where he first came to Curzon's attention. He was absent on leave when the British mission there was besieged. Unable to get orders to return to duty immediately and rush to the rescue of his comrades, he cajoled *The Times* into giving him an assignment as correspondent. With these somewhat dubious credentials he somehow manœuvred to beat the relief column to the beleaguered garrison in Chitral. Another interlude in his career found him in South Africa where he covered the Jameson Raid for *The Times* and found time to take a wife as well. Back in India – somewhat suspect in Headquarters because of his forays into journalism and his penchant for publicity—he was buried as third assistant to the Political Agent in Rajputana. But by 1902, having again favourably come to Curzon's attention, he was rehabilitated and made British Resident in Indore.

Younghusband seemed fated to become involved with Tibet. Unbeknown to him, he had been twice requested by the Lt Governor of Bengal in 1888 for duty on the Tibetan frontier. Without consulting him, the Government of India replied that he was 'unavailable'. In the following year he had plotted a trip to Lhasa, disguised as a Turk from Central Asia. But his unimaginative Colonel had snorted disapproval and refused to grant leave for this unorthodox venture. Thus, on 1 May 1903, when orders arrived describing his new mission to Tibet, Younghusband was elated. He later recalled with much youthful enthusiasm; 'Here indeed, I felt was the chance of my life. I was once more alive. The thrill of adventure again ran through my veins.'[1]

Younghusband reported to the Viceroy at Simla over a very civilized Viceregal lunch with Lord Curzon at the gymkhana downs. Here he heard for the first time details of his mission. Unimpressed by the stylish gentlemen and ladies around them performing 'every feat of equestrian skill and equestrian nonsense', they plunged into the subject at hand. In the shade 'of the glorious pine trees of Simla', Curzon transmitted to Younghusband his enthusiasm as well as his plans. 'The Viceroy had no intention of being stopped,' wrote Younghusband. 'One thing he

[1] Francis Younghusband, *op. cit.*, p. 96.

The Imperialists

made perfectly clear to me from the start, he meant to see the thing through; he intended the mission to be a success . . . he had his whole heart and soul in the undertaking.'[1]

Second in command of the Tibet Frontier Commission, as the mission was to be called, was John Claude White, Resident in Sikkim. It was intended that White would supply the intimate knowledge of Sikkim-Tibet border politics, which would be needed. Captain Frederick O'Connor, a skilled Tibetan linguist, was named Intelligence Officer and later Secretary of the Commission while Ernest Wilson was borrowed from the China Consular Service for his Chinese language proficiency. A 200-man military escort, drawn mainly from the 32nd Sikh Pioneers under Captain Bethune, would provide not only protection against possible rash and unfriendly acts by the Tibetans, but would supply the implicit force necessary to make the negotiators' voices better heard. With that certain touch that all good soldiers of the Empire had with the 'natives', Younghusband specified that the 32nd Pioneers pack their full dress uniforms to provide proper 'ceremonial effect'.

On the eve of his departure from Gangtok, Younghusband received amended orders by telegram. He was specifically instructed not to enter Tibetan territory unless he had certain knowledge that Tibetan envoys of sufficient rank awaited him at Khamba Dzong. The aggressive Younghusband, however, was not easily stopped. As he was often to do in the coming months, he found this time a formula which got around the problem without giving too much offence to his conscience. He simply interpreted the orders to apply to him, personally, and sent on O'Conner and White ahead while he waited at the head of the Sikkim valley, ostensibly to dry out his rain-soaked equipment.

The rain-soaked part of the story was only too true. As Younghusband later revealed: 'The rain never ceased: bucketsful and bucketsful came drenching down.' His description of the Pioneers' camp is a pathetic one. Not only were the miserable soldiers inundated with rain, but 'the heat was stifling, the insect pests unbearable'. 'Fever sapped the life out of the man,' he added, and 'one shuddered at the misery of life under such

[1] *Ibid.*, pp. 96, 97.

314

conditions, day after day, week after week, month after month, digging and blasting away at a road which as soon as it was made was washed into the river again . . . tormented with insect pests at work and in camp by night and by day.'[1]

White and O'Connor crossed into Tibet with their military escort on 4 July, while Younghusband remained behind at Tangu. They were met by the Commandant, or *Jongpen*, of Khamba Dzong, who earnestly sought to stop the Mission at the border. To frustrate Curzon's strategy of holding negotiations inside Tibetan territory, Lhasa had sent two high-ranking lamas to the border. It was for this reason that the *Jongpen* so frantically tried to hold back the two British officers.

O'Connor's own account of this incident, important as it indicates the nature of things to come, gives an idea of the atmosphere: 'I rode forward and was met by the *Jongpen* of Khamba Dzong at the wall, which the Tibetans claim as their frontier. He importuned me to dismount, and to persuade Mr White to do the same in order to discuss matters. I told him that no discussion was feasible here.' After further efforts by the *Jongpen* to get the British to 'discuss matters' at the border, O'Connor made it clear once again that 'any talks must be deferred until their arrival at Khamba Dzong, in accordance with the instructions of the Government of India, and after the arrival of Colonel Younghusband and the other commissioners.' 'The *Jongpen*,' relates O'Connor, 'followed us, and made repeated efforts to induce me to halt for a day at our next camp, Gyamt-sonang, in order to confer with the two [Lhasa] officials. He was in a very excited and agitated state, and hinted more than once at possible hostilities.' 'You may flick a dog once or twice without his biting,' the *Jongpen* said, 'but if you tread on his tail, even if he has no teeth, he will turn and try to bite you.'[2]

White and O'Connor reached Khamba Dzong on 7 July without further incident. Camp was struck by a small stream on the plain beneath a fairy-book fort perched high atop a massive rock outcropping. In the distance one could see Mount Everest and Kanchenjunga.

---

[1] *Ibid.*, p. 108.
[2] Samuel Louis Graham Sandberg, *op. cit.*, pp. 268, 269.

It was soon discovered that the Chinese representative, Mr Ho Kuang-hsi, held a very minor rank, clearly less than that empowered to reach agreement. Nor had the yellow-robed Tibetans, whom O'Connor sighted only rarely in the distance, plenipotentiary authority. One was a general named Wang Chhuk while the other was the lama Lo-pu Tsang, who held only a minor position in the Tibetan Government. Despite his instructions to await confirmation that representatives of appropriate rank would be on hand, Younghusband arrived in Khamba Dzong on 18 July. He had learned from White that the Tibetan delegates not only were of insufficient rank, but they had already made it clear that no negotiations would be held inside Tibetan territory. Only at Giaogong would they talk. Younghusband was anxious, however, to form his own on-the-spot impressions and understandably did not want to be left behind.

The first meeting with the Tibetans took place on 20 July and 22 July. They steadfastly reiterated their refusal to talk anywhere but Giaogong. After listening restlessly to a carefully prepared speech delivered by Younghusband for the record, the Tibetan delegates 'shut themselves up in the fort and sulked'. There was no further significant exchange for the nearly five months in which the British Frontier Commission remained at Khamba Dzong.

The time passed pleasantly for the British party. The weather was ideal and the endless, rolling plains well-stocked with game. Members of the Commission, following their own particular bent, collected fossils, bird and plant specimens, and made geological survey trips in the neighbourhood. This was a unique opportunity to confirm the topographical findings of the 'pundits' with modern instruments. While professionally frustrated, Younghusband remembered he 'did not care a pin how long these obstinate Tibetans kept us up there'.[1]

After the Viceroy protested by letter to the Chinese *Amban* in Lhasa that Ho's rank was inadequate, the cheerful Chinese emissary was withdrawn only to be replaced by one of even lower rank. While the Lhasan delegates never again put in an appearance, Younghusband did receive a deputation from the

---

[1] Francis Younghusband, *op. cit.*, p. 123.

Teshu Lama (Panchen Lama) in whose territory Khamba Dzong was located. The burden of this group's plaintive message was that the Lama had been 'put to great trouble with the Lhasa authorities by [the British] presence at Khamba Dzong; that the Lhasa authorities held him responsible for permitting [them] to cross the frontier. . . .'[1] After this preamble they begged Younghusband to withdraw to Giaogong.

This deputation was followed by a visit from the Head Lama of Tashilhunpo monastery. Reflecting Tibetan official concern with the seeming military nature of Younghusband's mission, the Abbot volunteered to remain with the British Commission as hostage if half of its military escort would be withdrawn. This, of course, was unacceptable to the British.

The Head Lama supplied O'Connor with some useful information. For example he revealed that there was a sizeable concentration of Tibetan troops nearby – crucial intelligence for the Commission's small bodyguard. But any hope that the Abbot could influence the Panchen Lama to bring the Tibetans to the conference table faded as the weeks slipped by. The Tashilhunpo Abbot had done his best to moderate Lhasa's stand but, as Younghusband later learned, Lhasa officialdom and policy was controlled by the National Assembly and this was made up mainly of Lhasa monks, uncompromisingly hostile to the British.

The Abbot was much attracted to the novelties of the British camp. Although he soon realized that his role was limited, he spent hours with gramophones, typewriters, pictures, photographs at the camp and generally revelled in this novel social experience. A charming, if not well-informed conversationalist, he vigorously disputed Younghusband's assumption that the world was round. 'It was not round, but flat, and not circular, but triangular, like the bone of a shoulder of mutton,' he insisted.

Younghusband was personally convinced that there was no hope of settlement anywhere short of Lhasa. But he recognized that 'it was high treason . . . to whisper the word Lhasa, such agitation did the sound of it cause to England.' The restless

---

[1] *Ibid.*

Commissioner was clearly exasperated and frustrated by the Home Government's inaction. In retrospect he complained:

I quite realized the difficulty which my Government at home has in securing support from the House of Commons in a matter of this kind. Such methods are very costly, very risky, and very ineffective; but as long as what an officer in the heart of Asia may do is contingent on the will of 'men in the street', of grimy manufacturing towns in the heart of England, so long must our action be slow, clumsy and hesitating, when it ought to be sharp and decisive.[1]

Younghusband urgently sought other approaches to end the stalemate: 'I racked my brains and everyone else's brains to think of alternative measures to advance on Lhasa, which might be exhausted before this proposal could be made.'[2] Shining through this statement, however, is the feeling that he saw in such alternative measures so little chance of success that he believed them useful only as proof that a march on Lhasa was the only right course of action.

One approach recommended by Younghusband was to encourage Nepal to exert pressure on Tibet. He believed that concrete evidence that the Nepalese were on the British side would have a great effect on the Tibetans. The Commissioner specifically proposed that the Nepalese Government provide the Mission yak herds to be used as beasts of burden. The sudden appearance of a gift herd of shaggy beasts lowing before the camp would, he felt, 'be a sign which the Tibetans could not mistake that the Nepalese were on our side.'[3] And, if coordinated with this move, the British escort could be augmented by the 23rd Pioneers standing by at Jelap Pass, the Chumbi Valley astride the main route to Lhasa could be easily occupied. Then, added Younghusband, 'the Mission might, transported by Nepalese yaks, march across to Gyantse'.[4]

Younghusband was on sound ground in anticipating Nepalese assistance. The Nepal Government had been no less apprehensive than the British about Russian intrigues in Lhasa. Although Nepal had a treaty relationship with Tibet in which it was bound to come to Tibet's assistance if the latter country were

---

[1] *Ibid.*, p. 133.　　[2] *Ibid*　　[3] *Ibid.*, p. 132.　　[4] *Ibid.*, pp. 132, 133.

attacked, Kathmandu knew the overriding importance of its relationship with India. The Nepalese Prime Minister on a visit to Delhi had in fact assured Curzon that Nepal would cooperate with India in whatever way possible. He had also taken the trouble to write the Tibetan Council in Lhasa and advise it to reach agreement with the British.[1]

Captain O'Connor all this while was busy collecting intelligence. The usefulness of his information (however inaccurate it may have been) in convincing London that the Tibetans were essentially hostile was not overlooked by Younghusband. This perhaps was the best way he could make his points although he did not hesitate to accompany such 'factual' reports with lengthy analyses and hypotheses of his own – all calculated to advance his thesis that Lhasa must be taken. In one such analysis, he painted a grim picture of a link-up of the Russian Central Asian Empire with the French South-east Asian Empire over the prostrate body of Tibet. In a letter to his father, Younghusband related quite frankly: 'It will all depend upon Government – especially the Home Government – and my own idea is that I shall have much more delicate work in managing them than with the Chinese and Tibetans. I shall have to carry them with me step by step.'

It was with considerable apprehension that the border Commission learned that there were some 2,600 Tibetan soldiers occupying the heights and passes between Phari and Shigatse. The Lhasa Command had been issued 1,000 rifles and 500 each had been given to the Phari and Shigatse Commands. Then, on 7 September, a monk-agent whom O'Connor had sent to spy in Lhasa returned with the information 'that the Lhasa authorities have quite made up their minds to fight, though they will make no move until the late autumn when the crops are gathered in ... 2,000 rifles have been given out, and the people generally have been warned to be ready for war.'[2]

Two of O'Connor's low-level spies – Sikkimese from the town of Lachung – were caught by the Tibetans and allegedly beaten and jailed in Shigatse. At least this was the information

[1] Ekai Kawaguchi, *op. cit.* pp. 523–4.
[2] Samuel Louis Graham Sandberg, *op. cit.*, p. 285.

reported in early August by another Sikkimese agent of unknown reliability. On the basis of a gossamer-thin cover story which described them as simple traders, Younghusband lodged an immediate protest. Failing to get satisfaction, all the Tibetan-owned livestock found grazing on the Sikkimese side of the frontier was seized as indemnity. Because this otherwise trifling incident tended somehow to substantiate Curzon's thesis that the Tibetans were hopelessly hostile and had to be dealt with in Lhasa itself, the Viceroy blew it up out of its true proportion. In a long despatch dated 5 November 1903, the Viceroy observed, 'the most conspicuous proof of the hostility of the Tibetan Government and of their contemptuous disregard for the usages of civilization has been the arrest of two British subjects [which they technically were] from Lachung at Shigatse, whence they have been deported to Lhasa and, it is credibly asserted, have been tortured and killed.' The latter allegation, which was quite untrue, represented Curzon's embroidery calculated, one presumes, to stir up London. If that was the Viceroy's objective, it was quite successfully realized since a strong diplomatic protest was made in Peking. Younghusband, himself, paid scant attention to the incident, perhaps not realizing at the moment its usefulness as ammunition. But the general tenor of his messages were fast reaching a crescendo of pessimism. He was convinced that 'the result of all our moderation in the present and previous years was nil ... I could no longer hold out any hope to Government of a peaceful solution of the question.'[1]

The time for decision had come. Younghusband was summoned to Simla for consultation with the Viceroy. The Commissioner left Khamba Dzong on 11 October, daring to hope that he could get agreement for more than an occupation of the Chumbi Valley. The Balfour Government was struggling for its existence and it seemed unlikely that it would adopt a forward posture on Tibet. But a message on 1 October from Lord George Hamilton to the Government of India provided unexpected encouragement: if negotiations proved impossible, London would be willing to consider not only the occupation of the Chumbi Valley, but an advance to Gyantse.

[1] Francis Younghusband, *op. cit.*, p. 138.

In Simla Younghusband found a sympathetic audience for his views. He and Curzon had always thought alike, and with this kind of encouragement from London, neither had difficulty in convincing himself of the righteousness of their cause. The Viceroy's reply enumerated the reasons why an advance into Tibet was mandatory: the Tibetans had refused to talk, no Chinese delegate of sufficient rank had appeared, the warlike preparations of the Tibetans, the imprisonment of two British subjects and the overall conclusion that the policy of forbearance followed for the past twenty-five years had simply been interpreted by the Tibetans as British weakness. And Gyantse as a goal had several advantages. It was here that the British proposed to establish a trade mart, thus there was symbolic value to be had. To stop short of the true Himalayan watershed at the end of Chumbi Valley would have no more symbolic value than remaining in Khamba Dzong: if the Tibetans wouldn't talk at Khamba Dzong, it was unlikely they would talk at Chumbi.

The Secretary of State in a fateful telegram dated 6 November flashed the green light. 'In view of the recent conduct of the Tibetans,' it read, 'His Majesty's government feel that it would be impossible not to take action, and they accordingly sanction the advance of the Mission to Gyantse.' The message made clear, however, that 'this step should not be allowed to lead to occupation or to permanent intervention in Tibetan affairs in any form.' 'The advance should be made for the sole purpose of obtaining satisfaction, and as soon as reparation is obtained a withdrawal should be effected.'[1] The telegram concluded that His Majesty's government was not prepared to establish a permanent mission in Tibet.

The Viceroy had got what he wanted. If the objective was more limited than Curzon would have liked, time and events, he was sure, would change London's attitude.

---

[1] *Papers Relating to Tibet, 1904* (London, His Majesty's Stationery Office, 1904), p. 294.

18

On to Lhasa

The risk implicit in the decision to move on Gyantse involved possible Russian countermoves. Lansdowne informed the Czar's Ambassador in London, Count Benckendorff, that 'owing to the outrageous conduct of the Tibetans . . . it has been decided to send a commission, with a suitable escort, further into Tibetan territory.' The British Foreign Secretary assured him, however, that this step did not indicate 'any intention of annexing or even of permanently occupying Tibetan territory'.[1] Benckendorff, of course expressed regret and apprehension. Russia, he said, could not help feeling that the invasion of Tibetan territory by a British force was calculated to involve a grave disturbance of the Central Asian situation. This was a predictable grumble, yet its tone, judged in the context of the mysterious jargon of diplomacy, was mild – certainly not such as to give the British pause. And London, moreover, could find some comfort in the fact that Russia was also distracted by problems in Manchuria and Korea which would soon plunge it into war with Japan.

The Chinese, too, were upset by the British decision to move to Gyantse. On 16 November Peking protested vigorously to Lansdowne, expressing hope that Younghusband would delay his advance, at least until the new *Amban* (who allegedly had been proceeding post haste to Lhasa for more than a year) arrived and could look into the problem. But Chinese objections weighed even less heavily than Russian; Lansdowne could pointedly remind Peking that the Tibetans had systematically disregarded the injunctions of the Emperor who demonstrably had no real influence in controlling his 'vassals'.

---

[1] *Ibid.* [Blue Book], p. 294, 'Lansdowne to Spring-Rice, 7 November 1903'.

Younghusband found the 6 November authorization to move up to Gyantse puzzling. As an outsider, Russia would logically assume that British actions were motivated by a geo-political necessity to ensure British paramountcy in Tibet: this, after all, was what the Great Game was all about. But Whitehall did not seem to have this objective in mind; at least not if Younghusband's instructions were taken literally. The puzzled Commissioner complained that the instructions 'said that the advance was to be made for the sole purpose of obtaining satisfaction', but, as he pointed out, 'it was always understood . . . that this was not a punitive expedition to obtain satisfaction and get reparation. It was a mission despatched to put our relations with the Tibetans on a regular footing, to establish ordinary neighbourly intercourse with them.' Nothing had really changed since Warren Hastings's times and Younghusband viewed his mission as having the same ultimate objective as Bogle's. Russian intrigues in Lhasa were a complicating factor and lent a note of urgency, but, fundamentally, Britain needed a friendly buffer to protect India's northern flank. This could be brought about only by a tripartite understanding reached with Tibet as well as its suzerain, China. There were advantages to a weak China: at least it would provide no threat to India in the same sense Russia did. But because Peking could not control its vassal, the British were forced to intervene and bring the Tibetans to heel. It was no wonder that Younghusband later commented: 'It is remarkable that a document which was so often quoted to the Russian Government, to the Indian Government, to the Chinese Government . . . should have described with so little precision the real purpose of the advance – and this at the culminating point of thirty years efforts on the part of the Government of India!'[1] If Younghusband later strayed from the spirit of his instructions, he could not be wholly blamed, particularly since he knew that Curzon viewed them more as licence to pursue India's destiny as he saw it rather than a rigid and inhibiting blue print of policy. As the dedicated Commissioner took his leave of the Viceroy before setting out on his new adventure, he promised to do his very best 'to get the thing through', and that is exactly what he did.

---

[1] Sir Francis Younghusband, *op. cit.*, p. 141.

The escort of more than a thousand fighting men for the march to Gyantse was assembled in Darjeeling in November and December 1903 under Brigadier-General J. R. L. Macdonald. The force consisted of the number 7 Mountain Battery of the Royal Artillery, a Maxim gun detachment of the Norfolk Regiment, two guns – seven-pounders – of the 8th Gurkhas, a half-company of the 2nd Sappers, eight companies of the 23rd Sikh Pioneers, six companies of the 8th Gurkhas; and the usual field hospital, engineer field park, ammunition column, postal and survey detachments.

For transport, Macdonald's escort force had counted heavily on a large herd of yaks donated by the Nepalese Government, which had been organized into the 1st, 2nd and 3rd Yak companies – surely one of the strangest cavalries the world has known. Unfortunately the animals were decimated by disease. Only a handful of the beasts ever reached the British Mission and they were too weak to use. The officers in charge of the yak corps told a pathetic story of hardship and endurance in the long drive from Nepal. This unhappy saga, never fully treated in the voluminous literature of empire, spelled near catastrophe for the British Mission. Only with brilliant improvising was Major Bretherton, the logistics officer, able to put together a new supply train consisting of local yaks, Kashmir ponies, mules, bullocks, camels and, undoubtedly for the first and last time in history, 'zebrules'. These experimental half-zebra and half-donkey pack animals proved to be treacherous and unruly; they were cordially detested by men and beasts alike. Augmenting the pack animals was a corps of several thousand coolies, both men and women, who in Himalayan tradition were capable of carrying enormous loads on their bent backs.

The 14,000-foot Jelap Pass linking the Chumbi Valley with Sikkim was crossed by the British Mission on 12 December 1903. A midwinter crossing of the Himalayas was difficult and held obvious risks, but Younghusband was satisfied that it was possible and infinitely preferable to waiting for the spring thaw. The snow drifts were enormous and the biting cold took a heavy toll of the ponies who had climbed suddenly from tropical rain forests to the ice-bound pass, nearly three miles high.

As the force descended into Chumbi it would soon become clear whether or not the Tibetans would fight. If they did, the role of the military commander would be an important one. The Tibet Frontier Commission was a political mission, not a military campaign: the military component, however large, was an escort only. But the chance of combat was high and in such a contingency, Macdonald would of necessity have the last word on tactics and deployment of troops even though Younghusband was senior political officer. Inevitably there was a grey area of command in which friction between Younghusband and Macdonald could easily arise. Only with a good personal relationship could they overcome such frictions.

Nothing appears in available correspondence to suggest that Younghusband was aware of Macdonald's record in the Uganda Railway Survey in 1892. But if the Commissioner had known that Lugard, as survey head, had clashed dreadfully with Macdonald at that time, he might have been less optimistic than when he wrote his father in October: 'Macdonald is an excellent sound, solid fellow and we shall get on capitally.' He added, 'Of course in actual military operations I have nothing to say.'[1] This suggests that he realized that combat would not only test the General's metal but would test their ability to properly balance command responsibility between the military and the political.

Macdonald was a very difficult person to get on with. He was childishly concerned with rank and prerogatives. But more serious, he was inexperienced and incompetent as a field commander. Among other faults, he was inordinately cautious and found making decisions painful. The kind of behaviour which had caused Lugard to record Macdonald's shortcomings and leave them in a sealed envelope in the Foreign Office was to repeat itself with Younghusband and jeopardize the success of the Mission. But when they started out from Sikkim, Macdonald's insistence that the Khamba Dzong force be safely withdrawn to Sikkim rather than risk a lateral march across Tibetan territory to join the Gyantse expedition, was the first hint Younghusband had of his escort's excessive caution.

Younghusband was met in Yatung on the border by Captain Parr, a British subject who served the Chinese Emperor as customs officer. This enigmatic expatriate, who found himself in

---

[1] Peter Fleming, *Bayonets to Lhasa* (London, Rupert Hart-Davis, 1961), p. 111.

the difficult position of having to satisfy his Chinese employer without appearing disloyal to his own countrymen, informed Younghusband that the Tibetans expected the British to make clear their objective before penetrating further into their country. If, for example, the British intended to make war they should declare war! Intelligence reports suggested that Tibetan arrogance could be traced to the close relations established by the Russians in Lhasa. Dorjiev specifically was blamed by Younghusband.

According to Filchner's reconstructed account of Zerempil's activities,[1] that shadowy Buriat had been sent to the Chumbi Valley by Dorjiev to gain intelligence on the British advance and advise the Tibetans on their defences. When the British crossed Jelap Pass, Zerempil allegedly ordered the Tibetans to evacuate Phari and fall back to a more defensible position to meet the advancing enemy. Macdonald in fact found the fort at Phari unoccupied, and posted two companies of the 8th Gurkhas and one seven-pounder in the strong masonry bastion, astride the junction of the Lhasa road and the main road to Bhutan.

Younghusband, who had assured the *Jongpen* of Phari that his mission would take no hostile act if the Tibetans were also peaceful, privately blamed Macdonald for occupying the fort – an act which suggested unfriendly intentions. While this incident happily did not overly offend the local Tibetans (certain officials even continued to live in the fort alongside the Mission force), it was a warning to Younghusband that Macdonald could not be relied upon to be guided by political considerations when military factors were at stake.

At Phari it was discovered that a Tibetan general and representatives of the three great monasteries of Lhasa were in town. The lamas whom Captain O'Connor tried to engage in discussion snarled their refusal to talk anywhere but back in Yatung. They showed no awe of the British force and like the rest of the townsfolk seemed supremely confident that the thousands of Tibetan troops on the other side of the pass with their newly-issued

---

[1] W. Filchner, *Sturm Uber Asien* (Berlin, 1924). A translated summary appeared under the title, 'A Story of Struggle and Intrigue in Central Asia', *Journal of the Central Asian Society*, 1927–28, Vol. XIV, Part IV, p. 366.

modern rifles were more than a match for the British and could prevent the Mission's advance.

Phari was a grimy place which the British were anxious to leave as soon as possible. A particularly unpleasant description of this Tibetan town was filed by the *Statesman* correspondent – one of several pressmen covering Younghusband's mission:

I looked down from the roof this morning on Phari town, lying like a rabbit warren beneath the fort. All one can see from the battlements are the flat roofs of low black houses, from which smoke issues in dense fumes. The roofs are stacked with straw and connected by a web of coloured praying flags running from house to house, and sometimes over the narrow alleys that serve as streets. Enormous fat ravens perch on the walls and there are innumerable flocks of twittering sparrows. For warmth's sake most of the rooms are underground, and in these subterranean dens Tibetans, black as coal heavers, huddle together with yaks and mules. Tibetan women, equally dirty, go about, their faces smeared and blotched with caoutchouc, wearing a red hooplike head-dress ornamented with alternate turquoises and ruby-coloured stones. In the fort the first thing one meets of a morning is a troop of these grimy sirens climbing the stairs, burdened with buckets of ice and sacks of yak dung, the two necessaries of life.[1]

Landon of *The Times* was no more flattering:

The collection of sod-built hovels, one or at most two stories in height, cowers under the southern wall of the *Jong* [fort] for protection against the wind from the bitterest quarter. The houses prop each other up. Rotten and misplaced beams project at intervals through the black layers of peat, and a few small windows lined with crazy black match-boarding sometimes distinguish an upper from a lower floor. The door stands open; it is but three black planks, a couple of traverses, and a padlock. Inside, the black glue of argol smoke coats everything. . . . In the middle of the street, between the two banks of filth and offal, runs a stinking channel, which thaws daily. In it horns and bones and skulls of every beast eaten or not eaten by the Tibetans . . . lie till the dogs and ravens have picked them clean enough to be used in the mortared walls and threshholds. The stench is fearful.[2]

---

[1] *The Statesman* (London, 22 March 1904).
[2] Sir Francis Younghusband, *op. cit.*, pp. 71, 72.

Tang La (Tang Pass) was crossed in the face of a whiplash wind and sub-zero temperature. Although the ascent was gradual, it was a thousand feet higher than Jelap Pass, which made this mid-winter crossing of the Himalayas particularly difficult for those unused to high altitudes. Well beyond the pass at the hamlet of Tuna the Mission gratefully halted and dug in under the protection of four companies of the 23rd Pioneers and a Maxim gun detachment. Tibetan troops nearby whose intentions were not yet clear made necessary a strict and alert guard. If Phari was disagreeable, Tuna was worse. Younghusband described it as the filthiest place he had ever seen – 'only the white Himalayan wall guarding the approaches to Bhutan in the distance and the majestic Chumalhari peak rising closer at hand provided relief to this sordid scene.'

The bleak, cold and inhospitable introduction to trans-Himalaya was too much for Macdonald. Pleading inadequate fuel and forage, the Mission commander insisted that Tuna be evacuated and the Mission force turned back. Younghusband, who would not conceive of retreating before they had barely begun and who was acutely conscious of the effect this would have on the watchful Tibetan force poised nearby, would not hear of it. By agreeing to take full responsibility for the decision to stay he was able to get Macdonald to reverse himself, but this was yet another forewarning of the difficulties he could expect from Macdonald.

On 12 January, Younghusband received a message from the Lhasan officials who had come to Tuna to intercept the Mission, asking for an interview. In a preliminary conversation with O'Connor, who acted as Mission spokesman, the Tibetans at least seemed willing to talk even though they reiterated the familiar refrain that only in Yatung could discussions take place. In a significant aside they intimated that if the British remained on Tibetan soil, 'another power' would come to their rescue.

Tired of 'fencing about' and eager 'to get a move on' – an Americanism which delighted him – Younghusband decided to beard the lamas in their lair. Using a technique which had often worked on the North-west Frontier, the Commissioner marched into the midst of his antagonists at Guru, unarmed and escorted only by O'Connor and one junior officer. Facing the startled and surly lamas, Younghusband explained the purpose of his call: he came not in formal capacity as British Commissioner, but informally as friend to make clear his position.

The Tibetans' reaction was illuminating. In short, fervent phrases the monks revealed the basis for their intransigence. They agreed solemnly, one with another, that since their religion must be preserved, no European could ever be permitted to enter their land! No amount of logic or persuasion by the British Commissioner would shake them from their position that talks could be held only at Yatung: negotiations within Tibet were unthinkable.

Younghusband raised the issue of Dorjiev and Russian influence in Lhasa only to be rebuffed by his angry antagonists who swore that the Buriat was a simple monk – nothing more. To have discussed this subject at all was a diplomatic blunder, as Curzon later pointed out to Younghusband. His Majesty's Government could not admit that the Mission had been mounted because of a Russian threat, and for that matter it was not at all clear that London had in fact justified it on this basis. Ostensibly, at least, it had been undertaken on the grounds that Tibet had not lived up to its trade and boundary treaty obligations.

The situation became ugly as the three Englishmen started to leave. The monks, 'looking as black as devils', shouted stop. The atmosphere was electric. The agitated monks refused to let them pass until they promised to set a date when the escort force would leave Tuna. Younghusband finally talked his way out of the circle of highly agitated monks and returned with his comrades to camp. 'It had been a close shave,' as Younghusband put it. But however reckless he had been, he had gained new insight and was now convinced that 'not until the monkish power had been broken, should we ever make a settlement'. 'Yet,' recalled the Commissioner with a note of frustration, 'it was still treason to mention the word "Lhasa" in any communications to Government, and I had to keep these conclusions to myself for many months yet for fear I might frighten people in England who had not yet got accustomed to the idea of our going even as far as Gyantse.'[1]

An effort was made to use Bhutanese good offices in a last

---

[1] Sir Francis Younghusband, *op. cit.*, pp. 166, 167.

effort to bring the Tibetans to the negotiating table. Trimpuk Jongpen, a Bhutanese envoy who visited Younghusband at Tuna, pledged political support and promised that his country would provide badly needed supplies for the escort force. He also invited the Tibetans to talk with him with the intention of trying to convince them to negotiate with the Mission. But nothing useful came of this initiative. The Tibetans were adamant. No alternative remained but to march on Gyantse despite new intelligence that a large force of Tibetan troops blocked the way. The crucial moment was approaching when the Tibetans must give in or fight.

Adding to Younghusband's worries was the nagging problem of Macdonald. In an earlier exchange of telegrams with Government the Commissioner had sought guidance on the never-quite resolved issue of command: in the event of fighting who would be in charge, he or Macdonald? To Younghusband's dismay the reply made it clear that Macdonald would be in command until the force arrived in Gyantse. While there was logic to this decision, Younghusband simply had no confidence in his escort commander. So strongly did he feel about this matter that he asked to be relieved 'of such a delicate political matter as the conduct of our relations with Tibet', and be allowed to return to India to await Macdonald's arrival in Gyantse. Younghusband was convinced that Macdonald would commit grievous political as well as military errors in the course of the campaign – errors with which he did not care to be associated. Only after Foreign Secretary Dane personally urged him to stay on did Younghusband agree to do so.

As the British column advanced across a wind-swept, gravelly plain toward Guru, the site of Younghusband's tense meeting with the Lhasa lamas, the Tibetan positions came into view. At 1,000 yards distance Macdonald drew up his troops as a small cavalcade of Tibetan officers galloped up out of the dust. The now-familiar General from Lhasa reigned up and joined Younghusband and Macdonald, squatting on the ground, in a last, futile parley. He again insisted that the British Mission return to Yatung, hinting that he was under orders from Lhasa to resist with arms if it didn't. Younghusband was exasperated: 'There was no possible reasoning with such people; they had over-weening confidence in their Lama's powers.' He later wrote:

'How could anyone dare to resist orders of the Great Lama? Surely lightening would descend from heaven or the earth open up and destroy anyone who had such temerity!'

Younghusband stubbornly refused to compromise. He gave the Tibetans fifteen minutes to give way once the General had returned to his lines; otherwise the British would use force to break through. The Lhasan General heard this without sign of emotion. Either he had supreme confidence in his larger force, perched advantageously on rocky outcroppings above the British and dug in behind a barricade erected across the defile, or he didn't dare defy orders from Lhasa.

Younghusband was faced with a difficult dilemma. Macdonald's force of 100 Englishmen and 1,200 Indians was outnumbered by the Tibetans. To advance slowly, challenging the Tibetans to fire first, was to risk close combat in which British arms of precision and longer range firepower could not be brought to bear. Yet to take the initiative in attacking on British terms, while protecting the lives of the troops and ensuring victory, would incur the politically unacceptable onus of attacking the Tibetans. Younghusband wrote his father: 'Twice Macdonald asked me to be allowed to commence fighting, but each time I refused.'[1] If the Commissioner was privately annoyed by Macdonald, he described the incident fairly and with restraint in print:

If General Macdonald had had a perfectly free hand and had been allowed to think of military considerations, he would have attacked the Tibetans by surprise in their camp, without giving them any warning at all. . . . As it was, in order to give them a chance up to the very last moment, he abdicated both the advantage of surprise of long-range force, and his troops advanced up the mountain side on less than even terms to the fortified position of the Tibetans.[2]

The General, who clearly had had the authority to override Younghusband and use his best military judgment, must here be given credit for courage. To satisfy Younghusband's political requirements he took a tremendous risk since any moment the

---

[1] Peter Fleming, *op. cit.*, p. 147.
[2] Sir Francis Younghusband, *op. cit.*, p. 176.

Tibetans could have opened fire with a destructive volley at the British force advancing up the open hill toward the Tibets' protected positions in the rocks.

Fortunately for the British the Tibetans showed great indecision. The British line came face to face with the Tibetans without a shot being fired. The sepoys, whose courage and discipline had held through this ordeal, obeyed orders to shoulder their opponents out of the way 'as London policemen would disperse a crowd from Trafalgar Square', in the face of a thousand rifles stilled trained on them at close quarters.[1]

Younghusband and Macdonald consulted and agreed to try to disarm the Tibetans who were 'huddled together like a flock of sheep behind the wall'. The Indian infantry were in position on the hillside only twenty yards above them on the one side, on the other Maxims were trained on the Tibetans at less than 200 yards distance. The mounted infantry were in readiness in the plain only a quarter of a mile away. The Mission troops were actually standing up to the wall, with their rifles pointing over at the Tibetans within a few feet of them. And the Lhasa General, himself, with his staff was on the British side of the mass in among the sepoys.

The Tibetans milled about in a sea of confusion. They had neither orders to retreat nor resist. A growing murmur from the ranks, revealed their frustration and anger as the Sikhs began to disarm them. Some struck back with fists, others threw stones or wrestled to retain their weapons, but none yet dared fire. Then suddenly at high noon tragedy struck. The Lhasa General, overcome by the enormity of his humiliating *de facto* surrender, screamed hysterically to his men to resist. Drawing his own revolver, he blew off the jaw of a nearby Sikh sepoy. After a dreadful silence which lasted perhaps three seconds, a rifle went off – probably by accident since a Sikh and a Tibetan were struggling for the weapon. Landon of *The Times* was eyewitness to the mayhem which ensued:

. . . the Tibetans hurled themselves with drawn swords against the thin line of Pioneers leaning up against the wall. Such of them as had their

---

[1] *Ibid.*, p. 177.

pieces ready fired point-blank at the Indian guard, and then dropping them flung themselves with their long, straight, heavy swords into the mêlée. . . . By this time the storm had broken in full intensity, and from three sides at once a withering volley of magazine fire crashed into the crowded mass of Tibetans. . . . Under the appalling punishment of lead, they staggered, failed and ran. Straight down the line of fire lay their only path of escape. Moved by a common impulse, the whole mass of them, jostling one against another with a curious slow thrust, set out with strange deliberation to get away from this awful plot of death. Two hundred yards away stood a sharply squared rock behind which they thought to find refuge. But the Gurkhas from above infiltrated this position and the only hope they had lay in reaching the next spur half a mile away. . . . Men dropped at every yard. Here and there an ugly heap of dead and wounded was concentrated, but not a space of twenty yards was without its stricken and shapeless burden. At last, the slowly moving wretches – and the slowness of their escape was horrible and loathsome to us – reached the corner, where at any rate, we knew them safe from the horrible lightening storm which they had themselves challenged.[1]

Younghusband admitted that it had been a 'terrible and ghastly business', but he refused to accept the description used in Parliament: 'a massacre of unarmed men'. Nor did he like disapproving journalistic commentary, typified by a *Punch* article which snidely observed: 'We are sorry to learn that the recent sudden and treacherous attack by the Tibetans on our men at Guru seriously injured the photographs that the officers were taking.' 'Looking back,' wrote the Commissioner, 'I do not see how it could possibly have been avoided. The Tibetans' irrational belief that their religion was in danger, blind fear and overweening confidence conspired to bring disaster upon them.'[2]

Except for one further and quite minor engagement at the Tsamdang Gorge, the British force was able to advance unopposed to Gyantse.[3] Entering the town on 1 April, the Mission was received, surprisingly enough, by an apparently friendly people. Younghusband could also be cheered by a telegram of congratulations from Curzon waiting for him. The Viceroy

---

[1] Perceval Landon, *The Opening of Tibet* (New York, 1905), pp. 82, 83.
[2] Peter Fleming, *op. cit.*, p. 154.
[3] Sir Francis Younghusband, *op. cit.*, p. 178.

YOUNGHUSBAND'S
ROUTE TO LHASA

•••••• Younghusband's route

0 10 20 30 40 50 60
miles

offered 'grateful recognition of the cheerfulness, self-restraint, and endurance exhibited by all ranks in circumstances un-exampled in warfare, and calling for no ordinary patience and fortitude.'[1]

The Commandant, or *Jongpen*, sat dutifully guarding the fort at Gyantse when the British Mission arrived. His soldiers, he explained, had run away. Exclaiming that if he surrendered the fort he would be executed by the Dalai Lama, he pleaded with the British to leave him in peace. Understandably, however, the Mission had to search this vast citadel, and eased aside its lone defender. Exploration of the seemingly endless labyrinth beneath the fort revealed one macabre chamber inexplicably jammed with severed heads – perhaps centuries old. Archi-tecturally the fort, rising high above the town, was fascinating. It conjured up images of a feudal world which might equally have belonged to medieval Europe.

It was impractical to garrison the monstrous fort: for one thing the water source would have been inaccessible in the event of siege. So the Mission was bivouacked on the plains near Gyantse at a place known as Chang-lo. Once settled in, Mac-donald and part of his force returned to Chumbi to look into logistical problems attendant to the now-extended supply line. He left four companies of the 32nd Sikh Pioneers, two companies of the 8th Gurkhas, fifty Mounted Infantrymen and two maxim guns, now affectionately nicknamed 'Bubble' and 'Squeak' – five hundred men in all – to guard the Mission while Younghusband awaited properly accredited Tibetan negotiators.

The Chinese *Amban* at Lhasa wrote that he intended to proceed to Gyantse, but somehow unconvincing excuses for his lack of action was all that ever reached the Mission. Quite obviously the Tibetans themselves were making no move to send an envoy to meet with the Mission. Younghusband's patience was exhausted: on 22 April he finally recommended officially that the Mission move up to Lhasa. 'This,' he said, 'would be the most effective and only permanent way of clinching matters.'[2] He argued that British prestige was high; Nepal and Bhutan had shown re-markable solidarity with the British and the Lamas were, for the

---

[1] *Ibid.*, p. 181.   [2] *Ibid.*, p. 184.

moment, stunned as a result of the British victory at Guru. Mission intelligence also suggested that there were elements in Lhasa who were urging the Dalai Lama to give in. Only the 'evil' influence of Dorjiev seemed to stand in the way of success.

It was difficult to know just what was occurring in Lhasa. The Japanese agent, Kawaguchi, related that as recently as 1903 many Lhasans were beginning to have doubts about the ability of the Russians to rescue them. Aside from Russia's preoccupation with Japan, which the Tibetans were probably only dimly aware of, the Czar was simply too far away. The 'Warrior' priests specifically were hostile to Dorjiev, and they were worthy adversaries indeed.[1] With the humiliating defeat of the Tibetan army at Guru – which it was rumoured had been due to the faulty strategy of Dorjiev and his lieutenant, Zerempil – one could only assume that the pro-Russian clique in Lhasa was beginning to lose face and thus influence.

That no Tibetan negotiators appeared in Gyantse was proof enough however, that resistance to the British had not yet collapsed. Younghusband was inclined to think that Macdonald's temporary withdrawal with part of the Mission force, 'may have had the effect of re-arousing the Tibetans'. Whatever the case, worrisome news began to filter through that Tibetan forces were collecting again for an assault against the British garrison. Stout walls were also being constructed across Karo Pass north of Gyantse on the road to Lhasa to block a further British advance.

In what Macdonald and others later criticized as a rash act, Colonel Brander in whose charge the Mission escort had been left, marched two-thirds of his force out to engage some 1,500 Tibetans at Karo Pass. No sooner had they gone when ominous reports reached Chang-lo that an army from Shigatse was moving up toward Gyantse. Then on 4 May, Tibetan patients in the Mission sick bay slipped out, one by one and returned home. A few of the patients hinted before they left of an imminent attack, although none of them obliged the uneasy doctor with any useful details. Still, the Mission was now prepared to believe that something was afoot and kept its guard up.

A reconstruction of events reveals that late on 4 May, some

---

[1] Ekai Kawaguchi, *op. cit.*, p. 514.

1,600 Tibetan soldiers from Shigatse stole through the night and infiltrated Gyantse. Half of them reoccupied the fort in secret while the other half moved into position at the edge of the British encampment at Chang-lo. There they remained from 3:00 a.m. until just after 4:00. So stealthy were their movements that they very nearly avoided being spotted altogether. But a single sepoy, a new recruit so ill at ease that he couldn't sleep, made out a shadowy movement at the southern entrance to the camp and fired a warning shot. The jittery camp leapt into action at the sound of the report and instantly made for their battle stations. Landon, who was among those suddenly aroused, related dramatically:

The effect of a shot at night upon a defended post is something which should be experienced to be fully understood; the whole place is galvanized as though it had received an electric shock. And every other sentry realized in a second the danger that lay in the swarming black ring of men, which now for the first time were seen clearly enough encircling the whole post. The Tibetans also were . . . startled into action; they stood up under our very walls and actually used our own loop-holes, thrusting the muzzles of their matchlocks into the Mission compound.[1]

Younghusband, who was awakened by the post doctor, recalled:

I was in my pyjamas and only half awake, and the first thought that struck me was to go to the rendezvous agreed upon beforehand in what we called the citadel. But I ought . . . as I think always should be done in cases of any sudden attack – to have made straight for the wall with whatever weapon came to hand, and joined in repelling the attack during the few crucial moments.[2]

What may have saved the day was the fact that the loop-holes had been constructed to accommodate the tall Sikhs: the shorter Tibetans could thus not aim through them with any precision. Their 'network of flashes and humming bullets struck in every direction over the enclosure', according to Younghusband's recollection, but few found their mark. Daylight broke in time

---

[1] Perceval Landon, *op. cit.*, p. 148.
[2] *Sir Francis Younghusband*, op. cit., p. 188.

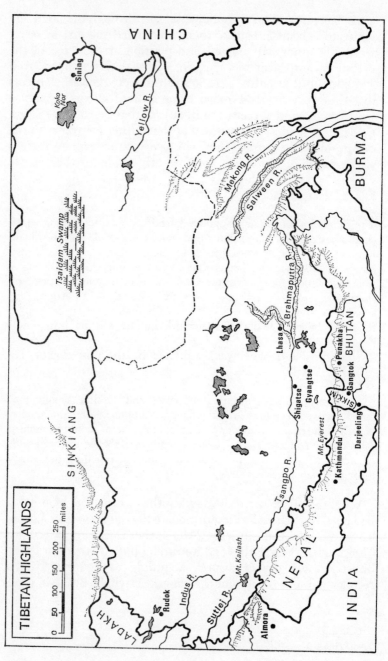

to make them defenceless targets of the sepoy defenders, now thoroughly roused to action. Those Tibetans who could make it, found sanctuary with their comrades within the fort.

It was not until the 7th that news reached Younghusband that Colonel Brander had been finally successful in clearing away the Tibetan defenders at Karo Pass. The Tibetans had been strongly entrenched behind a loop-holed wall, 800 yards long, built across the high pass. After an abortive frontal attack the Tibetan flank was turned by Gurkhas who had scrambled up an 18,000-foot ridge to pour fire on the hapless Tibetans.

When a worried Macdonald wired Brander from Chumbi, 'Fear your action will be considered as attempt to force hand of Government,' he was right in his apprehension. Brander and Younghusband had taken a gratuitous and dangerous initiative north of their Gyantse limit. But the Tibetan attack on the Mission camp at Chang-lo one day earlier saved them both from strong criticism in England. Brander's plea that such 'recon-naissance' was vital to the protection of Chang-lo would certainly not have stilled the vociferous critics at home had attention not been diverted by the Chang-lo attack. Younghusband wrote Curzon after Chang-lo saying: 'The Tibetans . . . have played into our hands.' And in fact the Tibetan attack with its flavour of treachery accomplished what Curzon had not been able to accomplish: cause the Home Government to sanction a march to Lhasa. Chang-lo was interpreted as conclusive proof that the Tibetans would not negotiate, and His Majesty's Government now agreed that recent events made it inevitable that the Mission advance to Lhasa. Accompanying the new authority was a caveat impressing upon the Government of India that there had been no change of policy since the 6 November telegram. But this was but a sop to conscience. Curzon had had his way.

Younghusband was impatient with his instructions to give the Tibetans a month to reconsider before beginning the march. He feared this delay would give the Tibetans time to marshall their forces to stop them. But he recognized realistically that there was strong opposition in the House of Commons which Govern-ment had to contend with. As he later commented with con-siderable understatement: 'There was no enthusiasm for the enterprise in the country. We had only recently emerged from the South African War; the Russo-Japanese War was causing anxiety; and we had not yet concluded the agreement and formed the *Entente Cordiale* with France.'[1]

Taking advantage of the unavoidable delay, Younghusband went to Chumbi to consult Macdonald. There were a myriad of details to be settled before the Mission could move on. *En route* to Chumbi the Commissioner stopped at a British outpost at Kangma. Early on 6 June he was rudely aroused by the battle cries of several hundred Tibetan attackers. The day was an exhausting one with Younghusband personally fighting in the line to defend the compound from attacking Khamba tribesmen. While tired and still tense that night he composed a long telegram to the Government of India giving his views on future courses of action. With little grace or diplomacy Younghusband set forth his ideas, the most controversial of which was his insistence that the Mission should plan to spend the winter in Lhasa. He was sure that negotiations with the dilatory Chinese and Tibetans would take that long.

This produced a stinging response in which Government found it necessary to remind Younghusband that his proposals should be in conformity with the policies of His Majesty's Government and that these policies were based on 'considerations of international relations wider than relations between India and Tibet'.[2] The Commissioner was icily told that 'it was impossible to argue the necessity of remaining at Lhasa during the winter until he had arrived there and gauged the situation.'[3]

This 'God-Almighty-to-a-black-beetle' telegram, as Younghusband described it to his father in a gloomy letter home, elicited his prompt offer of resignation. What the Commissioner did not discover until later was that the Government's message had been intended to provoke his resignation. Lord Ampthill, acting Viceroy during Curzon's absence in England, and Kitchener both had concluded that the forward policy in Tibet could only lead to disaster. Younghusband, who was associated with the aggressive posture into which the Government of India had been manœuvred, was the most convenient scapegoat. But once faced with Younghusband's resignation, Ampthill realized that a

---

[1] *Ibid.*, p. 192.   [2] *Ibid.*, p. 199.   [3] *Ibid.*, p. 200.

storm would erupt in press and Parliament if he let it go through. Moreover Curzon, fighting for his forward policies in London, predictably took issue with Ampthill and his old antagonist Kitchener, accusing them both of wanting to see the failure of a mission before it had accomplished its objectives. Ampthill therefore decided to hold on to Younghusband – at least until negotiations with the Tibetans had been concluded. Younghusband didn't then realize it, but his act of resignation had placed him in a much stronger position *viz-à-vis* Government. Ampthill in his zeal to reverse policy, had crawled into a box from which it was difficult to crawl out again, while Younghusband, by successfully meeting the Acting Viceroy's challenge, had won the round.

Russia of course still worried London. It was now harder to support earlier British assurances that there was no intention to establish a permanent mission in Lhasa or to enforce trade facilities with a seizure of Lhasa, much less a prolonged occupation of Tibet's capital. Younghusband could see that with the Russians now at war with Japan, London had to be careful. Moreover, he recognized intellectually that it was 'hardly worth endangering our relations with Russia, especially when her adhesion to our arrangement with France in regard to Egypt was required.'[1] But the bogy of Dorjiev in Lhasa still haunted the Commissioner. So long as this 'Russian subject, who had been accustomed to go backwards and forwards between Lhasa and St Petersburg' was calling the tune in Tibet's capital, it seemed 'hard that the Government of India, now at the climax of all their efforts, should have been tied down through deference to the distant power.'[2] This, to give his critics their due, was a highly parochial view point, which revealed a political myopia difficult to justify. But Younghusband, after all, had been very close to the affair for a long time and, moreover, had been under a great deal of strain.

Of more immediate concern to Younghusband was the fact that the Chang-lo garrison was under siege from the Tibetans. While their maiden attack had been repulsed, they were still strongly entrenched in the area surrounding Chang-lo and still held the Gyantse fort. They also had received reinforcements

---

[1] *Ibid.*, p. 202.   [2] *Ibid.*, p. 203.

from the surrounding countryside. Younghusband, therefore, was understandably eager to return to Chang-lo after his brief consultation with Macdonald in Chumbi. Macdonald returned after his long – and much noticed – absence from the scene of action. With him came reinforcements in the form of a unit of Royal Fusiliers, the 40th Pathans and the 29th Punjabis, bringing the total Mission strength up to about 800. The situation around Gyantse was a stalemate which had to be broken before an advance could take place. While the Tibetans held a 10 to 1 superiority over the Mission force, they were no match in fire power, and were forced to content themselves with a defensive posture and ineffectual bombardment of Chang-lo. Macdonald, while able to clear the countryside, was faced with a difficult military problem in trying to dislodge the Tibetans from the massive, well-defended fort.

A last effort at a negotiated settlement was made, using Tongsa Penlop, ruler of Bhutan, as intermediary. But tedious parleys produced nothing; deadlines came and went until Younghusband despaired of talking the Tibetans out of their *idée fixe*. The armistice simply provided the Tibetans more time to reinforce their defences at the fort. On 5 July, when the last deadline set by Younghusband had passed, the signal for attack was given. Macdonald, whose health and morale had suffered with a return to Chang-lo, hesitated up to the last minute. With prodding from Younghusband, who was by now thoroughly dis-illusioned with his dilatory and ineffectual escort commander, Macdonald reluctantly undertook the assault of the Tibetans' last stronghold.

The objective was not an easy one. Younghusband remembered afterward:

We were right in the heart of Tibet, with all the strength that the Lamas, with a full year of effort, could put forth. The fortress to be attacked from our little post in the plain looked impregnable. It was built of solid masonry on a precipitous rock rising sheer out of the plain. It was held by at least double and possibly treble our own force, and they were armed — with Lhasa-made rifles, which carried over a thousand yards. In addition there were several guns mounted.[1]

---

[1] *Ibid.*, p. 216.

During the afternoon of 5 July, operations began. Two guns, six companies of infantry and one company of mounted infantry made a feint on that side of the fortress to which the monastery was attached. But after nightfall an 'unfortunate incident', not otherwise described except as unexpectedly heavy fire, forced the three columns to be pulled out and reorganized into two columns made up of twelve guns, twelve infantry companies, a company of mounted infantry and half a company of sappers, which took up new positions south-east of Gyantse.

As dawn broke Tibetan rifles, which could now be trained on the assaulting troops, cracked sharply. The seven-pounder known as Bubble was used with devastating effect at point-blank range while Lieutenants Gurdon and Burney led their troops gallantly in storming the houses at the southern base of the rock. Gurdon gave his life in this engagement, probably as a result of flying debris dislodged by his own cannon fire. Resistance was now stilled along the eastern and southern bases of the rocks. But, as Younghusband put it, 'the real business had yet to be accomplished. The Dzong, [or fort], with 5,000 or 6,000 Tibetans inside it, still had to be assaulted.'[1]

Landon, who as usual covered the campaign at close quarters, related:

The Rock of Gyantse is so steep that it seemed accessible nowhere except along the main approach, which . . . was well defended. Any attack here would have been made not only in the teeth of the gunfire of the Tibetans holding the gate, but also at great danger from the stones rolled down by the enemy from the high bastion which flanked the road. . . . But at the point which Colonel Campbell chose there was just a bare possibility of scaling the Rock.[2]

Macdonald's reaction to Campbell's request to proceed was very much in character. The indecisive General's instinct was to abandon the attack that day. But he finally gave in to Campbell's repeated urgings and ordered concentrated fire from all points upon the wall at the head of this steep climb. The ten-pounders blasted away, savagely tearing a ragged hole in the wall.

---

[1] *Ibid.*, p. 218.
[2] Perceval Landon, *The Opening of Tibet*, pp. 265, 266.

The Gurkhas could be seen inching upward from the houses at the base of the Rock. Climbing is their forte and their performance that day was in their best tradition. Risking not only point blank enemy fire but their own close cover fire, as well as dislodged rubble, they climbed upward on their hands and knees.

Younghusband's own account of the climax is moving:

Very, very gradually . . . or so it seemed to us in our suspense below, the Gurkhas, under Lieutenant Grant, made their upward way. First a few arrived just under the breach, then more and more. Then came the crisis and Grant was seen leading his men straight for the opening. Instantly our bugles all over the field rang out the cease-fire so as not to endanger our storming party. The Tibetans too now stopped firing; and where a moment before there had been a deafening din there was now an aching silence. We held our breath and in tense excitement awaited the results of the assault. We saw the little Gurkhas and Royal Fusiliers, who formed the storming party, stream through the breach. Then we watched them working up from building to building. Tier after tier of the fortifications was crowned, and at last our men were seen placing the Union Jack on the highest pinnacle of the *Dzong*. The Tibetans had fled precipitously and Gyantse was ours.[1]

Leaving a garrison at Gyantse, the rest of the Mission force began its 150-mile march to Lhasa in high spirits on 14 July. All were in high spirits, that is, except the ailing Macdonald who gloomily predicted all kinds of catastrophes. 'Retiring Mac', as the troops now referred to their commander, still felt that renewed efforts at negotiations with the Tibetans should be made at Gyantse. But his views, dutifully forwarded by Younghusband, were swept aside by the Government of India, now convinced of the need to proceed to Tibet's capital.

From a military point of view, the march to Lhasa was relatively uneventful: Tibetan resistance had been broken at Gyantse. At Nagartse on Lake Yamdok-Tso, Younghusband spent seven hours in talks with Tibetan officials sent from Lhasa, but this produced no more results than the many talks before. Clearly the Tibetans were anxious to prevent the British from entering

---

[1] Sir Francis Younghusband, *op. cit.*, pp. 219, 220.

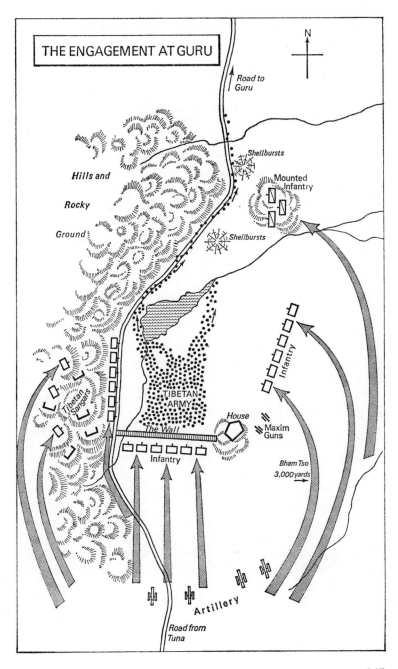

THE ENGAGEMENT AT GURU

N

Road to
Guru

Shellbursts

Hills and

Rocky

Ground

Mounted
Infantry

Shellbursts

Infantry

Tibetan
Sangars

TIBETAN
ARMY

House

Maxim
Guns

The Wall

Infantry

Bham Tso
3,000 yards

Artillery

Road from
Tuna

their holy city, Lhasa, but they were unable to stop them by force and were unwilling to reach a negotiated agreement, if indeed they had the power to do so.

Macdonald, of course, urged Younghusband to remain at Nagartse. Heel-dragging to the end, the Mission Commander had incurred the resentment of his officers and men. Dark rumours sprang up that some of the officers had even considered seizing command from the reluctant commander if he refused to go on. While such mutinous thoughts never came close to action, they were indicative of the exasperation felt by most members of the Mission.

The crossing of the swift-running Tsangpo was a feat of no mean proportion. It was a cruel twist of fate that Major Bretherton, whose logistical genius deserved much of the credit for the success of the Mission, was drowned when a small raft capsized in the midst of his greatest logistical triumph.

On the banks of the great river, Younghusband received still another Tibetan appeal to stop short of Lhasa. This time it was the *Tsongdu*, or Tibetan Assembly, which urged them not to 'press forward hastily to Lhasa'. This appeal encouraged Macdonald, whose tent was but a stone's throw from Younghusband's, to launch a strange correspondence with the Commissioner. In the first of three letters he composed for delivery 'next door', the General demanded to see the authority by which Younghusband justified his continued advance on Lhasa in the face of Tibetan promises to negotiate. He wrote accusingly, 'would be glad to know whether you propose to grant their [Tibetan] prayer for peace, or if I am to continue military operations and force my way to Lhasa.'[1] Younghusband, obviously annoyed by the General's continuing obstructionism, shot back a note making it unequivocally clear that they would go on.

Meeting little resistance (except that offered by Macdonald), the Mission force made good time. It came within sight of its long-sought goal on 2 August 1904. The sight of the Potala with its gilded roof thrust high above the city meant the end of a long quest. A final frantic plea by the Tibetan officials, who were still dogging the Mission's tracks, only served to make the prize seem

---

[1] Peter Fleming, *op. cit* , p. 227.

sweeter. These were the first Europeans to penetrate the citadel of Lamaism since the eccentric Manning, nearly a hundred years earlier. Younghusband memorialized this moment by writing:

The goal of so many travellers' ambitions was actually in sight! The goal, to attain which we had endured and risked so much, and for which the best efforts of so many had been concentrated, had now been won. Every obstacle which nature and man combined could heap in our way had been finally overcome, and the sacred city, hidden so far and deep behind the Himalayan ramparts, and so jealously guarded from strangers, was full before our eyes.[1]

But once a European army occupied Lhasa, however briefly and peacefully, the spell of mystery would be broken. No longer could Lhasa provide the same stuff of dreams for Western travellers; no longer could it resist completely the virus of progress. Robbed of its innocence, it must join the modern world and suffer the consequences of material progress. However inevitable, this was somehow sad.

---

[1] Sir Francis Younghusband, *op. cit* , p. 250.

Epilogue

The Potala's Chief Magician had once predicted that 1904 – the year of the Wood Dragon – would bring disaster to Tibet. How true this must have seemed to the Dalai Lama as he fled Lhasa on the eve of Younghusband's entry. The twenty-eight year old God-King, who had never before been away from his holy See or faced life without the panoply of his court, now leaned heavily on Dorjiev. His pitiful party struggled through the bleak, robber-infested northern plains of Tibet in the direction of Mongolia. Finally in November it reached Urga where the Dalai Lama found sanctuary with the Head Lama of Mongolia.

For nearly four years the Dalai Lama remained in Mongolia's capital. Although he found the somewhat licentious Mongolian Lama a trying host, and the existence of two such high ranking lamas in the same city posed awkward protocol problems, he had no choice but to remain there until he could be assured safe passage home. The Russians on whom he depended were properly attentive in Urga. The local Consul saw him frequently, and early in his stay the Russian Minister came over from Peking to consult with him. Dorjiev continued to serve as adviser, and soon after the Dalai Lama's *hegira* travelled to St Petersburg to petition the 'Great White Khan', for support.

Russian agent Zerempil's movements during the months following the British occupation of Lhasa were more difficult to track. This shadowy figure somehow managed to escape the scrutiny of history, although the German Tibetologist, Filchner, alleged that he hid in Kumbun Monastery near Koko Nor and from this sanctuary attempted to incite Tibet's Lamaist clergy to revolt. Armed with a secret decree from the God-King, calling upon all Lamaist monasteries to rise against the Chinese, Zerempil sought desperately to stop what inevitably would be a strong Chinese move to tighten its grip on Tibet.[1] The late spring of 1905 did in fact see a major uprising of monks. Prematurely triggered by the assassination of a special Chinese emissary as he passed through Batang *en route* to Lhasa, the revolt succeeded only in provoking a major Chinese punitive offensive against Tibet. Zerempil's traces were again lost for the moment as he fled before Chao Ehr-feng's forces sweeping into eastern Tibet.

While the exiled Lama languished in Urga, Younghusband sought to reach agreement with the Tibetans. He found Lhasa in complete confusion, however. The Tibetan ministers shrank from treating with their new conqueror lest one day a vengeful Dalai Lama punish them for their collaboration. The Chinese *Amban* danced attendance on Younghusband but lacked authority to do anything very constructive.

Had it not been for a courageous and strong-minded lama known as Tri Rimpoche, who had been hastily named Regent by the fleeing Dalai Lama, Younghusband would once again have searched in vain for someone with whom to negotiate. With perfunctory approval of the Tibetan Assembly, Tri Rimpoche reached an agreement with Younghusband on the relationship between Tibet and Great Britain. Notably absent from the document was the *Amban*'s signature. Peking could thus repudiate the pact, and avoid any implication that by co-signing as an equal with Tibet China had abandoned its suzerain preeminence.

The Agreement was signed in the Potala with much pomp and flourish. Key points in the document adjudicated the Sikkim-Tibet border, made provision for opening British-staffed trade marts in Gyantse, Gartok and Yatung, laid the groundwork for negotiating new trade regulations, and foreclosed the possibility that any foreign power (meaning Russia) would exercise political influence in Lhasa. It was, however, Younghusband's inclusion of a staggering indemnity of over £500,000 and the stipulation that British forces could garrison the Chumbi Valley until the indemnity was paid in full which caused London to erupt with indignation. Younghusband had not only exceeded his instructions, but he was suspected of hastily arranging the withdrawal of

---

[1] W. Filchner, 'A Story of Struggle and Intrigue in Central Asia', *Royal Central Asian Journal*, Vol. XV, Part I, 1928, p. 89.

his mission before Whitehall could reach him with instructions to delete these stringent and unauthorized terms from the Agreement.

Younghusband as man-on-the-spot had consistently assumed as much authority as possible. This was in the best tradition of British colonial servants. But this time he had clearly overreached in presuming to sign a protocol of international significance without explicit and detailed authority from London. Moreover he no longer had Curzon to back him up; the 'forward thruster', a victim of London politics, had been removed as Viceroy during Younghusband's march to Lhasa.

As Bogle had warned more than a century before, Britain could not sustain suzerain responsibilities in Tibet; communication lines were simply too long. But the immediate crux of the problem was Russian-British relations – an *entente cordiale* in which spheres of influence were clearly delineated from Persia to the Pamirs where the two empires dangerously met had to be reached if peace were to be preserved. In his zeal Younghusband had not seen all this in clear perspective and had, therefore, to be censured. More important, the Agreement had to be modified.

Younghusband made a convenient scapegoat for an unpopular Tibet policy. In a letter to Curzon, who was after all the real architect of the forward policy, Broderick, Secretary of State for India, wrote revealingly: 'It seems impossible to avoid throwing over Younghusband to some extent, and the great point to avoid is the appearance of doing so under pressure from Russia. . . . Arthur Balfour considers the honour of the country is involved in repudiating Younghusband.' Prime Minister Balfour, himself, wrote:

The only chance of any permanent arrangement with . . . [Russia] in Central Asia depends on the mutual confidence that engagements will be adhered to; and if, as I fear, Colonel Younghusband in acting as he had done, wished to force the hands of the Government . . . he has inflicted upon us an injury compared with which any loss to the material interest affected by our Tibetan policy is absolutely insignificant.[1]

---

[1] Peter Fleming, *op. cit.*, p. 272.

Younghusband believed that his settlement 'would admirably meet all . . . local requirements'. But what of the broader requirements? Equally revealing of Younghusband's limited viewpoint was his conclusion that London's action in amending his treaty and censuring him was symptomatic of new, restrictive ground rules for the agents of empire. No longer would the man-on-the-spot be given his head. Whitehall, admired in domestic politics, would call the tune without really knowing what the true state of affairs was at the end of the line. Younghusband, who never accepted the dots and dashes of a field radio as a master to be taken seriously, wrote eloquently in his own defence: 'I knew that I was not acting within my instructions. I was using my discretion in very difficult circumstances with what the Government of India afterwards described . . . as 'a fearlessness of responsibility', which it would be a grave mistake to discourage in any of their agents.'[1]

Younghusband was perhaps the last of the major players in the Great Game. But he failed to understand the Greater Game of twentieth-century European power politics. Tibet was a pawn to be manipulated according to the requirements of big power politics. The Game, a strategic one rather than a tactical one, was suddenly being played in the chanceries of Europe, not in the deserts of Trans-Himalaya.

The Thirteenth Dalai Lama was also a casualty of the Greater Game. Thanks to the influence of Dorjiev, the young God-King had pinned everything on the faulty premise that Russia would protect him against both England and China. But where were the Czar's armies when Younghusband approached Lhasa? Where were the Cossacks he needed to convey him back to Lhasa, and why had the agitations of Russian agents failed to rally Tibetan monks in an effective defence of Tibet against the army of Chao Ehr-feng?

It was the Anglo-Chinese Convention of 1906 which modified Younghusband's 1904 accord with Tibet. This new treaty in effect guaranteed Chinese paramountcy in Tibet. It recognized Chinese rights in Tibet to a degree the Chinese had previously been unable to exercise them. Since a weak, nearly prostrate

---

[1] Sir Francis Younghusband, *op. cit.*, p. 299.

China was no threat to Britain's Asian Empire this formula admirably suited London; it filled a vacuum without requiring that Whitehall assume the burden of defence. A year later Russia and Great Britain reached a *modus vivendi* in Asia by the Anglo-Russian Convention of 1907 in which Chinese suzerainty over Tibet was again recognized. The Dalai Lama now knew that he had no choice but to make terms with Peking if he were ever to see Lhasa again.

On September 1908 the Dalai Lama, still accompanied by Dorjiev, set out for Peking. Upon arrival he was received with honours but the court soon made it clear that he was still considered a vassal. The first scheduled audience was in fact cancelled because the Dalai Lama had let it be known that he would not *kow tow* before the throne in the traditional posture of vassalage.

The Dalai Lama, using Dorjiev as intermediary, sought Russian support, but Korostovetz, the Russian Minister, informed the Buriat emissary that the Dalai Lama had no choice but to return to Lhasa on Peking's terms. Much the same advice was given by the American Minister, W. W. Rockhill, whose help the God-King also solicited. Rockhill told him frankly: 'Whatever may have been the sovereign rights of the Dalai Lama before the present dynasty came to the throne, his present position was that of a vassal prince whose duties, rights and prerogative had been fixed by the succeeding emperors.'[1]

Rockhill, an accomplished Central Asian scholar as well as a skilled diplomatist, provides an interesting view of Dorjiev, the man, in a despatch to President Theodore Roosevelt written from Peking. He found the Buriat 'a very quiet, well-mannered man, impressionable like all Mongols and apparently but very little less ignorant of politics and the world in general than the Tibetans, though he has travelled over Europe and Asia.' 'He is devoted to his religion and to the head of his Church, the Dalai Lama, whom he has sought to assist as best he could.' As for Dorjiev, the *éminence grise*, who very nearly brought the empires of Britain and Russia into collision, Rockhill observed naively: 'I

---

[1] W. W. Rockhill, American Legation, Peking Despatch No. 1041, 10 November 1908, enclosure to President Theodore Roosevelt, The U.S. National Archives, Washington, D.C.

do not think he was or is more of an intriguer than any Asiatic would be when confronted for the first time with, to him, such a new and intricate question as Tibet's policy in Central Asian politics and in relation to the great empires, its neighbours.'[1]

The Dalai Lama sought two important concessions from the Manchu court: a guarantee of the supremacy of the Yellow Hat sect, and the right to address, or 'memorialize' the Emperor directly without going through the *Amban*. The latter request was denied him, thus the Dalai Lama set out for Lhasa full of bitterness and foreboding. Revolutionary 'reforms' were already being carried out in Tibet which eroded his power, and he could well conclude that Chao Ehr-feng's campaign would soon culminate in total domination of the country. The new and more ornate title awarded the Dalai Lama by the Empress Dowager on the occasion of her seventy-fifth birthday was small compensation for the by now obvious fact that he was returning to his See stripped of almost all temporal power. Rockhill was accurately prophetic when he wrote at the time: 'His [the Dalai Lama's] pride has suffered terribly while here, and he leaves Peking with his dislike for the Chinese intensified; I fear he will not cooperate with the Chinese . . . serious trouble may yet be in store.'[2]

As Chao Ehr-feng's forces pressed closer to Lhasa the newly returned Dalai Lama realized that his position would soon be untenable. He appealed to London for diplomatic support, but a mild British protest had no effect whatsoever, and Chao Erhfeng's soldiers in February 1910 marched unopposed into Lhasa.

Once more the Dalai Lama fled before a foreign invader. This time his destination was India where he sought the protection of the British. He must finally have seen his erstwhile Russian 'protectors' in true perspective when they chose to respond negatively to his last and secret plea to them for help through the good offices of his British hosts in India.

Seen in the hindsight of history, Chao Ehr-feng's Tibet campaign was a death rattle of the dynasty. The Republican Revolution which swept the tottering Manchus from power in 1911 provided the Tibetans with an opportunity to throw out the Chinese occupation forces with considerable ruthlessness. The Dalai Lama

---

[1] *Ibid.*   [2] *Ibid.*

returned to Lhasa in June 1912 and ruled his country for the duration of his thirteenth incarnation. In his last will and testament, drawn up shortly before his death in 1931, the God-King foresaw the Communist threat to Asia and warned his people: 'Unless we can guard our own country, it will happen that the Dalai Lama and Panchen Lama, the Father and the Son, the Holder of the Faith, the Glorious Rebirth, will be broken down and left without a name.'[1]

Western adventurers would for a while continue to brave the hazardous approaches to Lhasa to join the select few who had seen the Potala. But the Thirteenth's remarkable prophesy came all too true when the armies of a new dynasty occupied Tibet in 1950 under the red banner of Communism, and set in motion events which less than a decade later would force his successor also to flee to India. Tibet again became a denied area.

While Younghusband's mission momentarily opened the door to Tibet a crack, it remained for Communist China with its new roads and air routes to bring Tibet into touch with the brutal realities of the modern world. It is tragic that the instruments of progress have in Tibet been used to destroy the heart and religion of a people. How pathetic now is the ring of Bogle's valedictory prayer for Tibet written to his sister on the eve of his departure from Lhasa at the conclusion of the first British mission to Tibet:

Farewell ye honest and simple people. May ye long enjoy the happiness which is denied to more polished nations, and while they are engaged in the endless pursuits of avarice and ambition, defended by your barren mountains, may ye continue to live in peace and contentment, and know no wants but those of nature.[2]

---

[1] Sir Charles Bell, *Portrait of the Dalai Lama* (London, 1946), p. 380.
[2] Sir Francis Younghusband, *op. cit.*, p. 24.

Bibliography

AMIOT, F., *Memoires Conçernant L'Histoire Les Sciences, Les Arts, Les Moers, Les Usages, Des Chinois Par Les Missionaires de Pekin*, Paris, 1783.

ANDRADE, A. DE., *Novo Descrobrimento do Gran Cathayo ou Reinos de Tibet*, Lisbon, 1626. From a letter by Andrade dated 8 November 1624.

[Anonymous] 'The Buddhist Monastery at Ghoosery', *Bengal, Past and Present*, Vol. XXVI, Calcutta, 1923.

ASTLEY, THOMAS, *New General Collection of Voyages and Travels*, Vol. IV, London, 1747.

BAILEY, F. M., *China, Tibet, Assam, A Journey, 1911*, London, 1945.

BELL, SIR CHARLES, *Tibet, Past and Present*, Oxford, 1924.

— *The People of Tibet*, Oxford, Oxford U.P., 1928.

— *Portrait of the Dalai Lama*, London, Collins, 1946.

BERNARD, P. HENRI, *Le Père Matthew Ricci, La Societé Chinoise de Son Temps, 1552–1610*, 2 Vols., Tientsin, 1937.

— (Ed.) *Lettres et Memoires d'Adam Schall*, Tientsin, 1942.

Bogle Papers, India Office Library, Mss Eur-E-226, Vol. 53, London.

BOSMANS, H., *Documents Sur Albert Dorville de Bruxelles, Missionaire de La Companie de Jesus au XVIIe Siècle et Notamment Sur les Episodes de Son Voyage vers Lisbonne et La Chine*, Louvain, 1911.

CAMMANN, SCHUYLER, *Trade Through the Himalayas*, Princeton, 1951.

— 'The Panchen Lama's Visit to China in 1780', *Far Eastern Quarterly*, Vol. IX, 1949.

CANDLER, EDMUND, *The Unveiling of Lhasa*, London, E. Arnold, 1905.

CORDIER, H., *L'Expulsion de MM Huc et Gabet du Tibet*, Paris, 1909.

CURZON, G. N., *Russia in Central Asia*, London, 1889.

D'ANVILLE, JEAN BAPTISTE BOURGIGNON, *Nouvel Atlas De La Chine, De La Tartarie-Chinoise et Du Thibet*, The Hague, 1737.

DAS, SARAT CHANDRA, *Narrative of A Journey to Lhasa*, Calcutta, 1885.

— *Journey to Lhasa* (ed. W. W. Rockhill), London, Murray, 1904.

DAS, TARAKNATH, *British Expansion in Tibet*, Calcutta, 1929.

DAVIES, A. MERVYN, *Warren Hastings, Maker of British India*, London, Weidenfeld & Nicolson, 1935.

DAWSON, CHRISTOPHER, *The Mongol Mission*, New York, 1955.

DE FILIPPI, FILIPPO (ed.), *An Account of Tibet, The Travels of Ippolito Desideri of Pistoia, S.J., 1712–1727*, London, George Routledge & Sons Ltd, 1931, Revised Edition, 1937.

DISALKAR, D. B., 'Bogle's Embassy to Tibet', *The Indian Historical Quarterly*, Vol. IX, 1933, Calcutta.

— 'The Tibeto-Nepalese War, 1788–1793', *Journal of the Bihar and Orissa Research Society*, Vol. XIX, 1933, Patna.

DUNNE, GEORGE H., *Generation of Giants*, Notre Dame, University of Notre Dame Press, 1962.

EDEN, ASHLEY, *Political Missions to Bootan*, Calcutta, 1865.

EVANS-WENTZ, W. Y., *The Tibetan Book of the Dead*, New York, Oxford U.P., (Galaxy paperback edition).

FILCHNER, W., *Sturm Über Asien*, Berlin, 1924.
[A summary of this book entitled 'A Story of Struggle and Intrigue in Central Asia' appeared in the *Journal of The Central Asia Society*, 1927–1928, Vol. XIV, Part IV.]

FLEMING, PETER, *Bayonets to Lhasa*, London, Rupert Hart-Davis, 1961.

FLEURE, H. L., 'Tibet', *Encyclopedia Britannica*, 14th Edition.

FOREST, SIR GEORGE W., *Selections from the Letters, Despatches, and Other State Papers Preserved in The Foreign Department of the Government of India, 1772–1785*, 3 Vols, Calcutta, 1890.

FOSTER, WILLIAM, *The English Factories in India, 1642–45*, Oxford U.P., 1913.

FRANKE, WOLFGANG, *China and The West*, New York, 1967.

GROUSSET, RENÉ, *Conqueror of the World, The Life of Ghingiz Khan*, New York, 1966.

HEDIN, SVEN, *Trans-Himalaya*, 3 Vols, London, Macmillan & Co Ltd, 1913.

— *Jehol, City of Emperors*, New York, E. P. Dutton & Co, 1933.

HENNESSY, J. B. N., 'Report on the Explorations Made by A-K, 1879–82', Dehra Dun, 1884, India Office Library, W/2189, London.

HEISSIG, WALTHER, *A Lost Civilization, The Mongols Rediscovered*, New York, 1966.

HOLDICH, SIR THOMAS, *Tibet, The Mysterious*, London, Alston Rivers Ltd, 1906.

HUC, E., *Christianity in China, Tartary and Tibet*, 2 Vols, Lazarist Press, Peking, 1857.

— *Souvenirs of A Journey Through Tartary, Tibet and China, 1844, 1845, 1846*, 2 vols, Peking, 1931 edition.

KAWAGUCHI, EKAI, *Three Years in Tibet*, Benares, 1909.

KIPLING, RUDYARD, *Kim*, London, 1901.

KIRCHER, ATHANASIUS, *China Monumentis Qua Sacris, Qua Profanis Nec Non Variis Naturae et Artis Spectaculis, Aliarumque Rerum Memorabilium Argumentis Illustrata* (short title, *China Illustrata*) Amsterdam, 1667.

KIRKPATRICK, COLONEL WILLIAM, *An Account of The Kingdom of Nepaul*, London, 1811.

KOMROFF, MANUEL, *Contemporaries of Marco Polo*, New York, Tudor Publishing Co, 1928.

— (ed.), *The History of Herodotus*, New York, Tudor Publishing Co, 1956.

LACH, DONALD F., *Asia in The Making of Europe*, Vol. I, *The Century of Discovery, Book One*, Chicago, 1965.

LAMB, ALASTAIR, *Britain and Chinese Central Asia: The Road to Lhasa, 1767–1905*, London, Routledge & Kegan Paul, 1960.

— 'Some Notes on Russian Intrigue in Tibet', *Journal of The Royal Central Asian Society*, January 1959.

LANDON, PERCEVAL, *Lhasa, An Account of The Country and People of Central Tibet and of The Progress of The Mission Sent There by The English Government in 1903–4*, 2 vols, London, 1905.

— *The Opening of Tibet*, New York, Doubleday, Page & Co, 1905.

LATTIMORE, OWEN, *Inner Asian Frontiers of China*, New York, 1951.

LEE, WEI-KUO, *Tibet in Modern World Politics*, New York, Columbia U.P., 1931.

LI, TIEH-TSENG, *Tibet: Today and Yesterday*, New York, Bookman Associates, 1960.

LUDWIG, ERNEST, *The Visit of the Teshoo Lama to Peking*, Peking, 1904.

MACLAGAN, SIR EDWARD, *The Jesuits and The Great Mogul*, London, Burns, Oates & Washbourne Ltd, 1932.

MARKHAM, SIR CLEMENTS, *Narratives of The Mission of George Bogle To Tibet, and of The Journey of Thomas Manning to Lhasa*, London, 1876.

MARSDEN, WILLIAM (ed.), *The Travels of Marco Polo, The Venetian*, Garden City, Garden City Books, 1948.

MASON, LT COLONEL KENNETH, 'Great Figures of 19th Century Himalayan Exploration', *Journal of The Royal Central Asian Society*, Jul/Oct 1956, Part III, IV.

MEHRA, PARSHOTAM, 'Tibet and Russian Intrigue', *Journal of The Royal Central Asian Society*, January 1958.

— 'Kazi U-gyen, A Paid Tibetan Spy', *Journal of The Royal Central Asian Society*, Jul/Oct 1964, Parts III, IV.

MITCHELL, R. (ed.), *The Chronicle of Novgorod*, Camden Society, 1914.

NEWTON, ARTHUR P. (ed.), *Travel and Travellers of The Middle Ages*, London, Routledge & Kegan Paul Ltd, 1926.

O'CONNOR, F., *On the Frontier and beyond: A Record of Thirty Years Service*, London, Murray, 1931.

OTTLEY, W. J., *With Mounted Infantry in Tibet*, London, E. Smith, 1906.

PANIKKAR, K. M., *Asia and Western Dominance*, London, Allen & Unwin, 1953.

Papers Relating to Tibet, 1904 (Blue Book I), London, 1904.

Bibliography

PARIS, MATTHEW, *Chronica Majora* (ed. H. R. Luard), 7 Vols, London, 1872–1883.

PETECH, L., *China and Tibet in the Early 18th Century: History of the Establishment of a Chinese Protectorate in Tibet*, Leiden, E. J. Brill, 1950.

PETECH, L., 'The Missions of Bogle and Turner According to Tibetan Texts', *T'oung Pao*, 1949.

POLO, MARCO, *The Travels of Marco Polo*, Baltimore, 1967.

PREJEVALSKY, N., *Mongolia, The Tangut Country and Solitudes of Northern Tibet*, London, 1876.

PRINCEP, H. T., *Tibet, Tartary and Mongolia*, London, 1852.

RICHARDSON, H. E., *A Short History of Tibet*, New York, E. P. Dutton & Co, Inc, 1962.

RICCI, MATTEO (Pietro Tacchi, ed.), *Opere Storiche*, 2 vols, Macerata, 1911.

ROCKHILL, WILLIAM WOODVILLE, *The Dalai Lamas of Lhasa and Their Relations With the Manchu Emperors of China, 1644–1908*, Leyden, 1910.

— *The Journey of William of Rubruck to The Eastern Parts of the World, 1253–55*, London, Bedford Press, 1900 (Hakluyt Society Second Series, No. IV).

SANDBERG, SAMUEL LOUIS GRAHAM, *The Exploration of Tibet: Its History and Particulars, 1623–1904*, Calcutta, Thacker, Spink & Co, 1904.

SARCAR, S. C., 'A Note on Puran Gir Gosain', *Bengal, Past and Present*, Vol. XLIII, Calcutta, 1932.

— 'Some Notes on the Intercourse of Bengal with the Northern Countries in the Second Half of the 18th Century', *Bengal, Past and Present*, Vol. XLI, Calcutta, 1931.

SCHALL, ADAM (ed. P. Henri Bernard), *Lettres et Memoires d'Adam Schall*, Tientsin, 1942.

SEYMOUR, M. C. (ed.), *The Bodley Version of Mandeville's Travels*, London, Oxford U.P., 1963.

SHAKABPA, TSEPON, W. D., *Tibet, A Political History*, New Haven, Yale U.P., 1967.

SKELTON, R. A.; MARSTON, THOMAS; PAINTER, GEORGE, *The Vinland Map and the Tartar Relation*, New Haven & London, Yale U.P., 1965.

SLESSAREV, V., *Prester John, The Letter and The Legend*, Minneapolis, 1960.

THEVENOT, *Relations de Divers Voyages Curieux*, Vol. IV, Paris, 1672.

TOSCANO, G. M., *La Prima Missione Cattolica Tibet*, Rome, 1951.

TRONNIER, RICHARD, 'Die Durchquerung Tibets Seitens der Jesuiten Johannes Grueber und Albert de Dorville Im Jahre, 1661', *Berlin Zeitschrift der Gesellschaft Für Erkunde*, Berlin, 1904.

TURNER, SAMUEL, *An Account of An Embassy to the Court of the Teshoo Lama in Tibet*, London, W. Bulmer & Co, 1800.

WADDELL, L. A., *Lhasa and its Mysteries*, London, Murray, 1905.

WALEY, ARTHUR, *The Secret History of the Mongols*, London, Allen & Unwin 1963.

WESSELS, C., *Early Jesuit Travellers in Central Asia, 1603–1721*, The Hague, Martinus Nijhoff, 1924.

WHITE, JOHN CLAUDE, *Sikkim and Bhutan*, London, E. Arnold, 1909.

WILBUR, MARGUERITE EYER, *The East India Company*, New York, 1945.

WITTE, COUNT, *Memoirs* (translated and edited by A. Yarmolinsky), London, Heinemann, 1921.

WOODRUFF, PHILIP, *The Men Who Ruled India*, Vol. I, *The Founders*, London, Jonathan Cape, 1953.

YOUNGHUSBAND, SIR FRANCIS, *India and Tibet*, London, John Murray, 1910.

YULE, COLONEL HENRY, *Cathay and The Way Thither*, Vols I, II, III, (new edition edited by Henri Cordier and printed for the Hakluyt Society), Cambridge, 1914.

— (editor), *The Book of Ser Marco Polo, The Venetian Concerning The Kingdoms and Marvels of The East* (3rd edition, revised by Henri Cordier and printed for the Hakluyt Society), 2 vols, Cambridge, 1903.

Index

Index

Baian Kara Ula Range, 280
Baian Kars Range, 52
Baiju, 8, 9
Baikal, Lake, 190
Baldwin II, Emperor of Byzantium, 12
Balfour, Prime Minister Arthur, 309, 350
Balfour Government, Great Britain, 320
Balkash, Lake, 15, 156
Baltistan, 252
Banog, India, 254
Baranoff, 287
Barantola, Kingdom of (Tibet), 52
Barkul, 279
Bashkir Tribe, 156
Bassein, Portuguese Colony, India, 61
Batang, Tibet, 263
Battle of Perwan, 7
Batu, Mongol of Great Khan, 3, 7, 8, 12
Beauvais, Vincent of, 8
Behar District, India, 116, 117, 138
Beligatti, Casiano (of Macerata), 105–110, 262
Bell, Sir Charles, 285, 295
Benares, India, 57
Benckendorff, Count A., 310, 322
Benedict of Poland, Friar, 4
Bengal, India, 27, 42, 116, 117, 125, 128, 137, 141, 149, 160, 161, 166, 190, 211
Bengal Government, 298, 299
Bethune, Captain, 314
Bexley, England, 228
Bhutan, 40, 41, 117–119, 128, 132, 133, 137, 138, 164, 166, 178, 180, 212, 302, 326, 329, 335, 342
Bhutan, Rajah of, see Deb Judhur
Bhutia Boarding School, Darjeeling, India, 267
Bijapur, Nepal, 155
Bir Singh, 252
Bishop of Gabala, Syria, 1
Bishop of Winchester, 3
'Black Buran', 230
'Black Death', 25
Boddhisatva Avalokitesvara, 123
Bodh Gaya, 161
Boer War, South Africa, 309, 339
Bogdanovitch, see Orlov, Colonel
Bogle, George, (Chapters 6, 7, 8, 9), 124, 151, 153, 155, 157–170, 174–179, 183, 184, 188, 189, 196, 260, 303, 323, 350, 354
Bokhara, 252, 256, 301
Bombay, 49

Bon Religion, Tibet, 43
Bootieas (Bhutanese), 138
Bort, Captain, 50
Bosmans, Father, 50
Bottan (Tibet), 29
Boxer Rebellion, 304
Brahma, 65
Brahmaputra River, 133, 190, 218, 263, 265
Brander, Lieut. Colonel, 336, 339
Bretherton, Major, 346
British Consul General, Odessa, 296
British East India Company, see East India Company
British in Tibet, Chapters 6–10, 12, 14, 15, pp. 282, 284, 285, 288–292, 295, 301, 302, 305, 306, Chapters 17, 18
British sartorial mores, India, 215
Broderick, St. John, 350
'Bubble', 335, 343
Bubonic Plague, 25
Buddha, 16, 234
Buddhism, 14, 15, 17, 60, 234
'Buffer' concept, 251, 302
Bunyan, John, 21
Buriat Mongols, 165
Burkhan Buddha Range, 52, 280
Burma, 204
Burney, Lieut., 343
Buxadewar, India, 179

Cabral, Father João, 39–42
Cacella, Father Estevão, 39–42
Caesarea, Palestine, 11
Cailac, Mongolia, 15
Calamatty, India, 178
Calcutta, 125, 129, 161, 165, 167, 178, 206, 227, 241, 288, 294
Calicut, India, 26
Calo Chu Lake, Tibet, 136, 214
Calumba herb, 61
Cambay, Gulf of, India, 49
Campbell, Colonel, 276, 343
Canbaluc (Ancient Peking), 18, 19, 30, 31
Cantalbari (Kathal-bari), 212
Canton, 169, 210, 211, 218
Cape of Good Hope, 26
Capuchin Catholic Mission, Tibet, 68, 69, 76, 81, 82, 100–103, 105, 106, 108–110, 121, 245
Carpini, Friar John of Plano, 4–8, 18, 19
Casals, Princess, 71, 72, 74
Cathay, 15, 16, 25, 26, 28–31, 33, 39

Index

Index

Index

367

Index

Index